The Four Faces of Nuclear Terrorism

Charles D. Ferguson

William C. Potter

with Amy Sands, Leonard S. Spector,

and Fred L. Wehling

ABOUT THE CENTER FOR NONPROLIFERATION STUDIES

The mission of the Center for Nonproliferation Studies (CNS) is to combat the spread of weapons of mass destruction by training the next generation of nonproliferation specialists and disseminating timely information and analysis. Dr. William C. Potter is the director of CNS, which is headquartered in Monterey, California, and has offices in Washington, DC, and Almaty, Kazakhstan. CNS is the largest nongovernmental organization in the United States devoted exclusively to research and training on nonproliferation issues. CNS gratefully acknowledges the support of the following funders and thanks them for their commitment to our mission: the Carnegie Corporation of New York, the Center for Global Partnership, the Compton Foundation, the Ford Foundation, the Japan-United States Friendship Commission, the John D. and Catherine T. MacArthur Foundation, the Nuclear Threat Initiative (NTI), the Ploughshares Fund, the Prospect Hill Foundation, and the Scherman Foundation. CNS particularly is very grateful to the Ploughshares Fund, the MacArthur Foundation, and NTI for providing funding for this book.

The Four Faces of Nuclear Terrorism

Copy Editor: Lisa Sanders Donohoe

Cover Design: Aubrie Ohlde

Cover photos from top to bottom: tactical missile launch, photo credit: Lawrence Livermore National Laboratory (LLNL); mushroom cloud from Muskegon nuclear test on May 11, 1962, photo credit: LLNL; Watts Bar Nuclear Power Plant, photo credit: David Lochbaum, Union of Concerned Scientists; radioactive source transport container, photo credit: International Atomic Energy Agency.

ISBN 1-885350-09-0
Monterey Institute of International Studies

ACKNOWLEDGEMENTS

This study was made possible by the generous support of the Nuclear Threat Initiative, which provided funding for research and publication; the Ploughshares Fund, which provided funding for research and writing; and the John D. and Catherine T. MacArthur Foundation, which has supported the CNS Scientist-in-Residence Program.

The lead authors are particularly grateful for the important and extensive contributions of Amy Sands, Leonard S. Spector, and Fred L. Wehling. Amy Sands was the principal author of Chapter 2 of this volume, covering the motivations of terrorist organizations that might lead them to escalate their violence to the nuclear level. Leonard Spector contributed extensively to the analysis of political developments in countries with nuclear assets of potential interest to terrorists and to the assessments of U.S. nonproliferation and threat reduction programs. Fred Wehling contributed several early drafts of key material, especially in Chapter 3, addressing intact nuclear weapons. All technical judgments concerning the dangers posed by specific nuclear instrumentalities are solely the work of the principal authors.

The authors wish to express their deep appreciation for the guidance provided by the members of the Advisory Board for this project: Therese Delpech, Siegfried Hecker, Patricia Lewis, Morten Bremer Maerli, Michael May, and Marvin Miller. The advice they provided is solely their own and does not represent their organizations.

The authors also thank those individuals who provided comments on specific chapters and sections of the study, including John Bickel, Oleg Bukharin, Matthew Bunn, Richard Garwin, Neil Joeck, Michael Levi, Edwin Lyman, Richard Meserve, Alistair Millar, Robert S. Norris, Bennett Ramberg, Gregory van Tuyle, Peter Zimmerman, and others who prefer to remain anonymous.

A number of Center for Nonproliferation Studies staff and consultants, including Praveen Abhayaratne, Gary Ackerman, Caitlin

Baczuk, Natasha Bajema, Anjali Bhattacharjee, Adam Dolnik, Nicolas Florquin, Bill Gibson, Gaurav Kampani, Joel Lubenau, Jennifer Machado, Kevin Moran, Maya Nakamura, Hugh Naylor, Darby Parliament, Kaleb Redden, David Steiger, Jeremy Tamsett, Kathleen Thompson, and Jonathan Tucker, contributed to the research for this study and related projects or to the production of this book. The authors are especially appreciative of the editorial work done by Lisa Donohoe and the cover design created by Aubrie Ohlde.

The book would not have been possible without the assistance of the individuals and organizations named. Of course, any errors in the volume are strictly the fault of the authors and are not a reflection on the advisers, reviewers, or commentators.

TABLE OF CONTENTS

Acknowledgements   iii

Foreword   vi

Chapter 1   The Growing Threat   1

Chapter 2   The Nuclear Terrorists: 14
                Who, Why, and How Capable?

Chapter 3   Seizing the Bomb: 46
                Theft, Diversion, and Instability

Chapter 4   Making the Bomb: 106
                Loose Materials and Know-How

Chapter 5   Releasing Radiation: 190
                Power Plants and Other Facilities

Chapter 6   Dispersing Radiation: 259
                The Dirty Bomb and Other Devices

Chapter 7   Meeting the Challenge: 318
                A Plan for Urgent Action
                against Nuclear Terrorism

Selected Bibliography   337

Index   363

About the Authors   375

FOREWORD

When we launched the Nunn-Lugar Cooperative Threat Reduction program thirteen years ago, we understood the threat posed by the potential nexus of nuclear proliferation and international terrorism.

As this excellent volume by Bill Potter and his colleagues at the Center for Nonproliferation Studies at the Monterey Institute of International Studies makes clear, the threat of nuclear terrorism comes in many forms. The most destructive but least likely nuclear terror scenarios involve the theft or purchase by terrorists of a nuclear weapon from the arsenals of the United States, Russia, or other nuclear powers. This is the least likely, but not impossible. Major international efforts, including the Nunn-Lugar Cooperative Threat Reduction Program and the G-8 Global Partnership Against the Spread of Weapons and Materials of Mass Destruction, have helped make this worst-case scenario less probable. However, much work remains in Russia and in other nuclear weapons states, including the United States.

The gravest danger, however, and the one requiring the most urgent attention is the possibility that terrorists could obtain highly enriched uranium (HEU) or plutonium for use in an improvised nuclear device (IND). This book correctly highlights the priority of securing, consolidating, and eliminating HEU, while maintaining rigorous security around plutonium. It is here that the G-8 Global Partnership Against the Spread of Weapons and Weapons Materials must focus its diplomatic and fiscal resources. It is here that all nations must join the fight against catastrophic terrorism.

The huge quantities of weapons-usable fissile material in Russia; the smaller but terrorism-significant stocks remaining in Ukraine, Belarus, Uzbekistan, and other former Soviet and Eastern European states; and the unknown amounts of HEU and plutonium in North Korea and other countries greatly increase the risk of nuclear terror. The nuclear smuggling network set up by A. Q. Khan and his international partners demonstrates the relative ease by which nuclear material and technology can be obtained illicitly.

The Proliferation Security Initiative is an important measure to interdict shipments of weapons of mass destruction (WMD) and goods that could be used to create WMD, but it alone cannot prevent terrorists from acquiring dangerous materials, such as HEU. Combating nuclear terrorists is a battle that must be fought on all fronts. Current efforts to reduce the quantity of weapons-usable material in all countries and to move Soviet-origin material to safer storage in Russia or elsewhere must be accelerated.

Less destructive but more likely terrorism dangers come from attacks on nuclear facilities that use or process nuclear material. While most of these facilities were designed with security in mind, many reactors were not designed to resist the level of terrorist threat that materialized on September 11th. The standards for security of nuclear facilities must be revised, implemented, and realistically tested against likely terrorist threats. Means to protect spent fuel pools, research reactors, and other facilities with weaker levels of or nonexistent containment structures must also be developed and implemented.

The ease with which terrorists could build and detonate radiological dispersal devices—"dirty bombs"—or use radioactive material for other harmful purposes and the accessibility of potent radioactive sources make this kind of nuclear terrorist attack especially concerning. Because radioactive sources are used for a wide variety of beneficial purposes in medicine, science, and industry, the amount of radioactive material potentially available to terrorists is very large. Unfortunately, our system for keeping track of these radioactive sources is not adequate, and many remain unaccounted for—"orphaned." While most of these orphan sources would not make powerful dirty bombs, explosion of any radioactive device could cause damage and serious psychological shock, and their presence underscores the need to strengthen regulatory controls further and to dispose of disused sources safely and securely.

For better or worse, the world has entered a new nuclear age in which we face very different nuclear threats. This thought-provoking and well-researched book points to specific, prioritized steps, which, if implemented in a timely manner, could block many of the pathways by which terrorists might unleash nuclear or radiological attacks. It builds on the tradition of outstanding scholarship the Center for Nonproliferation Studies is known for and should be read by policy makers and anyone interested in a better understanding of the threats we face today.

Richard G. Lugar

Chairman, U.S. Senate
Foreign Relations Committee

Member of the Board of
Directors, Nuclear Threat Initiative

Sam Nunn

Co-Chairman
and Chief Executive Officer,
Nuclear Threat Initiative

1

THE GROWING THREAT

The United States has faced the threat of nuclear terrorism for many years, but this peril looms larger today than ever before. Terrorist organizations have escalated the destructiveness of their acts, as the events of September 11, 2001, the bombing in Bali in October 2002, and the Madrid bombings of March 2004 so tragically showed. Controls over nuclear and radioactive materials remain fragmentary and uncertain in many states where terrorist groups operate, often with popular support. And the list of incidents demonstrating terrorist interest in unleashing nuclear mayhem is growing more frightening by the month.

Certain nuclear arms within at least two states may be at heightened risk for terrorist seizure. Russia continues to deploy a number of its most portable nuclear weapons on its front lines, where security controls are weakest—weapons Senator Richard Lugar, Chairman of the U.S. Senate Foreign Relations Committee, and former Senator Sam Nunn have emphasized are the most attractive to terrorists.[1] Russia, however, is unwilling to relocate all of its tactical nuclear weapons to central storage or to implement fully and expeditiously the 1991-1992 Presidential Nuclear Initiatives, and the United States has neither pressed the matter nor provided assistance to enhance the security of these weapons. In Pakistan, where President Pervez Musharraf survived two assassination attempts in December 2003, new investigations have revealed unauthorized sales of sensitive nuclear technology by Pakistani nuclear scientists supportive of a fundamentalist Islamic agenda, developments that raise questions about the security of that country's nuclear arsenal. The new revelations echo earlier disclosures in November 2001 that Pakistani nuclear scientists provided aid of unknown dimensions to al Qaeda.

Nuclear materials suitable for nuclear arms are perhaps at even greater risk than the nuclear weapons themselves. Hundreds of tons of plutonium and weapons-usable uranium in Russia have yet to receive even rudimentary security improvements, while stocks of Soviet-origin, weapons-usable uranium remain vulnerable at research centers in other former Soviet states and elsewhere around the globe. Comparable U.S.-origin material in certain foreign locations may also be at risk. Even fissile material stocks in the United States, where security is considered far stronger than in the former Soviet Union, may be vulnerable to attack because of flaws in protective measures.[2]

Although protective measures have been increased at many nuclear power plants throughout the world, these installations remain alluring targets for terrorists. The August 2003 arrest in Ontario, Canada, of nineteen individuals (the same number of attackers involved in 9/11) on charges of conspiring to destroy a nuclear power plant on the shore of Lake Ontario was a chilling reminder of the interest of terrorist organizations in exploiting nuclear facilities to cause grievous harm to the United States and its friends.[3]

Meanwhile, criminal activities involving radioactive materials are on the rise. In Ecuador in December 2002, thieves held five stolen radioactive sources ransom but returned only three, after the ransom was paid, suggesting the other two are now available on the black market, perhaps accessible to terrorist buyers or their intermediaries. In another recent case, a radioactive source stolen in a carefully planned operation in Nigeria later turned up in Western Europe, again highlighting the growing scale of illicit trafficking in these materials. Most dangerous of all the cases that have come to light, however, was the theft in 2003 of three of the world's most potent radioactive sources—Russian "nuclear batteries"—each potentially containing enough radioactivity to make an urban area the size of the District of Columbia uninhabitable.[4] Fortunately, the thieves discarded the radioactive materials, retaining the pure metal container housing them, which they planned to sell as scrap.

These disturbing developments highlight the four "faces" of nuclear terrorism. Terrorists have essentially four mechanisms by which they can exploit military and civilian nuclear assets around the globe to serve their destructive ends:

- The theft and detonation of an intact nuclear weapon
- The theft or purchase of fissile material leading to the fabrication and detonation of a crude nuclear weapon—an improvised nuclear device (IND)
- Attacks against and sabotage of nuclear facilities, in particular nuclear power plants, causing the release of large amounts of radioactivity
- The unauthorized acquisition of radioactive materials contributing to the fabrication and detonation of a radiological dispersion device (RDD)—a "dirty bomb"—or radiation emission device (RED).

The first two classes of incidents would involve nuclear explosions, the most horrific form of nuclear terrorism. Hundreds of thousands of lives could be lost from the blast, immediate property damage could run to many billions of dollars, and radioactive contamination could cause tens to hundreds of billions of dollars' worth of lost economic activity, property damage, and long-term health effects. Total costs, in monetary terms, could soar to several trillion dollars.[5]

Consequences stemming from a terrorist-detonated nuclear weapon in an American city would emanate beyond the immediate tens or hundreds of thousands of fatalities and the massive property and financial damage. Americans who were not killed or injured by the explosion would live in fear that they could die from future nuclear terrorist attacks. Such fear would erode public confidence in the government and could spark the downfall of the administration in power. The tightly interconnected economies of the United States and the rest of the world could sink into a depression as a result of a crude nuclear weapon destroying the heart of a city.

The destruction of a nuclear power plant would probably cause considerably less damage. However, loss of the plant itself and permanent or temporary loss of use of any co-located nuclear power reactors would still run into many billions of dollars, and widespread radioactive contamination could lead to tens to hundreds of billions of dollars in lost economic activity, property damage, or long-term health effects. The consequences of use of an RDD in the form of a dirty bomb are scenario dependent. Under certain circumstances, use of an RDD in the form of a dirty bomb could result in hundreds of prompt casualties and tens of billions of dollars' worth of lost economic activity, property damage, and long-term health effects.[6] The costs of panic and evacuation must also be added to the toll in each of these cases.

While the probability of nuclear terrorism remains much smaller than the likelihood of terrorism involving conventional means of violence, the danger of high-end terrorism is growing. The February 2003 U.S. *National Strategy for Combating Terrorism,* for example, warned that, "The probability of a terrorist organization using a chemical, biological, radiological, or nuclear weapon, or high-yield explosives, has increased significantly during the past decade."[7] The strategy reflects anxieties at the highest levels of the U.S. government. Indeed, it has been reliably reported that within a few weeks of September 11, 2001, President Bush "ordered his national security team to give nuclear terrorism priority over every other threat to the United States."[8] More recently, Vice President Cheney was reported as warning that "'the major threat' facing the nation is the possibility that terrorists could detonate a biological or nuclear weapon in a U.S. city."[9]

Despite these statements of concern, there is little evidence that the U.S. government has developed a comprehensive plan that effectively prioritizes how the United States and its allies should combat the threat of nuclear terrorism. Addressing the Vice President's fear of biological terrorism, the White House was reportedly, as of mid-December 2003, "nearing completion of a classified 'Biodefense End-to-End Assessment' that systematically catalogues the gaps in the nation's safeguards against biological attack and begins to develop strategies for filling them."[10] But no such thorough effort has been announced to assess defenses and other strategies to combat nuclear terrorism. In particular, the U.S. government has neither undertaken a comparative assessment of the risks of the principal types of nuclear terrorism nor sought to prioritize strategies for addressing them.

A starting point for developing such a plan is a comprehensive understanding of the nature of nuclear terrorism, beginning with an appreciation of the relative risks posed by its principal forms. Risk can be defined as the probability of an event multiplied by its consequences. Thus, the greater the probability *or* the greater the consequences, the higher the overall risk. Quantifying risk presents many difficulties, especially when there is a paucity of information about the occurrence or likelihood of an event. Fortunately, to date, no detonations of illicitly obtained nuclear weapons or INDs have occurred, nor have there been any dirty bomb attacks. Nuclear facilities have experienced some terrorist attacks, but none of these has resulted in off-site releases of radioactivity. However, from the perspective of risk analysis, this minimal data set significantly constrains the ability to perform a quantitative risk assessment. Consequently, decision makers must rely upon the qualitative examination of the risks of the different faces of nuclear terror.

Nuclear terrorism experts generally agree that the nuclear terror acts with the highest consequences are the least likely to occur because they are the most difficult to accomplish.[11] Conversely, those acts with the least damaging consequences are the most likely to take place because they are the easiest to carry out. Constructing and detonating an improvised nuclear device, for example, is far more challenging than building and setting off a radiological dispersal device, because the former weapon is far more complex technologically and the necessary materials are far more difficult to obtain. Thus, an IND presents a less likely threat than does an RDD. In contrast, the consequences from an IND explosion are orders of magnitude more devastating than the damage from use of an RDD. Taking into account both the magnitude of potential consequences and the relative difficulty of execution, all four faces of nuclear terrorism pose potentially grave and imminent dangers, and the United States and other concerned states must work to address all of them.

Striving for maximum risk reduction demands a rigorous examination of both the probability and consequence factors of the risk equation. If national and international efforts can shrink the probability of an event, the risk is reduced. Similarly, if the consequences of a nuclear terrorist attack can be reduced to a low level, terrorists potentially can be dissuaded from launching such an attack because it would be less likely that they could achieve their goals of inflicting massive damage and terror.

Knowing where and how to apply efforts to reduce risk requires understanding the chain of necessary conditions for a nuclear terror act to occur.[12] In the case of the detonation of an intact nuclear weapon or an IND, this chain of events consists of the following steps:

1. A terrorist group with extreme objectives and the necessary technical and financial resources must organize itself.
2. The group must then choose to engage in an act of nuclear terrorism.
3. These terrorists must seize an intact nuclear weapon or acquire fissile material (either highly enriched uranium or plutonium) to make an IND.
4. They must determine how to bypass or defeat any safeguards in an intact nuclear weapon or how to assemble an IND from the fissile material.
5. Then the terrorist group must be able to transport the IND (or its parts) or the intact nuclear weapon to a high-value target.
6. Finally, the terrorists must detonate the IND or intact nuclear weapon to complete their plan.

Should any link in this chain be severed, the nuclear terrorist plan would be thwarted. Thus countermeasures can be effective at many different points in the evolution of a nuclear terror act, and multiple countermeasures, even if individually imperfect, can combine into an increasingly effective system. The global war on terrorism, for example, has disrupted some terrorist organizations, removed certain safe havens, and interfered with terrorist financing activities. The United States is also moving to improve port and border security against the illicit introduction of nuclear and radioactive materials into this country, initiatives that will require years of additional work to complete.[13] New radiation sensors are being installed around certain cities considered likely terrorist targets, and commercial air travel security has been significantly tightened to reduce the chances that a commercial aircraft might be used as an instrument of a terrorist attack.

The benefits from these initiatives and those directed more specifically at protecting nuclear assets are cumulative and mutually reinforcing, and in time, they will combine into a "multilayered defense" to reduce the overall danger of nuclear terrorism to acceptable levels. For now, however, the most rapid advances can be made by focusing on the nuclear dimension of the problem, in particular improving security over nuclear assets and preparing for nuclear terror incidents in order to mitigate their consequences. Indeed, an overall strategy of risk reduction should strive to *reduce the probability of nuclear terror acts with the highest consequences and mitigate the consequences of the nuclear terror acts that are the most probable.*

The following chapters of this book will review these issues in depth, beginning with an examination of the motivations and capabilities of the terrorist organizations that might seek to escalate their agenda for destruction into the nuclear realm. Subsequent chapters will scrutinize each of the four faces of nuclear terrorism to provide a technical understanding of the dangers they pose, the steps terrorists must take to accomplish them, and the key strategies needed to reduce the risks they pose. The concluding chapter will summarize findings and will make recommendations for both immediate and longer-term action by the United States and other concerned nations.

As will be seen, averting the most destructive forms of nuclear terrorism depends on ensuring *secure custody* over nuclear arms and the materials needed to manufacture them. The most severe challenges are in Russia, at locations in a number of former Soviet republics, and in Pakistan.

In the former Soviet space, the overarching objectives should be to secure, consolidate, and, where possible, reduce stocks of nuclear arms and fissile material. A number of U.S. and international programs are in place to advance these goals, but they need to be accelerated and redirected to achieve faster risk reduction. Significantly, these efforts, with budgets of hundreds of millions of dollars annually, have not been realigned to recognize the new realities of international security since the events of September 11, 2001. Prior to that date, the greatest concern of U.S. policy makers was that nuclear assets might fall into the hands of proliferant states. Even a handful of nuclear weapons or the plutonium or highly enriched uranium (HEU) needed to make them might have provided Iraq, Iran, or Libya with a small nuclear deterrent virtually overnight—or allowed North Korea to double or triple its arsenal. After September 11, however, the danger of terrorists obtaining such assets has emerged as an even more chilling prospect. Some terrorist organizations have openly declared their hopes of wreaking massive destruction on the United States, and others may well follow suit.

Fortunately, the technical and financial resources of terrorists are far more limited than those of states. For this reason, terrorist organizations seeking the ultimate weapon will find some nuclear assets more valuable than others because they are easier to exploit. As detailed in the following chapters, weapons-usable enriched uranium would be vastly easier for a terrorist organization to transform into an improvised nuclear device than would plutonium. The U.S. and Russian governments, however, have been reluctant to acknowledge this changed calculus and modify their nonproliferation priorities accordingly. The senior Russian atomic energy official, for example, continues to deny the possibility that non-state actors have the technical skills to manufacture a nuclear bomb. Some senior U.S. government officials echo this view and appear to project on to terrorists their concerns that weapons would have to meet rigorous safety requirements and produce reliable and predictable explosive yields.[14] However, nuclear terrorists could reach their objectives of massive destruction by detonating nuclear weapons that fell far short of exacting military specifications, but still resulted in a devastating explosion. Employing weapons-usable uranium would vastly simplify their work.

In Pakistan, the greatest challenges to secure custody of nuclear assets derive from instabilities in the Pakistani political system, questions about the reliability of the military and nuclear chain of command, and the commitment of the nation's leaders to abandon past ties with radical Islamic causes. Prior to 9/11, Pakistan supported the Taliban-led government in Afghanistan, and many within Pakistan's intelligence service, the ISI, were sympathetic to the Taliban and to al Qaeda. Soon after 9/11, Pakistani President Pervez Musharraf pledged his support for President Bush's "War on Terror," and quickly became a key ally in helping to disrupt and destroy terrorist units within his country. Despite this effort, al Qaeda operatives continue to reside in the border region between Pakistan and Afghanistan and, until recently, the central government has been reluctant to pursue them.

Musharraf's backing of the U.S.-led War on Terror has made his own position precarious. A coup in Pakistan could elevate the risk of terrorists or their supporters seizing nuclear assets. These terrorists, moreover, could potentially tap technical expertise in Pakistan. And, as noted earlier, "rogue" Pakistani nuclear scientists are believed to have met with al Qaeda. Moreover, as the International Atomic Energy Agency (IAEA) revealed in early 2004, Dr. Abdul Qadeer Khan, the former head of Pakistan's nuclear weapons program, led a clandestine nuclear smuggling network that provided sensitive uranium enrichment technology and possibly a nuclear weapon design to Iran, whose nuclear program is controlled by governmental elements who are also believed to support international terrorism. No less disturbing, in his public confession that he provided nuclear assistance to Iran, Libya, and North Korea, Khan declared that Pakistan's military and civilian leaders were unaware of all of these transactions, a position publicly reaffirmed by President Musharraf. If true, these declarations would raise serious questions about the effectiveness of security over Pakistani nuclear assets— and if the declarations are not true, it would mean that Pakistan's current leaders share responsibility for providing nuclear weapons technology to a government that the United States has accused of being a sponsor of international terrorism. Unless a strategy can be mounted to promote internal and regional stability, the risk that Pakistan's nuclear weapons or fissile material could fall into the hands of terrorists will continue to grow.

Protecting nuclear facilities in the United States against terrorist attack and sabotage presents a more manageable but not inconsequential challenge. The United States has made considerable progress in enhancing protective measures at its nuclear power plants and other nuclear facilities, but questions remain as to whether these measures fully address the terrorist challenge.

For a terrorist organization, attacking or sabotaging a nuclear facility would require that it identify a nuclear power plant or other nuclear facility that is potentially vulnerable. To facilitate the success of their mission, the terrorists would likely try to enlist the support of at least one insider. They must then decide how to strike the facility. Attack modes include airplane crashes; commando raids by land, water, or air; or cyber assault. The terrorist must then disable or destroy enough vital equipment at the facility to cause an offsite release of radioactivity. Though far from easy, these steps would not require technical capabilities as advanced as those needed for the fabrication of an IND.

With certain qualifications, U.S. nuclear power plants, and those of similar design elsewhere, present considerable barriers to successful terror acts that might cause a significant release of radioactivity. For example, they employ defense-in-depth safety systems that would mitigate the consequences of a terror attack or sabotage. Moreover, the U.S. Nuclear Regulatory Commission stepped up its security efforts immediately after 9/11 and continues to work on security enhancements. Nonetheless, concerns persist as to whether its efforts have gone far enough. A small number of U.S. nuclear power reactors, for example, have features that provide significantly less protection than typical facilities, suggesting the need for additional measures at these sites to compensate for these vulnerabilities. More broadly, it appears that the "design basis threat" adopted by the U.S. Nuclear Regulatory Commission (NRC) does not fully reflect the magnitude of the September 11th attack: 19 motivated and well-trained assailants operating in four separate teams.

The United States also operates numerous research reactors, many in urban centers and universities. Although the inventory of radioactive materials in such facilities is far smaller than that of nuclear power stations, security at most research reactors is very limited, which could make them potentially attractive targets for terrorist groups.

Nuclear arms, fissile materials, and—obviously—nuclear facilities, are situated at locations known to responsible authorities, who, in turn, have the ability to implement effective protective measures. In contrast, so many potent radioactive sources are now used in medicine, industry, and research around the world, and so many have fallen outside regulatory control, that it will be many years, if ever, before secure custody of these items can be achieved. Moreover, there is considerable evidence of ongoing international illicit trafficking in these radioactive commodities and of terrorist interest in obtaining them for use in a dirty bomb. Creating such a device would be a simple task for any group that had such materials; indeed, the simplest dispersion devices would require little more than a familiarity with the use of high explosives. An RED—basically, the emplacement of a radioactive source in a heavily traversed area—would be even simpler, although this would not offer a terrorist group the immediate impact of an explosion that could spread radioactive debris with the potential for contaminating a large area.

Given these factors, reducing the probability of a terrorist incident may be a less effective risk-reduction strategy in the short term than seeking to mitigate the consequences of an RDD attack, an event which must be considered highly likely to occur in coming years. Therefore, even as strategies are implemented to improve controls over these materials slowly but steadily, preparing for the actual use of an RDD would be the most urgent priority. Preparatory measures can include education efforts to immunize the public psychologically against panic in the face of an RDD attack, which is unlikely to cause mass casualties; investment in the development of technologies for wide-area decontamination; training of first responders and governmental authorities; and advance stockpiling of emergency response equipment and therapeutics.

One additional, overarching component of efforts to combat nuclear terrorism deserves special attention: the need for effective intelligence. Intelligence is essential to every element of the multilayered defense against nuclear terror. It is crucial for guiding the war on terror, including efforts to identify and disrupt groups that might consider acts of nuclear terror. It is fundamental for helping to determine locations of nuclear weapons and fissile materials in the former Soviet Union and Pakistan needing security upgrades, to track patterns of nuclear trafficking, to monitor the effectiveness of chains of command responsible for these assets, and to alert U.S. policy makers to signs of impending political instability. It is critical for allocating limited resources for port and border security. And it is vital for providing warning of impending attacks. Given the global nature of the nuclear terror threat, moreover, to be effective, intelligence must be coordinated with that of friendly states and relevant international organizations.

Finally, it is important to take stock of existing and potential international mechanisms for combating different nuclear terrorist threats. A surprisingly large number of legal instruments, programs, and non-binding agreements relevant to some dimensions of the terrorism problem have been in play for an extended period of time. They range from the EURATOM Treaty of 1960 to various Nuclear-Weapon-Free Zone treaties to ongoing efforts to amend the 1980 Convention on Physical Protection of Nuclear Material. An effort is made in the chapters that follow to examine the utility of these extant international measures and to specify what more is required to meet the different challenges of nuclear terrorism.

The multi-faceted challenges of nuclear terrorism are technically and politically complex. However, they can be countered effectively by a strategy employing a combination of preventive measures and those that address law enforcement, public education, and emergency response. The remainder of this book elaborates on the nature of the four faces of nuclear terrorism and what can and must be done to reduce these threats.

---

[1] U.S. Senate, Foreign Relations Committee, Testimony of Sam Nunn, Co-chairman of the Nuclear Threat Initiative, July 23, 2002, and Richard G. Lugar, "The Next Steps in U.S. Nonproliferation Policy," *Arms Control Today*, December 2002.

[2] In a report released in January 2004, the Department of Energy Inspector General disclosed that guards at the Y-12 Plant, in Oak Ridge, Tennessee, had received advanced warning of mock terrorist attacks, calling into question the effectiveness of their training; see, U.S. Department of Energy, Office of Inspector General, Office of Inspections and Special Inquiries, "Protective Force Performance Test Improprieties," Inspection Report, DOE/IG-0636, January 2004. Y-12 reportedly contains the U.S. reserve stockpile of about 5,000 "secondaries," which are the key components for thermonuclear weapons, and it is the main processing center for enriched uranium in the United States.

[3] DeNeen L. Brown, "Canada Arrests 19 As Security Threats," *Washington Post*, August 23, 2003, p. A20.

[4] Peter D. Zimmerman with Cheryl Loeb, "Dirty Bombs: The Threat Revisited," *Defense Horizons*, January 2004, Center for Technology and National Security Policy, National Defense University.

[5] Matthew Bunn, Anthony Wier, and John P. Holdren, *Controlling Nuclear Warheads and Materials: A Report Card and Action Plan* (Washington, D.C.: Nuclear Threat Initiative and the Project on Managing the Atom, Harvard University, March 2003), < http://www.nti.org/e_research/cnwm/cnwm.pdf>.

[6] In a few, highly specific scenarios, however, an RDD might lead to much more serious consequences, resulting in tens of thousands of long-term fatalities.

[7] United States Government, *National Strategy for Combating Terrorism*, February 2003.

[8] Barton Gellman, "Fears Prompt U.S. to Beef Up Nuclear Terror Detection," *Washington Post*, March 3, 2002, p. A1.

[9] Mike Allen, "Chemical, Nuclear Arms Still 'Major Threat,' Cheney Says, "*Washington Post*, December 17, 2003, p. A15.

[10] Ceci Connolly, "Classified Look at U.S. Biodefense Nearly Finished," *Washington Post*, December 16, 2003, p. A2.

[11] See, for example, Matthew Bunn and George Bunn, "Strengthening Nuclear Security Against Post-September 11 Threats of Theft and Sabotage," *JNMM* (Spring 2002), pp. 48-60, Siegfried S. Hecker, "Nuclear Terrorism," in Committee on Confronting Terrorism in Russia, *High-Impact Terrorism: Proceedings of a Russian-American Workshop* (Washington, DC: National Academy Press, 2002), pp. 149-155, and "Nuclear and Radiological Threats," Chapter 2 of Committee on Science and Technology for Countering Terrorism, National Research Council, *Making the Nation Safer: The Role of Science and Technology in Countering Terrorism* (Washington, DC: National Academy Press, 2002).

[12] Matthew Bunn, et al., *Controlling Nuclear Warheads and Materials*, discuss this chain of conditions in detail in a section termed the "Terrorist Pathway to the Bomb." Their report, however, addresses only the nuclear terror threats of an IND or an intact nuclear weapon.

[13] Michael Richardson, *A Time Bomb for Global Trade: Maritime-related Terrorism in an Age of Weapons of Mass Destruction* (Singapore: Institute of Southeast Asian Studies, 2004).

[14] For example, in May 2003, Russian Minister of Atomic Energy Aleksandr Rumyantsev discounted the possibility that terrorists could construct an IND; see Robert Serebrennikov, "Russian Minister: No Terrorist Organization Can Manufacture an Atomic Bomb," ITAR-TASS, May 19, 2003. See also, Stephen M. Younger, Director, U.S. Defense Threat Reduction Agency, remarks at the Conference on Counter-Proliferation at Ten, Alexandria, Virginia, December 8, 2003.

2

THE NUCLEAR TERRORISTS
WHO, WHY, AND HOW CAPABLE?

Would a terrorist organization actually take the step of killing 100,000 innocent people and destroying a city? Would it engage in the lesser but still extreme acts of destroying a nuclear installation and causing hundreds of billions of dollars of losses to a modern society or of contaminating historic and/or financial critical sites with radiation?

Even in the decade leading up to 9/11, U.S. policy makers have treated all of these threats as credible and serious. In the post-Cold War world, the attention to the threat of terrorism involving chemical, biological, radiological, and nuclear (CBRN) weapons has resonated at all levels of policy making in the United States and internationally. Several factors, including the proliferation of CBRN technologies and materials, the alarming destructiveness of state-sponsored and transnational terrorism, and an ominous trend toward fewer but higher-casualty terrorist incidents, have given rise to a new and challenging security environment.

The tragic events of September 11, 2001, further heightened concerns about mass casualty/mass destruction terrorism. With this one event, terrorists demonstrated their willingness to kill thousands, cause billions of dollars of destruction, and wreak havoc on the American psyche. In retrospect, the growing lethality of conventional terrorist attacks in the last two decades and the increasingly strident anti-American rhetoric and goals of certain terrorist groups were obvious. Starting with the destruction of Pan Am 103, in which 270 people were killed, the next 13 years were filled with high-casualty incidents and failed attempts at mass-casualty events. (See Figure 2.1) Culminating with the 9/11 attacks, terrorism has become more violent and more deadly.[1] Although the number of incidents has not increased during this time, the lethality of each act of terror has.

This trend in the lethality of individual terrorist attacks is ominous, as it may reflect a shift upward in the terrorists' threshold for inflicting pain on their targets. The possibility that terrorists could acquire and use weapons of mass destruction, including chemical, biological, radiological, and nuclear weapons, therefore, should not be beyond imagina-

FIGURE 2.1
HISTORY OF TERRORISM DISTURBING AND CLEAR

1988	Pan Am #103	270 dead
1992	Car bomb, Buenos Aires	242 dead
1993	Truck bomb, World Trade Center	6 dead and 1,042 injured (goal was 50,000 dead)
1995	Truck bomb, Oklahoma City	168 dead and 500 injured
1996	Truck bomb, Sri Lanka,	90 dead and 1,400 injured
1996	Truck bomb, Saudi Arabia	19 dead and 515 injured
1998	Truck bomb at U.S. Embassy, Kenya	212 dead and 4,022 injured
1999	Bombs in Moscow apartment block	200 dead
2001	World Trade Center, Pentagon, and Pennsylvania	3,062 dead
2002	Bali	190 dead, 300 injured
2004	Madrid	191 dead and 1,800 injured

Since the 1988 terrorist attack on Pan Am 103, which killed 270 people, there has been a greater propensity for large death tolls and injuries in many high-profile terrorist attacks, indicating that political considerations may no longer be the major driving force behind today's most dangerous terrorism threat, although instilling fear in a larger audience still motivates terrorists.

tion. The written materials about these agents found in the al Qaeda caves in Afghanistan,[2] terrorist links to Pakistani nuclear scientists,[3] the ricin-contaminated letters in early 2004,[4] and the anthrax-laced letters of fall 2001 provide strong indications that today we confront terrorists willing and actively seeking ways to cross the weapons of mass destruction threshold.

Historically, terrorists have attempted to force the hand of political leaders by fueling fear in a wider audience. However, trends dating from at least the 1990s indicate that political considerations may no longer be the major driving force behind today's most dangerous terrorism threat, although instilling fear in a larger audience still motivates terrorists. Rather than inspire terror for the sake of achieving limited political objectives, today's terrorism is often fueled by extremist religious ideologies that rationalize destruction, vengeance, and punishment as both necessary ends in themselves and as tools to achieve a better world.[5] Today's terrorists, particularly those steeped in religion, hold all nonbelievers at risk, blurring the line between combatants and noncombatants in ways that could justify pursuing catastrophic terrorism.

For many years, most analysts of terrorism thought that groups with motives to use CBRN weapons were not likely to possess the resources necessary to do so. However, the unthinkable became a reality with Aum Shinrikyo's 1995 sarin attack in the Tokyo subway. This apocalyptic terrorist group, under the leadership of Shoko Asahara, a charismatic cult leader, sought to overthrow the Japanese government, initiate a world war and Armageddon, and eventually impose a bizarre theocratic state on the world. The group explored chemical, biological, and even nuclear weapons as means to achieve its goals. In the end, the incident in March 1995 was fortunately not very effective or successful, resulting in 12 deaths, 1,000 injured and over 5,000 "worried well"[6]; but it also caused the Japanese government to crack down on its activities by arresting its leaders and disbanding the cult.[7]

The emergence of a terrorist organization with the motivation and the means to carry out an attack involving weapons of mass destruction cast a spotlight on the issue of mass casualty terrorism, sounding an alarm in the U.S. national security arena. It changed the way many experts thought about the *potential* of CBRN terrorism in today's context, but it did not really change what experts *expected* the outcome to be because even Aum, with unprecedented access to technical capabilities and financial resources, had still not been very successful. The Oklahoma City bombing a month later in 1995 with its 500 injuries and 169 fatalities became more symbolic of what a terrorist might attempt. Using readily available, inexpensive, highly effective bomb-making materials, two individuals, who believed that some innocent people might have to die in order to win the war against a "tyrannical" government, did far more damage than Aum Shinrikyo did with its sarin attack.[8] The airplane strikes on the World Trade Center and the Pentagon in 2001 have left no doubt as to the immediacy of the threat of mass casualty terrorism. Mass casualties, however, do not necessarily demand weapons of mass destruction: the attacks of 9/11, the 1993 bombing of the World Trade Center, the almost simultaneous bombing of two American embassies in Africa, and the bombing of the *U.S.S. Cole* were all carried out by conventional means.

Although most terrorist groups are not likely to turn to CBRN weapons to cause mass destruction, some may. The available open-source data clearly indicate an increased interest by terrorists in CBRN weapons and agents. According to information in the Center for Nonproliferation Studies' WMD Terrorism Database, the number of terrorist incidents involving some type of CBRN has been growing in the past decade, even if the scale of each event remains low.[9] Terrorists in Europe, Southeast Asia, and South Asia have been found with literature on CBRN weapons or in some cases small amounts of CBRN agents.[10] Also, some al Qaeda hideouts in Afghanistan contained rudimentary sketches of improvised nuclear devices. When such interest is combined with the increasing lethality of terrorist incidents and the more virulent, militant, and anti-Western nature of many current terrorists, the possibility of some type of catastrophic terrorist incident involving CBRN weapons or materials becomes much more probable.

While there is no doubt that terrorist groups exploring the possible use of dangerous chemical and biological agents exist now, the greatest danger to the public emerges from the increased potential for terrorists to pursue the most horrific types of nuclear terrorism involving nuclear detonations. Moreover, even lower-scale radiological events not involving the actual detonation of a nuclear weapon or an IND could have severe economic and psychological consequences because of public fears concerning radioactivity.

TERRORIST GROUPS THAT MIGHT PURSUE NUCLEAR TERRORISM

Terrorist groups most likely to pursue one or more types of nuclear terrorism may be organized in the following categories: apocalyptic groups, politico-religious groups, traditional nationalist/separatist groups, and single-issue groups.

Apocalyptic Groups

Apocalyptic groups include those who believe that the end of the current world order is close, that they need to take some active role in promoting this event, and that this apocalyptic event is an imperative to be furthered with the use of violence. Most apocalyptic groups will not direct violent action at the community around them; if they do act, often their violence is focused internally.[11] However, throughout history, there have been apocalyptic groups, such as certain Jewish or Islamic extremists or factions of the Christian Identity movement, whose faith entails a deep belief in the need to cleanse and purify the world via violent upheaval to eliminate nonbelievers. These types of groups, driven by an urgency and religious passion, often have characteristics—charismatic leaders, isolation and alienation from the larger society, sense of paranoia and grandiosity—that make them of great concern as potential nuclear terrorists.

Politico-Religious Groups

Of equal concern in today's context are the "new terrorists" who have come to dominate the post-9/11 dialogue on terrorism. These groups are hybrids in that they have both political *and* religious motivations and objectives, which are tightly intertwined with their rhetoric, ideology, and action. Groups included in this politico-religious category range from the very broad, transnational al Qaeda network to the more geographically focused Hezbollah and the Hindu fundamentalist extremist group. Such hybrid groups are not without historical precedent, but today they have potential access to CBRN materials and to very high-value targets, making the scope and scale of their terrorist destruction unique. At least one group, al Qaeda under the leadership of Osama bin Laden, is known to have an interest in inflicting mass casualties on Western targets and, specifically, in acquiring and using CBRN materials to do so. What is less certain is whether other such groups exist and whether the loose network of terrorist cells and sympathizers affiliated with al Qaeda are quite so dedicated to such catastrophic terrorism or would be willing to pursue such objectives for bin Laden. Even the team that caused the 191 deaths and 1,800 injuries on the trains bound for Madrid's central station in March 2004 might not be prepared to escalate to acts that might cause 200,000 to die and destroy the heart of a centuries-old city. Whether or not these smaller, subsidiary groups are willing to undertake nuclear terrorist acts that cause mass casualties, they still remain a substantial threat for lesser types of nuclear terrorism that could result in dire economic consequences.

Nationalist/Separatist Groups

Traditional nationalist/separatist terrorist groups cover those terrorist organizations whose purpose is focused on achieving some type of political objectives for a given ethnic or tribal group. Examples include the Irish Republican Army (IRA) in Ireland, the Tamil Tigers in Sri Lanka, and the Kurds in Turkey, and their objectives may range from political independence to political revenge, but these groups' willingness to resort to nuclear terrorism may be constrained by the values of their base constituency. In addition, their own location may make them extremely vulnerable to retaliatory attacks or to concerns of harming their own people from a nuclear attack that took place too close to their homeland areas. Given their sensitivity to such issues, traditional nationalist/separatist terrorist groups are less likely to find the most dangerous types of nuclear terrorism an attractive means to achieving their goals. However, such groups might benefit from appearing to have a capability to inflict harm on their oppressors through nuclear means in order to force state authorities to negotiate an end to hostilities or to provide increased political rights.

Single-Issue Terrorists

The final category of terrorist groups, single-issue terrorists, is defined by a commitment to act as a catalyst to change policies or behavior as it relates to a very clearly defined social or political issue. Animal liberation activists, anti-abortion advocates, pro-environmentalist groups, and even the anti-nuclear movement conceivably could attract extremists who might advocate nuclear terrorism as a way to force the public and government to recognize a perceived problem or concern. Groups of this type have very targeted goals that do not include killing thousands or even causing mass disruption. On the other hand, factions within these groups might turn to the lesser forms of nuclear terrorism, such as radiological dispersion devices, or even nuclear hoaxes, much the way anthrax hoaxes have been used to disrupt abortion clinics. Finally, there could also be members sympathetic with the other, more violent groups mentioned above, thus perhaps making more high-end forms of nuclear terrorism, such as trying to build an IND, more attractive. An anti-abortion radical who is also a member of the Christian Identity might be an example of such possible mixed commitments that could result in nuclear terrorism. In fact, in *The Turner Diaries* by American neo-Nazi William Pierce, the protagonist Turner becomes a martyr by crashing a plane armed with a nuclear weapon into the Pentagon.

While it is impossible to know with certainty which terrorists might resort to some form of nuclear terrorism, these four broadly defined groups cover the general categories of greatest concern. Determining what might cause these types of terrorists to make the decision to resort to nuclear terrorism requires a more thorough evaluation of terrorist motivations, as well as capabilities. In doing so, the following analysis will provide a better understanding of why a terrorist organization would focus on nuclear terrorism in particular, and why such an organization would pursue one form of nuclear terrorism in lieu of another.

CATALYSTS TO NUCLEAR TERRORISM

Nuclear Terrorism and Terrorist Groups

The Iranian Revolution in 1979 marked the advent of modern religious terrorism, sparking militant fundamentalist Islamic movements in states such as Algeria, Egypt, and Saudi Arabia. By the mid-1980s, the impact of religious terrorism had become highly visible. The war against the Soviet Union in Afghanistan further radicalized key Islamic fundamentalist groups. By 1995, religious terrorists, despite carrying out only one-quarter of known terrorist incidents, were responsible for almost two-thirds of terror-related fatalities.[12] Today, many terrorists pride themselves on claiming a religious allegiance and a religiously focused set of objectives, making it very difficult to categorize accurately the core motivations of many regional groups. However, there is no doubt that a growing number of terrorists have established international links and consider themselves part of a transnational, global Islamic fundamentalist movement aggressively seeking change through violent means.

From a motivational standpoint, the acquisition of a working nuclear weapon would represent the ultimate capability for *apocalyptic and politico-religious terrorist groups*. Groups with nuclear capability could assume a quasi-state nature and rely upon the prestige associated with the possession of these weapons to manipulate adversaries into making political concessions. With regard to actually employing such a device, apocalyptic groups who are externally oriented are most likely to pursue this option. They may believe that detonating a nuclear warhead would spark a broader nuclear conflict, enabling them to hasten the end of the world. In this same vein, an improvised nuclear device could also result in mass terror, death, and destruction, making it a close second choice for apocalyptic groups. (As discussed further below, however, although a group may have the desire to cause cataclysmic nuclear destruction, it may lack the necessary skills and resources to execute such a vision.)

On the lower end of nuclear terror acts, the notion of attacking a nuclear facility or detonating a radiological dispersal device does not seem particularly well suited for apocalyptic-type groups. Lacking a nuclear explosive yield, these variants of nuclear terrorism are less likely to meet the standards of spectacular devastation that can often drive apocalyptic terrorists.[13] While both forms of terror might release a significant amount of radiation, the consequences might not be great enough to merit serious investment. If a nuclear weapon or an improvised nuclear device does not represent a technically viable option for an apocalyptic group seeking to cause massive immediate casualties, the organization is probably more likely to pursue non-nuclear avenues of mass destruction, as evidenced by Aum's decision in the early 1990s to forgo the nuclear and biological routes in favor of chemical weapons.[14] Notably, the main constraints on Aum were technical, not motivational.

For a *politico-religious group* such as al Qaeda, the desire to control a nuclear weapon is twofold. First, publicizing the acquisition of a nuclear weapon would have an extraordinary psychological impact on the target audience. The credible threat created by controlling a nuclear weapon would significantly bolster any political goals of the terrorist group. Second, the group might decide that the benefits of detonating the weapon outweighed the value of the threat alone. The blast from such a device would immediately fulfill the group's strategic objective of striking a devastating blow against the perceived enemy. The physical damage would be catastrophic, just as the psychological and economic impact on the survivors would be overwhelming.[15]

As with apocalyptic groups, politico-religious groups unable to acquire a nuclear weapon could attempt to produce an improvised nuclear device instead. An IND would still serve the dual goals of a politico-religious group: manipulation and mass devastation. Also, producing an IND may bring more prestige to a terrorist group than acquiring an intact nuclear weapon. Such production ability would greatly enhance the threat posed by a terrorist group.

Unlike apocalyptic terrorists, politico-religious terrorists are not concerned merely with bringing death and destruction. The lingering psychological impact of an attack carries significant weight as well, as seen in the wake of 9/11. Thus, a radiological dispersal device could also prove advantageous for a politico-religious group. A powerful conventional bomb coupled with radiological material could lead to hundreds of casualties, and it could also cause physical damage, making an area of economic or symbolic importance unusable for decades. Finally, it would leave an indelible mark on the psyche of the target audience. Likewise, an attack on a nuclear power plant or storage facility would also carry a great psychological impact, as well as the potential for substantial property damage and long-term medical challenges.[16] Since both an RDD and an attack on a nuclear facility may have somewhat similar consequences, the allure of either one will depend to a large degree on the terrorists' capabilities and objectives. The case of José Padilla is instructive in this regard. An American convert to militant Islamic fundamentalism arrested in 2002 in the United States, Padilla appears to have been tasked to do a feasibility study for an RDD, illustrating current terrorist interest in using nuclear materials for malicious intentions, while inadvertently demonstrating their limited capabilities. [17]

For the more traditional *nationalist/separatist terrorist groups,* the advantages of acquiring a nuclear weapon do not hinge on the desire for mass destruction. Rather, the prestige factor would be the driving force behind the acquisition of an intact nuclear warhead or improvised nuclear device. More traditional terrorist groups are primarily motivated by political goals. For these groups, a nuclear weapon would offer great strategic value. Possession of either a nuclear warhead or an improvised nuclear device would enable a nationalist/separatist terrorist group, such as the rebels in Chechnya, to gain international recognition and feign some of the attributes of a state, thereby advancing their nationalist objectives. The likelihood of such a group actually detonating a nuclear device or an IND is extremely low, due to the fear of an overwhelming international backlash. Nonextremist members of the ethnic or national group the terrorists claim to represent may also react negatively to the use of weapons of mass destruction. However, nationalist/separatist terrorist groups might find significant value in using a nuclear weapon (whether stolen or an improvised nuclear device) to blackmail their adversary into achieving their political goals. In this scenario, the terrorists would have to be able to prove they had a credible nuclear capability, which they could operationalize in an attack against the adversary or its interests. The leaders of the target country would then be faced with giving into the terrorists' demands, taking a chance that their threat was a bluff, or living with the disastrous consequences of a nuclear weapon explosion on its territory.[18] Realistically, very few of these groups will possess the technical or financial resources to develop or acquire a nuclear weapon, but their ability to have such weapons might appear be more plausible today given the poor security surrounding critical nuclear materials and the publicly available information on nuclear weapon designs.

The political aims of traditional nationalist/separatist groups severely limit their options with respect to nuclear terrorism. In order to pursue their goals, these groups cannot afford to alienate their target audience with a full-fledged nuclear yield. Thus, radiological dispersal devices appear to be the most promising candidate for nuclear terrorism among traditional groups, assuming that such weapons can be used without harming assets that the perpetrator is seeking to protect. The radiological fallout and lingering psychological effects offer greater potency than mere conventional attacks, but given the lower scale of consequences leave the door open to negotiations. Attacking a nuclear facility would create the same powerful symbolism, but the threat of lingering physical effects from radiation would be greater. Traditional groups are unlikely to target sites on their own territory, where the physical effects would harm members of their community and could weaken support for their cause.[19] Concern for their support base, however, does not necessarily preclude an attack against a nuclear facility located a safe distance away. Attacks against facilities that are not yet in operation might also be carried out in order to discourage an adversary's presence in disputed territory. The attack by the Basque terrorist group ETA on the unfinished Lemoniz nuclear facility in Spain in 1977 is an example of terrorists trying to signal rejection of their government's presence and willingness to target a nuclear power plant in the future if necessary.[20]

Single-issue terrorist groups—particularly extremist environmental and anti-nuclear groups—also factor into the nuclear terror equation. Such groups would not focus on mass destruction; rather, they would be intent upon exposing the dangers of nuclear technology or lashing out at the nuclear power industry. In this situation, an anti-nuclear group would not necessarily use a nuclear weapon or blow up a nuclear facility. They would most likely take over a facility to show its vulnerabilities.

The key condition pushing a terrorist group toward one type of nuclear terrorism may be the ease of access to critical materials, people, and/or facilities. The one exception might be the single-issue anti-nuclear-power terrorist groups, since their purpose is to undermine public confidence in nuclear energy and to prevent continued reliance on nuclear power. These groups evolved in the 1970s when nuclear power emerged as an alternative form of energy, and they were most active during that decade, although there were several groups still active in the 1980s.[21] Such terrorist groups were organized around extremist political beliefs, with their objectives hinging on influencing policy rather than punishing an adversary.[22] Consequently, the majority of attacks by anti-nuclear groups against nuclear facilities have occurred during the construction phase.[23] As nuclear energy reemerges as an option to address global warming problems, these groups could reappear.

The political goals of such groups dictate that, for the most part, they discriminate in their activities[24] and develop operations with limited objectives, targets, and scale. The possibility exists, however, that fringe groups might view an attack on a nuclear facility that resulted in a radiation leak as a prime option for illustrating to the public the dangers of nuclear power. These groups may also attack nuclear fuel or waste in storage or transit in an attempt to dramatize the environmental dangers the material poses. In such cases, the single-issue group would probably not claim responsibility for the attack in order to protect what it sees as its legitimate political standing.

In addition, the possibility that a *lone individual* might attempt some type of nuclear terrorism can not be dismissed, especially for those types that require limited technical and operational capabilities. There have been numerous times when individuals have made highly effective terrorists—the Alphabet Bomber of the 1970s and the more recent Unabomber provide just two examples of loners who successfully terrorized communities by engineering random acts of terror.[25]

Strategic Considerations

Whatever their category, all terrorist groups must make a conscious decision to resort to nuclear terrorism. Such a decision can be broken down into many parts, but it always involves some assessment of how well a nuclear terrorist incident, regardless of type, will appear both to promote the strategic goals of the group or individual and be technically viable. Nuclear terrorism is most inviting to groups seeking highly visible and psychologically potent results and having little regard for the possible consequences. With respect to the various forms of nuclear terrorism, the potential vulnerability of certain facilities and ease of access to nuclear and radiological materials will strongly influence which mode a group may choose to pursue. The wide array of destructive capabilities within the arena of nuclear terrorism provides a range of options and will strongly influence the group's choice as it tries to find the right fit between means and ends. Given the various types of nuclear terrorism possible, a terrorist group might exist that perceives one or more type of nuclear-related event as being congruent with its objectives. Before the terrorists pursue such an option, there will be many decision points, with the final event reflecting a combination of strategic and tactical considerations. Recognizing that terrorists must make numerous choices on the path to nuclear terrorism means there will be several points at which terrorists can be thwarted or diverted.

When examining terrorists' motivations to pursue some type of nuclear terrorism, it is helpful to analyze the necessary decision-making process such groups might enter into. A critical first-order decision relates to the scale and scope of the intended violence: Would it be to cause mass destruction, mass disruption, or a more limited, symbolic event with few casualties? The choice made at this very first point would most likely reflect the core objectives and ideology of the group and be strongly influenced by the group's leadership. The group, presumably, would consider engaging in acts of terrorism also because of the psychological dimension of this type of violence. Especially when considering nuclear terrorism, terrorists would try to exploit the public trauma from a terrorist incident involving nuclear materials. Imagine the public's reaction if the Chernobyl accident had been intentional or if al Qaeda could credibly claim to have a nuclear weapon.[26]

Terrorists recognize that pursuing some type of nuclear terrorism would be perceived as crossing a major threshold and would entail enormous risks. The question still remains, then, why nuclear? Is there something unique to "things nuclear" that would make nuclear terrorism more attractive and effective than chemical, biological, or conventional attacks? Nuclear terrorism has the feature of achieving a unique type of public fear and trauma because of the negative societal association with almost anything nuclear. Thus, nuclear terrorism of any type could be an obvious means to achieve one goal common to all terrorism—causing a psychological reaction within the target community. Even more than the events of the fall of 2001, an attack using nuclear materials, whether in a nuclear weapon, from a nuclear power plant, or from a radioactive source, would cause a residual fear in the population about their safety and the safety of their environment due to possible physical contamination, their own exposure to radiation, and the long-term effects of radioactive fallout.[27] Experts have noted the public's irrational fear of radiation, which clearly terrorists could try to exploit. [28]

The growing lethality of terrorist attacks also points to a desire to create a more impressive spectacle. Consider the impact should a nuclear weapon be detonated inside the United States—terrorists would achieve the goals not only of killing many Americans, but also of psychologically scarring the American public, perhaps even undermining the public's willingness to be global leaders or causing the U.S. government to strike out in excessive retaliation. An attack with an intact nuclear weapon or an IND represents the ultimate in highly visible attacks. The grandiosity of the event would definitely appeal to apocalyptic cults as well as politico-religious terrorists because it would demonstrate an enormous capability and heighten their own sense of power. In addition to the sheer destructive impact of a nuclear explosion, the aura of fear and myth surrounding nuclear weapons would afford a terrorist organization significant political capital. Some nationalist terrorists might find the appearance of having leveled the playing field between the United States and a much weaker terrorist group, even if briefly, as well worth the effort. It would provide a huge boost to the credibility and reputation of the terrorists involved, perhaps creating a sense of being equivalent to a state.[29] Some might imagine that by claiming to have additional nuclear weapons, they could hold the United States hostage, in a manner resembling the way weaker states such as North Korea have been able to parlay possible WMD capabilities to offset enormous asymmetries in power. Of course, the risks to the terrorists would be equally substantial since U.S. authorities would stop at nothing to eliminate such a threat. But what would it take to deter the United States? It is unlikely that the United States would risk having a credible nuclear terrorist group blow up an American city, making it feasible for terrorists to be able to use the "great equalizer" to their benefit. Moreover, the intelligence problem of identifying where the nuclear terrorists have their nuclear weapon(s) would pose an enormous challenge.

The threat of a terrorist attack alone would have a powerful psychological impact on the public and could perhaps force a government into negotiations with the terrorist group. Finally, a personal preoccupation with nuclear weapons by terrorist leaders might drive a group to pursue the nuclear option. Such was the case with Aum Shinrikyo in the late 1980s. Although the group also experimented with chemical and biological weapons, the cult's leader, Shoko Asahara, predicted a violent end to humanity, sparked by a nuclear cataclysm.[30] Asahara was hoping to catalyze a nuclear war between the United States and Japan, claiming that Aum members would survive such a catastrophe.

While it may be relatively easy to target the few groups whose goals and capabilities might be consistent with detonating some type of nuclear weapon, determining those that might pursue the lesser types of nuclear terrorism is more problematic. The strategic value of these less destructive nuclear incidents would be tied to the actual target (such as nuclear power), the disruption effect due to contamination, or the sense of vulnerability to radiation they might instill. These results might not be seen as substantial enough to opt for some type of low-end nuclear terrorist attack without other tactical considerations entering into the decision-making process of the terrorists. For example, how easy is access to needed nuclear materials or nuclear facilities? The choice of weapon may be decided more by opportunistic access to resources, technical expertise, or targets than by a specific motivation. When technical and operational issues facilitate a terrorist group's ability to pursue a nuclear-related incident, it may then have the final means or encouragement to go through with the event.

Tactical Issues

A plan to resort to some type of nuclear terrorism might not merely reflect a strategic decision; it might also be the result of organizational dynamics, ease of access to needed materials/targets, successful use elsewhere, or a leader's obsession.

The issue of precedence represents an important factor in evaluating the threat of nuclear terrorism. Aum Shinrikyo's sarin attack is the most significant instance of CBRN terrorism to date. Although Chechen rebels accepted responsibility for placing a radioactive container in Ismailovsky Park in Moscow in 1995, they have stopped short of detonating a "dirty bomb," despite their proven ability to acquire radioactive material and penetrate the heart of Moscow.[31] An explanation for the Chechen rebels' apparent reluctance in carrying out a radiological attack could be that "the Russian government has adopted an even harder public line every time the Chechens have threatened to carry out acts of CBRN terrorism in Russian cites."[32] The fact that there has been no precedent for a nuclear or radiological terrorism attack may be credited in large part to a lack of will on the part of terrorist organizations. The attacks of 9/11, highly imaginative yet ultimately conventional in nature, have resulted in the U.S.-led overthrow of two regimes and opened the floodgates for American military activity around the world. Clearly the impact of a nuclear terrorist attack could be devastating for both the target of the attack and the terrorist support base. Given the attention and fear that would result, even an RDD attack would in all likelihood hold disastrous consequences for the culprit.

The lack of a precedent stands out as a major deterrent to nuclear terrorism by suggesting that other groups have found this option too difficult or too dangerous in view of the scale of likely retaliation. Once that precedent has been set, however, the playing field will change dramatically. Two factors in particular will determine the actions of other would-be nuclear terrorists. First, the effectiveness of an attack will either encourage or discourage its perpetrators. Due to a make-shift means of delivery, Aum's chemical attack was able to cause only a small fraction of the fatalities generally associated with WMD.[33] The low number of casualties highlights the limitations of terrorism involving chemical weapons. The difficult task of effectively dispersing a chemical agent has arguably acted as a significant deterrent to other terrorist groups. On the other hand, any nuclear attack—including one by a state—that appeared successful at causing panic, destruction, the breakdown of governmental authority, and substantial human casualties raises the possibility of copycat events, as the impact of a nuclear attack will have been visibly demonstrated. Second, the consequences for the perpetrators of a nuclear or radiological attack will have sizeable influence on the plans of other terrorists. Should the detonation of a nuclear weapon, an attack on a nuclear facility, or use of an RDD be met with only a moderate response, the perceived taboo against such terrorist methods might erode considerably.

Terrorists groups may also be pushed toward nuclear terrorism because of internal organizational issues. These might range from the leader's fascination with "things nuclear" to an internal power struggle that results in the group becoming fractionalized. Often when such fissures occur within a terrorist organization, one segment may be much more radical and seek ways to demonstrate the correctness of its approach, often resulting in the use of more extreme methods to achieve the group's objectives than had been adopted by the pre-schism parent organization. In such a case, the resort to nuclear terrorism might provide the new, more violent faction with just the right display of innovative destructiveness to claim center stage and power within the larger terrorist organization.

Another aspect of an organization that might facilitate the nuclear choice involves the group's mix of personnel and their comfort level with different types of technologies. Clearly a group that decides to go down the path of a nuclear incident will need some technical capabilities that go beyond conventional bomb making. Such a group would probably go out and recruit or take hostage the necessary experts. But, if a group already had in its midst (or had access to) sympathetic nuclear scientists and technicians, it might consider some type of nuclear terrorist incident much more readily than would a group with chemists or biologists. The assistance that Pakistani nuclear scientists reportedly offered to al Qaeda is an important case in point, as it would provide the terrorists with the technical personnel to explain and potentially operationalize some of the materials they were already collecting about nuclear facilities and weapons, making it possible for them to make their rhetoric about wanting nuclear weapons a reality.[34]

An additional organizational characteristic relevant to the decision to pursue nuclear terrorism revolves around the nature of the group's leadership.[35] A charismatic, authoritarian leader, such as Asahara of Aum Shinrikyo, will dominate all of the decisions made about what methods to use to further the group's goals. Asahara appears to have been convinced that Armageddon would result from a global nuclear war pursued by the United States; thus he needed nuclear weapons to confront this threat. Despite various efforts, he did not make much meaningful headway in acquiring these weapons. Terrorist leaders, such as Osama bin Laden, have also stressed their need and right to have the same weapons as their enemies, leading to a justification for RDDs, INDs, or nuclear weapons as demonstrated in his now famous comment:

> Acquiring weapons for the defense of Muslims is a religious duty. If I have indeed acquired these weapons, then I thank God for enabling me to do so. And if I seek to acquire these weapons, I am carrying out a duty. It would be a sin for Muslims not to try to possess the weapons that would prevent the infidels from inflicting harm on Muslims. [36]

In addition, leaders may promote efforts to obtain and use nuclear weapons against the United States so as to be seen as challenging the direct symbol of American power and punishing the Great Satan for its past nuclear uses.[37]

A final catalyst pushing terrorists toward nuclear terrorism is ease of access to necessary nuclear materials or nuclear targets. While their

capabilities and skills may be limited, terrorists are typically both ratio-
nal and pragmatic in their planning—they will try to exploit vulnerabilities and use available resources as much as possible. Thus, terrorists'
ability to get their hands on radioactive sources, fissile materials, or even
nuclear weapons easily may encourage them to explore how best to use
these items in the pursuit of their strategic goals. Prevent access to materials or targets, and the terrorists' decision-making calculus changes.
Even if the goal is to create some type of mass-casualty disaster, without access to the nuclear materials, most terrorists will likely seek other,
very effective non-nuclear options. An RDD becomes less attractive if
the radioactive sources are more difficult to obtain or an attack on a
nuclear waste facility or power plant may just not be worth the effort in
light of adequate containment and security precautions.[38] Thus, terrorists may be deterred from nuclear terrorism by being denied access to
key materials and/or targets. When this happens, the terrorists would
be unable to overcome their inadequate capabilities regardless of the
strength of their motivations.

DISINCENTIVES FOR THE PURSUIT OF NUCLEAR TERRORISM

While terrorists may have strategic reasons and tactical opportunities
to pursue nuclear terrorism, few in fact have contemplated such an
incident. Even fewer have ever attempted to develop a plan to pursue
one of the types of nuclear terrorism, and only a handful has actually
operationalized their interest.[39] The factors influencing terrorists who
decide not to resort to nuclear terrorism are numerous and can be
divided into four groups: implementation challenges, philosophical or
moral issues, response fears, and insufficient capability. Except for the
last item, the specific factors that will ultimately influence any one group
or individual will be rooted in the terrorists' basic motivation.

Implementation challenges are the primary barriers to any type of
nuclear terrorism—even for terrorist groups set on mass destruction,
such as al Qaeda. This group has major global changes as its core objective and justifies the use of any type of violence necessary to reach that
goal. It is not worried about crossing the nuclear threshold and causing
a new level of destruction; nor is it concerned with retaliation or its

followers' reactions. Al Qaeda's belief system fully justifies resorting to whatever means necessary to attack the West and specifically the United States as a means toward their ultimate goal of returning the Muslim world to global dominance under their guidance. If this group can develop the capabilities and believes it can operationalize them effectively, there is little doubt that it will resort to nuclear terrorism.[40]

While nationalist and single-issue terrorists might be deterred by being unable to acquire the necessary capabilities and operational capacity, these groups could also be influenced by other factors such as moral questions, fears of severe retaliation, or constituency backlash. For example, an ecoterrorist group would probably have severe, moral reservations about contaminating the environment with radioactive fallout; it might choose to take over a nuclear power plant for a few days to demonstrate the potential for disaster rather than try to blow one up. Ethnically based groups with identifiable home territories, such as the Chechens or Tamil Tigers, could believe they have much to lose from severe retaliation or constituency-group alienation in response to a decision to attempt any type of nuclear terrorism. Not only might the target of their attack feel justified in retaliatory strikes that ultimately eliminate the group, but the group's own followers and others who were sympathetic to it might decide that nuclear terrorism was a threshold not to be crossed, leaving the perpetrators isolated from the constituency group. In these contexts, the public fear of "things nuclear" might actually deter terrorists by acting as a constraint rather than as an incentive.

However, the possibility that other, more extreme factions could alter this dynamic should not be dismissed. As pointed out by Jeffrey Bale, "…one can easily envision another possible scenario, one that is perhaps even more worrisome" than a scenario purely designed to advance nationalist-separatist goals. "It seems probable that the radical Islamist components of the Chechen resistance movement would be more likely, for ideological reasons, to have recourse to radiological or nuclear terrorism than the traditional nationalist or moderately religious components."[41]

A final disincentive to terrorists considering the option of nuclear terrorism could be that the planning, training, and acquisition of necessary capabilities might create unique "signatures," making them more vulnerable to discovery by intelligence operatives and law enforcement agents. In addition, since a nuclear terrorist incident would involve a terrorist group in novel, complex, technical, and untried activities, the potential for accidents and the emergence of unforeseen problems would be much greater than what might be expected for more conventional terrorism. Groups with limited resources would not necessarily want to endanger their long-term viability by early detection or disastrous accidents, especially if there were less risky alternatives.

Understanding the disincentives at work could provide the basis for a counter-terrorist strategy. For example, by finding it harder to obtain intact nuclear weapons, fissile materials, or radioactive sources, terrorists might be dissuaded from their pursuit of nuclear terrorism. Improving security at nuclear facilities and containment at nuclear waste facilities might considerably diminish the attraction of attacking a nuclear facility by making destructive and psychological consequences more difficult to achieve. Another component of a nuclear terrorism prevention program might involve stimulating a more public vetting of the immorality of resorting to nuclear terrorism, recognizing that certain religions and communities might contain strong anti-nuclear sentiments. Additionally, if countries clarified through publicly stated policies a commitment to severe retaliatory response, some terrorists, weighing the costs and benefits of trying to cross the nuclear threshold, might opt for other avenues to achieve their objectives.

CAPABILITIES NEEDED TO CONDUCT NUCLEAR TERRORISM

The capabilities necessary for a successful attack vary greatly for each form of nuclear terrorism. The ability to acquire and deliver an intact nuclear weapon requires a large organization with substantial financial resources. Depending on the target and the source of the nuclear weapon, it could also require multinational operational capabilities. A strong central authority would likely be necessary to coordinate the numerous operatives involved in acquisition and delivery. State sponsorship could be invaluable: A rogue state could theoretically develop a nuclear weapon and pass it on to a terrorist organization in order to strike out at its enemies in the hope of avoiding any negative consequences. The Bush administration, in promoting its strategy of preemption and in many of its arguments for military action against Saddam Hussein's Iraqi regime in 2003, demonstrated how seriously this scenario is taken by U.S. policy makers.[42] Should the terrorist organization lack a state sponsor, it might successfully obtain a nuclear weapon with assistance from a senior-level official in the nuclear chain of command of a state. Without support of this kind, even if the group obtained the support of one or two lower-level custodians, it would most likely require a highly organized and well-armed military wing capable of stealing an intact weapon. (Indeed, in order to steal a nuclear weapon from a military installation, insider support would be extremely advantageous and perhaps essential.)

Developing an improvised nuclear device represents the most challenging type of nuclear terrorism. An attack involving an IND requires extensive financial and technological resources, in addition to a secure facility in which to develop and construct the weapon. The construction of an IND would in all likelihood demand a well-organized international network of agents charged with locating fissile material and recruiting scientists to develop the device itself. However, if the terrorists acquired enough HEU to build a gun-type IND, the simplest nuclear weapon, the level of technical expertise needed to assemble the device would be far less than that required by more technically challenging weapon designs, such as implosion-type devices, which would be necessary for INDs using plutonium as their core.[43]

Like the scenario involving an intact nuclear weapon, a terrorist plot involving an improvised nuclear device would benefit significantly from state sponsorship. The terrorist group would need a safe haven in which to establish the necessary production and staging facilities without risking detection by counterterrorism and nonproliferation agencies. An effective delivery method would require a well-coordinated, well-funded network of operatives across several nations, capable of arranging transport and detonation of the device without detection. It might be possible to construct the IND in the targeted country, thereby avoiding the problem of transportation of an IND or fissile materials across international borders. However, this scenario requires finding an in-country safe place to do the necessary assembly.

An attack on or sabotage of a nuclear facility also requires a highly organized, well-funded, and well-armed group of operatives, although it does not necessarily require a multinational capability. While the size of the terrorist network need not be nearly as large as that for groups seeking intact nuclear weapons or INDs, it would have to be well coordinated in order to carry out an attack against a nuclear facility. The financial resources of such a group might range from moderate to high, depending on the plan of attack. A commando-type raid on a facility would require relatively modest financial resources, although in order to achieve success it would almost certainly need insider cooperation. A suicide attack on a nuclear reactor or spent nuclear fuel storage pool with an aircraft, on the other hand, would require funds to train the pilots for a direct hit on the facility, unless trained individuals were already part of the terrorist team.[44]

An RDD would require significantly fewer technical skills and financial resources than the other forms of nuclear terrorism. Widespread access to radioactive sources essentially obviates the need for a multinational network. An RDD may be effectively delivered via a conventional bomb packed with radioactive material or through other dispersion modes. Alternatively, the radioactive source could be used to cause injury by means of an RED, for example, by using a suitcase filled with an unshielded radioactive source that is intended to expose passersby to dangerous gamma radiation. The relative ease of delivery of an RDD makes it a viable option for smaller groups with limited financial resources and technical know-how.

Depending on the scenario, moving a weapon, IND, or RDD to the target could require a substantial transportation network that could operate without detection, further taxing the organizational and financial resources of a terrorist group.

Several other factors could enhance the capability of terrorists to undertake nuclear terrorism by facilitating their access to materials or facilities or by providing them with a safe haven where planning and training can occur without fear of detection. These factors, including state sponsorship, insider assistance, and links to organized crime, might be considered "wild cards" given the uncertainty of the relationships involved and the potential impact on the terrorist group. The difficulty of detecting and evaluating links to states, organized crime, or relevant insiders could provide terrorists the element of surprise. It may not be necessary for the terrorists and these "wild cards" to have the same motives, but should some type of connection exist, the wherewithal for an act of nuclear terrorism could be bolstered.

The more collaborative relationships might involve partnerships in which terrorists carry out a state's bidding using nuclear weapons or materials. Alternatively, states might turn a blind eye to activities occurring within their boundaries, thereby permitting terrorists to organize complex operations such as might be involved in a nuclear terrorist attack. Other collaborations might involve sales of weapons, materials, or blueprints. Finally, insiders might be sympathizers or might be blackmailed into granting access to sensitive facilities or materials. Such relationships might act as a catalyst to action since they could provide the crucial missing piece—weapons-usable fissile material, access, or a safe haven—needed for the terrorists to proceed with a nuclear terrorist attack.

When all of these factors are taken together, it becomes evident that few terrorist groups, in fact, have both the motivational orientation and the capabilities to attempt some type of nuclear terrorist incident. As Table 2.1 indicates, at the present time al Qaeda is likely the only network with all the requisite characteristics discussed above to pursue nuclear terrorism of the most extreme form, either by acquiring or developing a nuclear weapon. While other terrorist groups might show an interest in nuclear terrorism, their interest will most likely be in less extreme forms of nuclear terrorism, and their abilities to operationalize such an interest may be limited. Trying to identify further the number and type of terrorists capable of any type of nuclear terrorism will help counterterrorist efforts to target certain groups with the hope of disrupting any operational efforts and denying access to required materials.

TABLE 2.1
CRITERIA FOR PURSUING ACTS OF NUCLEAR TERROR

	Stolen Nuclear Device	Improvised Nuclear Device	Radio-active Release from Nuclear Facility	RDD
Motivation	Extreme; desire to cause mass deaths, destruction; likely limited to apoca-lyptic and politico-religious groups	Extreme; desire to cause mass deaths, destruction; likely limited to apocalyptic and politico-religious groups	Very high; desire to cause great property damage, disruption, some loss of life	Very high; desire to cause great property damage, disruption, some loss of life
Organiza-tional skills needed	Very high	Very high	Very high	Moderate
Geo-graphic reach needed	Multicountry capability required to detonate Russian, Pakistani, or Indian device in U.S.	Multicountry capability required to detonate device built from foreign-origin, weapons-usable, fissile material in U.S.	Single country	Single country sufficient

TABLE 2.1(CONTINUED)
CRITERIA FOR PURSUING ACTS OF NUCLEAR TERROR

	Stolen Nuclear Device	Improvised Nuclear Device	Radioactive Release from Nuclear Facility	RDD
Financial resources needed	High	High	Moderate to high	Modest
Technical skills needed	High	High; moderate for some scenarios	Moderate to high	Modest
Number of groups (2004)	Few; (possibly none currently able to meet all criteria for foreign country incident)	Few; (possibly none currently able to meet all criteria for foreign country incident)	10+	10s-100s

FINAL CONSIDERATIONS

The Impact of Innovation

By choosing nuclear terrorism, a terrorist group heads down an unknown path. While terrorists are not opposed to innovation, they have tended to be conservative in their choice of methods, shifting to new ways or new technologies either because of necessity, new or radicalized leadership, or demonstrated success by others. The decision to attempt a nuclear terrorist operation would require new capabilities in terms of personnel, equipment, and materials; it would involve new operational skills and knowledge; and it would demand developing new types of plans and networks. All of these innovations would present unknown challenges, pitfalls, and risks.

Equally important to a group's willingness to innovate will be its mind-set. A terrorist organization would need a high level of technological awareness, which would require some level of interaction with the broader scientific and technical community. This requirement for interaction with outsiders might be difficult for groups that need isolation to sustain their organization. In addition, the terrorists, especially the leaderships, would have to be open to new ideas. Members would need to feel comfortable putting forward their own proposals, taking initiative, and trying out new approaches. In many terrorist organizations, control and suppression of the individual are critical, and the diversity of views and opinions is seen as a threat to the security and stability of the group. Finally, a terrorist group considering nuclear terrorism would need to perceive the risk involved in such an operation as positive because it provides stimulation and generates group solidarity.[45]

As the terrorists proceed through their decision tree toward implementing a nuclear terrorist attack, doing something innovative could be seen either as a burden and deter the group from acting, or as a statement with the potential for multiplying the impact of conventional terrorism. If some of the negative aspects of pursuing such an innovative strategy were diminished, perhaps through the help of a state or an insider, the recognition that nuclear terrorism might serve a group's interests could make the decision to move forward much more attractive and more likely.

Is Crossing the Nuclear Threshold Significant?

That some terrorists today may have already made the decision to cross the nuclear threshold is a prevailing concern. If true, these terrorists probably do not see a threshold to cross. The most militant Islamic extremists are dedicated to killing as many Americans as possible. They can accomplish this goal in various ways, with nuclear terrorism providing the added terror resulting from the nuclear character of the incident. To most officials, communities, and experts, however, a nuclear terrorist attack would be seen as crossing a threshold, as it would vastly increase the level of destruction and fear resulting from one incident. Also, if successful in killing thousands and creating societal trauma, such an incident would be recognized by other groups, quickly leading to other attempts and hoaxes. For groups considering less destructive types of nuclear terrorism, an actual event could signal that a terrorist group had crossed a threshold because it was willing to raise the stakes for itself and for its target audience. But it could also reflect tactical decisions relating to ease of acquiring the necessary nuclear materials or gaining access to nuclear facilities. Thus, it is important not to assume that resorting to nuclear terrorism would necessarily be a difficult decision for terrorist groups and equally important to recognize that once a successful nuclear terrorist event of any type occurs, it will change fundamental assumptions about American and global security.

What About Nuclear Hoaxes?

Terrorist groups may be able to leverage their nuclear capabilities effectively without ever actually exploding a nuclear weapon or a radiological dispersion device. Although there have been many nuclear weapon hoaxes in the past 25 years, none has succeeded in the sense that the perpetrators were able to achieve their demands. However, government officials have still had to respond to what eventually are determined to be hoaxes, putting into play numerous intelligence and government assets such as the Nuclear Emergency Search Team (NEST) to assess quickly the credibility of the threat and initiate appropriate responses.[46] For a terrorist group such as al Qaeda, pursuing a strategy of attempting a nuclear hoax would not appear worth the consequences since its interest is in causing a nuclear catastrophe, not in threatening to do so. Nonetheless, such a group might attempt a hoax to blackmail the United States, for example, into stopping support for Israel. On the other hand, if the hoax were found to be an empty threat, the terrorist group would lose credibility. However, other terrorist groups, such as the Basque ETA, the Chechens, or Hezbollah, might see great value in being able to threaten to detonate a nuclear weapon inside Europe, Russia, or the United States, or in being able to claim to have a powerful RDD. Single-issue groups with little interest in causing significant human or physical damage, however, might find the most value in attempting a nuclear hoax as it would temporarily instill fear in the public and force a government to acknowledge vulnerability without putting much at risk. Hoaxes, then, would appear to serve the purposes of only a few terrorist groups and primarily to provide short-term benefits, such as news media attention or a momentary distraction.

For all of these scenarios, though, groups would have to be able to provide enough proof that their nuclear threat was real in order to be taken seriously. While providing such proof might not appear to be so difficult given the availability throughout the globe of nuclear materials and expertise, terrorists would have to do more than just show that they had nuclear materials and theorctical capabilities. Whether a terrorist group could deceive the United States or another country with a nuclear hoax is an open question, but so far none has done so.

The Role of the News Media and the Meaning of Success

Two final points about terrorists' interest in nuclear terrorism involve the role of the news media and the question of identifying what a successful nuclear terrorist incident is. These two issues are intertwined because the news media will play a central role in defining the public's perception of the event and in framing the ongoing discussion. Terrorists thrive on media coverage because it multiplies the effect of an attack by bringing it into the homes of the public and, thus, making any event more personalized. With a nuclear incident, all of these media-induced consequences will be amplified as the public tries to grapple with pictures of death and disaster that could resemble those from Hiroshima, while also wondering whether their community might be affected by radioactive fallout, or whether it might be the next target. It is possible that media overreaction could make even a low-level or failed nuclear incident a success in terms of creating fear in the public, causing high-impact economic disruption, and bringing broad attention to the cause of the terrorists.

Whether this level of success would be sufficient for the perpetrators depends largely on their ultimate goals. If a nuclear incident achieved the group's primary goals—whether to cause mass casualties or to strengthen anti-nuclear sentiment in a country—it would have to be defined as successful. But terrorists pursuing nuclear terrorism may not be able to operationalize their plans because of the technical challenges involved. In these cases, will the effort alone to resort to nuclear terrorism have been enough? In some cases, it may be, especially if there has been some release of radiation. A failed high impact attack that has some low-level consequence may still cause considerable public fear and have substantial economic implications. However, hoaxes and incidents that result in no unique nuclear signature will probably not provide terrorists with the gains they had hoped for by choosing the nuclear option. At this point they may decide to try again, having gained enormous experience from the first failed effort, or they may shift their attention to other available options. Regardless of the actual outcome, if the effort is significant enough and becomes public, it will result in more attempts at nuclear terrorism. These copycats, if not adequately responded to, will lead to an increase in the perceived value of nuclear terrorism and eventually to a successful attack.

[1] Bruce Hoffman, "Terrorism Trends and Prospects," in Ian Lesser, ed., *Countering the New Terrorism,* RAND Corporation document MR-989-AF, 1999, pp. 10-27; Nadine Gurr and Benjamin Cole, *The New Faces of Terrorism: Threats from Weapons of Mass Destruction* (London and New York: I.B. Taurus, 2000), pp. 22-23;

Gavin Cameron, *Nuclear Terrorism: A Threat Assessment for the 21st Century* (New York: Palgrave Macmillan, 1999), p. 138.

[2] Jacquelyn S. Porth, "U.S. Goal: Keep Weapons of Mass Destruction Out of the Hands of Terrorists," 2002 United States Special Weapons Nuclear & Missile Proliferation News, March 13, 2002, <http://www.fas.org/news/usa/2002/index.html>, accessed on April 8, 2004.

[3] Peter Baker, "Pakistani Scientist Who Met Bin Laden Failed Polygraphs, renewing Suspicions," *Washington Post*, March 3, 2002, p. A1.

[4] Associated Press, "White House Was Also Ricin Target," CBSNews.com, February 4, 2004, <http://www.cbsnews.com>.

[5] Bruce Hoffman, *Inside Terrorism* (New York: Columbia University Press, 1998), pp. 87-88; Yigal Carmon, "Contemporary Islamist Ideology Permitting Genocidal Murder," The Middle East Media Research Institute (MEMRI), Special Report #25, January 27, 2004.

[6] The term "worried well" refers to individuals who believe they have been hurt or affected by an event but in reality they are fine. They are worried about having been hurt and convince themselves that they may need medical help even if they might have been miles away from an incident.

[7] David Kaplan, *The Cult At the End of the World* (New York: Crown Publishers, 1996), pp. 278-284; OPCW, Responding to Chemical Terrorism, "Chemical Terrorism in Japan: The Matsumoto & Tokyo Incidents," <http://www.opcw.org/resp/html/japan.html>, accessed on April 9, 2004.

[8] For more information on the Oklahoma City bombing see: David J. Whittaker, *Terrorism: Understanding the Global Threat* (Longman, 2002), p 87; John Kifner, "Terror in Oklahoma City: The Overview," *New York Times*, April 20, 1995.

[9] WMD Terrorism Database, annual review, in *Nonproliferation Review* 7 (Summer 2000), pp. 157-174.

[10] Ibid.

[11] Examples of cults that have been internally oriented but extremely lethal include the "Order of the Solar Temple" and "The Peoples Temple." In both cases, most of the members of the cult committed mass suicide.

[12] Bruce Hoffman, "Terrorism and WMD: Some Preliminary Hypotheses," *Nonproliferation Review* 4 (Spring-Summer 1997), p. 47.

[13] Gavin Cameron, "WMD Terrorism in the United States: The Threat and Possible Countermeasures," *Nonproliferation Review* 7 (Spring 2000), p. 166; Walter Laquer, *The New Terrorism: Fanaticism and the Arms of Mass Destruction* (New York: Oxford University Press, 1999), pp. 241-243; David E. Kaplan, "Aum Shinrikyo," in Jonathan B. Tucker, ed., *Toxic Terror: Assessing Terrorist Use of Chemical and Biological Weapons* (Cambridge, MA: MIT Press, 2000), pp. 213-218.

[14] Ibid.

[15] Kenneth Hyams, et al., "Responses to Chemical, Biological or Nuclear Terrorism: The Indirect and Long-Term Health Effects May Present the Greatest Challenge," *Journal of Health Politics, Policy and Law* 27 (April 2002); Alexander Kelle and Annette Schaper, "Terrorism Using Biological and Nuclear Weapons: A Critical Analysis of Risks After 11 September 2001," PRIF Report No. 64, Peace and Research Institute, Frankfurt, 2003, pp. 28-29.

[16] Cameron, *Nuclear Terrorism*, pp. 133-135; Morten Bremer Maerli, "Relearning the ABCs: Terrorists and 'Weapons of Mass Destruction,'" *Nonproliferation Review* 7 (Summer 2000), p. 108.

[17] Amanda Ripley, "The Case of the Dirty Bomber," Time Online Edition, June 16, 2002, <http://www.time.com>.

[18] Cameron, *Nuclear Terrorism*, pp. 142-143.

[19] Jessica Stern, *The Ultimate Terrorists* (Boston, MA: Harvard University Press, 2001), pp. 78-79.

[20] Gordon Thompson, "War and Nuclear Power Plants," Institute for Resource and Security Studies, Cambridge, March 1996; Laquer, *The New Terrorism*, pp. 72-73.

[21] Ely Karmon, "Olympic Bomb Plot to Blow up Sydney Nuclear Reactor Foiled. How Serious the Threat?" International Policy Institute for Counter-Terrorism, Herzliya, Israel, September 3, 2000.

[22] Cameron, *Nuclear Terrorism*, p. 117; Hoffman, *Inside Terrorism*, 1998, pp. 157-160; Brent L. Smith, *Terrorism in America: Pipe Bombs and Pipe Dreams* (New York: State University of New York Press), 1994, pp. 36-39.

[23] Karmon, "Olympic Bomb Plot to Blow up Sydney Nuclear Reactor Foiled"; Laquer, *The New Terrorism*, pp. 72-73.

[24] Gurr and Cole, *The New Face of Terrorism,* p. 115.

[25] For more information on the Alphabet Bomber see: Jeffrey D. Simon, "The Alphabet Bomber," in Tucker, *Toxic Terror,* pp. 71-94; William M. Carley, "A Time to Heal: Unabomber's Package Leaves Decade of Pain and Shattered Dreams," *Wall Street Journal,* October 17, 1995, p. A1.

[26] Gary Ackerman and Dr. Jeffrey Bale of the Center for Nonproliferation Studies, Monterey Institute of International Studies, interview by author, Monterey, CA, January 23, 2004.

[27] Theodore Rockwell, "Radiation Chicken Little," *Washington Post,* September 19, 2003, p. A19; Michael A. Levi, "Radiation: The Real Deal," *Washington Post,* September 20, 2003, p. A29; Franz-Nikolaus Flakus, "Radiation in perspective: Improving comprehension of risks," IAEA Bulletin 37 (June 1995), pp. 7-13; Cameron, *Nuclear Terrorism,* pp. 135-143; Jim Stewart, "The Fear of Radiation," CBSnews.com, April 24, 2004, <http://www.cbsnews.com>.

[28] Jay Lehr, "An Interview with Bernard Cohen," *Environment News,* June 1, 2001; Scott R. Burnell, "Radiation a Mystery To Most People," *UPI Science News,* April 17, 2002.

[29] Richard A. Falkenrath, Robert D. Newman, and Bradley A. Thayer, *America's Achilles' Heel: Nuclear Biological, and Chemical Terrorism and Covert Attack* (Cambridge: MIT Press, 1998), pp. 207-208.

[30] Melissa Chirico, "Changing Preconceptions of the Nuclear Terrorism Threat: A Case Study of the Aum Shinrikyo Cult," paper for the department of Science, Technology and International Affairs, Georgetown School of Foreign Service, fall 1999.

[31] For more information on the Ismailovsky Park and Moscow Theater events see: CNN, "Chechen Guman Sieze Moscow Theatre," CNN.com, October 24, 2002, <http://www.cnn.com/2002/WORLD/europe/10/23/russia.siege/>; Tony Karon, "Behind the Moscow Theater Siege," Time, October, 25, 2002.

[32] Jeffrey M. Bale, "The Chechen Resistance and Radiological Terrorism," NTI Issue Brief, April 2004, <http://www.nti.org/e_research/e3_47b.html>, accessed on May 18, 2004.

[33] Kaplan, "Aum Shinrikyo," pp. 218-220.

[34] David Albright and Holly Higgins, "A Bomb for the Ummah," *Bulletin of the Atomic Scientists* (March/April 2003), pp. 49-55.

[35] Laquer, *The New Terrorism,* pp. 95-97; Stern, *The Ultimate Terrorists,* pp. 82-86.

[36] Rahimullah Yousafsai, ABCNEWS Interview with Osama Bin Laden December 1998, published September 26, 2001, <http://www.abcnews.com>.

[37] Gary Ackerman and Dr. Jeffrey Bale of the Center for Nonproliferation Studies, Monterey Institute of International Studies, interview by author, Monterey, CA, January 23, 2004.

[38] Falkenrath et al., *America's Achilles' Heel,* pp. 322-324; Stern, *The Ultimate Terrorists,* pp. 87-106.

[39] For more examples, see data contained in the WMD Terrorism Database, developed by the Center for Nonproliferation Studies, Monterey Institute of International Studies.

[40] Jessica Stern, *Terror In the Name of God: Why Religious Militants Kill* (New York: Harper Collins Publishers, 2003), pp. 254-258, 296; "Dealing with the Unthinkable," *Economist,* November 3, 2001, p. 12; Graham Allison, "Could Worse be Yet to Come?" *Economist,* November 3, 2001, pp. 19-21.

[41] Bale, "The Chechen Resistance and Radiological Terrorism."

[42] The White House, *U.S. National Security Strategy; National Strategy to Combat Weapons of Mass Destruction;* and *National Strategy for Combating Terrorism,* Washington, DC, 2002.

[43] The relative difficulty of manufacturing different types of INDs is discussed in Chapter 4.

[44] Edwin S. Lyman, "Vulnerability of Nuclear Power Plants Containment Building to Penetration," Nuclear Control Institute, September 21, 2001; Douglas Chapen, et al., "Nuclear Power Plants and Their Fuel As Terrorist Targets," *Science,* September 9, 2002, p. 297. The 9/11 attackers required less than $1 million to learn to fly and conduct their operations, but they were not training to hit a nuclear containment structure. If they were targeting other vulnerable buildings at nuclear facilities that might be easier targets, they might not need the same degree of training or funds.

[45] Adam Dolnik, "All God's Poisons: Re-evaluating the Threat of Religious Terrorism with Respect to Non-conventional Weapons," study prepared for Defense Threat Reduction Agency under contract to Center for Nonproliferation Studies, Monterey Institute of International Studies, Summer 2003, pp. 20-22.

[46] See Chapter 3 for more information about NEST.

3

Seizing the Bomb

Theft, Diversion, and Instability

Detonation of a nuclear weapon in a major city is the ultimate nuclear terrorism nightmare. The use of an intact nuclear weapon from any of the existing arsenals could completely destroy the heart of a large metropolis, taking potentially hundreds of thousands of lives. Devastating ripple effects, including untold economic losses and potentially severe restrictions on civil liberties, would reverberate throughout the United States and much of the rest of the world.

While nuclear-armed states usually maintain tight controls over their nuclear weapons, the seizure of an intact nuclear weapon by terrorists cannot be ruled out. Certain classes of these weapons pose special risks of theft or diversion. Many experts, as well as current and former government officials, have expressed particular concern about the security of "tactical" nuclear weapons in Russia.[1] Testifying before the Senate Foreign Relations Committee, former Senator Sam Nunn highlighted this concern when he warned,

> Tactical nuclear weapons are another piece of unfinished business. These weapons have never been covered in arms control treaties. We can only guess at the numbers in each other's inventories as well as the locations. Yet these are the nuclear weapons most attractive to terrorists—even more valuable to them than fissile material and much more portable than strategic warheads.[2]

In addition to concerns surrounding many Russian nuclear weapons are post-9/11 fears of loose nuclear weapons in Pakistan, which have been underscored by the perilous political and security environment in that country.

Have terrorists already acquired intact nuclear weapons? Uncorroborated reports from as early as 1993 indicate that al Qaeda operatives have embarked on expeditions to obtain nuclear armaments, and some news reports even suggest that these efforts were successful.[3] Although most analysts are skeptical of these accounts and believe that, by now, al Qaeda would have sought to use any nuclear weapons in its possession, one must still take seriously Osama bin Laden's call for his organization to acquire such weapons of mass destruction as "a religious duty."[4]

This chapter will describe the nuclear arsenals of today's nuclear-armed states, and, after examining the potential consequences of terrorist use of an intact nuclear weapon, will analyze the chain of events required for a terrorist group to accomplish this heinous act. It will then review security arrangements covering nuclear arms and identify areas where improvements are most urgently needed. This background will provide the basis for identifying the most effective interventions for reducing the overall risk of terrorist use of an intact nuclear weapon, issues that are discussed at the conclusion of this chapter.

EXISTING NUCLEAR ARSENALS

Today, the nuclear arsenals of the nine nations known or believed to possess nuclear weapons (China, France, India, Israel, North Korea, Pakistan, Russia, the United Kingdom, and the United States) contain more than 30,000 such weapons. This total includes more than 10,000 weapons that are in reserve and retired but not yet dismantled. From the perspective of guarding against nuclear terrorism, certain categories of the world's nuclear weapons are more vulnerable to terrorist acquisition than others. The following discussion of categories of nuclear weapons provides essential background information for understanding this aspect of nuclear terrorism.

The classification system for nuclear weapons stems from the U.S.-Soviet arms control negotiating process, which began in the 1960s. This system classifies nuclear warheads according to the range and military application of the delivery systems for which they were designed or on which they are deployed. Strategic weapons, in the U.S.-Russia context, can deliver nuclear warheads over intercontinental distances, greater than 5,500 kilometers (km). These weapons include intercontinental ballistic missiles (ICBMs), which are land-based missiles with ranges of more than 5,500 km; ballistic missile submarines (SSBNs), which carry submarine launched ballistic missiles (SLBMs); and heavy bombers, which can travel over intercontinental distances. Non-strategic (tactical) nuclear weapons are typically limited to distances of less than intercontinental range. Nuclear warheads for missile systems with ranges between 550 and 5,500 km are classified as intermediate or theater weapons, while warheads for missiles with ranges of less than 500 km, bombs for aircraft other than heavy bombers, and artillery shells are considered tactical weapons.[5]

As will be discussed below, tactical nuclear weapons represent a particular concern from the standpoint of nuclear terrorism because of a combination of their physical properties and policies for their deployment and employment. Some strategic weapons, however, also share with tactical nuclear arms the trait of "relative portability," making them more vulnerable to terrorist seizure and use. In particular, nuclear warheads based on ballistic missiles—either sea-based SLBMs or land-based ballistic missiles, such as ICBMs—would not be considered portable or accessible to terrorists while these warheads are mated to the missiles. In contrast, bombs designated for either strategic or tactical aircraft would be far more portable. Similarly, air launched cruise missiles (ALCMs) and submarine launched cruise missiles (SLCMs) would be more portable than warheads mated on SLBMs or ICBMs. Table 3.1 lists the estimated numbers of nuclear weapons categorized by their relative portability. The warheads in the inactive category (those in reserve stockpiles or awaiting dismantlement) would be deemed relatively portable because they are not mated to delivery systems such as SLBMs or ICBMs.

The nuclear arsenals of the other states known or believed to possess nuclear weapons are much more difficult to enumerate with any accuracy. Table 3.2 presents a range of estimates for the total nuclear

TABLE 3.1
ESTIMATED NUCLEAR ARSENALS OF THE NUCLEAR WEAPON STATES

	United States	Russia	France	United Kingdom	China
Active unmated warheads, including bombs and cruise missiles	2,850	4,200	60	0	250
Active weapons mated to ICBMs and SLBMs, which are not readily portable	4,800	4,000	288	200	130
Total active weapons	7,650	8,200	348	200	380
Weapons considered to be relatively portable	3,000	8,000-10,000	Unknown	Unknown	Unknown

Source: Natural Resources Defense Council (NRDC) Nuclear Notebook, "Chinese Nuclear Forces, 2003," *Bulletin of the Atomic Scientists*, November/December 2003; NDRC Nuclear Notebook, "Russian Nuclear Forces, 2002," *Bulletin of the Atomic Scientists*, July/August 2002; NRDC Nuclear Notebook, "British Nuclear Forces, 2001," *Bulletin of the Atomic Scientists*, November/December 2001; NRDC Nuclear Notebook, "French Nuclear Forces, 2001," *Bulletin of the Atomic Scientists*, July/August 2001; NRDC Nuclear Notebook, "U.S. Nuclear Forces, 2003," *Bulletin of the Atomic Scientists*, May/June 2003. For purposes of this chart, "nuclear weapons states" are those that had detonated nuclear explosions prior to January 1, 1967, as defined by the Nuclear Non-Proliferation Treaty (NPT). According to the latest published estimates from the International Institute for Strategic Studies, the numbers of nuclear warheads in the active arsenals are: 7,094 for the United States; 8,626 for Russia; 348 for China; 410 for France; and 185 for the United Kingdom. The International Institute for Strategic Studies, *The Military Balance*, 2003-2004 (Oxford: Oxford University Press, 2003), p. 229.

TABLE 3.2
ESTIMATED NUCLEAR ARSENALS OF DE FACTO NUCLEAR WEAPON STATES, 2001-2002

State	Total Nuclear Weapons
Israel	75-200
India[i]	30-35
Pakistan[i]	24-48
North Korea[ii]	1-2, possibly as many as 8

[i] According to some experts, India and Pakistan keep nuclear warheads separated from nuclear delivery vehicles, both aircraft and missiles. Gaurav Kampani, Center for Nonproliferation Studies, correspondence with author, April 6, 2004.

[ii] Although little other open source evidence directly supports this claim, the U.S. government estimates that North Korea has probably produced up to two nuclear weapons; see National Intelligence Council, "Foreign Missile Developments and the Ballistic Missile Threat Through 2015," National Intelligence Estimate, December 2001, <http://www.cia.gov/nic/pubs/other_products/Unclassifiedballisticmissile final.htm>, accessed on April 24, 2003. Further, North Korea would likely be able to produce an additional five or six nuclear weapons with the weapons-grade plutonium residing in the 8,000 spent fuel rods unloaded from its 5-megawatt (MWe) reactor. Furthermore, depending on the capabilities of its uranium enrichment program, North Korea could produce several additional nuclear weapons in the next few years. See NRDC Nuclear Notebook: "North Korea's Nuclear Program, 2003," *Bulletin of the Atomic Scientists*, March/April 2003, pp. 74-77, and the Center for Nonproliferation Studies' (CNS's) analysis of North Korean nuclear capabilities on the Nuclear Threat Initiative (NTI) Web site, <http://www.nti.org/ e_research/e1_nkorea_1.html>, accessed on April 24, 2004. Press reports on April 24, 2003, indicated that the North Korean delegation at the talks in Beijing with the United States and China admitted that North Korea has nuclear weapons. Sonni Efron, "North Korea Says It Has Nuclear Arms," *Los Angeles Times*, April 25, 2003, p. A1; Charles Hutzler, "China Fuels Fear North Korea Has Nuclear Weapon," *Wall Street Journal*, July 18, 2003, p. A7.

Source: NRDC Nuclear Notebook, *Bulletin of the Atomic Scientists*, <http://www.thebulletin.org/ issues/nukenotes/nukenote.html>, accessed on May 19, 2004. According to the latest published estimates from the International Institute for Strategic Studies, the numbers of nuclear warheads in the active arsenals for these states are: 200 for Israel, 40+ for India, 40+ for Pakistan, and ± 2 for North Korea. The International Institute for Strategic Studies, *The Military Balance*, 2003-2004, p. 229.

weapons possessed by Israel, India, Pakistan, and North Korea. Insufficient information is available from open sources to determine which of these weapons are mated with missile delivery systems in a fashion that would make them less vulnerable to seizure by terrorists.

Finally, it is worth noting that the nuclear weapons in all of the foregoing arsenals can be found in a number of settings: deployed with, or near to, their delivery systems; in storage (either centralized or dispersed);

in transit; or at manufacturing, refurbishment, or dismantlement sites. Security measures covering nuclear arms in such settings are discussed, in detail, below.

EFFECTS AND CONSEQUENCES OF A NUCLEAR EXPLOSION

Nuclear weapons are not merely extremely powerful conventional weapons; in addition to generating a devastating blast, they cause extraordinary thermal and radioactive effects.[6] Roughly 50 percent of the released energy of a nuclear detonation goes into the blast. The blast wave can create tremendous overpressures that can knock down the most solidly constructed buildings. Second, heat radiation, manifested as a flash of light, comprises about 35 percent of the energy of the weapon. This heat can start large-scale fires and inflict lethal burns.[7] Third, about 5 percent of the energy is emitted as prompt radiation in the form of gamma rays, electrons, and neutrons. Fourth, the remaining 10 percent of energy shows up in secondary radiation from radioactive fallout of fission products. Because terrorist use of a nuclear weapon would likely be a ground burst instead of an air burst, fallout would be maximized and result in long-term contamination in the local area of the explosion and perhaps hundreds of miles downwind, depending on the weather conditions.

Table 3.3 lists the radius for the effects of prompt radiation, fallout radiation from a surface burst, severe blast damage, and moderate blast damage for explosive yields from one ton to one megaton (MT) TNT equivalent. The smaller yields in the table exemplify those that could be produced through the explosion of an IND, as discussed in the following chapter. The larger yields are typical of those of tactical and strategic nuclear weapons. (The 500-rem dose was chosen because an exposure of this amount of ionizing radiation would likely kill more than 50 percent of the affected population within 60 days.) For comparison, the "Little Boy" bomb dropped on Hiroshima in August 1945 produced an estimated yield of 12.5 kilotons (KT). Such a bomb could destroy the central area of a large city and kill a hundred thousand or more people, depending on the population density. A March 2003 report by a Harvard University team estimated 500,000 deaths resulting from a Hiroshima-

TABLE 3.3
NUCLEAR EXPLOSIVE EFFECTS AS A FUNCTION OF YIELD

	Radius for Indicated Effect (meters) [i]			
Explosive Yield Measured in Tons of TNT Equivalent (Surface Burst)	500-Rem Prompt Gamma Radiation	Fallout from Surface Blast (500-Rem Total Dose) [ii]	Severe Blast Damage (10 psi)	Moderate to Light Blast Damage (3 psi)
1 ton	45	30-100	33	65
10 tons	100	100-300	71	140
100 tons	300	300-1,000	150	300
1 KT (1,000 tons)	680	1,000-3,000	330	650
10 KT	1,280	3,000-10,000	710	1,500
100 KT	1,800	10,000-30,000	1,500	3,300
1 MT (1 million tons)	2,400	30,000-100,000	3,250	7,100

KT: kiloton
MT: megaton
psi: pounds per square inch
ton: metric ton; equivalent to explosive blast from 1,000 kg, or 2,200 pounds of TNT

---

[i] Effects for 1 ton through 1 KT adapted from Kevin O'Neill, "The Nuclear Terrorist Threat," Institute for Science and International Security, August 1997, and references therein, p.6; effects for 10 KT, 100 KT, and 1 megaton (MT) are adapted from Dietrich Schroeer, *Science, Technology, and the Nuclear Arms Race* (Ontario: John Wiley & Sons Canada Ltd., 1984), pp. 37, as based on Glasstone and Dolan, *Effects of Nuclear Weapons.*
[ii] The range of fallout effects depends on wind and rain conditions, which explains the large range of uncertainty in this column.

sized device exploded at Grand Central Station in Manhattan on a typical work day.[8] Moreover, the report projected more than a trillion dollars worth of economic damage from such an event. The psychological costs would also be immense.

Determining the explosive yield of a "typical" intact nuclear weapon presents a number of problems. For many arsenals, such as those of India, Israel, and Pakistan, reliable estimates of the yields are very uncertain. Based on the May 1998 nuclear tests in India and Pakistan, those countries' nuclear weapons may have yields in the low tens to many tens of kilotons,[9] although this testing data may have since led to construction of warheads with higher yields. The yields of many Russian and American warheads are better known. In the view of some observers, Russian strategic nuclear weapons have yields from about 100 to 750 KT.[10] The yields of Russian tactical nuclear weapons are less well known and could range from about 1 KT to several hundred KT. U.S. strategic nuclear weapons, according to some unofficial sources, have yields from 150 to 475 KT, and its non-strategic warheads have yields that may be as high as 150 KT and as low as 0.3 KT, for instance in the case of the "dial-a-yield" B61 bomb.[11]

THE CHAIN OF CAUSATION

The principal elements that would have to coalesce for a terrorist group to detonate an intact nuclear weapon at a high-value target, such as an American city, include the following steps:[12]

1. A terrorist group with extreme objectives and the necessary technical and financial resources to execute this scheme must organize and begin operations.
2. The group must then choose to engage in an act of nuclear terrorism at the highest level of violence.
3. These terrorists must then acquire an intact nuclear weapon through gift, purchase, theft, or diversion.
4. They must next determine how to bypass or defeat any safeguards against unauthorized use incorporated into an intact nuclear weapon.
5. The terrorist group must be able to transport the intact nuclear weapon to a high-value target.
6. Finally, the terrorists must detonate the intact nuclear weapon to complete their plan. [13]

Terrorist Groups with Motivation and Capabilities to Acquire and Use Nuclear Weapons

As discussed in Chapter 2, the number of terrorist organizations highly motivated to employ nuclear weapons in pursuit of their goals is small but not zero. However, one must guard against complacency in assuming that the small number is known precisely or that the figure will remain constant. In this respect, it is useful to recall that the apocalyptic Japanese group Aum Shinrikyo took intelligence analysts by surprise when it used sarin gas in the 1995 Tokyo subway attack. Aum's efforts to acquire nuclear weapons, although unsuccessful, also blindsided experts. A prudent analysis, therefore, should assume that additional terrorist groups motivated to acquire and use nuclear weapons may already exist or could appear unexpectedly. Intelligence assets must be focused on discerning such developments.

The financial and technical resources necessary to implement a plan to obtain and detonate an intact nuclear weapon would be considerable, and many obstacles would need to be overcome. Most variants of a terrorism scenario involving an intact nuclear weapon would require the group in question to have access to many millions of dollars in order to have a realistic prospect of purchasing a weapon, suborning nuclear weapon custodians, mounting a raid against a weapons storage site, and moving the weapon clandestinely to its target.[14] In addition, considerable organizational skills would be required to permit the group to operate internationally. Finally, the group would need a considerable degree of technical competence to overcome any safeguards integrated into the weapons themselves, such as coded safety locks (known as permissive action links, or PALs) and to detonate the weapon.

Acquisition of an Intact Nuclear Weapon

In the chain of causation outlined above, the most difficult challenge for any terrorist organization would be acquiring the nuclear weapon itself. There are a wide range of scenarios in which a terrorist organization could do so. Most notably, a state might voluntarily share a nuclear weapon with a terrorist group or sell one to it; a senior official or governmental element with authorized access to such weapons might, for ideological or mercenary motives, provide one to terrorists, without the express approval of governmental leaders; the immediate custodians of the weapons might, for money or ideology, or under duress, provide one to the organization or assist it in seizing one by force or stealth; or terrorists might obtain a weapon by force or stealth without insider help. Finally, nuclear weapons could come into the hands of terrorists during a period of political turmoil, including one brought on by a coup or revolution.

Vulnerabilities can be identified in all states possessing nuclear weapons that might lead to such weapons falling into the hands of terrorists. These vulnerabilities appear particularly acute in Pakistan and Russia. In Pakistan they stem from the country's volatile domestic political situation and history of the Pakistani military's support for radical Islamists. In Russia, nuclear weapons are considered at higher risk because of the large numbers of weapons in that country's nuclear arsenal at a time when the impoverishment of the military structures responsible for their custody lead to seriously weakened security arrangements. Much of the discussion below concentrates on these two states, while also addressing the security of nuclear arms in other nations.

Deliberate Transfer by a National Government

The most direct means for a terrorist group to acquire an intact nuclear weapon would be to obtain it directly from a sympathetic government. This would greatly simplify the requirements for the terrorist groups, making it unnecessary to defeat security systems protecting such weapons or devise means to bypass any internal safing mechanisms. Financial and organizational requirements for the organization would thus be significantly reduced. Operational weapons could be given to terrorist groups by a state that intended to use them against an opponent behind a veneer of plausible deniability in the hope of avoiding retaliation.

Such a combination of "rogue state" and mass-casualty terrorists is a "worst case scenario" that has shaped U.S. foreign policy toward such states and fueled public fears of nuclear terrorism. The Bush administration considered Iraq under Saddam Hussein, for example, to pose a major threat in part because of concerns that the state might provide weapons of mass destruction to terrorists. Although this assertion has become controversial because of questionable evidence for such a nexus, other cases can be identified where the transfer of a nuclear weapon to a terrorist organization is not totally implausible.

In Pakistan, for example, Dr. A.Q. Khan, a leading figure in Pakistan's nuclear weapons program, has admitted that between 1989 and 2003, he provided Iran, Libya, and North Korea with highly sensitive matériel for their respective nuclear weapon programs.[15] Although in his public confession he asserted that he did this without the knowledge or approval of successive Pakistani governments, a point that Pakistani President Pervez Musharraf has sought to reaffirm, many question this claim.[16] At the time of the transfers, all three recipient nations were deemed by the United States to be sponsors of terrorism. If the government of Pakistan was, in fact, complicit in the transfers, it was, at the least, indifferent to the question of whether nuclear arms might ultimately find their way into the hands of terrorists.

During the 1990s, Pakistan's political and military leaders (including Pervez Musharraf, who served as Army Chief of Staff and then president during this decade) strongly supported the Taliban leadership in Afghanistan, at a time when it was providing a haven for al Qaeda. Individual Pakistani nuclear scientists also interacted with that terrorist organization and probably provided at least basic information related to various weapons of mass destruction capabilities. After 9/11, President Musharraf agreed to support the United States and its allies in the War on Terror and in deposing the Taliban in Afghanistan. Some senior elements of the Pakistani political establishment, however, oppose this change of position. With Musharraf the target of two assassination attempts in December 2003, which were allegedly mounted with the assistance of insiders, there is reason for concern that individuals supportive of radical Islamist groups may come to power in Pakistan. Such a development might give rise to the possibility of an intact Pakistani nuclear weapon being transferred to a terrorist organization, even if it is assumed that the Musharraf government would not, itself, do so.[17]

It is also worth noting that in April 2003 a North Korean official told his U.S. counterpart that Pyongyang might be prepared to "take physical action" such as testing or transferring nuclear material to others if the United States did not agree to a nonaggression pact and other concessions.[18] Although the statement by Li Gun, deputy director of American Affairs for North Korea's Foreign Ministry, was most likely a rhetorical ploy, and although North Korea did not specifically mention sales to terrorists or sales of intact nuclear weapons, such statements are highly disturbing, especially in view of North Korea's past ties to international terrorism and history of selling strategic goods, in particular missiles, to the highest bidder.[19]

Iran is a state that is widely believed to be seeking nuclear arms and simultaneously to be supporting international terrorism. Although, to date, there is no indication that the Iranian government has shared WMD with terrorist organizations, the possibility remains that it might do so in the future.[20]

As of mid 2004, it is difficult to identify any of the other nuclear-weapon states (or aspirants) that might contemplate the transfer of a nuclear weapon to a terrorist organization. As a practical matter, it is highly unlikely that even states that might provide active support for terrorists groups would be prepared to hand over an intact nuclear weapon. The transferring state would have to be extraordinarily reckless, desperate, or possess an unusual degree of confidence in the recipient terrorist organization, given the probability that the weapon(s) would be traced back to the state of origin. The resulting risk of retaliation, especially if the weapons were actually used, therefore likely serves as a significant deterrent to such transactions. Indeed, prior to 9/11, the U.S. Department of Defense (DOD) concluded, in its January 2001 analysis of proliferation threats that, "the likelihood of a state sponsor providing such a weapon to a terrorist group is believed to be low."[21]

Unauthorized Assistance from a Senior Official

Even if a state's political leaders were not prepared to transfer a nuclear weapon to a terrorist organization, it is conceivable that other senior officials with access to the country's nuclear assets might take this step, for financial or ideological reasons, without the formal authorization of their superiors. If General Musharraf and A.Q. Khan are to be believed, the latter's unauthorized sale of nuclear know-how demonstrated the feasibility of such transfer, and involved provision of a nuclear weapon design to Libya and, possibly, Iran and North Korea. Were Iran to acquire nuclear arms, one also would need to be concerned that hard-line factions aligned with the weapons custodians might consider sharing nuclear arms with terrorist organizations without the express approval of the country's political or spiritual leadership.

This nuclear transfer scenario would entail a breakdown in the chain of command over nuclear weapons at such a high level that subordinates with physical custody of nuclear arms would obey the orders of their superiors. Under this scenario, the senior official also would be able to assist the terrorist organization in surmounting any internal safeguards within the acquired weapon and conceivably assist in moving the weapon to a target site.

Assistance from Custodians of Nuclear Weapons

Aid from one or more insiders lower down the chain of command, such as guards at a nuclear weapon storage or deployment site, also could facilitate the transfer of a nuclear weapon into terrorists' hands. Custodians might provide assistance because of sympathy with the terrorists' cause or bribery, or they might be coerced through threats of violence to themselves or family members.

Reliance on this mode of assistance would require considerable effort by a terrorist group, possibly in collaboration with organized criminal elements, to identify the relevant insiders and arrange for the exploitation of their assistance at the location where the weapon in question was held. A terrorist group might also place one of its members into a facility as a custodian or guard, perhaps years before any action is contemplated. Such an individual could act as a "sleeper," waiting to be activated upon receiving a command from another operative. Without cooperation from multiple parties, it would be extremely difficult to purloin such a weapon without early detection. In most scenarios, terrorists would have to defeat loyal guard and response forces, escape with the weapon, and then move the weapon over considerable distances to a target.

Since the demise of the Soviet Union, a particular concern is that poorly paid and demoralized nuclear weapon custodians in Russia might be susceptible to subornation by terrorists or others. In addition, the vast scale of the Russian nuclear arsenal and the infrastructure needed to produce, transport, and maintain it, greatly adds to the difficulty of ensuring the security of all Russian nuclear arms. To date, there are no confirmed instances of the loss or sale of a Russian nuclear weapon, although there have been a number of confirmed cases of diversion and illicit trafficking of small amounts of Russian nuclear-weapon materials. Nonetheless, as discussed later in this chapter, the nuclear weapons protection program covering Russia's arsenal is beset by many weaknesses, and U.S.-assisted efforts to improve weapons security there have had only limited success, leaving potentially serious vulnerabilities.

Seizure without Insider Help

A terrorist organization planning to seize a nuclear weapon without insider assistance would need to invest in training and arming a force able to defeat all security measures protecting the weapons, including the intervention of guards and response teams. Among other challenges, the organization would have to gather information about the security measures it would confront, beginning with the location of the weapons themselves, and would need to plan an escape route, which would probably involve travel over sizeable distances. The task would be so daunting in most settings, unless security at the facility is sufficiently lax, as to appear more the stuff of fiction than a practicable approach for a terrorist organization.

Coups d'État and Political Unrest in a Failing State

Finally, terrorist groups might take advantage of a coup, political unrest, revolution, or a period of anarchy to gain control over a nuclear weapon.[22] Nuclear weapons could change hands, for example, because of a coup or revolution instigated by insurgents allied to or cooperating with terrorists. Although the failed coup attempt against Soviet President Mikhail Gorbachev during August 1991 did not involve terrorists, during the crisis Gorbachev reportedly lost control of the Soviet Union's nuclear arsenal to his would-be successors when they cut off his communication links.[23] It is also possible that during a period of political turmoil, nuclear custodians might desert their posts or be swept aside in the tide of events.[24] The collapse of the Soviet Union in

1991 could have led to such turmoil in a number of successor states where nuclear weapons were deployed. Fortunately, political transitions unfolded there with little violence, and discipline was maintained throughout the nuclear chain of command.

Today, it is highly unlikely that political unrest would threaten nuclear controls in most weapon states. The situation is less clear cut, however, in the case of Pakistan and North Korea. Here, the possibility of a breakdown of political order during the next several years—and with it the crumbling of the layers of security surrounding nuclear weapons—cannot be ruled out. A period of violent clashes among political factions in Pakistan that left the nature of the future government in doubt, or the more general disintegration of central government authority, might permit elements allied with terrorist groups or, even the members of such groups, to gain control of a Pakistani nuclear weapon. In North Korea, economic collapse and political instability might lead to a massive outflow of refugees into China, Russia, and South Korea and to wholesale desertions from the country's armed forces. These events, in turn, could lead to loss of governmental control over the country's nuclear weapons, their seizure by remnant elements of the Kim Jong Il regime, and, possibly, their sale on the international black market to a terrorist group.

Although one cannot discount the possible loss of state control over nuclear weapons during extreme political unrest or a coup d'état, all regimes can be expected to regard nuclear weapons as crucial symbols of political power and to employ the most reliable military or state security forces to guard them. Though political instability and uncertainty may create greater incentives and opportunities for nuclear custodians to cooperate in the illicit transfer or sale of nuclear weapons, elite security forces are most likely to continue to perform their protective duties during and after regime change. Under some circumstances, they also may be charged with destroying or evacuating the weapons to prevent them from falling under hostile control. Moreover, in the event of a successful coup in a nuclear-armed state, the new regime will have the same motivations as its predecessor to guard its nuclear arsenal, although, depending on the orientation of the new leadership, it may be more sympathetic to the nuclear aspirations of terrorists.

In sum, the probability that terrorists could acquire nuclear weapons directly from state sponsors is very small, but still significant enough to merit serious concern. Acquisition of a weapon with the assistance of a senior official or group of officials but without the approval of a country's political leaders is somewhat more likely, especially in countries in which senior nuclear weapons custodians have considerable political autonomy. Terrorist collusion with insiders at nuclear weapons sites—possibly with the assistance of criminal elements—in the form of covert theft or overt raids against a vulnerable nuclear weapons site represents remote but more probable pathways for acquisition. Russia's huge arsenal of nuclear weapons and problematic security measures pose the greatest concern for this scenario. Political turmoil could also lead to terrorist groups gaining access to intact nuclear weapons. Because of the vulnerability of Pakistan's government and the strength of radical Islamic groups in that country, Pakistani nuclear weapons appear most vulnerable to acquisition through this path, but political disintegration in North Korea could also lead to loss of control over nuclear arms.

Defeating Safeguards

Should a terrorist organization ultimately become able to obtain an intact nuclear weapon, in most instances it would still need to overcome mechanisms in the weapon intended to prevent its use by unauthorized persons. Permissive action links, designed to ensure that nuclear weapons cannot be exploded without inputting proper codes, are among the most effective warhead security mechanisms. While early PALs were based on mechanical combination locks, modern PALs integrate electronic locking mechanisms with multiple six- or twelve-digit codes integrated into the warhead's design. These electronic locks allow only a limited number of tries to enter the correct codes; if the limit is exceeded, circuits in the arming mechanism self-destruct, disabling the warhead.[25]

Nuclear weapons may also be safeguarded against unauthorized use through safing, arming, fusing, and firing (SAFF) procedures. For example, the arming sequence for a warhead may require changes in altitude, acceleration, or other parameters verified by sensors built into the weapon, designed to ensure that the warhead can be used only according to a specific mission profile. Finally, weapons may be protected from unauthorized use by a combination of complex procedural arrangements (requiring participation of many individuals in the chain of command) and authenticating codes authorizing each individual to activate the weapon and/or launch-related delivery systems.[26]

All operational U.S. nuclear weapons have PALs.[27] Most authorities agree that Russian strategic nuclear weapons (long-range missiles and bombers) and modern Russian nuclear weapons associated with shorter-range systems also incorporate these safeguards. In addition, many of these Russian weapons are believed to be outfitted with other devices that would prevent their detonation unless a strict SAFF sequence took place. According to one leading authority, both the warheads and delivery vehicles for Russian non-strategic systems also are fitted with PALs, many of which are mechanical locks.[28] Other experts, however, contend that an unknown number of older Russian tactical nuclear weapons do not incorporate PALs.[29] Many of these older weapons have been dismantled or are awaiting dismantlement at central storage locations, but it is possible that some remain deployed at forward bases.[30]

Because the United States has shared PAL technology with Britain and France, it is likely that operational British and French nuclear weapons (with the possible exception of French SLBM warheads) are also protected by PALs.[31] Chinese nuclear weapons are not believed to have PALs, but one U.S. scientist contends that China sought U.S. assistance with PALs in 1990 and, when the United States refused, approached Russia for help with its warhead security systems.[32]

The security safeguards on warheads of the other nuclear armed states—India, Israel, North Korea, and Pakistan—cannot be determined from open sources, but it appears likely that these countries rely on procedures and codes rather than PALs to prevent unauthorized use.[33] According to one report by a well-known Pakistani analyst, all procedures involving nuclear weapons in Pakistan are governed by a "three-man rule," requiring the concurrent decision of three persons. Pakistani weapons are believed not to use PALs,[34] but most, if not all, Pakistani weapons are reportedly stored in disassembled form, with the nuclear components separated from the non-nuclear elements. This situation has led at least one senior Pakistani military officer to suggest that PALs are unnecessary.[35] Reportedly, the United States considered providing Pakistan with information about PALs shortly after September 11, 2001, but this controversial option was rejected.[36] However, other reports indicate that Pakistan has sought help from the United States to improve precautions against unauthorized or accidental launch of its nuclear weapons,[37] though this would not necessarily include security devices on the warheads themselves. It is likely that the United States has provided Pakistan with information on other mechanisms for enhancing the security of its nuclear arsenal.[38] India also is thought to keep its weapons in disassembled form during peacetime and has sought, and may have received, advice and assistance from the United States and Russia on enhancing the security of its nuclear arsenal and related infrastructure.[39]

Assuming that a terrorist group had acquired a weapon protected by PALs or other features preventing easy detonation, the group might attempt to disable or bypass these mechanisms at a safe location prior to transporting the weapon to its final target, or it might make preparations to do so at the detonation site. Unless assisted by sympathetic experts, terrorists would find it difficult, though not necessarily impossible, to master this requirement. Modern PALs, particularly those integrated into the weapon itself, are more difficult to defeat than older-generation PALs, which may still be characteristic of some Russian weapon systems. Facing these impediments, terrorists might attempt to open the weapon casing to obtain fissile material in order to produce their own improvised nuclear device, a strategy discussed in the next chapter.[40] However, the act of prying open the bomb casing might result in terrorists blowing themselves up with the conventional high explosives associated with nuclear warheads. Thus, terrorists might require the services of insiders to perform this operation safely.

Transporting the Weapon to its Target

Assuming a terrorist organization could obtain a nuclear weapon and had the ability to overcome any mechanisms built into the device to prevent its unauthorized detonation, it would still face the task of taking the weapon to the group's intended target. For the scenarios of greatest concern to the United States—the use of the weapon against a city in the United States or one of its allies—the distance between the point of acquisition and the target could be quite substantial.[41] If the loss of a nuclear weapon were detected, as would be expected unless a state provided one to a terrorist organization, a massive hunt for the weapon would be launched, involving law enforcement and military personnel from many nations, assisted by nuclear specialists. This effort would be accompanied by greatly intensified security over transportation links and points of entry.

These factors would present considerable challenges to the terrorist organization, underscoring the need for such a group to have extensive resources and networks of collaborators. Unfortunately, intensive searches for high-value items (e.g., Osama bin Laden) and the record of U.S. efforts to interdict the massive influx of illicit narcotics is not reassuring. It also is possible terrorists might adopt strategies that minimized transportation, such as detonating the weapon at a near-by, less-than-optimal target, or even at the place of acquisition. Nuclear detonation by a non-state group virtually anywhere would terrorize citizens in potential target countries around the globe, who would fear the perpetrators had additional weapons at their disposal. The organization could exploit such fears in order to blackmail governments into political concessions—for example, demanding the withdrawal of military forces or political support from states the terrorists opposed. Indeed, the group might achieve these results without a nuclear detonation, by providing proof that it had a nuclear weapon in its possession at a location unknown to its adversaries.

Detonation

If a nuclear weapon were successfully transported to its target site, and any PALs disabled, a degree of technical competence would nonetheless be required to determine how to trigger the device and provide the necessary electrical or mechanical input for detonation. Moreover, detonation could be daunting unless the detonators and the arming and firing sequence mechanisms had been preserved. Here, again, insider assistance would be of considerable help. Thus, even this seemingly straightforward aspect of the chain of causation would pose an obstacle to the terrorists' goals.

NUCLEAR WEAPONS SECURITY AT THE STATE LEVEL

The foregoing analysis of the steps terrorists would have to take to acquire and use an intact nuclear device makes clear that this event is highly unlikely. Very few organizations have the necessary motivation and resources, and any organization making the attempt would have to surmount a series of extremely challenging obstacles. That being said, however, much would depend on the state of physical protection of the weapons themselves. Effective, national safeguards can defeat almost all paths to terrorist acquisition of a nuclear weapon, except for the transfer of such a device by a sympathetic government.

Precise information about the security of nuclear weapons understandably is closely controlled in all countries, but it can be assumed that the weapons are under tight security during their entire life cycle, including production, transit, storage, and deployment. Broadly speaking, nuclear weapon security systems have a number of mutually reinforcing components, including: personnel reliability programs to verify the loyalty and emotional stability of custodians, physical protection measures (e.g., barriers, alarms, controlled access arrangements, armed guards, and response forces), careful weapon accounting practices, procedures requiring more than one individual to access and/or detonate a weapon (two-man rules), and PALs or other mechanisms or procedures to prevent unauthorized use of the weapons. Provision for weapon recovery after theft or loss would also be an element of most security arrangements.

Certain general observations can be made about these security systems. As arsenals grow and become more diverse, for example, the scale of protective activities must expand and increase in complexity to keep pace,[42] raising costs and placing new demands on management structures. If a state lacks the resources to meet these new requirements, weapons become more vulnerable to loss, a problem observed following the collapse of the Soviet Union, which led to U.S. assistance in the form of the Nunn-Lugar Cooperative Threat Reduction (CTR) Program. Within larger arsenals, weapons that are physically integrated into ballistic missiles are more difficult to access and thus inherently more secure against theft than weapons that are self-contained and are more portable, such as gravity bombs, artillery shells, and air- and sea-launched cruise missiles. When weapons in the latter categories—particularly physically smaller and lighter tactical nuclear weapons—are forward deployed, vulnerability to theft or diversion increases significantly. As their arsenals grow, moreover, developing nations are likely to encounter greater difficulty in implementing security arrangements than more advanced states, where the general level of technology integration into military operations is higher, and the overall national infrastructure is more mature.[43] These factors could erode the effectiveness of security measures in India and Pakistan in coming years as security requirements become more complex, a problem that could be especially acute if weapons are dispersed to multiple locations and military units during a crisis.[44] Finally, while all states must contend with the danger that a nuclear custodian might assist outsiders to obtain a nuclear weapon, the disloyalty of more senior elements in the military chain of command or in that of the nuclear establishment can be especially damaging. This danger appears most salient today in Pakistan.

Judging from the open literature, most observers consider nuclear weapon security systems in the United States, Britain, France, China, Israel, and North Korea to be generally effective against threats from terrorists, although no security system is foolproof, and, from time to time, weaknesses have been identified in even the most well-developed systems.[45] Following is a review of the security of nuclear weapons in these states; then security arrangements will be examined in Russia, Pakistan, and India, where more pervasive weaknesses may be present.

The United States

The United States is believed to employ all of the protective measures described above, including PALs on all nuclear weapons, and its nuclear arms are generally considered to be highly secure in all phases of their life cycle. In testimony before a congressional committee in June 2003, the U.S. General Accounting Office (GAO), the investigative arm of the U.S. Congress, noted the high security levels provided nuclear weapons at the U.S. Pantex assembly/disassembly facility in Amarillo, Texas. The testimony states that the Department of Energy (DOE) and the National Nuclear Security Administration (NNSA), which administer this facility and other elements of the U.S. nuclear weapons production complex, have applied a "graded-threat approach" to ensure that facilities handling nuclear *weapons* have in place the most rigorous security measures in the complex:

> Under the 2003 DBT [design-basis-threat], ...the theft of a nuclear weapon or test assembly is judged to be more attractive to terrorists, and sites that have these assets are required to defend against a substantially higher number of adversaries than are other DOE and NNSA sites that possess other forms of Category I quantities of special nuclear material [such as weapons-usable forms of highly enriched uranium and plutonium]. For example, the Pantex Plant, which, among other things, assembles and disassembles nuclear weapons, is required to defend to a higher level than sites such [as] Los Alamos or Y-12 [at the Oak Ridge National Laboratory], both of which fabricate nuclear weapons components.[46]

DOE and NNSA completed their post-9/11 design basis threat revision in May 2003. Nonetheless, several reports have suggested vulnerabilities may exist at certain facilities within the U.S. nuclear weapons complex. In March 2004, for example, the DOE Inspector General questioned whether guards at such facilities had received adequate training on repelling attacks by terrorists and, in a separate report earlier in the year, disclosed that defenders at certain U.S. nuclear weapon complex installations had received advance warning of drills involving mock terrorist attacks, undercutting the effectiveness of the exercises as tests of plant security capabilities.[47]

Unlike any other nuclear-armed state, the United States continues to deploy a small arsenal of about 150 tactical nuclear weapons—in the form of gravity bombs—outside its territory. These weapons are stationed in six European NATO countries, according to unofficial sources.[48] Although these deployed U.S. non-strategic nuclear weapons are believed to be highly protected and are held at military bases, the weapons undoubtedly serve as a powerful symbol of the U.S. military presence abroad and can be expected to attract terrorist attention. Indeed, while no credible open source evidence exists that terrorists have contemplated the seizure of nuclear weapons in the United States, at least one reported incident points to possible terrorist targeting of nuclear weapons in Europe in the recent past. In November 2002, Belgian authorities announced that they had detained Nizar Trabelsi, a Tunisian, in possession of a large quantity of explosives, who said that he wanted to bomb the Kleine Brogel Air Base, which is used by NATO and allegedly houses U.S. tactical nuclear arms.[49]

The United Kingdom, France, and China

Little information is available from open sources to assess the security measures employed to protect British, French, and Chinese nuclear weapons.[50] The governments of these three states rarely publish statements concerning this subject, and when they do publish such information, it is usually terse. France's Atomic Energy Commission (CEA), for example, reported in 2001, "Concerning the struggle against nuclear terrorism, the Ministry of Defence and the Ministry of the Interior carry out coordinated action. This action draw[s] upon the competencies and means of the CEA since several years."[51]

Arguably, the security risks involving British nuclear weapons have diminished significantly since July 1998, when the Labor Party government announced changes in Great Britain's nuclear posture, stemming from its Strategic Defence Review.[52] First, Great Britain decreased its nuclear stockpile to about 200 warheads of only one type (a variation of the U.S. W76 warhead), which is solely deployed on Vanguard ballistic missile submarines, a deployment pattern that provides particularly strong protection against terrorist access to these arms. Second, because of the shift to one warhead type, the British government has consolidated nuclear weapons storage at a single site—the Coulport submarine base. Third, the movement of nuclear weapons between the storage site and the submarines base has also decreased because the number of submarine patrols has significantly lessened to only one patrol at any given time.[53]

Like Great Britain, France has also reoriented its nuclear arsenal, whose weapons number in the hundreds. In 1996, President Jacques Chirac announced "the withdrawal of several obsolete weapons systems and the modernization of others" and by 1998, France had dismantled all of its intermediate range ballistic missiles.[54] However, unlike Britain, France maintains more than one type of nuclear weapon, relying on submarine-based ballistic missiles, land-based aircraft, and sea-based aircraft. Nonetheless, the removal of older nuclear weapons and the consolidation of France's stockpile into fewer storage sites have reduced some security risks.[55]

China has been gradually modernizing its nuclear arsenal. However, at this time, it is unclear whether this modernization program will increase or decrease security risks that terrorists might exploit. While more Chinese nuclear weapons might mean more opportunities for theft, a modernized force might incorporate more up-to-date security procedures. Isolated storage and transportation links could pose increased risks for any nation's nuclear weapons security program. China is believed to assemble nuclear warheads at a number of nuclear facilities, and the Lop Nur test site may contain a storage facility for Chinese nuclear weapons (although it is probably unused, since China has not tested a nuclear weapon since 1996).[56] Lop Nur is remotely located in northwest Xinjiang province, where nationalist/separatist organizations have been campaigning for autonomy from Beijing. Although Xinjiang separatist groups have not openly expressed interest in acquiring nuclear weapons, some reports have alleged that Uighur separatists may have stolen radioactive sources from Lop Nur in 1993.[57]

It is difficult to offer an overall assessment of the security of China's nuclear arms against terrorists because Beijing has a long-standing practice of not publishing sensitive information. In addition, China shows little concern (at least openly) that nuclear terrorism can occur on Chinese soil. While this lack of concern may be justified, the Chinese government still has to factor in security threats posed by Xinjiang separatists and other groups that may engage in terrorism in China. Nonetheless, the dominant role of the Chinese Communist Party and its security apparatus in Chinese society, and the limited presence of terrorist groups in China, appear to reduce substantially the danger that a terrorist organization might gain control of an intact nuclear weapon in that country.

Israel

Although Israel is widely perceived to possess a small but potent nuclear arsenal, it has never acknowledged this capability. Its declaratory policy states, "Israel will not be the first country to introduce nuclear weapons in the Middle East." Not surprisingly, very little information is available about the security of Israel's nuclear arsenal. What is known is that Israel maintains a nuclear weapons facility at Dimona, a remote site in the Negev desert. Dimona contains a plutonium and tritium production reactor, a chemical separation plant, and nuclear weapons fabrication facilities.[58] Israeli authorities undoubtedly surround Dimona—as well as deployed Israeli nuclear weapons at air and missile bases—with tight security. Israel may have tactical nuclear weapons, such as nuclear artillery shells and nuclear mines, which, according to some reports are stored at the Eilabun facility which is located west of the Sea of Galilee.[59] Reportedly, Israel has modified U.S.-supplied Harpoon cruise missiles to carry nuclear warheads on its diesel-powered submarines.[60] Depending on the transportation security procedures to and from the submarines, this particular Israeli nuclear capability might be the target of terrorists during the transport of these weapons. Although terror attacks are a frequent occurrence in Israel, no attacks against an Israeli nuclear site are known to have taken place.

North Korea

No open source information is available about the security of North Korea's presumed nuclear weapons arsenal, usually estimated to consist of between two and eight nuclear weapons. Given the totalitarian nature of the North Korean regime, it is highly unlikely that these weapons might be seized or diverted by a non-state organization, since none could operate within that country. As noted earlier, the only conceivable means by which a North Korean nuclear weapon might fall into the hands of terrorists is through the sale of such a weapon by the

North Korean government or the sale by a remnant of the regime during a period of political turmoil.

Russia

The size of Russia's nuclear arsenal (more than 12,000 warheads stored at more than 100 sites and at least 24 operational strategic weapons bases), the slow progress of warhead security upgrades, and concerns about the reliability of guard forces create small but significant risks of theft or diversion of an intact Russian nuclear weapon.[61] As will be discussed below, at particular risk are those more portable weapons, some of which are at forward bases and may not be equipped with PALs.

Officials of the 12th Main Directorate of the Ministry of Defense (responsible for the security and safety of Russia's nuclear weapons) have repeatedly stated that Russia's arsenal is secure from terrorists, the only possible exception being a case in which insiders might collude in the attempt.[62] However, the U.S. National Intelligence Council found in 2002 that warhead security forces suffer from wage arrears and poor working conditions at many sites.[63] The same report also found that terrorists attempted to reconnoiter Russian nuclear weapons storage sites at least twice and attempted to reconnoiter warhead trains on two separate occasions.[64] While acknowledging that in the previous three years, Moscow had "elevat[ed] its concern about the security of its nuclear weapons and materials," the Council warned that the decline in Russia's military funding throughout the 1990s has "stressed the country's nuclear security system."[65]

The clearest evidence that Russian nuclear weapons security falls short of meeting current challenges is that the Russian armed services have sought and are receiving assistance from the United States to improve their security capabilities. For the past decade, the United States has provided nearly $1 billion through programs implemented by the U.S. Departments of Defense and Energy.[66] Through the CTR Program, the Defense Threat Reduction Agency (DTRA) is working with Russia to improve the security of Russian nuclear weapons in storage or transport. Its Nuclear Weapons Storage Security Program has provided more than 100 security fencing and sensor systems for warhead storage sites (most not installed, as yet), training and equipment for military guards, and computers for warhead accounting. The Nuclear Weapons Transportation Security Program has funded railcars for warhead transport, emergency vehicles, and weapons recovery equipment, and it has provided containers, blankets, and other equipment for warhead transport and storage. The DOE's Weapons Protection, Control, and Accounting program has undertaken parallel efforts, concentrating initially on work with the Russian Navy and the Ministry of Atomic Energy and expanding recently into working with the Russian Strategic Rocket Forces (responsible for Russia's land-based intercontinental missiles). These programs still have far to go, however, before they adequately ensure the security of the Russian nuclear arsenal.

In March 2003, the U.S. GAO published a report that identified extensive gaps in the security of Russian nuclear weapons and highlighted the significant impediments preventing full implementation of U.S.-Russian cooperative programs to improve their protection.[67] The report is the most detailed publicly available review of these programs and of the overall security of Russia's nuclear arsenal. The document reviewed the security assistance programs of the U.S. DOD and DOE, covering three categories of sites holding Russian nuclear weapons: storage sites (sites for long-term maintenance and the longer-term storage of nuclear weapons), operational sites (sites that support the deployment of nuclear weapons), and rail transfer points (sites for securing weapons during transport stopovers). In addition, it reviewed U.S. programs to improve security over the transportation of such weapons as they move through the Russian rail system. The most fundamental, although implicit, finding of the report is that the U.S. government believes that without the assistance provided by DOD or DOE programs, virtually no Russian nuclear weapon site or transportation link can be considered secure by Western standards.

The report notes that "DOD plans to improve security at all storage sites," a clear indication of the breadth of DOD's concerns.[68] In reviewing progress through early 2003, the report states that to improve security at such installations, "the 12th Main Directorate has stated that it needs 123 kilometers of new perimeter fencing for 52 geographic locations throughout Russia."[69] By late 2002, however, the GAO notes, the DOD had installed only "about one third of the fencing—42 kilometers at 52 locations" and was two years behind schedule in this effort, indicating that even by Russian standards, the bulk of Russia's nuclear weapon security sites were inadequately protected. Moreover, as of March 2003, the GAO reported that the DOD had "not yet provided comprehensive upgrades—security systems that protect against internal and external threats—at *any* of the storage sites" (emphasis added).[70]

Some details of DOD's efforts to provide assistance in this area emerged in the testimony of two Bush administration officials before Congress that took place after the GAO report was completed. In March 2003, Assistant Secretary of Defense for International Security Policy J. D. Crouch II testified that DOD concluded agreements with the Russian Ministry of Defense in February 2003 "that will guarantee CTR personnel the access necessary to oversee security upgrades."[71] The formal agreement is called the Nuclear Weapons Storage Site Security Protocol and is focused on consolidating and securing *decommissioned* nuclear warheads. In March 2004, Deputy Under Secretary of Defense Lisa Bronson testified, "In Autumn 2003, [DOD] delivered 60 small-arms training sets and 1200 hand-held radios to support nuclear weapons storage security forces at all 60 sites [DOD] believe[s] to be active or used for training."[72]

As noted earlier, the insider threat is the one that the 12th Main Directorate had identified as particularly worrisome.[73] DOE has made considerably more progress working with the Russian Navy to upgrade the security of stored naval weapons. By late 2002, all stored naval nuclear warheads had received rapid security upgrades through DOE's Navy Complex Program, and comprehensive upgrades were completed at 6 of Russia's 36 naval warhead storage sites, covering 40 percent of Russian naval weapons.[74] By March 2004, security over many more of these sites had further improved. Specifically, DOE has "secured 77% (30 sites) of the 39" sites that DOE was assisting—which includes the 36 naval sites, mentioned previously, and 3 Russian Strategic Rocket Forces sites.[75]

The situation at operational sites appears to be more dangerous, however, because the United States has generally excluded them from assistance or, in some cases, ended assistance before their security upgrades could be completed. The GAO report notes, for example, that some eighteen of the vulnerable Russian Navy sites where DOE began its security upgrades have been deemed to be operational sites, and under a January 2003 interagency decision, security upgrade work there has been frozen:

> The January 2003 U.S. interagency guidelines precluded further DOE assistance to many operational sites. The guidelines permitted assistance to storage sites and rail transfer points that support warhead storage, consolidation, dismantlement, or force reductions. However, while it allowed for exceptions, the policy prohibited assistance to operational sites where mated or unmated warheads may be handled in the course of training or deployment, such as piers where submarines loaded with nuclear weapons are docked. The change in policy reflected concern that U.S. assistance might enhance Russia's military capability. To implement this policy, DOE curtailed its plans to provide comprehensive security improvements at operational sites where it had already installed rapid upgrades. In addition, DOE will not provide further assistance to operational sites that do not meet the policy's guidelines.[76]

According to the GAO report, security upgrades for most rail transfer sites are also lacking.

> DOD has considered expanding its assistance to rail transfer points, locations used to transfer warheads between trains and trucks and for temporary warhead storage. While the U.S. interagency guidelines permit assistance to rail transfer points, DOD has not yet developed a security assistance plan for rail transfer points because the 12th Main Directorate has provided little information on these sites. *DOD officials stated that warheads are most vulnerable at rail transfer points.* The absence of a security plan for these sites is a significant gap in DOD's current plans for enhancing security around Russian nuclear warheads.[77] (emphasis added)

Recognition by DOD of the seriousness of the problem at rail transfer sites recently appears to have led to a change in U.S. policy in which assistance is reviewed on a case by case basis.[78] As for rail transportation, the GAO stated:

DOD is providing assistance to improve the security of nuclear warheads during transportation by rail to consolidation and dismantlement sites. According to DOD officials, security experts consider warheads to be highly vulnerable to theft during transport....

DOD also provided security and safety enhancements for 100 nuclear weapon cargo railcars and 15 guard cars that accompany the cargo cars. For each railcar, DOD paid to install tampering and intrusion detection sensors, fire detection, and thermal insulation. DOD continues to pay for the maintenance of these railcars. The Russian Ministry of Defense has also requested new railcars because the condition of those that it is currently using is deteriorating to the point where they can no longer be used. DOD has not yet agreed to this request, partly because it is concerned that the new railcars may enhance Russia's operational capability for transporting deployed nuclear warheads.[79]

Soon after the GAO report was completed, DOD reported that it intends to purchase ten replacement warhead transportation cars. "Russia agreed to destroy two unusable warhead transport cars at its own expense in exchange for each new car CTR provides."[80] Consequently, security arrangements covering this highly vulnerable aspect of Russia's nuclear weapons operations appear to be improving, but more assistance may be needed to ensure that all transport cars operate reliably and securely.

Apart from the self-imposed restrictions on U.S assistance, the GAO noted that a key challenge facing both DOD and DOE is that "the departments do not know the total number of sites they plan to assist because Russia has provided only limited information about site locations and security conditions."[81] Although discussions between DOD and the Russian Ministry of Defense resulted in U.S. experts gaining some access to nine Russian warhead storage sites to help with security upgrades, the issue of access and assurances continues to be a major obstacle to U.S.-Russian cooperation.[82]

As evident from the GAO report, a number of serious gaps remain regarding the security of Russian nuclear arms. At particular risk from the standpoint of nuclear terrorism are tactical nuclear weapons

(TNW)—the category of nuclear arms least regulated by arms control agreements.[83] The terrorism risks posed by Russian tactical nuclear weapons stem from their physical properties as well as the policies for their deployment and employment. More specifically, these threats include:

- *Vulnerability to theft and unauthorized use.* The relatively small size of TNW and the absence among older warhead generations of PALs make them more attractive targets for theft than less portable warheads for most strategic delivery vehicles. TNW also are often stored separately from their delivery vehicles, which may be dual use and thus more susceptible to theft than their strategic counterparts, which are more likely to be mated to missile delivery systems.

- *Forward basing.* The intended use of TNW in battlefield and theater-level operations encourages their forward deployment. Russia sees TNW as a counterweight to NATO conventional forces and is reluctant to withdraw them to truly central storage sites, especially as additional U.S. forces are deployed in Central Asia and the Caucasus.

- *Delivery systems.* In addition to their relatively small size, TNW may be attractive to terrorists because of the dual-use nature of many of their delivery systems. These systems are much more readily available on the international market than are those for strategic weapons.

- *Inadequate safeguards.* The security of TNW also is compromised by the lack of adequate storage facilities to handle the influx of warheads pending elimination. TNW for aircraft pose special risks since they are not kept at central storage sites and are supposed to be available for rapid deployment. A potentially serious problem involves the growing number of retired officers who previously guarded nuclear weapons sites. Many of these individuals continue to live within the storage site's outer perimeter since they are entitled to housing by law, even though they work elsewhere. There have been cases in which these retirees have assisted local criminal elements to penetrate several layers of security at nuclear storage sites, although the target of these activities appears to have been conventional rather than nuclear arms.[84]

A major positive step to enhance the security of TNW was taken following the parallel, unilateral Presidential Nuclear Initiatives of 1991-1992. In their respective declarations, the American and Russian presidents declared that they would eliminate many types of tactical nuclear weapons, including artillery-fired atomic projectiles, tactical missile nuclear warheads, and atomic demolition munitions, and would place most other classes of TNW in "central storage."[85] Although Russia proceeded to dismantle several thousand TNW, it has been unwilling to withdraw unilaterally all of its remaining TNW from forward bases or even to relocate to central storage in a timely fashion those categories of TNW covered by the 1991/1992 declarations. The precise number of remaining TNW and their locations are not known publicly or to U.S. officials due to the failure of the 1991/92 informal regime to provide for any data exchange or any verification and transparency measures.[86]

Pakistan

Extremist Islamic groups within Pakistan and the surrounding region, a history of political instability, uncertain loyalties of senior officials in the civilian and military nuclear chain of command, and a nascent nuclear command and control system increase the risk that Pakistan's nuclear arms could fall into the hands of terrorists. Little definitive information is available, however, on the security of Pakistan's nuclear weapons.

One important revelation on this subject came on the heels of two assassination attempts against Pakistani President Pervez Musharraf in December 2003. According to a January 2004 press report, electronic jamming equipment provided by the United States prevented the first attempt from being successful by delaying the detonation of the explosive intended to destroy the car in which Musharraf was riding.[87] That same report also stated that, "The United States has been working to induce Pakistan to improve its safeguards including the transportation and accounting of nuclear [weapons] and nuclear-related material since the Sept. 11 attacks."[88] On February 6, 2004, details of U.S. nuclear security assistance to Pakistan were first revealed on NBC Nightly News. The news broadcast stated that, "Meeting every two months, [the U.S. Liaison Committee is] helping Pakistan develop state-of-the-art security, including secret authorization codes for the arsenal."[89] This committee has reportedly "spent millions of dollars to safeguard more than 40 weapons in Pakistan's nuclear arsenal."[90] In a wire service story dated the same day, moreover, a senior U.S. government official, speaking on condition of anonymity, told Reuters that the United States has been careful to adhere to restrictions under U.S. law and the nuclear Non-Proliferation Treaty to not provide "direct involvement" with Pakistan's nuclear weapons. The official also said, "We [U.S. government nuclear experts] have had discussions with Pakistan on the need for Pakistan to safeguard its technology and its nuclear material. We are confident they are taking the necessary steps."[91]

An earlier news report from 2001, citing unnamed U.S. government sources, claimed that the United States had prepared contingency plans to gain control of Pakistan's nuclear arsenal in the event of a coup or widespread political instability.[92] Responding to that report, Pakistani spokesmen stated that concerns over the country's nuclear arsenal were exaggerated and that Pakistan's nuclear assets were protected by a "well organized, clearly delineated, maximum-security structure manned by the armed forces."[93] Indeed, by this time, reacting to the events of September 11, 2001, President Musharraf reportedly had ordered Pakistan's military to move its nuclear weapons to at least six new highly secure sites, and he moved to strengthen the military oversight of these weapons.[94] Moreover, "The existing security arrangements were reinforced for all nuclear installations, especially the nuclear installations in Kahuta, Khushab, Chaghai Hills, and missile sites around Sargodha."[95] As of this writing, General Khalid Kidwai heads the Strategic Plans Division, a joint military command, which is in charge of the operational security of Pakistan's nuclear weapons and oversees other aspects of the Pakistani nuclear program, including production, research, and development.[96]

Still, doubts about Pakistan's nuclear weapons security have continued. At a press conference in New Delhi, India, on December 4, 2002, for example, Russian President Vladimir Putin expressed concern that terrorist groups may acquire access to Pakistan's nuclear weapons and fissile material.[97] Indian newspapers and analysts also continue to sound an alarm about terrorist acquisition of Pakistan's nuclear weapons.[98] These concerns have been accentuated by news of the clandestine sales of Pakistani nuclear technology by A.Q. Khan and uncertainties about the discipline and loyalty of personnel in Pakistan's nuclear command structure.

It has been widely reported that, during peacetime, Pakistan keeps the nuclear and non-nuclear components of its nuclear weapons separate, a measure which, if true, would greatly complicate efforts to seize an intact nuclear device. During a military confrontation, however, the two elements would be mated and most likely the complete weapon would be mated with Pakistan's missile and aircraft delivery systems; thereafter, the missiles, all of which are road mobile, might be moved to avoid the threat of a preemptive attack. Dispersing missiles in this fashion would greatly complicate security arrangements. Pakistani weapons are thought to lack internal safety and security features, such as PALs, and if acquired by a terrorist organization would be considerably easier to detonate than devices containing such safeguards.[99]

India

Little is known about the operational security of India's nuclear arsenal. Like Pakistan's, India's arsenal is thought to contain a relatively small number of nuclear weapons, easing the challenge of maintaining a high level of security. Also, as in the case of Pakistan, it has been widely reported that, in peacetime, nuclear and non-nuclear weapon components are stored separately, a measure which, if it is indeed utilized, would add a significant barrier against theft or seizure.

Assembled Indian nuclear weapons, like their counterparts in Pakistan, are not known to be equipped with advanced safety and security features, and therefore might be easier for terrorists to use directly or to disassemble in order to procure fissile material for improvised nuclear devices. India relies on the Central Industrial Security Force (CISF), a paramilitary force under the Ministry of Home Affairs, to guard nuclear installations. However, nuclear weapons stationed at Bhabha Atomic Research Centre (BARC) facilities are controlled by military forces. BARC also reportedly has an active research program devoted to developing advanced physical protection systems for its facilities.[100]

Although there have been no reports of the United States directly sharing information on nuclear weapons security with India, it is likely that Washington has offered to do so and that a dialogue on these subjects has taken place. The United States and India are engaged in building a close strategic relationship and, given heightened U.S. concerns about terrorism since September 11, 2001, this subject would be a natural one for the two states to review, even if fears of anti-U.S. terrorism and of political instability are less pronounced in India than they are in Pakistan.

PREVENTION, ENFORCEMENT, AND RESPONSE MECHANISMS

The foregoing discussion has highlighted the steps that a terrorist organization would need to complete in order to acquire an intact nuclear weapon, examined potential vulnerabilities of such weapons to terrorist seizure in key states, and reviewed, selectively, some of the principal initiatives undertaken by the United States to address these vulnerabilities. This section will briefly explore a number of complementary activities now under way to reduce further the threat of terrorism involving intact nuclear weapons. Together with programs such as those of the U.S. DOD and DOE focused directly on improving security of nuclear weapons, these complementary measures form a layered defense against nuclear terrorism.

Law Enforcement and Intelligence Capabilities

Physical security often is considered to be the first line of defense against nuclear terrorism. Law enforcement and intelligence, however, also play integral roles in preventing that line of defense from being tested. Even before a terrorist organization might launch an effort to acquire and detonate an intact nuclear weapon, it would be at risk of being detected and disrupted by U.S. and foreign law enforcement and intelligence agencies, including the Federal Bureau of Investigation (FBI) and the Central Intelligence Agency (CIA). In the event that a group made an explicit threat to detonate a nuclear device, the FBI would take the lead in investigating the action and would be expected to coordinate its efforts with the Federal Emergency Management Agency (FEMA), NEST, and other federal response services.[101] To facilitate effective communication and coordination with federal, state, and local agencies and officials, the FBI has formed the National Joint Terrorism Task Force and the Joint Terrorism Task Forces in each of the 56 FBI field offices.[102]

In response to the bombing of the Federal Building in Oklahoma City in 1995—the first act of mass-casualty terrorism on U.S. soil—the U.S. government moved decisively to strengthen the authority and capabilities of federal, state, and local law enforcement agencies to respond to threats of terrorism with weapons of mass destruction, including nuclear weapons.[103] After the al Qaeda attacks of September 11, 2001, law enforcement agencies were given further powers to investigate suspected terrorist organizations. In October 2001, the Uniting and Strengthening America by Providing Appropriate Tools Required to Intercept and Obstruct Terrorism (USA PATRIOT) Act gave federal, state, and local law enforcement agencies expanded powers to conduct searches and detain individuals suspected of planning terrorist attacks. This law has been criticized, however, for its potential impact on the civil liberties and privacy of American citizens.[104] The Foreign Intelligence Surveillance Act (FISA) and the U.S. Visitor and Immigration Status Indicator Technology (VISIT) immigration tracking system, enacted with similar goals in mind, have been subject to similar criticism. In March 2003, the newly created Department of Homeland Security (DHS) took over responsibility for coordinating domestic programs for prevention and response to terrorism. The DHS Office of Domestic Preparedness, formerly part of the Department of Justice, provides training and technical support for terrorism prevention and response to state and local agencies.[105]

Both the Clinton and George W. Bush administrations have worked to increase international cooperation to thwart and apprehend terrorists and to stop the flow of funds and arms to terrorist organizations. In May 2003, President Bush announced the Proliferation Security Initiative (PSI) in response to North Korean exports of missiles and to reports that Pyongyang might attempt to sell nuclear weapons or materials for making them.[106] While some states have raised concerns that certain aspects of the PSI could violate international law, 11 states—Australia, France, Germany, Italy, Japan, the Netherlands, Poland, Portugal, Spain, the United Kingdom, and the United States—agreed to participate in the PSI in 2003. The exposure in 2003-2004 of the illicit nuclear trade network developed by A.Q. Khan, the Pakistani metallurgist often called the "father of the Pakistani bomb," prompted further strengthening of laws against nuclear and WMD smuggling.[107] Other countries and international organizations made similar moves to strengthen the antiterrorist capabilities of law enforcement agencies after 9/11. INTERPOL, for example, created its Fusion Task Force to assist national police agencies in sharing information on terrorist threats and improving methodology for investigation and threat assessment.[108]

There is widespread agreement that cooperation and information sharing between law enforcement and intelligence agencies will be vital for prevention of future terrorist attacks, including attempts by terrorists to utilize nuclear weapons.[109] However, the statutory and institutional obstacles to closer cooperation are formidable.[110] Coordination among agencies was a major topic for the hearings conducted in 2003-2004 by the National Commission on Terrorist Attacks upon the United States (a.k.a. the "9/11 Commission").[111] International cooperation among intelligence agencies is often impeded to an even greater degree by national laws, political interests, and the need to protect national security information. Nevertheless, in the wake of 9/11, intelligence cooperation between the United States, its allies, and other states generally has been enhanced, resulting in the apprehension of a number of leading figures in al Qaeda and other transnational terrorist organizations. Nevertheless, much room remains for improvement, including greater use of intelligence officers serving as liaisons between agencies.[112] A detailed analysis of these issues, however, is beyond the scope of this book.

Border Security

To import a nuclear weapon into the United States, a terrorist organization would have to breach border security measures, and, at a later stage, any in-country nuclear detection systems, such as those surrounding some major U.S. cities. Currently, the United States employs nuclear detection systems at ports, border crossing points, and international airports; however, with respect to port security, large vulnerabilities exist. Efforts to enhance security are under the purview of the DHS.[113] The coordination and coalescence of port security efforts by subsidiary organizations within DHS—most notably the Coast Guard, the Bureau of Customs and Border Protection, and the Transportation Security Administration—are progressing but will inevitably take additional time. Unlike DOD and DOE programs that assist Russia in safeguarding nuclear weapons and fissile material, which have had more than a decade to mature, many of the port security efforts are still in their conceptual or early implementation stages.

The Container Security Initiative, for example, has made substantial progress in concluding agreements with foreign nations operating "megaports," which will allow U.S. agents to inspect U.S.-bound cargo there before it departs for the United States, but officials behind the effort are still wrestling with the modalities of implementing these agreements and expanding the program to other ports of concern.[114] As of March 2004, DOE reported to Congress that it had launched the Megaports Initiative at the Port of Rotterdam, which is being equipped with detection gear.[115] Others initiatives, like standardized security regulations mandated under the Maritime Transportation and Security Act (MTSA), which was signed into law in November 2002, were to be finalized by the end of 2003. However, as of early 2004, many vessel and maritime facility owners were behind schedule in submitting security plans to the U.S. Coast Guard.[116] Consequently, while these programs may provide a substantial barrier against acts of nuclear terrorism in the future, they are unlikely to have a significant impact in the near term.[117] (Table 3.4 shows some current U.S. port security initiatives and, where applicable, their current level of funding.)

U.S. RESPONSE MECHANISMS

As previously discussed, even after terrorists acquired a nuclear weapon, they typically would have much to do before they could detonate it, particularly if they wished to transport the weapon to a distant site. As they pursued this course, the country whose weapon had been seized, and potentially many other states, including the United States, would launch massive recovery efforts to regain control over the lost nuclear arm.

Since the mid-1970s, the United States has had a rapid response capability, known as the Nuclear Emergency Search Team, to address such a contingency. NEST is composed of weapons specialists from DOE's NNSA and the national laboratories—the organizations responsible for developing, producing, and maintaining U.S. nuclear weapons.[118] These teams are equipped to search for, identify, and dispose of nuclear materials. Up to 600 team members from a potential pool of 750 can respond to the site of a terrorist threat; however, deployments have usually involved fewer than 45 people.[119] Search Response Teams consisting of seven members can deploy within four hours of receiving a call. Joint Technical Operations Teams can cooperate with military ordnance disposal units to contain, disable, or destroy a nuclear device. NEST travels with a large suite of sophisticated radiation detectors and other gear that can diagnose and disable a nuclear weapon, improvised nuclear device, or radiological dispersal device. After receiving news of a nuclear terror threat, NEST begins to analyze the "technical and psychological validity" of the threat. To assist with this assessment, "NEST maintains a comprehensive computer database of nuclear weapon design information—from reports in scientific journals to passages from spy novels."[120]

Because NEST can tap a database of nuclear weapon designs, in the event that an intact nuclear weapon is detonated, it can attempt to match the characteristics of the weapon—including explosive yield and isotopic composition of the radioactive fallout—with those in the existing arsenals. This attribution capability can point back to the original owner of the weapon. Among other benefits, this capability may contribute to deterring a nuclear armed state from deliberately transferring a nuclear weapon to a terrorist organization for fear that the United States could trace the weapon back to its country of origin and hold it accountable. As reported in July 2003, the DHS, which now oversees the NEST operation, has been striving to improve attribution capabilities.[121]

Given fears concerning the security of nuclear weapons (and nuclear weapon materials) in Russia and Pakistan, it is likely that the United States has deployed teams with nuclear search capabilities in Europe and in the Persian Gulf region or on the U.S. airbase on the Indian Ocean island

TABLE 3.4
SELECTED CURRENT U.S. PORT SECURITY INITIATIVES

Program	Goal	Status
Actions taken abroad		
Creation of International Standards for Maritime Security	Create international standards for maritime safety, uniform customs procedures and supply chain security, standardized devices for security containers, standardized identification and credentialing of seafarers, procedures for the transport of dangerous goods	Varies by initiative; negotiations are ongoing at the International Maritime Organization, the World Customs Organization, the International Organization for Standardization, the International Labor Organization, and the UN Subcommittee of Experts on Transportation of Dangerous Goods. Each of these efforts has made progress in deliberations, and several have concluded binding agreements.[i]

---

[i] The International Maritime Organization adopted a new International Ship and Port Security (ISPS) Code in December 2002 through amendments to its SOLAS (International Safety of Life at Sea) Convention, which will come into effect in July 2004. The World Customs Organization adopted several measures in June 2003, including Guidelines on Advanced Cargo Information, guidelines for arrangements between WCO members and private enterprise for improving supply-chain security, and a WCO Data Model and list of essential data required to identify high-risk cargo. The WCO also passed a resolution in June 2002 pledging to develop a worldwide system similar to the Container Security Initiative. The International Organization for Standardization (ISO) signed a Memorandum of Understanding in May 2003 with the Strategic Council on Security Technology to develop their Smart and Secure Tradelanes Initiative (SST), launched as a pilot program that has been implemented in more than 12 of the world's busiest trade routes. The International Labor Organization (ILO) adopted a Convention on Seafarers Identity in June 2003. The United Nations Subcommittee of Experts on Transportation of Dangerous Materials (UN Subcommittee) met June 30-July 4, 2003, to discuss a number of measures including harmonization of recommendations on the transport of dangerous goods, United National packaging requirements, and procedures for incident reporting. The UN Subcommittee also approved the text of a Globally Harmonized System of Classification and Labeling of Chemicals.

of Diego Garcia. It is also likely that the United States has developed contingency plans for using specialized military forces and naval assets to intercept terrorists attempting to transport a nuclear device into the territory of the United States or one of its friends or allies. Other nuclear weapon states also are likely to have specialized nuclear search capabilities, although no details are publicly available regarding these capabilities.

TABLE 3.4 (CONTINUED)
SELECTED CURRENT U.S. PORT SECURITY INITIATIVES

Program	Goal	Status
Actions taken abroad		
Container Security Initiative (CSI)	Station U.S. agents in major ports of interest abroad to inspect U.S.-bound cargo before transport to the United States begins	*First phase:* 19 of 20 countries with major ports, which account for 68 percent of goods entering the United States by sea, have concluded bilateral agreements to host U.S. inspectors. CSI is currently operational in 13 ports worldwide. However, as of March 20, only 20 inspectors had actually been deployed overseas. *Second Phase:* Another 20-25 ports, accounting for more than 80 percent of cargo arriving at U.S. seaports, will be added, including strategically chosen ports in such areas as the Middle East, Turkey, and Malaysia.

CONSEQUENCE MANAGEMENT

In the Cold War security paradigm, an all-out nuclear war was deemed to be so overwhelming that the government, at best, paid lip service to civil defense and in reality made little or no effort to prepare the public for the onslaught of a thermonuclear conflict involving upwards of thousands of nuclear detonations. In the new security environment, in which the explosion of a nuclear weapon by a terrorist group appears more likely than thermonuclear war, consequence management preparation plays a greater role in readying first responders and American citizens to weather the ravages of a nuclear detonation. Unlike a massive nuclear weapons exchange in a nuclear war scenario, the most plausible worst-case nuclear terror act involves a single nuclear explosion. Almost certainly, an intact nuclear weapon releasing hundreds of kilo-

TABLE 3.4 (CONTINUED)
SELECTED CURRENT U.S. PORT SECURITY INITIATIVES

Program	Goal	Status
Actions taken prior to arrival at ports		
Proliferation Security Initiative (PSI)	Create a coalition of nations that will interdict high-risk shipments in territorial waters and airspace	Members of 11 countries met in Madrid in June 2003 to establish basic principles underpinning this program. A second meeting of these states occurred in July 9-10, 2003, in Australia to begin to create guidelines, examine potential areas for action given current legal mandates, and consider ways to expand legal mandates for interdiction under international law. As of June 2004, PSI contains 14 states. In addition, Liberia and Panama have signed boarding agreements that could permit ships flying their flags to be stopped and searched. This is significant because these two states are responsible for almost one-third of shipping using "flag of convenience" states, which typically have minimal registration procedures and weak or essentially nonexistent regulatory oversight.

tons worth of energy would create far more damage than an improvised nuclear device built by terrorists, the subject of Chapter 4.

While a nuclear detonation could overwhelm any city's emergency
response system, much can be done to mitigate the consequences and
save many lives. Within the immediate area surrounding ground zero
where the effects of blast and prompt radiation would be overpower-
ing, almost all people would be killed, hospitals destroyed, emergency
personnel killed, and nearby resources inundated. Nevertheless, just
outside this catastrophic zone, first responders can work to rescue

TABLE 3.4 (CONTINUED)
SELECTED CURRENT U.S. PORT SECURITY INITIATIVES

Program	Goal	Status
Actions taken prior to arrival at ports		
Operation Liberty Shield	Conduct large-scale expansion of Coast Guard activities aimed at detecting and defending against terrorist acts on U.S. ports	Coast Guard activities are currently undergoing large-scale expansion and Coast Guard forces are being modernized.[i] However, other complementary programs (e.g. the Integrated Deepwater System, which aims to modernize the Coast Guard fleet over 20 years) and other Coast Guard activities (e.g. drug interdiction and fisheries enforcement) are suffering as a result of reprioritization of funding for these programs.

[i] Coast Guard patrols are being doubled, with 700 new Homeland Security Response boats replacing outdated models. The Sea Marshal Program, which places armed guards on high-interest ships, will expand and add 50 new personnel. The number of Maritime Safety and Security Teams is being doubled from 6 to 12.

trapped and injured people, fight fires, decontaminate individuals and property, and seal off highly radioactive and very heavily damaged areas.

Many American cities have been developing and implementing catastrophic emergency response plans. Soon after 9/11, the U.S. government took steps to provide for the continuity of government under the conditions of a major terrorist attack.[122] Although a detailed examination of these plans is beyond the scope of this book, it is worthwhile to highlight several aspects of ongoing efforts to shape effective consequence management plans.[123]

One of the most contentious issues concerns the formula for distributing homeland security dollars for consequence management. To date, a tendency to emphasize equality among states over likely terrorist targets has worked to the disadvantage of states such as New York and

TABLE 3.4 (CONTINUED)
SELECTED CURRENT U.S. PORT SECURITY INITIATIVES

Program	Goal	Status
Actions to protect and strengthen ports		
Operation Safe Commerce (OSC)	Promote R&D to enhance the security of containers throughout the supply chain	$58 million in new funding released in June; currently being tested on a pilot program basis by ports in Los Angeles/Long Beach, Seattle/Tacoma, and New York/New Jersey
Customs Trade Partnership Against Terrorism (C-TPAT)	Encourage awareness and voluntary measures by private entities to improve container security	As of November 2002, 1,100 companies had agreed to participate in C-TPAT, and 197 importers, 16 brokers, and 22 carriers had been certified under the program. However, the program currently suffers because there is almost no presence of customs service personnel to monitor the compliance of private entities participating in the program.

Sources: Harold Kennedy, "U.S. Coast Guard Ratchets Up Port Security," *National Defense*, June 2003; Flynn, "The Fragile State of Container Security"; Hecker, "Container Security: Current Efforts to Detect Nuclear Materials, New Initiatives, and Challenges," pp. 5-6, 11-17; "Secretary Ridge Announces New Initiatives for Port Security," Department of Homeland Security, June 12, 2003, <http://www.dhs.gov/dhspublic/display?content=957>; "Australia to Host WMD meeting," *Herald Sun*, June 26, 2003, <http://www.heraldsun.news.com.au/common/story_page/0,5478,6656907%255E421,00.html>; "What is the ISPS Code?" Lloyd's Register, <http://www.lr.org/market_sector/marine/maritime-security/what_is_ISPS_code.htm>; "WCO Council approves several initiatives to improve the security and facilitation of the international Trade Supply Chain," World Customs Organization, July 4, 2003, <http://www.wcoomd.org/ie/En/en.html>; "91st annual Conference of the ILO concludes its work: Delegates debate action to end poverty through work, adopt Convention on seafarers security measures," International Labor Organization, June 19, 2003, <http://www.ilo.org/public/english/bureau/inf/pr/2003/35.htm>; "Strategic Partnership aims to secure the future of global supply chains," pp.18-19, ISO Bulletin, International Organization for Standardization, June 2003, <http://www.iso.ch/iso/en/commcentre/isobulletin/articles/2003/pdf/ships03-06.pdf>; "Department of Transportation, Research and Special Programs Administration: International Standards on the Transport of Dangerous Goods; Public Meetings," Federal Register, Vol. 68, No. 104, May 30, 2003, <http://www.unreports.com/public/DOT%20notice%20(23rd%20UNSCOE).pdf>; Jofi Joseph, "The Proliferation Security Initiative: Can Interdiction Stop Proliferation?" *Arms Control Today* (June 2004).

TABLE 3.4 (CONTINUED)
SELECTED CURRENT U.S. PORT SECURITY INITIATIVES

Program	Goal	Status
Actions to protect and strengthen ports		
Port security grants	Fund grant applications from individual ports to undertake security improvements there	$92 million was released in 2002 after an initial round of applications. An additional $75 million for specific projects was provided in the FY2003 supplemental appropriations. A second round of applications has been funded with $170 million in new grants to 198 different installations in the United States.
Detection of nuclear cargo at U.S. ports	Equip U.S. ports and agents with technology to detect nuclear cargo	As of November 2002, most inspectors had some means of detecting radioactive cargo, though customs officials admit shortcomings in this area. Most notable is the continued reliance on small detectors, while technology to scan entire containers remains under testing and development.[i]

[i] As of November 2002, 4,200 of 7,500 inspectors had radiation detection pagers. All inspectors were slated to have pagers by September 2003. These pagers have limited range and are not designed to detect weapons-grade fissile material. In addition, approximately 200 X-ray-compatible detectors had been deployed at U.S. ports. These detectors can scan small packages but not complete containers. No portal monitors, capable of scanning entire contents of containers or vehicles, had been deployed. A pilot test using portal monitors was under way at one U.S. port, and customs officials hoped to purchase 400 units by the end of fiscal year 2003. Additionally, 5,000 of 7,500 inspectors had been trained to identify activity or materials involved in the transport or production of nuclear weapons. Customs planned to provide further training in nuclear material detection to 140 inspectors in conjunction with U.S. national laboratories.

California. New York City, however, recently was informed by DHS that it would receive a supplemental grant worth tens of millions of dollars to support consequence management as well as radiation detection capabilities.[124] As of March 2004, the Fire Department of New York (FDNY) has equipped all firefighting units with basic radiation detection gear and has supplied hazardous material (HazMat) units with more advanced detection equipment that can determine precisely what radioactive isotopes are present at the scene of either a nuclear weapon explosion or a radiological dispersal device attack. Ideally, given enough funds, FDNY would equip all firefighting units with the advanced detectors. This capability would give each firefighting team the ability to characterize the radiological hazard in a local area.

A terrorist nuclear attack would most likely involve a surface nuclear explosion. Since the only nuclear bombings against cities (Hiroshima and Nagasaki) were air bursts, experiential data do not exist to guide emergency planning responses for surface bursts, which would create tremendous amounts of localized radioactive fallout. In the event of a surface explosion, one would anticipate that within ten to fifteen minutes, very highly radioactive fallout would rain down on the affected city, greatly complicating the ability of firefighters and other emergency personnel to provide rapid response. Firefighters are typically trained to rush to a damaged area within four minutes. By following traditional training practices in responding to a nuclear attack, they could find themselves a few minutes later suffering from the effects of radioactive fallout, contaminating themselves and their equipment. Response techniques, therefore, must be modified so that emergency responders are able to protect themselves while saving as many lives as possible.

Surface nuclear detonations in urban areas would also have other unpredictable effects for first responders and the public. For instance, tall buildings would tend to provide shielding against radiation exposure. In addition, there would likely be channeling effects in which very sturdy structures could deflect blasts away from some areas and toward others. Moreover, buildings with large glass surface areas would likely reflect thermal energy, igniting fires far from ground zero. Concurrently, some of the thermal energy would be transmitted through the glass, starting fires within buildings. In sum, the firefighting task would likely be extremely challenging with multiple fires over a large area. Quenching or containing these fires would be critically important for preventing coalescence into a firestorm.

Another challenge facing firefighters is the tendency of well-meaning personnel to "self-dispatch" by deciding on their own where to report during a crisis. This "freelancing" phenomenon occurred often in the aftermath of 9/11. The Incident Command System (ICS), a management organization tool, can help a commander determine where his personnel are and where they should be assigned. After-action reports comparing the responses of the Arlington County Fire Department (ACFD) at the Pentagon with the FDNY at the World Trade Center indicated that ACFD made much better use of the ICS than did FDNY. Wider adoption of management tools such as ICS could provide much better coordination of response efforts, resulting in fewer lives lost.[125]

A related issue is the need for federal, state, and local governments to put in place effective and interoperable wireless communications. Although the ability to communicate among various agencies and responders is essential during a crisis, and despite the fact that the post-9/11 Congress appropriated funds for this purpose, many problems remain, not all of which are of a financial nature. In November 2003, the GAO observed that "Effectively addressing these challenges requires collaboration of all first responders and all levels of government. Failure to do so risks spending funds ineffectively and creating new problems in our attempt to resolve existing ones."[126]

The problem of interoperable communications is a subset of the vast managerial challenges confronting the United States and any other country subject to a nuclear detonation. While the consolidation of many federal government offices into DHS has enhanced coordination among some key emergency response entities, many other relevant agencies remain outside DHS. Coordinating the efforts among this disparate group will remain challenging for the foreseeable future.

One of the federal entities involved with consequence management outside of DHS is DTRA, which provides needed support functions at the federal, state, and local levels.[127] Its Consequence Management Advisory Team (CMAT) can deploy 2 to 20 personnel at short notice to locations that have been attacked by weapons of mass destruction. The CMAT staff has extensive expertise in nuclear weapons operations, nuclear weapons maintenance, explosive ordnance disposal operations, and nuclear weapons effects modeling. Computer modeling tools, including Hazard Prediction and Assessment Capabilities (HPAC) and the Consequence Assessment Tool Set (CATS), are available for local emergency responders and the National Guard Support Teams. According to a DTRA fact sheet, "HPAC helps users accurately predict the effects of the hazardous materials and its [sic] impact on people. This integrated computer program uses meteorological and geographic information to identify potentially hazardous areas, giving officials a better picture of the situation. CATS is an automated, integrated geographical information system of hazard prediction and natural disaster models, and databases."[128] DTRA also works with the Armed Forces Radiobiological Research Institute, which has expertise in health physics, casualty treatment, and the effects of ionizing radiation.

Some governmental and nongovernmental organizations have issued guidance about how best to increase the probability of survival outside the high-damage zones of a nuclear weapon explosion.[129] Although it is vitally important to develop effective means of consequence mitigation and continuance of government, the greatest reduction in the risk of a nuclear weapon explosion perpetrated by terrorists can come about through reducing nuclear stockpiles and ensuring the highest level of security among those that remain.

PRIORITY ISSUES

Acquiring and detonating a nuclear weapon would pose a daunting challenge for any terrorist organization, and few are motivated or capable of executing the mission. Although prospects for terrorist success are very low, one also should recognize the significant gaps that exist in the web of preventive and protective measures arrayed against the threat. Every effort must be made to close these gaps as rapidly as possible.

Russian and U.S. Nuclear Weapons

The U.S. government has failed to integrate the preeminence of the terrorist threat fully into U.S. policy. Although the United States has invested heavily in countering some dimensions of nuclear terrorism, in other areas outmoded thinking has undercut the effectiveness of U.S. initiatives or caused valuable threat reduction measures to be overlooked. In particular, residual U.S. concerns over the military threat from Russia have impeded efforts to enhance protection of intact Russian nuclear arms against possible terrorist action. The DOD's Cooperative Threat Reduction program to assist Russia to secure its nuclear weapons has sought from its inception to prevent proliferation and encourage weapons reductions, while seeking to minimize the enhancement of Russian operational capabilities. To balance these trade-offs, proposed activities are examined case by case. [130] This doctrine was developed in the early 1990s, shortly after the collapse of the Soviet state. Today, this policy needs to be reexamined in light of greater terrorism threats, and some restrictions on providing security assistance to operational Russian nuclear weapon sites should be removed.

The Russian Navy, it should be recalled, requested U.S. nuclear weapon security assistance in the mid-1990s specifically because of episodes involving the theft of weapons-usable nuclear submarine fuel from a Navy fuel storage site. Yet under the current, restrictive U.S. policy, DOE may not be able to provide security assistance to Russian Navy nuclear weapon sites for which the Navy had specifically requested assistance based on fears that its nuclear weapons and/or weapons usable fuel were at risk. [131] Even if the current policy is left in place, at the very least, it is essential to alter the weighting of factors during case-by-case reviews in favor of providing assistance to improve security against terrorism, even when such assistance may marginally enhance Russian military operational capabilities.

Russia, too, it should be stressed, needs to reorient its thinking to give efforts to protect against nuclear terrorism a higher priority than those to enhance the operational capability of its nuclear forces. It needs to provide the United States with greater access to weapons sites or to develop procedures to allow confirmation that assistance is being used effectively without offering full access. Removal of all tactical nuclear weapons to central storage installations within Russia would provide an important additional measure of security for these high-risk arms, assuming that Russia implements needed security upgrades at these locations. At a minimum, Russia should implement fully the Presidential Nuclear Initiatives in a timely fashion by moving all non-air-based TNW to secure central storage sites.[132]

The continued deployment of U.S. tactical nuclear weapons in Western Europe raises similar issues. At this time, especially given the generally positive evolution of U.S.-Russian relations during the Bush and Putin administrations, the deployment of these weapons no longer serves a clear strategic purpose, and it is difficult to imagine a scenario in which these armaments might be employed. Moreover, most European allies in the NATO alliance do not believe having such weapons on their soil enhances their security. Their presence, however, may pose a target for terrorist action.

In light of the very serious nuclear terrorism risks posed by TNW, it is imperative that the United States, Russia, and the international community focus far more attention and energy on the one category of nuclear weapons for which no legally binding agreements are in place. It is disingenuous and dangerous to purport to take seriously the threats of high-consequence nuclear terrorism without taking concrete steps to enhance the security of existing stocks of TNW while seeking to reduce further their number.[133]

Pakistani Nuclear Weapons

Pakistan also poses a serious risk for terrorist acquisition of an intact nuclear weapon. This danger stems from the activity in the region of Islamic militant terrorist groups and the sympathy for such groups by segments of the Pakistani military and nuclear establishment. In light of the dangers and uncertainties surrounding the security of Pakistani nuclear assets, it is very much in U.S. interests to promote political stability in Pakistan and its neighbors, to reduce the influence of Islamic extremist groups, to eradicate elements of al Qaeda operating in Pakistan's Northwest Frontier Province, and to reinforce prudent physical protection and command and control practices associated with Pakistan's nuclear weapons. It also is essential for the United States to acquire much better intelligence about both the operation of terrorist groups in Pakistan and the condition and location of Pakistan's nuclear weapons. Far more problematic are the best means to accomplish these objectives and to sustain them over time.

An important first step is for the U.S. government to attach very high importance to these objectives and to invest resources commensurate with the challenge. Although short-term considerations may dictate provision of significant assistance to President Pervez Musharraf, the United States should avoid pinning most of its hopes on a single individual. It also must press President Musharraf—far more than has been indicated publicly—about the involvement of senior Pakistani government and military officials in A.Q. Khan's nuclear supplier network and the possible contact Khan and his associates may have had with Islamic extremists in Pakistan and other countries.[134] In addition, the United States should maximize, consistent with the Non-Proliferation Treaty and domestic U.S. law, the sharing of unclassified information on personnel reliability programs and other security mechanisms to help Pakistan protect its nuclear arsenal. The United States also must develop contingency plans, possibly involving the use of American nuclear recovery teams or specialized military forces, to help ensure that Pakistani nuclear assets do not fall into the hands of terrorist organizations or their sponsors. Given the limitations of U.S. intelligence, under most circumstances such protection/recovery efforts would require the cooperation of knowledgeable Pakistani authorities.[135]

[1] Alistair Millar, "Russia, NATO, and Tactical Nuclear Weapons after 11 September," in Brian Alexander and Alistair Millar, eds., *Tactical Nuclear Weapons: Emergent Threats in an Evolving Security Environment* (Washington, DC: Brassey's Inc., 2003), p. 80.

[2] U.S. Senate, Committee on Foreign Relations, *The Treaty Between the United States of America and the Russian Federation on Strategic Offensive Reductions,* Testimony by Sam Nunn, Co-chairman of the Nuclear Threat Initiative, July 23, 2002.

[3] See, for example, Reuters, "Arab Newspaper Says al Qaeda has Ukrainian Nukes," February 8, 2004, and Associated Press, "al-Qaida's No. 2 Claims to Have Nukes," March 22, 2004.

[4] Anonymous, *Through Our Enemies' Eyes: Osama bin Laden, Radical Islam, and the Future of America* (Washington, DC: Brassey's Inc., 2002), pp. 186-193, and references therein.

[5] U.S. Department of State, Glossary of Terms (Arms Control and Disarmament), <http://usinfo.state.gov/topical/pol/arms/stories/pt11.htm>, accessed on October 24, 2002.

[6] Samuel Glasstone and Philip J. Dolan, *Effects of Nuclear Weapons* (Washington DC: U.S. Government Printing Office, 1977).

[7] Lynn Eden, *Whole World on Fire: Organizations, Knowledge, & Nuclear Weapons Devastation* (Ithaca: Cornell University Press, 2004), describes in great detail how nuclear targeting planners have failed to factor in the damaging effects of fires. Her work draws heavily from the research of Theodore Postol and Harold Brode, who have calculated the devastating and widespread effects of fires ignited by nuclear weapons. In an article based on her book, Eden writes, "For nuclear weapons of 100 kilotons or more, destruction from fire will be substantially greater than from blast"; Lynn Eden, "City on Fire," *Bulletin of the Atomic Scientists* (January/February 2004), p. 40. This observation clearly has relevance for the consequences from terrorist detonation of an intact nuclear weapon because such weapons would typically have yields greater than 100 kilotons (KT).

[8] Matthew Bunn, Anthony Wier, and John P. Holdren, *Controlling Nuclear Warheads and Materials: A Report Card and Action Plan* (Washington DC: Nuclear Threat Initiative and the Project on Managing the Atom, Harvard University, March 2003), pp. 22-23.

[9] NRDC Nuclear Notebook: "Pakistan's Nuclear Forces, 2001," *Bulletin of the Atomic Scientists* (January/February 2002); and NRDC Nuclear Notebook: "India's Nuclear Forces, 2002," *Bulletin of the Atomic Scientists* (March/April 2002).

[10] NRDC Nuclear Notebook: "Russian Nuclear Forces, 2002," *Bulletin of the Atomic Scientists* (July/August 2002).

[11] NRDC Nuclear Notebook: "U.S. Nuclear Forces, 2002," *Bulletin of the Atomic Scientists* (May/June 2002).

[12] Matthew Bunn, et al., *Controlling Nuclear Warheads and Materials,* discuss in detail the components of this chain of necessary conditions in their report in a section titled the "Terrorist Pathway to the Bomb."

[13] Some variants on this basic model can be imagined, such as the decision to set off the device at a less-than-optimal site in order to reduce the risk of detection inherent in transporting the device across borders. Collaboration among terrorist organizations is another possibility. See Morten Bremer Maerli, *Crude Nukes on the Loose? Preventing Nuclear Terrorism by Means of Optimum Nuclear Husbandry, Transparency, and Non-Intrusive Fissile Material Verification,* Ph.D. dissertation, Faculty of Mathematics and Natural Sciences, University of Oslo, 2004.

[14] A network of transportation links capable of moving the weapon across land and probably water, for example, would be required in most scenarios. While it is possible that a small team could carry out the transport of the weapon, it appears more likely that a large, well-organized network would be necessary to coordinate the various stages of transport from the original storage site to the end target. Resources would also be needed to sustain a relatively large organization for some period, perhaps comparable to that needed to sustain the four teams of al Qaeda operatives who undertook the September 11, 2001, attacks. To maximize its chances of success, the terrorist organization would also, under most scenarios, require the resources and manpower to study multiple-storage nuclear sites and their vulnerabilities. However, the larger and more complex the organization becomes, the greater the likelihood that it will be discovered before its mission can be accomplished.

[15] David Rhode and David E. Sanger, "Key Pakistani Is Said to Admit Atom Transfers," *New York Times,* February 1, 2004, p. A1; Patrick Chalmers, "Police: Pakistan's Khan Arranged Uranium for Libya," *Washington Post,* February 20, 2004, <http://www.washingtonpost.com>; "Re-imposition of sanctions feared: US aid maybe jeopardized – official," *Dawn,* February 5, 2004, <http://www.dawn.com>. Glenn Kessler, "Pakistan's N. Korea Deals Stir Scrutiny: Aid to Nuclear Arms Bid May be Recent," *Washington Post,* November 13, 2002, p. A1; David E. Sanger, "In North Korea and Pakistan, Deep Roots of Nuclear Barter," *New York Times,* November 22, 2002, p. A1; John Lancaster and Kamran Khan, "Pakistan Fires Top Nuclear Scientist," *Washington Post,* February 1, 2004, p. A1; Peter Slevin, "Libya Made Plutonium, Nuclear Watchdog Says," *Washington Post,* February 21, 2004, p. A15.

[16] Indeed, during the investigation of his activities Khan himself reportedly stated that during the 1990s, the leaders of Pakistan's military, including Musharraf when serving as Army Chief of Staff, were knowledgeable

about the transfers. John Lancaster and Kamran Khan, "Musharraf Named in Nuclear Probe," *Washington Post,* February 3, 2004, p. A13; Seymour M. Hersh, "The Deal: Annals of National Security," *The New Yorker,* March 8, 2004, p. 32; Salman Masood and David Rohde, "Pakistan Opposition Charges Atomic Cover-Up," *New York Times,* February 17, 2004, p. A3; Joseph Siegle, "Pakistan: The Dangers of Despotism," *Los Angeles Times,* February 22, 2004, p. M2.

[17] Similar scenarios are discussed in Matthew Bunn, et al., *Controlling Nuclear Warheads and Materials.* Concerning the transfer issue, David Abright and Holly Higgins, "A Bomb for the Ummah," *Bulletin of the Atomic Scientists* (March/April 2003), pp. 49-55, state, "Some of Pakistan's nuclear scientists believe that the bomb should be shared with all of the Muslim community, even—or especially—with al Qaeda." Many South Asian experts, however, doubt that radical Islamists are likely to gain power in Pakistan in the near term, and some also question their readiness to transfer nuclear weapons to terrorists. Gaurav Kampani, Center for Nonproliferation Studies, correspondence with author, April 6, 2004.

[18] Glenn Kessler, "N. Korea Says It Has Nuclear Arms; At Talks with U.S. Pyongyang Threatens 'Demonstration' or Export of Weapons," *Washington Post,* April 25, 2003, p. A1; David E. Sanger, "North Korea Says It Now Possesses Nuclear Material," *New York Times,* April 25, 2003, p. A1.

[19] James Dao, "U.S. Official Says North Korea Could Sell Bomb Material," *New York Times,* February 5, 2003; Will Dunham, "U.S. Worries North Korea Will Sell Nuclear Bombs," Reuters, January 19, 2003.

[20] Indeed, in an unusual twist on this theme, in early March 2004, Iran threatened to launch terrorists against Libya because the latter was divulging details of Iran's secret attempts to develop nuclear arms. "Iran Threatens Terrorist Action in Libya If Tripoli Reveals Nuclear Information," Nuclear Security Newswire, March 1, 2004.

[21] U.S. Department of Defense, *Proliferation: Threat and Response* (Washington, DC: Government Printing Office, 2001), p. 61. See also, Matthew Bunn, et al., *Controlling Nuclear Warheads and Materials,* pp. 28-29.

[22] Gaurav Kampani, Center for Nonproliferation Studies, personal communication with author, October 13, 2003.

[23] Peter Vincent Pry, *War Scare: Russia and America on the Nuclear Brink* (Westport, CT: Praeger, 1999), p. 60.

[24] During China's Cultural Revolution of the mid-1960s, it may be noted, leaders of China's nuclear establishment feared that their institutes and China's Lop Nor nuclear test site might be overrun by Red Guard cadres rampaging throughout China at the time. This did not transpire, however, as China's leaders acted to protect the country's nuclear activities from such depredations. Leonard S. Spector, *Going Nuclear* (Cambridge, MA: Ballinger Publishing Company, 1987), p. 32. In 1961, planning for a coup of the French government took place while the fourth French nuclear test was being prepared in Algeria. The coup plotters coerced senior officers and other military personnel in Algeria to join forces with them. Fearing that they might overrun the test site, French nuclear authorities rushed the nuclear test, which outside observers believed was a "fizzle"— probably due to the test preparations done in haste. Ibid., pp. 27-30.

[25] For more on PALs, see Dan Caldwell and Peter Zimmerman, "Reducing the Risk of Nuclear War with Permissive Action Links," in Barry M. Blechman, ed., *Technology and the Limitation of International Conflict* (Washington, DC: SAIS, 1989), pp. 137-150, and Peter Stein and Peter Feaver, *Assuring Control of Nuclear Weapons,* CSIA Occasional Paper #2, Center for Science and International Affairs (Harvard University, 1987).

[26] Bruce Blair, *Strategic Command and Control* (Washington, DC: Brookings Institution Press, 1985), pp. 104-108, and Gurmeet Kanwal, "Command and Control of Nuclear Weapons in India," *Strategic Analysis* 23, January 2000, Columbia International Affairs Online, <http://www.ciaonet.org/olj/sa/sa_00kag01.html>, accessed on December 17, 2002.

[27] The United States began equipping its nuclear weapons with PALs in the 1960s. Today, all operational U.S. nuclear weapons are protected by them, including weapons on submarines, which were fitted with PALs in 1997. Ashton B. Carter, John D. Steinbruner, and Charles A. Zraket, eds., *Managing Nuclear Operations* (Washington, DC: Brookings Institution Press, 1987), pp. 46-51 and 167-168; Bruce G. Blair, John E. Pike, and Stephen I. Schwartz, "Targeting and Controlling the Bomb," in Stephen I. Schwartz, ed., *Atomic Audit: The Costs and Consequences of U.S. Nuclear Weapons Since 1940* (Washington, DC: Brookings Institution Press, 1998), pp. 220-221.

[28] Oleg Bukharin, personal communication with author, March 31, 2004.

[29] Nikolai Sokov, "Tactical Nuclear Weapons," NTI Web site, <http://www.nti.org/e_research/e3_10b.html>, accessed on December 17, 2002.

[30] See William C. Potter, Nikolai Sokov, Harald Müller, and Annette Schaper, *Tactical Nuclear Weapons: Options for Control* (Geneva: United Nations Institute for Disarmament Research, 2002); Joshua Handler, "The September 1991 Presidential Nuclear Initiatives (PNIs) and the Elimination, Storing and Security Aspects of Tactical Nuclear Weapons (TNWs)," Princeton University Program on Science and Global Security, <http://www.princeton.edu/~jhandler/CV/JH_UN_24_Sept_01_TNW_Talk.pdf>, accessed on October 23, 2002; Stephen Lambert and David Miller, *Russia's Crumbling Tactical Nuclear Weapons Complex: An Opportunity for Arms Control, Institute for National Security Studies,* Occasional Paper 12 (Colorado: USAF Academy), April 1997, <http://www.usafa.af.mil/inss/ocp12.htm>, accessed on October 23, 2002; and William Potter and Nikolai Sokov, "The Nature of the Problem," in William C. Potter, et al., *Tactical Nuclear Weapons,* pp. 1-18.

[31] See Robert S. Norris, Andrew S. Burrows, and Richard W. Fieldhouse, *Nuclear Weapons Databook, Volume V: British, French, and Chinese Nuclear Weapons* (Boulder, CO: Westview Press, 1994). British Trident warheads, incorporating the same technology used in U.S. Trident systems, may be assumed to have PALs, but because there may be technical and operational difficulties associated with PALs on submarine-based weapons, it cannot automatically be assumed that French SLBM warheads have PALs.

[32] Steve Coll, "The Man Inside China's Bomb Labs," *Washington Post,* May 16, 2001.

[33] Kanwal, "Command and Control of Nuclear Weapons in India." Pakistani, Indian, and North Korean nuclear weapons are generally considered less sophisticated than those of the more advanced nuclear powers and thus are less likely to contain integrated PALs.

[34] See, for example, Pervez Hoodbhoy, "Living with the Bomb," undated, <http://www.foil.org/politics/nonuke/hoodbhoy.html>, accessed on November 12, 2003.

[35] Landau Network-Centro Volta, quoting Gen. Khalid Kidwai of Pakistan's Strategic Plan Division (SPD), in "Nuclear safety, nuclear stability, and nuclear strategy in Pakistan," Pugwash Online Web site, <http://www.pugwash.org/september11/pakistan-nuclear.htm>, accessed on December 17, 2002. President Musharraf also has suggested that even if terrorists were to gain access to an actual warhead, they would be unable to work the triggering mechanism to detonate it. See "Musharraf denies govt role in proliferation," *Dawn,* March 29, 2004.

[36] Steven Mufson, "U.S. Worries about Pakistan Nuclear Arms," *Washington Post,* November 4, 2001, p. A27. As a nuclear weapon state party to the nuclear Nonproliferation Treaty, the United States is prohibited from assisting states deemed non-nuclear weapon states (NNWSs) under the treaty to develop nuclear weapons. All states except those that detonated a nuclear explosion before January 1, 1967, are considered to be NNWSs under the treaty. If U.S. information concerning PALs contained data on the design of nuclear weapons, its transfer to Pakistan would thus have been banned by the treaty.

[37] Agha Shali, Zulfiqar Ali Khan, and Abdul Sattar, "Securing Nuclear Peace," *The News* (Islamabad), October 5, 1999, and Tanvir Ahmad Khan, "A Command and Control System," *Dawn,* February 15, 2000.

[38] See Zia Mian, "A Nuclear Tiger by the Tail: Some Problems of Command and Control in South Asia," PU/CEES Report No. 328, Center for Energy and Environmental Studies, Princeton University, June 2001, and Gaurav Kampani, "Safety Concerns About the Command & Control of Pakistan's Strategic Forces, Fissile Material, and Nuclear Installations," Center for Nonproliferation Studies, September 28, 2001, CNS Web site, <http://cns.miis.edu/research/wtc01/spna.htm>, accessed on March 30, 2004.

[39] Bruce G. Blair, *Global Zero Alert for Nuclear Forces,* Brookings Occasional Papers (Washington DC: Brookings Institution, 1995).

[40] An IND could well require more nuclear weapon material than might be found in the particular nuclear weapon the terrorist group had obtained, since it may be assumed that nuclear arms produced by any nation embody efficiencies developed during years of research that enable that nation to maximize the number of weapons it can create from limited amounts of fissile material and/or to reduce the weight and size of its nuclear arms to facilitate their delivery by ballistic and cruise missiles.

[41] Of course, the terrorist group might not want to target the United States and in that situation may not have to transport the weapon over as long a distance. For example, certain terrorist groups might decide to try to detonate a Russian tactical nuclear weapon in Moscow.

[42] See Carter, et al., eds., *Managing Nuclear Operations,* and Scott D. Sagan, *The Limits of Safety: Organizations, Accidents, and Nuclear Weapons* (Princeton, NJ: Princeton University Press, 1993).

[43] Feroz Hassan Khan, "Challenges to Nuclear Stability in South Asia," *Nonproliferation Review* 10 (Spring 2003), pp. 59-74.

[44] This would also be a problem for North Korea, but the country's population is so tightly controlled that there seems little risk that terrorists could obtain one of this state's nuclear weapons without the approval of the Kim Jong Il government.

[45] In 2002, the National Research Council of the U.S. Academy of Sciences, for example, assessed the threat to state-owned nuclear weapons. It concluded that in the United States, the United Kingdom, China, France, and Israel, nuclear weapons are well protected and the threat level is low. For Pakistan and India, the council assessed a medium threat level because, although the weapons are secure, the "political situation is unstable." Finally, it determined a medium threat level for Russia because Russia has "large numbers of weapons with poor inventory controls." "Nuclear and Radiological Threats," Chapter 2 of Committee on Science and Technology for Countering Terrorism, National Research Council, *Making the Nation Safer: The Role of Science and Technology in Countering Terrorism* (Washington, DC: National Academy Press, 2002). As discussed in the text, recent events suggest that the risks in India and Pakistan should no longer be considered comparable; political instability is a considerably greater risk in the latter than in the former, and the integrity chain of nuclear command appears to be far more uncertain in Pakistan.

[46] U.S. House of Representatives, House Subcommittee on National Security, Emerging Threats, and International Relations, "Nuclear Weapons Security," Testimony of Robin M. Nazzaro, Director, Natural Resources and Environment Team, June 24, 2003.

[47] Dave Montgomery, "Federal Inspectors Question Security at U.S. Nuclear Facilities," Miami Herald.com, March 17, 2004, <http://www.miami.com/mld/miamiherald/business/national/8209473.htm>; Ted Bridis, "Watchdog: Nuke Guards Cheated in Drill," *Guardian Unlimited*, January 26, 2004, <http://www.guardian.co.uk/uslatest/story/0,1282,-3672300,00.html>. Shortcomings of this type have been a source of concern for some time. In 2001, for example, the Project on Government Oversight (POGO) drew attention to the human dimension of security in the U.S. nuclear weapons complex. POGO found that "the government fails to protect against [mock] attacks more than 50% of the time—although the exact figure is classified." The report goes on to state that "DOE employees and others who have raised security concerns have largely been ignored and subjected to retaliation over many years." The Project on Government Oversight, *U.S. Nuclear Weapons Complex: Security at Risk,* POGO Report, October 2001. See, also, U.S. General Accounting Office, *Nuclear Security: Lessons to be Learned from Implementing NNSA's Security Enhancements,* GAO-02-358, March 2002. It should be noted that the two reports just cited have pointed out potential shortcomings in the management of nuclear materials security and not the security of nuclear weapons themselves.

[48] NRDC Nuclear Notebook, "U.S. Nuclear Forces, 2003," *Bulletin of the Atomic Scientists* (May/June 2003), p. 76. As suggested earlier, portable weapons such as these, which are not integrated into long-range land- and sea-based ballistic missiles, lack the extra layer of protection found in the latter.

[49] Trabelsi was arrested on September 13, 2001, and on September 30, 2003, was convicted and sentenced to a ten-year prison term. During his trial, he testified that he had not sought to detonate nuclear warheads, but intended to kill American soldiers with a car bomb. He acknowledged having received training from al Qaeda. See "18 Guilty in Terror Trial in Belgium; 3 Linked to Plot on NATO," Associated Press, October 1, 2003; Constant Brand, "Al Qaeda Bomb Plotter Conviction in Belgium," *Washington Post,* October 1, 2003, p. A17; Sebastian Rotella, "18 Convicted in al Qaeda-Tied Belgian Trial; Sentences are Handed Down for, Among Other Crimes, a Planned Attack on a NATO Base," *Los Angeles Times,* October 1, 2003, p. A4.

[50] Security should not be presumed just because nuclear weapons reside in advanced countries that have had these weapons for many years. Scott Sagan examines how nuclear weapons accidents and shortcomings in safety and security could arise in complex systems such as the complicated organizational structures built up around nuclear weapons establishments. See Sagan, *The Limits of Safety.*

[51] French Atomic Energy Commission (CEA), "Contributing to National Defence," in CEA Annual Report, 2001, <http://www.cea.fr/gb/publications/AnnualReport>.

[52] Robert S. Norris, personal communication with author, November 12, 2003.

[53] NRDC Nuclear Notebook, "British Nuclear Forces, 2001," *Bulletin of the Atomic Scientists* (November/December 2001), pp. 78-79. Before the nuclear warheads are loaded onto the submarine, the SSBN travels to the U.S. submarine base at Kings Bay, Georgia, to receive 16 Trident II (D-5) ballistic missiles, which the British government rents from the United States. Once a British SSBN has a full complement of Trident missiles, it returns to Coulport, Scotland, to have the nuclear warheads mated to the missiles; then the

submarine goes on patrol. At the end of the patrol, the procedure is reversed; i.e., warheads are removed in Scotland, and the submarine returns to the United States. Thus, British nuclear warheads never touch American soil. Robert S. Norris, personal communication with author, April 1, 2004.

[54] NRDC Nuclear Notebook, "French Nuclear Forces, 2001," *Bulletin of the Atomic Scientists* (July/August 2001), p. 70. See also "Review of the Implementation of Article VI," Working Papers submitted by France to the 2000 NPT Review Conference, New York, April 14-May 19, 2000, NPT/CONF. 2000/WP.8.

[55] Robert S. Norris, personal communication with author, November 12, 2003.

[56] Joseph Cirincione with Jon B. Wolfsthal and Miriam Rajkumar, *Deadly Arsenals: Tracking Weapons of Mass Destruction* (Washington, DC: Carnegie Endowment for International Peace, 2002). China has not tested a nuclear weapon since 1996, however, making it unlikely that the test site currently holds any intact nuclear devices.

[57] Nathan Busch, "China's Fissile Material Protection Control, and Accounting: The Case for Renewed Collaboration," *Nonproliferation Review* 9 (Fall-Winter 2002), p. 98, and references therein.

[58] NRDC Nuclear Notebook: "Israeli Nuclear Forces, 2002," *Bulletin of the Atomic Scientists* (September/October 2002), p. 73.

[59] Ibid, p. 75.

[60] Douglas Frantz, "Israel's Arsenal is Point of Contention; The Nation can now Launch Nuclear Weapons from Land, Sea, and Air, Officials Say; The Issue Complicates Efforts to Rein in Iran's Ambitions," *Los Angeles Times,* October 12, 2003, p. A1.

[61] These risk factors are discussed in Matthew Bunn, *Preventing Nuclear Terrorism: A Progress Update* (Washington DC: Nuclear Threat Initiative and the Project on Managing the Atom, Harvard University, 2003).

[62] See, for example, statements by Gen. Igor Valynkin, Interfax, September 4, 2002; Valynkin, Interfax, October 8, 2002; and Col-Gen. Yuriy Baluyevskiy, ITAR-TASS, September 4, 2002.

[63] National Intelligence Council, "Annual Report to Congress on the Safety and Security of Russian Nuclear Facilities and Military Forces," Central Intelligence Agency, February 2002.

[64] Ibid.

[65] Ibid. In a 1999 examination of the likelihood of nuclear weapons theft, the Canadian Security Intelligence Service reached a similar conclusion: "Theft of an intact nuclear weapon is not considered very likely, given the stringent security measures in place in most of the nuclear-weapon states, although political instability and socioeconomic decay in some of them—including the former Soviet Union—must remain of some concern. Tactical nuclear weapons, whose security features may be more vulnerable to tampering, are of greater concern than strategic nuclear weapons in this regard." Canadian Security Intelligence Service report, "Chemical, Biological, Radiological, and Nuclear (CBRN) Terrorism," December 2, 1999.

[66] Of the approximately one billion allocated dollars, the U.S. Department of Defense nuclear warhead security program in Russia was allotted $796.1 million, and the U.S. Department of Energy's complementary program was appropriated $159.4 million during the same timeframe. U.S. General Accounting Office, *Weapons of Mass Destruction: Additional Russian Cooperation Needed to Facilitate U.S. Efforts to Improve Security at Russian Sites,* GAO-03-482, March 2003, p. 17.

[67] Ibid., Chapter III and Appendices.

[68] Ibid., p. 34.

[69] Ibid.

[70] Ibid., p. 37.

[71] U.S. House of Representatives, Committee on Armed Services, Testimony of Assistant Secretary of Defense for International Security Policy, J. D. Crouch II, March 4, 2003.

[72] U.S. Senate, Committee on Armed Services, Subcommittee on Emerging Threats and Capabilities, testimony of Lisa Bronson, Deputy Under Secretary of Defense for Technology Security Policy and Counterproliferation, March 10, 2004.

[73] Valynkin, Interfax, September 4, 2002 and October 8, 2002; Baluyevskiy, ITAR-TASS, September 4, 2002.

[74] Michael Roston and David Smigielski, "Accomplishments of Selected Threat Reduction and Nonproliferation Programs in Russia by Agency," RANSAC Report, May 2002; and "Interview: Ambassador Linton Brooks on U.S. Nuclear Policy," conducted by Leonard S. Spector, *Nonproliferation Review* 9 (Fall-Winter 2002), p. 1.

[75] U.S. Senate, Armed Services Committee, testimony by Paul M. Longsworth, Deputy Administrator for Defense Nuclear Nonproliferation, National Nuclear Security Administration, March 10, 2004.

[76] GAO-03-482, p. 38. In commenting on the GAO report, the National Nuclear Security Administration (NNSA), the unit of the Department of Energy responsible for nuclear weapons, stated that the decision to curtail assistance to operational Russian Navy nuclear weapon sites had been taken independently by the department in early 2002, predating the January 2003 interagency decision, and that "the primary reason for the restriction was not a concern with 'operational enhancement' of Russian warhead sites, but rather with estimates of 'residence times' for warheads associated with these sites. At sites where residence times are believed to be very low, NNSA does not believe that comprehensive upgrades are justified." See GAO-03-482, p. 85.

[77] Ibid., p. 35.

[78] U.S. government official, name withheld by request, interview with author, Washington, DC, April 2, 2004.

[79] GAO-03-482, p. 74.

[80] U.S. House of Representatives, J. D. Crouch II testimony, March 4, 2003.

[81] Ibid., p. 7.

[82] U.S. National Academies Committee and Russian Academy of Sciences Committee on U.S.-Russian Cooperation on Nuclear Non-Proliferation, *Overcoming Impediments to U.S.-Russian Cooperation on Nuclear Non-Proliferation,* Report of a Joint Workshop, The National Academies Press, Washington, DC, 2004; Matthew Bunn, et al., *Controlling Nuclear Warheads and Materials,* p. 7. The United States has also engaged Russia in developing new technologies for securing weapons. In 1994, the United States and Russia signed the Warhead Safety and Security Exchange Agreement (WSSX), which the two countries have applied to improving nuclear warhead safety and security and enhancing counterterrorism activities. As of late 2003, WSSX encompassed almost 50 projects totaling about $35 million. Technologies to improve safety, security, and transparency of warhead dismantlement include next-generation tags and seals as well as radiation measurement equipment. Activities involve monitoring and dismantling nuclear warheads. The WSSX program has investigated counterterrorism technologies, such as advanced nuclear and explosive materials detectors, consequence modeling and mitigation capabilities, and explosive containment chambers to disarm terrorist devices. Darby Parliament, "U.S. Government Programs Addressing the Threats of Nuclear Terrorism," Paper for the Center for Nonproliferation Studies, December 6, 2003; Department of Energy's Office of Nonproliferation and International Security Web site, "Programs," <http://www.nnsa.doe.gov>, accessed on December 6, 2003.

[83] See William C. Potter et al., *Tactical Nuclear Weapons.*

[84] For a more detailed discussion of these issues see William C. Potter, "Practical Steps for Addressing the Problem of Non-Strategic Nuclear Weapons," in Jeffrey A. Larsen and Kurt J. Klingenberger, eds., *Controlling Non-Strategic Nuclear Weapons* (Colorado Springs: U.S. Air Force Institute for National Security Studies, 2001), pp. 211-228.

[85] Ibid.; see "U.S. Presidential Nuclear Initiative, 1991," and "Soviet and Russian Responses to the Bush Initiative," pp. 273-290.

[86] Estimates of remaining Russian TNW vary wildly and range from several hundred to more than ten thousand. Cf. Amy F. Woolf, "Nuclear Weapons in Russia: Safety, Security, and Control Issues," Issue Brief for Congress, Congressional Research Service, Updated April 11, 2003; Potter, "Practical Steps for Addressing the Problem of Non-Strategic Nuclear Weapons," pp. 223-225.

[87] Dana Priest, "U.S. Aids Security of Musharraf," *Washington Post,* January 3, 2004.

[88] Ibid.

[89] NBC Nightly News, February 6, 2004.

[90] Ibid.

[91] Carol Giacomo, "U.S. Helps Pakistan Safeguard Nuclear Material," Reuters, February 6, 2004.

[92] Seymour Hersh, "Watching the Warheads: The Risks to Pakistan's Nuclear Arsenal," *New Yorker,* November 5, 2001.

[93] Mushahid Hussain, "Pakistan's nuclear safety," *Nation* (Lahore edition, Internet version), November 6, 2001, FBIS document SAP20011106000058; Kamal Matinuddin, "How safe are the nukes?" *The News* (Islamabad, Internet version), November 14, 2001, FBIS document SAP20011114000062.

[94] Molly Moore and Kamran Khan, "Pakistan Moves Nuclear Weapons: Musharraf Says Arsenal is Now Secure," *Washington Post,* November 11, 2001, p. A1.

[95] Rajesh M. Basrur and Hasan-Askari Rizvi, *Nuclear Terrorism and South Asia,* Cooperative Monitoring Center, Occasional Paper 25, Sandia National Laboratories (Albuquerque, NM: Sandia National Laboratories, February 2003), p. 55.

[96] Council on Foreign Relations, "Pakistan: Controls on Nuclear Technology," updated: January 29, 2004, <http://www.cfr.org/background/background_pakistan_nuclear.php>, accessed on February 2, 2004.

[97] The Acronym Institute, "News Review: Chilling Rhetoric, Ongoing Nuclearisation in South Asia," *Disarmament Diplomacy,* February/March 2003.

[98] See, for example, Akhileshwar, "Under the Mushroom Cloud," *The Pioneer* (New Delhi), in FBIS-SAP20031029000070, "Indian author fears Pakistani Nuclear Weapons May Fall into Hands of Terrorists," October 29, 2003; Editorial, "India Must Remain Vigilant," *Rashtriya Sahara* (New Delhi), in FBIS-SAP20030408000042, "Indian Daily Alarmed at Reported Terrorists' Access to Pakistani Nuclear Program," April 8, 2003.

[99] David Albright, "Securing Pakistan's Nuclear Infrastructure," in Lee Feinstein, James C. Clad, Lewis A. Dunn, and David Albright, "A New Equation: U.S. Policy Toward India and Pakistan after September 11," Carnegie Endowment for International Peace Working Paper Number 27, May 2002.

[100] Basrur and Rizvi, *Nuclear Terrorism and South Asia,* pp. 65-66. See also, Rajesh M. Basrur, "Nuclear Terrorism and Nuclear Posture in India and Pakistan," paper presented at the 13th International Security Conference, Sandia National Laboratories, Albuquerque, New Mexico, April 23-25, 2003.

[101] Legal jurisdiction for the FBI's role is based on the Atomic Energy Act, 18 USC 831 and 18 USC 2332a.

[102] Bernie Bogdan, "FBI Nuclear Counter Terrorism Program," presentation to the 44th Annual Meeting of the Institute of Nuclear Materials Management, Phoenix, Arizona, July 17, 2003.

[103] Legal authority for many of these measures is codified in 50 USC 40, Defense Against Weapons of Mass Destruction, sections 2301-2317.

[104] For contrasting views on the efficacy and civil liberties impact of the USA PATRIOT Act, see "Preserving Life and Liberty," U.S. Department of Justice Web site, <http://www.lifeandliberty.gov>, accessed on March 30, 2004, and "Surveillance Under the USA PATRIOT Act," American Civil Liberties Union Web site, <http://www.aclu.org/SafeandFree/SafeandFree.cfm?ID=12263&c=206>, accessed on March 30, 2004.

[105] Office of Domestic Preparedness Web site, <http://www.ojp.usdoj.gov/odp/>, accessed on April 1, 2004.

[106] For more on the PSI, see "Proliferation Security Initiative," Globalsecurity.org Web site, <http://www.globalsecurity.org/military/ops/psi.htm>, accessed March 30, 2004; "Fact Sheet: Proliferation Security Initiative Statement of Interdiction Principles," White House Web site, <http://www.whitehouse.gov/news/releases/2003/09/20030904-11.html>, accessed on March 30, 2004; and "The Proliferation Security Initiative: An Interview With John Bolton," *Arms Control Today* (December 2003), <http://www.armscontrol.org/act/2003_12/PSI.asp>, accessed on March 30, 2004; Jofi Joseph, "The Proliferation Security Initiative: Can Interdiction Stop Proliferation?" *Arms Control Today* (June 2004).

[107] Gaurav Kampani, "Nuclear Watch—Pakistan: The Sorry Affairs of the Islamic Republic," NTI Web site, <http://www.nti.org/e_research/e3_38a.html>, accessed on March 30, 2004.

[108] "The Fusion Task Force," INTERPOL Web site, <http://www.interpol.int/Public/FusionTaskForce/default.asp>, accessed on April 1, 2004.

[109] See, for example, Center for Strategic International Studies, *Wild Atom: Nuclear Terrorism,* Global Organized Crime Project, 1998, which recommended that "...innovative international arrangements [are needed] to share information promptly and to craft trafficker profiles jointly, identify patterns in the activities of nuclear criminals, determine the origin and route of seized nuclear materials, and assess the bomb-making capabilities of key rogue states and terrorist groups should they acquire sufficient fissile material. The United States needs to move beyond traditional bilateral intelligence liaison toward a multilateral pooling of information, analysis, and resources."

[110] Frederick P. Hitz and Brian J. Weiss, "Helping the CIA and FBI Connect the Dots in the War on Terror," *International Journal of Intelligence and CounterIntelligence* 17 (Spring 2004), pp. 1-41.

[111] Testimony given during the public hearings conducted by the commission is available at <http://www.9-11commission.gov/hearings/index.htm>. The commission's final report was not issued at the time of this writing.

[112] Stephane Lefebvre, "The Difficulties and Dilemmas of International Intelligence Cooperation," *International Journal of Intelligence and CounterIntelligence* 16 (Winter 2003), pp. 527-542.

[113] The Department of Homeland Security came into existence on January 24, 2003. President Bush signed legislation creating the department on November 24, 2002. The department was given one year to bring under its jurisdiction each of the 22 federal agencies slated to become part of the new department. President Bush

has stated that he expected most of this reorganization to be completed by March 1, 2003. As of February 10, 2004, close to the first anniversary of the Department of Homeland Security's official founding, DHS Secretary Ridge testified to Congress that DHS encompasses 22 agencies and 180,000 employees. Concerning port and border security, he said, The DHS "budget includes a $411 million increase for our Customs and Border Protection, Immigration and Customs Enforcement, and Coast Guard." He underscored that "potential enemies will not always arrive at a customs checkpoint. That is why we have more than $64 million to enhance monitoring efforts along the border and between ports." Moreover, DHS is "pushing [U.S.] perimeter security outward, making sure that [U.S.] borders are the last line of defense, not the first." U.S. Senate, Appropriations Committee, testimony of Secretary Tom Ridge on FY05 Budget, February 10, 2004.

[114] Jay Etta Z. Hecker, "Container Security: Current Efforts to Detect Nuclear Materials, New Initiatives, and Challenges," U.S. General Accounting Office, GAO-03-297T, November 2002; Stanford Study Group, "Container Security Report," CISAC Report, Stanford University, January 2003; U.S. Senate, Governmental Affairs Committee, Stephen E. Flynn, "The Fragile State of Container Security," written testimony, March 20, 2003; Tom Ridge, "Remarks by Secretary Tom Ridge at the Port of Newark, New Jersey," Department of Homeland Security, June 12, 2003, <http://www.dhs.gov/dhspublic/display?content=960>, accessed on April 12, 2004; Richard M. Stana, Director, Homeland Security and Justice, "Homeland Security: Preliminary Observations on Efforts to Target Security Inspections of Cargo Containers," U.S. General Accounting Office, GAO-04-325T, December 16, 2003.

[115] U.S. Senate, testimony by Paul M. Longsworth, March 10, 2004.

[116] "Protecting America's Ports," Department of Homeland Security, June 1, 2003, <http://www.dhs.gov/interweb/assetlibrary/MTSA_Port_Presskit.pdf>. In January 2004, it was reported that some 25 percent of vessel plans and 50 percent of facility security plans had not been submitted to the Coast Guard. Blank Rome LLP, Counselors at Law, New Maritime Developments Update, Newsletter, January 2004. DHS is seeking in FY05 "more than $100 million to implement the Maritime Transportation Security Act." U.S. Senate, testimony of Secretary Tom Ridge, February 10, 2004.

[117] Pete Williams, "Ridge moves to boost port security," NBC News, June 12, 2003, <http://msnbc.com/news/925811.asp?0sl=-32>; Sean Holstege, "Livermore lab unveils scanner capable of detecting radiation," *Oakland Tribune*, June 19, 2003, <http://www.oaklandtribune.com/Stories0,1413,82~1865~1464670,00.html>.

[118] U.S. government information on NEST is available at <http://www.doeal.gov>, accessed on February 7, 2004.

[119] Jeffrey T. Richelson, "Defusing Nuclear Terror," *Bulletin of the Atomic Scientists* (March/April 2002).

[120] Ibid.

[121] Tony Fainberg, Science and Technology Directorate, Department of Homeland Security, Presentation to the 44th Annual Meeting of the Institute of Nuclear Materials Management, Phoenix, Arizona, July 17, 2003.

[122] It is important to distinguish between crisis management and consequence management. "Crisis management focuses on causes and involves activities to address the threat or occurrence of a terrorist incident. It is predominantly a law enforcement and intelligence function that includes measures to anticipate, prevent, and resolve a threat or act of terrorism. The lead agency for crisis management is the Federal Bureau of Investigation (FBI). Consequence management addresses the effects of an incident on lives and property. It includes measures to protect public health and safety, treat persons injured, mitigate impacts, restore essential government services, and provide emergency relief to governments, businesses, and individuals affected by a terrorist incident. FEMA [Federal Emergency Management Agency] is the lead agency for consequence management; U.S. General Accounting Office, "National Preparedness: Integration of Federal, State, Local, and Private Sector Efforts if Critical to an Effective National Strategy for Homeland Security," testimony of Randall A. Yim, Managing Director, National Preparedness, April 11, 2002, GAO-02-621T, p. 5.

[123] A July 2003 report by a task force sponsored by the Council on Foreign Relations points out that the United States is ill-prepared in this regard and even lacks a methodology to determine the critical requirement for first responders. See Warren B. Rudman, Chair, Richard A. Clarke, Senior Adviser, and Jamie F. Metzl, Project Director, *Emergency Responders: Drastically Underfunded, Dangerously Unprepared,* Report of an Independent Task Force by the Council on Foreign Relations, July 2003, p. 7.

[124] Raymond Hernandez, "City to Get $64 Million to Counter Terrorism," *New York Times,* November 14, 2003, p. B6; FDNY Chief Michael Weinlein, presentation at West Point seminar on countering terrorism, Brooklyn, New York, March 2, 2004.

[125] Jim Matthews, "A Tale of 2 Fire Departments," *Homeland Security,* March 2004, p. 15.

[126] U.S. General Accounting Office, "Homeland Security: Challenges in Achieving Interoperable Communications for First Responders," testimonial statement of William O. Jenkins, Jr., Director, Homeland Security and Justice Issues, November 6, 2003, GAO-04-231T. For a discussion of difficulties in coordinating emergency response efforts in New York City, see "New York's Emergency Plan Stalled," *Washington Post,* April 4, 2004, p. A9.

[127] U.S. General Accounting Office, "Weapons of Mass Destruction: Defense Threat Reduction Agency Addresses Broad Range of Threats, but Performance Reporting Can Be Improved," GAO-04-330, February 2004.

[128] Defense Threat Reduction Agency, "DTRA and Consequence Management," Factsheet, March 2004, available at <http://www.dtra.mil/news/fact/nw_cm.html>, accessed on March 31, 2004.

[129] For example, in February 2003, the World Health Organization distributed through the Internet information on how to respond to a nuclear weapon attack; this document is available at <http://www.who.int/ionizing_radiation/en/WHORAD_InfoSheet_Nuclear_weapons21Feb.pdf>, accessed on February 7, 2004. Also in 2003, RAND published a guide to help individuals prepare for unconventional terrorist attacks; Lynn E. Davis, Tom LaTourrette, David E. Mosher, Lois M. Davis, and David R. Howell, *Individual Preparedness and Response to Chemical, Radiological, Nuclear, and Biological Terrorist Attacks: A Quick Guide* (Santa Monica, CA: RAND, 2003), available at <http://www.rand.org/publications/MR/MR1731.1/>, accessed on February 7, 2004. The U.S. government has published citizen guides at the Department of Homeland Security's Web site <http://www.ready.gov> and the Federal Emergency Management Agency's Web site <http://www.fema.gov>, which contains the publication, *Are You Ready? A Guide to Citizen Preparedness.* The U.S. Centers for Disease Control and Prevention also provides useful response information at <http://www.cdc.gov>, accessed on February 7, 2004.

[130] Senior Bush administration official, name withheld by request, telephone interview with author, January 2004.

[131] GAO-03-482, pp. 7-8.

[132] Warheads for tactical air force aircraft are not required to be withdrawn to central storage under the 1991/1992 declarations. President Yeltsin, however, did propose that the remaining air-borne TNW could, on a mutual basis, be withdrawn from air force units and relocated at centralized storage depots (January 29, 1992). Statement by the president of the Russian Federation, Boris Yeltsin, "On Russia's Policy in the Field of Limiting and Reducing Armaments," in Larsen and Klingenberger, pp. 284-289.

[133] For detailed recommendations about how to address the risks of TNW, see William Potter, "Practical Steps for Addressing the Problem of Non-Strategic Nuclear Weapons," in Larsen and Klingenberger, *Controlling Non-Strategic Nuclear Weapons,* pp. 211-228, and William Potter and Nikolai Sokov, "Practical Measures to Reduce the Risks Presented by Non-Strategic Nuclear Weapons," paper prepared for the Blix Weapons of Mass Destruction Commission, June 9, 2004. In addition, Graham Allison has recommended that the United States and Russia develop a new "International Security Standard" that "would require rapidly securing all nuclear weapons" as part of a strategy of "no loose nukes." Graham Allison, "How To Stop Nuclear Terror," *Foreign Affairs* (January/February 2004).

[134] Public commentary by senior officials in the Department of State and Defense which echo the denials of President Musharraf are not compelling. See, for example, Defense Secretary Donald Rumsfeld, who said, "I do not believe that there's any evidence or any suggestion that President Musharraf was involved." Chuck Neubauer, "Musharraf Has Rumsfeld's Support in Nuclear Case," *Los Angeles Times,* March 29, 2004, p. A3. In response to a question by Rep. Gary Ackerman (D-New York) in congressional testimony, Under-Secretary of State for Arms Control and International Security John Bolton, said "The decision about the policies the government of Pakistan is pursuing on A.Q. Khan is one that we have been considering very carefully, and I would say, Mr. Ackerman, to go back to your opening statement, this turns on a fundamental evaluation as to who in Pakistan was responsible for A.Q. Khan's activities. Based on the information we have now, we believe that the proliferation activities that Mr. Khan confessed to recently—his activities in Libya, in Iran and North Korea, and perhaps elsewhere—were activities that he was carrying on without the approval of the top levels of the government of Pakistan. That is the position that President Musharraf has taken, and we have no evidence to the contrary." U.S. House of Representatives, Committee on International Relations, John R. Bolton, "The Bush Administration and Nonproliferation: A New Strategy Emerges," March 30, 2004.

[135] The authors are grateful to George Perkovich for sharing his perspective on this point. George Perkovich, personal correspondence with author, March 31, 2004.

4

MAKING THE BOMB
LOOSE MATERIALS AND KNOW-HOW

Terrorists determined to unleash the most devastating forms of nuclear terrorism may try to acquire an intact nuclear weapon, as discussed in the previous chapter. If, however, they are deterred by the security measures surrounding nuclear armaments, they may instead seek to acquire fissile material by purchase, diversion, or force for the purpose of fabricating a crude nuclear bomb, known more formally as an "improvised nuclear device" (IND).

Two types of fissile material could be used for this purpose, highly enriched uranium or plutonium (Pu), but the former would be far easier to make into a successful IND, as explained in detail, below. These materials have been produced in great quantity in nuclear weapon and civilian nuclear energy programs around the world. Leaving aside material currently in nuclear weapons, themselves, many hundreds of tons of fissile material are currently dispersed at hundreds of sites worldwide, where they are being processed, used, or stored, often under inadequate security arrangements. Russia, alone, processes more than 34 metric tons of weapons-usable nuclear material annually.[1] According to the conservative figures used by the International Atomic Energy Agency, only 25 kilograms (kg) of HEU or 8 kg of plutonium would be needed to manufacture a weapon.

It is more difficult to maintain strict control over fissile materials than over nuclear weapons. Among other challenges, while the latter can be easily identified and counted, fissile materials are often handled in difficult-to-measure bulk form, introducing measurement uncertainties that can mask repeated diversions of small quantities of HEU or plutonium from process streams and storage areas.[2] Indeed, in the past decade a number of cases have been documented involving illicit trafficking in fissile materials; no similar cases have been confirmed involving the theft of nuclear weapons.[3] Although none of the fissile material cases involved quantities sufficient for a nuclear explosive, it is conceivable that such transactions have occurred without detection and that a terrorist organization might currently be in possession of such a quantity of material and in the process of developing a nuclear device.

This chapter will describe global fissile material holdings, and, after reviewing the impact of terrorist use of an IND, will analyze the chain of events that would be required for a terrorist group to accomplish this objective. It will then review security arrangements covering fissile materials and highlight areas where improvements are most urgently needed. This background will provide the basis for identifying the most effective interventions for reducing the overall risk of terrorist use of an IND, issues which are discussed at the conclusion of this chapter.

GLOBAL STOCKS OF FISSILE MATERIAL

Because the sizes of military stockpiles of fissile materials are classified and up-to-date records of civilian stocks are difficult to obtain, it is possible only to estimate the global inventory of these materials. Nonetheless, it is clear that the amount of fissile material that might theoretically be accessible to terrorists is staggering. Tables 4.1 and 4.2 present an overview of the world stockpiles of HEU and plutonium, as of 1999.

In international usage, HEU refers to uranium that has been processed to increase the proportion of one isotope of uranium, uranium-235 (U-235), from the naturally occurring level of 0.7 percent to 20 percent or more—the level at which its use for weapons becomes practicable.[4] Enrichment is performed in specialized facilities that use centrifuges, gaseous diffusion, or lasers to differentiate among uranium isotopes and slowly increase the concentration of the desired U-235. Although all uranium enriched to more than 20 percent is termed "highly enriched," the ease of causing a nuclear detonation is greatly increased at higher enrichment levels. Specifically, terrorists would find it much easier to develop a workable IND with material enriched to 80 percent or more, and military programs prefer material enriched to 90 percent or more for nuclear arms. (In Tables 4.1 and 4.2, "weapons-grade" uranium refers to uranium enriched to at least 90 percent.) HEU is used principally in nuclear weapons and as fuel in certain research reactors, certain nuclear power reactors,[5] and in propulsion reactors on submarines, certain surface warships, and Russian civilian icebreakers. Enrichment levels for these uses vary, but HEU enriched to 80 percent or more (referred to henceforth as "high-quality" HEU) can be found in all of these applications, except in power reactors.

Plutonium is produced by irradiating uranium fuel in a reactor and then processing the "spent fuel" chemically, in a "reprocessing" plant to separate the plutonium from the unused uranium and unwanted radioactive byproducts. Plutonium varies in quality. That intended for military purposes, or "weapons-grade" plutonium, is usually produced in specialized production reactors and has less than 6 percent of the isotope Pu-240 and much smaller percentages of other isotopes, such as Pu-238, Pu-241, and Pu-242, in order to improve weapon performance; therefore, it has about 94 percent of the isotope Pu-239, which is preferred for weapons.[6] Plutonium produced in nuclear power plants, known as reactor-grade plutonium, is irradiated for far longer periods and has higher concentrations of Pu-240, -241, -242, and -238, which are least desirable for nuclear weapons. However, as detailed in a later section of this chapter, reactor-grade plutonium can nonetheless be used to develop nuclear arms. Plutonium is used principally in nuclear weapons and, in a few states, in mixed oxide (MOX) fuel for nuclear power plants. MOX fuel is a mixture of plutonium and depleted uranium oxides and can be used as a substitute for low-enriched uranium (LEU) nuclear power plant fuel, the type most widely used in modern nuclear power reactors.[7]

Even if it were assumed that half of all materials listed in Tables 4.1 and 4.2 as produced for military uses were contained in weapons, the remaining fissile material in the military sector, together with that in the civilian sector, comprises a stockpile sufficient for tens of thousands of improvised nuclear devices.[8]

TABLE 4.1

ESTIMATED GLOBAL PLUTONIUM AND HEU INVENTORIES, END OF 1999

Material Type	Global Inventory (MT)
Military plutonium	250
Civil plutonium (separated)	208
Military HEU[i]	1,670
Civil HEU	20

[i] Figures for HEU are weapons-grade uranium equivalent.

Source: David Albright and Mark Gorwitz, "Tracking Civil Plutonium Inventories: End of 1999," Institute for Science and International Security, <http://www.isis-online.org/publications/puwatch/puwatch2000.html>, accessed on December 18, 2002; submissions of members of the International Plutonium Management Group detailing civil plutonium stocks as of December 1999, IAEA document INFCIRC/549, available at <http://www.iaea.org/Publications/Documents/Infcircs/Numbers/nr501-550.shtml>.

TABLE 4.2

ESTIMATED MILITARY STOCKS OF FISSILE MATERIAL, END OF 1999

Country	Military Plutonium (MT)	Military HEU (MT of Weapons-Grade Uranium Equivalent)
Russia	130	970
United States	100	635
France	5	24
China	4	20
United Kingdom	7.6	15
Israel	0.51	not known
India	0.310	small quantity
Pakistan	0.005	0.690
North Korea	0.03-0.04	not known
South Africa	None	0.4

Source: David Albright and Mark Gorwitz, "Tracking Civil Plutonium Inventories: End of 1999," Institute for Science and International Security, <http://www.isis-online.org/publications/puwatch/puwatch2000.html>, accessed on December 18, 2002.

Since 1999, global stocks of plutonium have increased, while those of HEU have probably declined. India, Israel, North Korea, Pakistan, Russia, and possibly China[9] have continued to produce plutonium for weapons. With an annual output of between 1 and 2 tons of new, separated military plutonium, Russia's stock comprises by far the largest increment in this area.[10] As shown in Table 4.3, France, Germany, Great Britain, India, Japan,[11] and Russia have continued to separate plutonium from civilian nuclear power plant fuel, output that exceeds new production of military plutonium. Pakistan, India, and possibly China, Israel, and North Korea[12] have added to their HEU stocks for weapons. However, these additions to global stocks of HEU (probably amounting to several tons, at most, since 1999) have been offset during this period by the blending down of 200 metric tons of Russian HEU to LEU nuclear power plant fuel, as of January 1, 2004, under a collaborative program with the United States.[13] (Low-enriched uranium is not readily usable for nuclear weapons.)

As noted, HEU and plutonium outside of nuclear weapons can be found at hundreds of sites worldwide. Although fissile material in any location is a potential target for terrorists, this chapter will concentrate on three settings of particular concern:

- Russia, where hundreds of tons of these materials are used, processed, or stored at dozens of Russian Federal Agency for Atomic Energy (formerly Ministry of Atomic Energy) and Ministry of Defense facilities under inadequate security

- Pakistan, where political instability and uncertain loyalties in the nuclear chain of command might result in fissile material coming into the hands of terrorists

- Research reactors using HEU fuel, including some two dozen Soviet-designed research reactor sites and research centers containing HEU outside of Russia in almost 20 nations, and several U.S.-origin research reactors outside the United States.

In addition, this chapter will briefly note the other settings in which fissile materials might be obtained by terrorists, including the complexes

TABLE 4.3
SEPARATED CIVIL PLUTONIUM (MT) AT REPROCESSING PLANTS AND OTHER LOCATIONS AS OF DECEMBER 31, 1999 AND DECEMBER 31, 2002

Country	Separated Civil Plutonium (12/1999)	Separated Civil Plutonium (12/2002)
Germany	0.5	0.0
France[i]	60.0	52.2
Great Britain[ii]	69.5	86.5
India	0.7	0.7 (est.)
Japan	0.9	1.2
Russia	30.9	36.0
United States[iii]	0.0	0.0
Total	162.5	176.6

[i] Includes material held for other states.

[ii] Ibid.

[iii] The United States does not separate plutonium in its civilian nuclear power program; however, it has declared 45.5 metric tons of military plutonium to be excess and irreversibly removed from military uses. Thirty-four tons of this material will be manufactured into MOX fuel and burned in nuclear power reactors; Russia does not include the equal quantity of military plutonium it will dispose of in this manner as part of its stocks of civilian plutonium.

Source: These numbers are derived from information obtained at the International Atomic Energy Agency's web site, www.iaea.org, except where otherwise noted. For amount of plutonium held by India as of 1999, see David Albright, *Separated Civil Plutonium Inventories: Current and Future Directions* (Washington, DC: Institute for Science and International Security, June 2000). In the absence of new information on Indian plutonium separation, the 1999 figure is repeated for 2002, although it is likely that Indian plutonium stocks grew slowly during this period.

supporting the nuclear weapon programs of the United States and the other nuclear weapon states, the marine propulsion programs of the United States and other states, research reactors in United States and other Western nations, and existing and emerging programs to use plutonium for the production of nuclear energy.

EFFECTS AND CONSEQUENCES OF IND DETONATION

The devastating consequences of a nuclear explosion were detailed in Chapter 3, which examined the impacts from blast, heat, and radioactivity. As a reminder of the horrific damage such an event would cause, the table from that chapter showing nuclear explosive effects as a function of yield is reproduced here. Of greatest relevance to an examination of INDs are the entries toward the top of the table, showing the impacts of lower-yield nuclear explosions.

As detailed in a later section, it is generally assumed that successful INDs would have yields in the 10-20-KT range (equivalent to 10,000-20,000 tons of TNT), while INDs that fizzled—i.e. did not detonate fully—might still produce a nuclear yield, which though far less powerful, could still cause very significant damage. A 20-KT yield, equivalent to the yield of the bomb that destroyed Nagasaki, could devastate the heart of a medium-sized U.S. city, while causing fire and radiation damage over a considerably wider area. At the lower end of the nuclear yield spectrum, it should be recalled that the conventional explosive that destroyed the federal building in Oklahoma City in 1995 used 5,000 pounds of fertilizer, and the truck bomb used in the 1993 attempt to destroy the World Trade Center in New York used some 1,500 pounds of fertilizer. In terms of TNT equivalent yields, these bombs produced about 1.8 tons and 0.5 tons, respectively.[14] Thus even a nuclear yield of a few tons could, under certain circumstances, cause the destruction of a number of skyscrapers potentially resulting in many thousands of casualties, as well as widespread contamination. Table 4.4 summarizes these effects.

Unfortunately, even an IND that detonated with no yield or one that was never even used but whose existence was disclosed could cause consequences of historic proportions, because terrorists could use the *threat* of a successful future nuclear detonation to blackmail target governments. Given the stakes, target-state leaders would be hard pressed not to give into the demands presented. Indeed, it is possible that a terrorist organization might be able to credibly threaten a nuclear detonation merely by demonstrating its possession of the requisite nuclear-weapon material, a possibility that underscores the critical importance of ensuring such fissile materials do not fall into the hands of such groups.

The Chain of Causation

The principal elements that would have to combine for a terrorist group to detonate an IND at a high-value target, such as an American city, include the following steps:[15]

1. A terrorist group with extreme objectives and the necessary technical and financial resources to execute this scheme must organize and begin operations.
2. The group must then choose to engage in an act of nuclear terrorism at the highest level of violence.
3. These terrorists must then acquire sufficient fissile material to fabricate an IND, through gift, purchase, theft, or diversion.
4. They must next fabricate the weapon.
5. The group must transport the intact IND (or its components) to a high-value target.
6. Finally, the terrorists must detonate the IND to complete their plan.[16]

Although variants of this chain of causation can be imagined, this outline can serve as a means to determine where to apply risk-reduction measures to lessen the probability that such an act of nuclear terror might occur. As stressed throughout this volume, all of these elements must be realized for a terrorist IND attack to succeed, and intervention at any stage can be sufficient to avert catastrophe.

Terrorist Groups with Motivation and Capabilities to Manufacture and Use an IND

As discussed in Chapter 2, there appear to be very few terrorist organizations that are highly motivated to detonate nuclear weapons of any kind to advance their objectives. Nonetheless, the potential number of such groups cannot be established with precision and can change over time—for example, as new groups form or as new alliances are built among existing groups.

Traditional nationalist/separatist terrorist groups, such as the IRA in Ireland, the Tamil Tigers in Sri Lanka, and the Kurds in Turkey, are less likely to resort to this extreme form of nuclear terrorism because they may be constrained by the values of the their base constituencies. In addition, their own location may make them extremely vulnerable to retaliatory attacks or to concerns of harming their own people from a

TABLE 4.4
NUCLEAR EXPLOSIVE EFFECTS AS A FUNCTION OF YIELD

	Radius for Indicated Effect (meters)			
Explosive Yield[i]	500 Rem Prompt Gamma Radiation	Fallout from Surface Blast (500 Rem Total Dose)	Severe Blast Damage (10 psi)	Moderate to Light Blast Damage (3 psi)
1 ton	45	30-100	33	65
10 tons	100	100-300	71	140
100 tons	300	300-1,000	150	300
1 kiloton (1,000 tons)	680	1,000-3,000	330	650
10 kilotons	1,280	3,000-10,000	710	1,500
100 kilotons	1,800	10,000-30,000	1,500	3,300
1 megaton (1 million tons)	2,400	30,000-100,000	3,250	7,100

rem = roentgen equivalent man; the dosage of ionizing radiation that will cause the same biological effect as one roentgen of X-ray or gamma-ray exposure
psi = pounds per inch

---

[i] Measured in tons of TNT equivalent (surface burst)

Source: Effects for 1 ton through 1 kiloton are adapted from Kevin O'Neill, "The Nuclear Terrorist Threat," Institute for Science and International Security, August 1997, and references therein, p.6; effects for 10 kilotons, 100 kilotons, and 1 megaton are adapted from Dietrich Schroeer, *Science, Technology, and the Nuclear Arms Race* (John Wiley & Sons, 1984), pp. 37, as based on Glasstone and Dolan, *Effects of Nuclear Weapons,* U.S. Government Printing Office, Washington, DC, 1977.

nuclear attack that took place too close to their homeland areas. Nationalist/separatist groups might, however, consider the development of an IND (in contrast to its use) to be an advantageous tool for gaining international recognition and/or for blackmailing adversary governments into making concessions. Single-issue terrorist organizations are also unlikely to seek to cause massive destruction by using an IND, but extremist factions within such groups might consider doing so.

Further limiting the number of terrorist organizations that might seek to develop an IND are the financial and technical assets that the group would need to pursue this course. Because the complexity of fabricating an IND is much greater than the technical demands of making an improvised explosive device (IED)—a conventional bomb—it is likely that the technical barriers alone would dissuade most terrorists from pursuing an improvised nuclear device. Nonetheless, as discussed in more detail later, a gun-type IND could be well within the capabilities of some terrorist groups.

Among other requirements, millions of dollars would likely be needed if the group sought to purchase fissile material, bribe or threaten members of security forces guarding them, or attack a fissile material storage or processing site. While the planning for an operation to seize weapons-usable nuclear material and other non-nuclear parts of an IND could take months, the actual mating of the fissile material (especially highly enriched uranium) with the rest of the weapon could require mere days or even less time, depending on the characteristics of the material—whether in solid metallic form, needing minimal or no processing, or combined with other elements, requiring separation and chemical processing of the fissile material–and on the type of bomb design employed. Moving the IND (or its components) clandestinely to its target would be costly and complicated for most scenarios.[17] Staff would have to be fed and housed for the potentially extended duration of the plot. In addition, considerable organizational skills would be required to permit the group to operate internationally.

Finally, the group would need a considerable degree of technical competence. Most analysts have assumed that to accomplish this task, the terrorist group in question would have to assemble a small team of specialists with expertise in such varied areas as nuclear physics or engineering, metallurgy, machining, and conventional explosives. Indeed, even if insider help were available at a fissile material site or from a nuclear weapon designer, still other specialists would have to be recruited to achieve success.[18] However, as discussed in detail in a later section, building the simplest type of IND, a gun-type device, might not require a large technical team. Acquiring the highly enriched uranium for this device is probably a more challenging task than actually assembling a workable crude gun-type nuclear weapon.

In early 2004, very few terrorist organizations would appear to possess the wherewithal to assemble such a team, but the possibility that a group like al Qaeda could do so cannot be ruled out. A team brought together under its aegis might be recruited from sympathetic Pakistani nuclear scientists with knowledge of nuclear weapon designs and/or access to fissile materials, anti-American Iraqi nuclear specialists, members of Iran's nuclear weapons development team, or technicians who participated in the A.Q. Khan nuclear network.[19] Conceivably, nuclear scientists from the former Soviet nuclear weapons program could also be lured into employment for the right price. Fortunately, however, there have been no confirmed instances to date of former Soviet or current Russian weapon scientists providing such assistance to terrorist organizations. These scientists appear loyal to Russian national interests, which are obviously opposed to nuclear terrorism. Finally, the nuclear weapon design that Khan supplied to Libya, and possibly to Iran and North Korea, may also now be available on the black market and might be obtained by terrorists, although, from what is known about the design, it appears to be considerably more complex than what would be needed for a crude nuclear device.[20]

Al Qaeda's interest in acquiring weapons of mass destruction sparked great concern following the September 11, 2001, attacks in New York and Washington, DC. The campaign in Afghanistan revealed that al Qaeda has been attempting to develop chemical and possibly biological agents.[21] Moreover, al Qaeda had reportedly attempted to launch a nuclear program in Afghanistan, seeking aid from Pakistan.[22] According to Jamal Ahmed Al-Fadl, a Sudanese national who testified against Osama bin Laden in 2001, al Qaeda had tried to obtain uranium in Khartoum in the early 1990s.[23] Furthermore, documents uncovered after the U.S. toppled the Taliban regime in Afghanistan revealed that al Qaeda operatives were studying nuclear weapons information.[24] Although the U.S. military intervention in Afghanistan and the capture of some of al Qaeda's top leadership appear to have upset these operations, these actions may have delayed, but not eliminated al Qaeda's pursuit of WMD. Moreover, al Qaeda has demonstrated in past terrorist operations that it tends to plan high-profile terrorist attacks patiently, such as in the bombing of the *U.S.S. Cole*, the bombings of the American embassies in Africa, and the September 11th suicidal plane crashes into the World Trade Center and the Pentagon. Consequently, the setbacks for al Qaeda could merely provide a pause before another round of even more catastrophic attacks. It is possible that such a round has already begun with the suicide bombers in Saudi Arabia, Morocco, Indonesia, Spain, and Iraq.

The level of technical sophistication of the September 11th attacks was demanding but manageable. Undoubtedly, the technical skills required to construct and detonate an IND would also be challenging. Because the 9/11 attacks and manufacture of an IND involve different skill sets, a direct comparison is difficult, if not impossible, to make. However, 9/11 did demonstrate that al Qaeda was able to assemble a large team of 19 people who carried out the attacks and an additional cadre who provided monetary and other logistical support. As discussed below, a comparably sized terrorist team or perhaps a smaller group— about the size of an al Qaeda cell—would likely be capable of carrying out an IND attack. Although uncertainty exists about whether al Qaeda possesses the requisite skills to build such a device, there is little question that al Qaeda seeks to launch devastating attacks. The question is less whether al Qaeda will attempt another spectacular incident but rather what means it might have available to cause mass casualties the next time it acts. An improvised nuclear device would represent the ideal weapon for al Qaeda. This terror network has clearly declared its motivations to use weapons of mass destruction and its intention to acquire such weapons. Al Qaeda and its affiliates almost certainly have the funding, organization, and logistical capability to acquire poorly secured HEU or plutonium and are making efforts to gain the technical capability needed to assemble weapons-usable fissile material into an IND. If an opportunity to obtain such material were to present itself, it is all too likely that the world will confront a nuclear-armed Osama bin Laden.

At the present time, it is difficult to identify other terrorist organizations whose extreme goals and substantial resources match those of al Qaeda. It is possible, however, that Chechen rebel factions might be motivated to acquire an IND to force concessions from Russia and might seek nuclear materials from sites in Russia, Central Asia, and other parts of the former Soviet Union. Central Asian national/separatist groups, such as the Islamic Movement of Uzbekistan, whose area of operations include Uzbekistan and Kazakhstan, might also consider seizing fissile materials from sites in these countries and using the threat to detonate an IND as a means to pursue their goals for political power and/or autonomy. In contrast to al Qaeda, however, it does not appear that any organizations in Russia or Central Asia would desire to cause massive casualties through the actual use of such a weapon.

Acquisition of Fissile Material

In the chain of causation, the most difficult challenge for a terrorist organization would be obtaining the fissile material necessary to construct an IND. The circumstances under which terrorists might be able to do so parallel, in many ways, the routes that might permit it to obtain an intact nuclear device. As described in Chapter 3 in addressing the latter subject, a state might voluntarily share fissile material with a terrorist group or sell the material to it; a senior official or governmental element with authorized access to such materials might, for ideological or mercenary motives, provide it to terrorists without the express approval of governmental leaders; the immediate custodians of the material, for money or ideology, or under duress, might provide HEU or plutonium to the organization or assist it in seizing the material by force or stealth; or terrorists might obtain the material by force or stealth without insider help. Finally, nuclear weapon materials could come into the hands of terrorists during a period of political turmoil, including one brought on by a coup or revolution.

Although the scenarios involving terrorist acquisition of an intact nuclear weapon and fissile material for an IND are similar in many respects, there are important distinctions between the two enterprises. A national government, for example, might be more inclined to provide fissile material and rudimentary nuclear-weapon design know-how to collaborating terrorists than to hand over a nuclear weapon, in the belief that an IND made from such materials would be less likely to be traced back to the provider than a complete nuclear explosive. Moreover, as will be seen, acquiring fissile material, though very difficult, would probably be less challenging than acquiring an intact nuclear weapon. As noted, for example, materials are far more difficult to keep track of than weapons, and the loss of fissile material over a period of time might go undetected—a factor that might encourage insiders to assist a terrorist organization in the belief that they could do so without exposing themselves to arrest. The undetected removal of a nuclear weapon is far less likely. In addition, whatever gaps may exist in national systems for securing these different assets, weapons have traditionally received the highest level of security, above that accorded fissile materials. This ranking is explicit, for example, in the U.S. Department of Energy's graduated safeguards system for securing nuclear items. A third indicator that acquisition of fissile material may be less daunting than acquisition of a complete nuclear weapon is the fact that, as previously mentioned, cases of illicit trafficking in fissile materials (and in other nuclear assets that might be needed to develop an IND) have been observed, but no similar cases involving clandestine transfers of nuclear weapons have come to light.

Technical Considerations

Manufacturing weapons-usable HEU from natural uranium, using current uranium enrichment techniques, would likely pose insuperable challenges for terrorists because of the sizeable facilities and extremely complex technology that would be required to produce quantities sufficient for nuclear weapons, even assuming that the organization began with uranium that was partially enriched. Nonetheless, at least one terrorist group did start down this path. In the early 1990s, Aum Shinrikyo tapped into its vast financial resources to buy Australian properties containing natural uranium deposits and, with scientists as members, also investigated purchasing uranium-enrichment technologies. It appears that the group never advanced beyond early studies of the issue, however.[25]

To produce plutonium on its own, a terrorist group would need a nuclear reactor. Without strong state sponsorship, the group could not feasibly embark on the path toward acquiring plutonium. Moreover, even if the terrorists somehow could afford to obtain a nuclear reactor, operating it clandestinely would be extremely difficult. Short of stealing previously produced and separated plutonium, the terrorist organization could try to reprocess spent nuclear fuel to extract plutonium, as discussed below.

Notwithstanding these caveats, which suggest that some terrorist organizations might conceive of developing an entire nuclear fuel cycle to produce fissile materials, all scenarios described in this chapter assume that terrorists seek and ultimately obtain either fissile material immediately usable for weapons, or a product from which fissile material can be separated and converted into a weapons-usable form with only moderate effort.[26]

Metallic HEU would be the most efficient form of the material for use in an IND. This material would most likely be found in nuclear weapon assembly/disassembly facilities and in national HEU stockpiles of the nuclear weapon states. Most fuels, such as those used in research reactors and marine propulsion systems, do not use pure HEU metal. Rather, HEU is combined with other materials, such as aluminum, and/or the HEU is found in the form of uranium oxide. At enrichment facilities, where HEU is produced, moreover, HEU is in the form of uranium hexafluoride, an extremely corrosive gas. Thus, in many scenarios, after a terrorist organization obtained HEU, it would need to process the material into a form usable in a nuclear device. Although the chemistry of uranium conversion is not considered unduly complicated, this step would add complexity to the endeavor, requiring the recruitment of additional technically trained cadres, the acquisition of additional equipment, and the setting up and operation of small-scale processing facilities (discussed immediately below)—all of which would extend the time required to produce a workable IND and increase the risk of detection. Plutonium, too, might require processing into metal if terrorists sought the form most useful in a nuclear explosive. Plutonium metal would most likely be found at nuclear weapon production facilities and at reprocessing plants producing plutonium for nuclear weapons. Plutonium in MOX fuel or awaiting fabrication into fuel at a MOX fuel fabrication facility would be in oxide form, as would most plutonium stored at civilian reprocessing plants. Thus, as in the case of HEU, after terrorists obtained plutonium, additional processing steps might be necessary, requiring added resources and time.

One phase of obtaining fissile material for weapons in many contexts is the chemical separation of the fissile material from other substances with which it is amalgamated—for example, in fissile-material-bearing nuclear fuels. This activity is generically known as reprocessing. In contrast to uranium enrichment methods, reprocessing technology might be accessible to terrorist organizations. This technology might be used to separate HEU from other fuel constituents in fresh or spent research reactor or marine propulsion fuel, to separate plutonium from fresh MOX fuel, or to separate plutonium from spent nuclear power reactor fuel, although this option would be more demanding because of the high levels of radiation such fuel emits.

The possibility of non-state actors separating plutonium from spent fuel has been the subject of government attention. Typically, concerns about plutonium extraction efficiency and radiation safety at the state level have compelled states to employ advanced chemical reprocessing techniques and technically sophisticated facilities containing hot cells using massive amounts of shielding. However, a 1977 report by the Oak Ridge National Laboratory about the feasibility of a "simple and quick" reprocessing plant concluded that a group using equipment "acquired from a small industry such as a winery, dairy, or oil refinery"[27] might be able to assemble such a plant in as little as four months and could then extract enough plutonium from spent nuclear power plant fuel for a weapon about a week later.[28] The relatively short time period of four to six months needed to construct such a facility and the very short operating time that might be required for processing raise the chances that the reprocessing activity might escape detection, assuming the terrorist organization had available a secure and clandestine haven, although theft of some fissile-material-bearing fuels (especially nuclear power plant spent fuel, which is usually well monitored) could be difficult to conceal and could trigger alarms at the site of the theft, as well as aggressive recovery efforts.

Because the technicians operating the simple and quick plant processing of spent nuclear power plant fuel would run the risk of acute radiation exposure and death, the terrorist organization would likely use some shielding and remote handling equipment for manipulating the spent nuclear power plant fuel.[29] Such precautions would not be required for processing fresh HEU or MOX fuels, and only modest shielding and more limited remote handling equipment would be needed for processing lightly irradiated HEU fuel or HEU fuel whose radiation level had been reduced by the passage of time. In 1975, Dr. Theodore Taylor, a former U.S. weapons scientist, testified before the U.S. Congress about the differences between commercial spent fuel reprocessing plants and the simple and quick method, stating,

> A commercially competitive nuclear fuel reprocessing plant…is a highly complex, sophisticated facility, costing at least several hundred million dollars. But a reprocessing facility designed only to extract plutonium for nuclear weapons could be much smaller, simpler, and less expensive. One could describe such a facility…[it] would require only a few months for construction and an operating crew of less than a dozen appropriately skilled people, using information that is widely published and materials and equipment that are commercially available worldwide.[30]

Although Taylor was addressing a scenario involving the extraction of plutonium from spent nuclear power plant fuel, these principles, again, would also apply to chemical separation facilities intended to extract HEU from fresh or spent research or marine propulsion reactor fuel or to extract plutonium from fresh MOX fuel.

Although the reprocessing phase might be manageable, terrorists would also face the major impediment of acquiring sufficient quantities of fresh or spent fissile-material-bearing fuel to put through the facility. Spent nuclear power plant fuel would not only be the most challenging to process, but would also likely be the most difficult to obtain. With plutonium comprising roughly 1 percent of typical nuclear power plant spent fuel, terrorists would have to obtain close to a metric ton of this dangerously radioactive material to meet their needs, taking account of processing losses, the weight of spent fuel hardware, and other factors. Since such material is usually stored at reactor sites in pools or dry casks and must be handled with remotely controlled cranes, it is difficult to envision that a ton of the material might be diverted without detection—and upon detection, would lead to active recovery efforts that might well succeed before the desired plutonium could be extracted.

A terrorist group might also attempt to extract HEU from fresh or spent HEU fuel used in research or propulsion reactors. Fresh fuel can contain up to 93 percent enriched uranium; thus, very little might be needed for an IND—perhaps no more than 50 kg of weapons-grade HEU, or roughly 100 kg of fuel assembly material, assuming that the HEU were bound with other substances (such as aluminum) in the fuel matrix. Spent HEU fuel contains a smaller concentration of U-235 than does fresh fuel, but if the original enrichment were high enough or if the fuel had been only partially used—or lightly irradiated—before it was seized, enrichment levels could easily remain close to the original concentration of U-235.[31] In fact, many research reactors are often used only intermittently, resulting in lightly irradiated fuel, which presents a reduced radiation safety hazard, greatly simplifying the HEU separation process.[32] Similarly, large quantities of Russian naval reactor HEU spent fuel have been stored for decades, much of its radioactivity having been dissipated, making it more attractive for terrorists; the enrichment level of much of this material is relatively low, however, especially after use, which might make it of less interest to such groups. As discussed further below, fuel stored at intermittently used research reactors, at remote Russian submarine bases, in largely abandoned Russian naval spent fuel storage areas, or at large-throughput fuel fabrication plants might be susceptible to theft without detection.

Another source of plutonium is fresh MOX fuel, which contains 4 to 7 percent plutonium oxide mixed with depleted uranium oxide, as mentioned earlier. If terrorists could acquire such fuel, they could, in principle, use a simple and quick reprocessing plant to separate chemically the weapons-usable plutonium from the MOX. Although this chemical process is somewhat challenging, it is a good deal simpler than traditional plutonium reprocessing methods and for this reason, historically, civilian MOX has normally required the same level of security as separated plutonium in international commerce. Depending on the plutonium concentration, terrorists would need to obtain in excess of 150 to 250 kg of fresh MOX fuel to obtain 8 kg of fissile material for a device, assuming that not all plutonium would be successfully recovered. One factor that facilitates the separation process is that fresh MOX fuel, unlike spent fuel, is not highly radioactive, making it unnecessary to carry out plutonium separation activities behind shielding and greatly simplifying certain chemical processes—although glove box enclosures would be preferred to contain the plutonium as it is being separated from the MOX. According to an August 2002 report by a well-known British expert, "a terrorist organization could relatively easily extract the plutonium and fabricate a nuclear explosive having first acquired MOX fuel."[33] (Later sections discuss additional issues related to MOX and civil plutonium reprocessing.)

Deliberate Transfer by a National Government

Acquiring weapons-usable fissile materials directly from a sympathetic government would significantly simplify the requirements for the terrorists, obviating the need to defeat security systems protecting such materials. Presumably, to further the purposes of the transfer, the state sponsor would also provide assistance in manufacturing an IND, perhaps by providing a design or the non-nuclear components or by machining the HEU or plutonium into appropriate shapes before handing it over. Such material might be provided to terrorist groups by a state that hoped to see an IND used against an opponent, but wanted to be in a position to deny its involvement and reduce the threat of retaliation.

Prior to Operation Iraqi Freedom in Iraq, the Bush administration feared Saddam Hussein might provide such support to terrorist groups. Today, the greatest sources of concern in this regard are Pakistan, North Korea, and, if it should begin/resume producing fissile material, Iran.

Regarding Pakistan, as discussed in more detail in the previous chapter, questions remain as to whether the government of Pakistan (including its current leadership) was complicit in Dr. A.Q. Khan's transfers between 1989 and 2003 of highly sensitive matériel for nuclear weapon programs in Iran, Libya, and North Korea—all of which were considered by the United States to be state sponsors of terrorism. If the government of Pakistan was involved, it was apparently unconcerned about whether terrorists might obtain fissile materials, and potentially, an IND, from these sympathetic governments. Moreover, although Pakistani President Pervez Musharraf has given his support to the U.S.-led War on Terror, including the ouster of the Taliban regime in Afghanistan and the elimination of al Qaeda, some senior elements of the Pakistani political establishment oppose this support. Musharraf was the target of two assassination attempts in December 2003. This history raises concerns that individuals supportive of radical Islamist groups may come to power in Pakistan and might give Pakistani nuclear weapon material to a terrorist organization, although it is assumed that the Musharraf government would not do so.[34]

Although some North Korean officials have provoked concern that North Korea might transfer nuclear materials outside of that country, their statements have not specifically mentioned transactions with terrorists.[35] In addition, there are no known ties between the North Korean government and extremist terrorist groups. However, North Korea has had ties to international terrorism in the past. Moreover, this state has sold ballistic missiles to other states of concern, and it has engaged in counterfeiting currency and selling illicit drugs. Such transactions speak to the desperate condition of North Korea and raise the risk that Pyongyang may decide to sell nuclear materials, either directly or indirectly, to terrorist groups. In April 2004, U.S. intelligence analysts revised their estimate of the size of the North Korean nuclear arsenal, assessing that its arsenal had grown from two to eight weapons. The increase would make it possible for North Korea to sell one or perhaps two weapons, or the fissile material needed to make them, while retaining a significant nuclear deterrent.[36]

In May 2004, news reports raised suspicions that North Korea may have sold uranium to Libya, a country that had been of proliferation concern until December 2003. According to the reports, North Korea in early 2001 may have provided Libya almost two metric tons of uranium that was not enriched for weapons use, but that could have been fed into a uranium enrichment cascade that Libya had been manufacturing.[37] Although evidence has yet to emerge that North Korea has used a nuclear trading network to sell nuclear material intentionally or inadvertently to terrorist organizations, the apparent North Korean-Libyan connection should serve as a warning about North Korean readiness to export nuclear commodities with little regard to the end user. That being said, there also are reports that North Korea is prepared to reassure the United States that it has no intention of providing nuclear materials to terrorists. Selig Harrison, an American analyst specializing in Northeast Asian security issues, reported in May 2004 that North Korean officials said that they would pledge never to transfer such materials to terrorists, suggesting that this commitment could be part of a larger security package between the United States and North Korea.[38]

Unlike North Korea, Iran presently has ties to Islamic terrorist groups. Although Iran is widely believed to be seeking nuclear arms,[39] there is no evidence to date to indicate that it has acquired these weapons. Moreover, there is no indication that Tehran has given WMD of any kind to terrorist organizations. Nonetheless, future transactions cannot be ruled out.

As of early 2004, no other states possessing sizable quantities of nuclear-weapons-usable materials are thought to have close ties to terrorist organizations. Moreover, as stressed in Chapter 3, even states that actively support terrorists groups would be highly unlikely to transfer such materials to terrorists. The transferring state would risk suffering massive retaliation from the United States and its allies if the material were traced back to the state. The fear of discovery would likely serve as an effective means of deterrence in most situations.

However, the greatest risk of such transactions would likely involve states that are facing imminent regime change. These states might have little to lose by handing the ingredients for an IND to a terrorist group as a last means of striking against an opponent.[40] For example, some observers expressed concern prior to the 2003 U.S.-led war against Iraq that regime change might provoke Saddam Hussein to transfer WMD-material to non-state actors.[41] Thus, an unintended consequence of over-throwing the governments of states possessing HEU or plutonium could be to provoke them to aid or abet nuclear terrorists.

Unauthorized Assistance from a Senior Official

Although leaders of a state may have little or no interest in transferring the wherewithal for an IND to a terrorist group or, even if they are interested, may be deterred from carrying out such transactions, senior officials within that state may be inclined to provide access to nuclear assets. These officials might be motivated by greed or ideological align-ment with the terrorists, and they could act without the knowledge or approval of the state's leadership. For instance, Khan's sale of nuclear know-how to three governments, allegedly without authorization from the government of Pakistan, pointed to the potential for a nuclear black market conduit to terrorists although there is no evidence to indicate that Khan's network is connected to terrorist organizations. While he did not arrange the actual transfer of HEU, Khan provided the blue-prints for a plant to produce this material, critical components for such a plant, raw materials (uranium in the gaseous form needed for enrich-ment), and a weapon design. Moreover, Khan's activities appear to have involved a number of other highly placed officials in the Pakistani nuclear weapons program, and the provision of gaseous uranium appears to have involved not merely the copying of documents (such as blueprints and weapon designs), but the physical removal of (non-weapons us-able) nuclear material from Pakistani stocks. Finally, although Khan is not known to have dealt with terrorists, other Pakistani nuclear scien-tists were allegedly providing assistance to al Qaeda prior to the U.S. war in Afghanistan.[42] In sum, by the time Khan was exposed, many of the elements of a conspiracy that could have led to the transfer of fissile material to terrorists were in place.

The exposure of Khan and his co-conspirators appears to make such transfers from Pakistan less likely in the future. If, however, Iran were to acquire substantial stocks of HEU or plutonium, there would be cause for concern that hard-line factions might consider sharing a portion of them with terrorist organizations, without the explicit approval of the country's political or spiritual leaders. Such radical factions could be responsible for Iran's current efforts to produce HEU as part of a clandestine nuclear weapons program. If the Pakistani case is a relevant model, it is also quite possible that such internal factions would also be responsible for designing nuclear weapons and might be in a position to share with their terrorist clients the know-how for fabricating an IND.

Assistance from Fissile Material Production Workers and Custodians

Some insiders at uranium enrichment or reprocessing plants are likely to have varying degrees of access to HEU or plutonium. As discussed in Chapter 3, their motives for providing these materials to a terrorist group might include sympathy with the terrorists' goals, greed, or coercion through threats of violence or blackmail to friends, family members, or themselves. Identifying susceptible insiders and arranging for their assistance present substantial challenges. Terrorists might seek collaboration with organized crime to facilitate this method of acquisition. If, by taking advantage of the difficulty of accounting for fissile materials and/or weak security arrangements, the perpetrators were able to divert material without detection, they would gain the ability to mask their future actions—fabricating an IND and transporting it (or its components) to the detonation site—without confronting intensive recovery efforts and heightened security at likely target locations.

As highlighted in the previous chapter, poorly paid and demoralized nuclear workers and security guards in Russia might be vulnerable to subornation by terrorists or criminals. Moreover, the huge size and complexity of the Russian fissile material stockpile and production infrastructure greatly adds to the difficulty of protecting HEU and plutonium. As detailed later in this chapter, security measures covering well over 50 percent of Russia's hundreds of tons of fissile material remain rudimentary, and even the most basic upgrades under U.S. assistance programs have yet to be implemented, raising fears that the illicit trafficking in these materials seen in the past may be continuing.

Seizure without Insider Help

Considerably greater effort and skill would be needed for a terrorist organization to seize fissile material without insider assistance, since this would mean the organization would need to train and arm a force able to defeat all security measures protecting the materials. In addition, the terrorists would have to determine what security measures they would confront, and they would need to map out a secure means of escape, which could involve travel over long distances. Although assaults would be more problematic against fissile material storage or processing areas deep within large, secure complexes, fissile materials are also found at sites in city centers, at smaller suburban research parks, and at isolated, stand-alone plants where armed assaults—perhaps accompanied by diversionary attacks—would be more practicable. Moreover, in Russia, tens of tons of fissile material are transported over substantial distances each year, creating opportunities for seizure at remote points on rail lines or at major rail junctions. HEU used in research reactors around the world, many of which are found in small, easily accessible research centers, is considered particularly vulnerable.

Coups d'État and Political Unrest

As in an attempted seizure of a nuclear weapon, political instability during a coup or a revolution could provide an opportunity for terrorists to gain control over fissile material. Insurgents allied to or cooperating with terrorists could trigger or be the main assault force behind a takeover of a state with weapons-usable nuclear material. Even if such an insurrection were unsuccessful, however, nuclear sites could fall behind "enemy" lines before fissile materials could be removed, permitting their transfer to terrorists or their allies. Or, during a period of civil strife, response forces might be drawn into the conflict, leaving fissile material sites vulnerable to assault. It is also possible that during a period of political turmoil, nuclear custodians might desert their posts or be swept aside in the tide of events.

Such scenarios are not far-fetched: Although the details remain murky and there is no indication that terrorists obtained the material involved, it appears that a small quantity of HEU (about 2 kg of 90 percent en-

riched), located at the Sukhumi Nuclear Research Center in the break-
away Georgian province of Abkhazia, was diverted during a period of
civil turmoil in the early 1990s.[43] More recently, terrorism attributed to
the Islamic Movement of Uzbekistan, led to increased concern about
the security of nuclear materials at the Institute of Nuclear Physics in
Ulugbek, near Tashkent, and to the removal to Russia of fresh HEU
research reactor fuel stored there.[44]

It was argued in the previous chapter that even during a period of
political turmoil elite security forces protecting nuclear weapons would
be most likely to continue to perform their duties during and after regime change. Whether guard forces responsible for fissile materials
would have the same dedication to their responsibilities is less clear.
Even in states possessing nuclear weapons, such materials represent a
more diffuse, less symbolically important national asset than intact
nuclear arms, themselves; in other states, such as those with HEU-using
research reactors, national political and military organizations may not
even be aware of the strategic importance of this material or of its exact whereabouts. This lack of attentiveness—and security—is especially
worrisome with respect to HEU that has been irradiated but could still
be processed for use in an IND.[45]

In sum, although the probability that terrorists could obtain nuclear
weapons material directly from state sponsors is quite small, it is significant enough to warrant serious concern. A senior official or group
of officials providing such assistance without the approval of a country's
political leaders is somewhat more likely, especially in states in which
senior nuclear officials have significant political independence. Collusion of insiders with a criminal organization is a more probable pathway for acquisition of nuclear weapons material. Russia's vast stocks of
HEU and plutonium and less-than-desirable security measures pose the
greatest concern. Political instability could also result in terrorist groups
accessing weapons-usable fissile materials. The vulnerability of Pakistan's
government combined with the power of radical Islamic groups in that
country highlight the potential for terrorist acquisition of Pakistani
materials through a successful or an attempted overthrow of the gov-

ernment. A politically imploding North Korea could also lead to leakage of materials needed for nuclear arms into the hands of terrorists.

Fabrication of an Improvised Nuclear Device

Assuming that terrorists would not have access to technologically sophisticated nuclear weapons design and fabrication infrastructures, such as those possessed by a limited number of states, terrorists who seek to build an improvised nuclear device would favor nuclear weapon designs based on first-generation, well-proven technology. First-generation nuclear weapons draw upon two designs: gun-type and implosion-type.

Gun-Type Device

The most basic type of nuclear weapon is a gun-type device. As its name suggests, like a gun, it fires a projectile—in this case a piece of HEU—inside a tubular shell. Moreover, like a gun, this device uses a gun barrel to direct the projectile. To ignite a nuclear explosion, the HEU projectile travels down the barrel to another piece of HEU at the other end of the tube. Each piece of HEU is subcritical; that is, each alone could not sustain an explosive chain reaction. Once they combined, however, they would form a supercritical mass.

Ideally, weapons-grade HEU[46] is the most effective fissile material for a gun-type device because of its very high concentration of U-235.[47] Gun assembly is an inefficient means of exploding HEU, mainly because it is a relatively slow way (compared to implosion assembly, as described below) to form a supercritical mass, and it does not appreciably compress or change the density of the fissile material.[48] Therefore, a gun-type device requires relatively large amounts of HEU and can fission only a small fraction of the HEU during the explosive chain reaction. Nonetheless, even HEU enriched to less than weapons-grade can lead to an explosive chain reaction. The gun-type Hiroshima bomb, for example, used about 60 kg of 80 percent enriched uranium. Also, South Africa's six gun-type weapons—each with an estimated 55 kg of about 80 percent enriched HEU[49] employed material below weapons grade.

Terrorists would probably need about 40 to 50 kg of weapons-grade HEU to have reasonable confidence that the IND would work.[50] A technically sophisticated terrorist group might be able to achieve the lower limit of efficiency for a gun-type device using weapons-grade HEU by reducing the necessary amount of material to about 25 kg; this, however, would require the use of a "reflector" made of beryllium—a closely regulated metal—to enhance the chain reaction.[51]

Most physicists and nuclear weapons analysts have concluded that construction of a gun-type device would pose few technological barriers to technically competent terrorists.[52] In 2002, the U.S. National Research Council in its report warned, "Crude HEU weapons could be fabricated without state assistance."[53] The council further specified, "The primary impediment that prevents countries or technically competent terrorist groups from developing nuclear weapons is the availability of [nuclear material], especially HEU."[54] Thus, this prestigious group of scientists emphasized the dangers posed by HEU over other types of nuclear material. In September 2003, several scientists under the auspices of the Union of Concerned Scientists signed a letter, which stated that HEU is "the easiest material in the world for terrorists to use to make a nuclear bomb."[55] Moreover, commenting on the relative ease of using HEU to make a nuclear weapon, Richard Garwin and Georges Charpak wrote, "Enriched uranium is the dream material for making bombs."[56] Frank von Hippel, a physicist who had served as the Assistant Director for National Security at the White House's Office of Science and Technology Policy, wrote in 2001, "It is generally agreed, however, that educated terrorists could turn weapon-grade uranium…into a gun-type nuclear explosive."[57]

While there appears to be little doubt among the experts that technically competent terrorists could make a gun-type device given sufficient quantities of HEU, the question remains as to how technically competent they have to be and how large a team would be needed. At one end of the spectrum of analysis is the view that a suicidal terrorist could literally drop one piece of HEU metal on top of another piece to form a supercritical mass and initiate an explosive chain reaction. Nobel laureate Luis Alvarez's oft-cited quote exemplifies this view. He wrote,

With modern weapons-grade uranium, the background neutron rate is so low that terrorists, if they have such material, would have a good chance of setting off a high-yield explosion simply by dropping one half of the material onto the other half. Most people seem unaware that if separated HEU is at hand it's a trivial job to set off a nuclear explosion...even a high school kid could make a bomb in short order.[58]

However, he did not specify what he meant by "high-yield" explosion. A January 2002 *New York Times* report elaborated that "a 100-pound mass of [weapons-grade] uranium dropped on a second 100-pound mass, from a height of about 6 feet, could produce a blast of 5 to 10 kilotons."[59] It should be noted that both statements suggest that there is no guarantee that this very crude method would work all the time or would always produce such a powerful explosion. This scenario also posits that the terrorist would be suicidal. With more technical effort, the terrorist group could significantly increase its chances of generating a high-yield explosion. The basic design specifications are well known and available through the Internet.

However, to make sure that the group could surmount any technical barriers, it would likely want to recruit team members who have knowledge of conventional explosives (needed to fire one piece of HEU into another), metalworking, draftsmanship, and chemical processing (for example, in order to extract HEU metal from other chemical forms, such as oxide or aluminum-based reactor fuel). A well-financed terrorist organization such as al Qaeda would probably have little difficulty recruiting personnel with these skills. Concerning the size of the team and the preparation time required, Albert Narath estimated, "Once the HEU in metallic form is in hand it might require only a dozen individuals with the right set of skills to accomplish the design and construction over a period of perhaps a year."[60] This approximate time for preparation would allow for "rapid turn around" —that is, after the group had obtained the material, "the device would be ready within a day or so." Carson Mark, et al., also assessed, "Such a device could be constructed by a group not previously engaged in designing or building nuclear weapons."[61] In a later analysis in November 2001, the Pugwash Council echoed this view by underscoring that "sub-national terrorist groups could accomplish the challenge."[62] In May 2004, a team of international security experts set out to demonstrate the feasibility of terrorists making a gun-type IND. After witnessing a simulation in Brussels, Belgium, of the Black Dawn scenario in which a small group of terrorists was able to build and detonate an IND using the gun assembly method, the government officials and technical experts present deemed the simulation very plausible.[63]

Because of the inherent simplicity of a gun-type device, designing and constructing it would be relatively straightforward. Testing the non-nuclear parts of the device would likely be required, and an appropriate testing area would be needed (such as a terrorist training camp where other explosives were routinely used) to avoid arousing suspicion. Assuming such tests could be accomplished and a sufficient amount of HEU obtained in the appropriate form, terrorists could have a moderate degree of confidence that their IND would result in a substantial nuclear yield. It may be recalled that U.S. scientists had such great confidence in the gun-type design prior to its actual use over Hiroshima that they believed it was unnecessary to test it through a nuclear detonation. One of the leading scientific administrators of the Manhattan Project, James Bryant Conant, then-president of Harvard University, assessed in early 1945 (months before the Hiroshima bomb was detonated) that "the gun method of detonation seemed 'as nearly certain as any untried new procedure can be.'"[64] Similarly, South African nuclear weapon designers had full confidence in the gun-type weapons they had built, even though that country is not known to have conducted a nuclear test. South Africa assembled these bombs in a warehouse—a relatively small building that escaped detection throughout its many years of operation.[65] Thus, the most formidable barrier to a gun-type weapon remains the acquisition of sufficient HEU.

It is impossible to achieve a large nuclear explosion by employing plutonium in a gun-type device because the speed of assembly of the critical mass is too slow to allow plutonium to be used efficiently.[66] However, some authorities have concluded that a relatively small explosive yield (not greater than 10 to 20 tons TNT equivalent) could be produced by using plutonium in a gun-type IND. Both weapons-grade and reactor-grade plutonium would result in this fizzle yield.[67] Although this yield is about three orders of magnitude less than that expected from a Hiroshima-type (HEU) bomb, it is much more powerful than typical conventional explosives. Thus, terrorists detonating a gun-type IND fueled with plutonium could cause tremendous blast damage within an area encompassing several city blocks—the destruction radius from ground zero would be about 100 meters—and could "produce radioactive fallout with a total intensity of a few tens of curies, as well as a cloud containing a few kilograms of plutonium oxide aerosol."[68] This aspect of the weapon's impact would, in effect, be similar to a very large radiological dispersion device (discussed in Chapter 6), and would be especially dangerous, inasmuch as small quantities of plutonium, if inhaled, are known to cause cancer. In sum, although weapons-usable HEU poses the greater threat by far because it could power a devastating gun-type device, plutonium could conceivably be used by terrorists to produce a significant, though lower-order, level of damage.

Implosion-Type Device

To cause a nuclear explosion, an implosion-type device squeezes a sphere of fissile material from a relatively low-density subcritical state to a high-density supercritical state. If the implosion does not occur smoothly, the bomb will be a complete dud or result in a fizzle yield, lower than expected from a properly designed implosion weapon. Thus, in contrast to a gun-type device, an implosion-type device requires more technical sophistication and competence. A terrorist group, for example, would need access to and knowledge of high-speed electronics and high explosive lenses,[69] a particularly complex technology. This equipment is necessary to effect a fast and smooth squeezing of the fissile material into a supercritical state. Unlike a gun-type device, an implosion-type device can employ HEU or plutonium because the speed of assembly is fast enough to allow the use of plutonium. An improvised implosion-type weapon would probably require approximately 25 kg of weapons-grade HEU or roughly 8 kg of plutonium in the highest density, or alpha, phase.[70] For comparison, the implosion bomb exploded over Nagasaki contained 6 kg of weapons-grade plutonium.

As noted earlier, weapons-grade plutonium is the most desirable type of plutonium both from the perspective of a weapon scientist employed by a state and of a terrorist organization, since it is most readily detonated. Even reactor-grade plutonium can result in an explosive chain reaction, however, depending on the skill of the weapons designers and builders.[71] While an IND fashioned from weapons-grade plutonium would require a neutron initiator, an IND made from reactor-grade plutonium would not, removing the need for terrorists to obtain or design a critical component.[72] Carson Mark, a former Los Alamos National Laboratory weapons scientist, cautioned against assuming that nuclear terrorists would seek only weapons-grade materials. He wrote,

> There is, of course, no question that weapons-grade material is preferable from a design standpoint; and if, as for the U.S., one has the option and is paying for the plutonium anyway, one chooses the most advantageous. So would the terrorist if he had a choice. But if he can't get weapons-grade material he would take whatever he can get, should any be open to him.[73]

Because reactor-grade plutonium would have a much higher chance of preignition, the bomb yield would likely be much less than that of a weapon made from weapons-grade plutonium. Nonetheless, even if terrorists were able to achieve only a "fizzle" yield from the device, it would be far greater than the yield from a powerful conventional explosion, thus giving the terrorists a potent weapon. Commenting on the yield of a fizzle reactor-grade implosion device, Garwin and Charpak wrote, "The major problem is that the much larger amount of plutonium-240 [in the reactor-grade material] than in weapons-grade plutonium makes even the implosion system very likely to preinitiate—and when it does so, it lowers the yield of the simplest system to as little as 2,000 tons of explosive, in contrast to a design yield of 20,000 tons (which would still be achieved a portion of the time)."[74] However, as noted, for the purposes of a terrorist group, a tendency toward preinitiation could offer an advantage in the sense that the bomb would not need an initiator. But this feature provides only one minor comparative advantage.

Implosion-type weapons, using reactor-grade plutonium, weapons-grade plutonium, or HEU, would pose design and construction challenges much greater than those of a gun-type HEU device. Iraq's nuclear weapon scientists, for example, appear to have required several years to achieve a workable nuclear weapon design based on implosion.[75]

Even if terrorists obtained a design that was known to work, manufacturing the components for the device and ensuring that they all worked together with the necessary precision would be a daunting technical challenge, requiring considerable time and extensive testing of the non-nuclear "triggering package," both of which would increase the risk of detection. Given these challenges, terrorists would likely have far less confidence that their implosion-based device would work than they would have in the case of a far simpler gun-type assembly using HEU. Additionally, since it is assumed that terrorists will have only limited quantities of plutonium available, a full-scale nuclear test undertaken simply to prove the design of the weapon the terrorists had built seems highly unlikely. More probable is that the first detonation using plutonium would be at a target, with the expectation that even if the device failed to produce a nuclear yield, its very existence would cause profound fear in the target state and permit blackmail based on the real or pretended existence of additional weapons. Moreover, as discussed earlier, even a very small nuclear yield or a mere conventional explosion that dispersed plutonium would comprise a radiological dispersion device of historic proportions.

Could a reasonably technically competent small terrorist group design and build an implosion device? A U.S. government-sponsored experiment in the 1960s sheds light on the technical capabilities required.[76] Deciding to prove that designing a first-generation-type nuclear weapon does not require Nobel laureates, the Lawrence Livermore National Laboratory hired two young Ph.D. physicists who had no prior experience with nuclear weapons to conduct the Nth Country experiment. These physicists, using access to only open source information, were able to design a workable implosion-type weapon in less than three years. They pursued the implosion design because they decided that a gun-type device was too simple and, thus, not enough of a challenge. Later in 1977, a Princeton undergraduate designed an implosion-type bomb for a term paper using only unclassified sources. His professor, Freeman Dyson, a physicist familiar with nuclear weapons-design, gave him an "A." The U.S. government classified the paper.[77]

Other technical hurdles could trip up terrorist construction of an implosion IND. For instance, an implosion device would require a neutron initiator to start the chain reaction at the time of maximum compression of the fissile material. While such initiating systems could be relatively easily acquired and adapted from neutron devices used in oil well logging, for example, terrorists might have difficulty figuring out how to time the initiation at the exact moment.[78]

Table 4.5 summarizes several of the properties and characteristics of gun-type and implosion-type devices. In sum, given a choice between building a gun-type or an implosion-type device, terrorists probably would choose to construct a gun-type device because it is more likely to result in a nuclear weapon producing a large explosive yield. However, if nuclear terrorists had access only to plutonium, they would be forced to build an implosion-type device to achieve high yields, or they could try to construct a low-yield gun-type device, as discussed in an earlier section.[79]

In sum, the basic knowledge of how to begin to construct a gun-type or an implosion-type IND is readily available. Nonetheless, significant technical hurdles would remain. Thus, terrorists who are motivated to build INDs and who do not have access to sophisticated technical skills would probably choose to acquire sufficient HEU to produce a gun-type device.

Transporting the IND (or Its Components) to the Target Site

Assuming that nuclear terrorists were able to acquire the necessary fissile material and manufactured an IND, they would then have to cross the next barrier to IND use. That is, they would have to find a way to deliver an IND to a target without being caught and stopped. For the scenarios of greatest concern to the United States, the use of the weapon against a city in the United States or one of its allies, the distance between the point of acquisition and the target could be quite substantial. If the loss of fissile material were detected, a massive hunt for the material would be launched, involving law enforcement and military personnel from many nations, assisted by nuclear specialists. This would

TABLE 4.5
COMPARISON OF GUN-TYPE TO IMPLOSION-TYPE IND

Characteristic/ Property	Gun-Type	Implosion-Type
Ease of construction	Relatively simple	More difficult
Fissile material	HEU (for yield > 20 tons TNT equivalent) Pu (for yield < 20 tons)	HEU or Pu (either weapons-grade or reactor-grade)
Amount of fissile material	~ 50 kg (for weapons-grade HEU)	~ 5-10 kg of Pu, depending on the grade and density or ~ 25 kg of weapons-grade HEU
Reliability	High	Lower
Risk of pre-ignition	Low for HEU Very high for Pu	High
Radiological hazard during construction	Low	Low if HEU used Medium if Pu used

be accompanied by greatly intensified security over transportation links and points of entry. Unfortunately, for many scenarios, material might be diverted without detection for some time or the diversion might not be acknowledged, providing the opportunity for the terrorist organization involved to cover its tracks and move the material to a safe location where it could undertake the manufacture of the IND.

Once the IND was completed, its transportation would not present insurmountable difficulties. Although an IND would likely be heavy—perhaps weighing up to a ton—trucks and commercial vans could easily haul a device of that size. In addition, container ships and commercial airplanes, such as those used to transport heavy equipment, could provide a means of delivery. As of late 2003, only about 2 to 3 percent of

TABLE 4.5 (CONTINUED)
COMPARISON OF GUN-TYPE TO IMPLOSION-TYPE IND

Characteristic/ Property	Gun-Type	Implosion-Type
Need for experimentation to prove design	Low	High
Need for complex non-nuclear components, such as high-explosive lenses	Low	High
Susceptibility to radiation detection during construction and transport	Low if HEU Medium if Pu	Low if HEU Medium if Pu
Effectiveness as RDD, assuming dud or very low-yield fizzle bomb	Low if HEU High if Pu	Low if HEU High if Pu

Source: Parts of this table are based on Morten Bremer Maerli, "The Characteristics of Nuclear Terrorist Weapons," Presentation at 14th Summer Symposium on Science and World Affairs, University of Illinois at Urbana-Champaign, July 2002. Other information was obtained from references, such as Carson Mark, Theodore Taylor, Eugene Eyster, William Maraman, and Jacob Wechsler, "Can Terrorists Build Nuclear Weapons?" in Paul Leventhal and Yonah Alexander, eds., *Preventing Nuclear Terrorism: The Report and Papers of the International Task Force on Prevention of Nuclear Terrorism* (Lanham, MD: Lexington Books, 1987), pp. 55-65; and Stanislav Rodionov, "Could Terrorists Produce Low-Yield Nuclear Weapons?" in National Research Council, National Academy of Sciences, in Cooperation with the Russian Academy of Sciences, *High-Impact Terrorism: Proceedings of a Russian-American Workshop* (Washington, DC: National Academies Press, 2002).

the containers entering the United States are thoroughly checked, a matter discussed in greater depth elsewhere in this volume. Nonetheless, terrorists would need extensive resources and networks of collaborators to move their IND over long distances, adding to the complexity of their plot.

Detecting uranium or even plutonium in transit is difficult. On September 11, 2002, ABC News reported that one of its correspondents traveled throughout Europe with a suitcase containing 15 pounds of depleted uranium shielded by a steel pipe with a lead lining. The package was headed toward the United States in a test of whether government authorities could detect the shipment. The suitcase escaped inspection and detection.[80] Although critics of this test charged that depleted uranium has a much weaker detection signal than HEU, the physicists at the Natural Resources Defense Council (NRDC) who provided the depleted uranium replied that they could have easily shielded the same mass of HEU to result in a detection signal comparable to the depleted uranium.[81] Exactly one year later, ABC News reported that it shipped the same depleted uranium from Jakarta, Indonesia, to the port of Long Beach without detection by U.S. Customs (now the Bureau of Customs and Border Protection).[82]

Every means of delivery, however, exposes terrorists to some risk of discovery. To reduce or eliminate this risk, a terrorist group might choose to detonate an IND on the spot where it was assembled. Piece by piece, terrorists could bring enough fissile material to a garage or some other innocuous structure—for example, at the outskirts of a major city at some distance from the group's most desired target —and build the IND at that location. A devastating blast even in such a location would cause great damage and many deaths and provide terrorists the opportunity to threaten to destroy more impressive targets with INDs it only claimed to possess. Alternatively, terrorists might try to assemble and detonate a gun-type device, but probably not a more sophisticated implosion-type device, at a fissile material storage site, assuming that this site contained sufficient quantities of readily usable HEU metal, that the terrorists were suicidal, and that the assault team included members versed in the relevant technical skills of gun devices.[83] As an illustration of this hypothetical scenario, the Project on Government Oversight reported, "In a test [in October 2000] at a Los Alamos facility, the [mock] 'terrorists' had enough time to construct an Improvised Nuclear Device."[84] Though information on any comparable tests in other countries is lacking, terrorists might be able to accomplish onsite assembly of an IND at sites in Russia, Germany, Japan, or elsewhere. As noted in Chapter 3, a nuclear detonation by a non-state group virtually anywhere would terrorize citizens in potential target countries around the globe, who would fear the perpetrators had additional weapons at their disposal. The organization could exploit such fears in order to blackmail governments into political concessions—for example, demanding the withdrawal of military forces or political support from states the terrorists opposed. Indeed, the group might achieve these results without a nuclear detonation by providing proof that it had an IND in its possession at a location unknown to its adversaries.

Detonation of the IND

Inasmuch as, by definition, terrorists constructing an IND would be familiar with its design, the act of detonating the device would be relatively straightforward and present few technical difficulties. However, as discussed above, an implosion device presents a much greater chance of producing a dud or fizzle yield than does a gun device.

NUCLEAR MATERIALS SECURITY AT THE STATE LEVEL

The foregoing analysis of the steps terrorists would have to take to acquire fissile material and then manufacture and use an IND makes clear the high degree of difficulty involved and the low probability of success. Very few organizations have the necessary motivation and resources, and any organization making the attempt would have to surmount a series of extremely challenging obstacles. That being said, much would depend both on the ability of the terrorist organization to recruit a suitable, technically competent team and on the state of physical protection and accounting covering the fissile materials needed for weapons. If effective, national safeguards can defeat almost all paths to terrorist acquisition of these materials, except in the case of the transfer of such materials by a sympathetic government (which might also provide assistance in nuclear weapon design and fabrication). As outlined earlier, the settings posing the greatest risk of terrorist acquisition of a nuclear weapon are found in Russia, Pakistan, at certain research facilities around the globe with HEU stocks, and, possibly, at plutonium processing and storage facilities in Japan.

Russian HEU and Plutonium

The huge quantity of fissile material in Russia poses a uniquely dangerous risk of terrorist acquisition of weapons-origin material for an IND. As of March 2003, the DOE estimated that Russia possessed roughly 600 metric tons[85] of weapons-usable plutonium and HEU outside of nuclear weapons—enough to make more than 20,000 nuclear warheads— stored at more than 50 military and civilian sites.[86] Numerous assessments citing the general state of decay of Russia's nuclear infrastructure, decades of inadequate nuclear materials accounting, and the impoverishment of Russian nuclear workers and scientists have concluded that most of this material is inadequately secured. In 2002, for example, the U.S. National Intelligence Council (NIC) concluded that, while Russia inherited a security system geared toward repelling external threats, this system is not prepared "to counter the preeminent threat faced today— an insider who attempts unauthorized actions." Alarmingly, the NIC "assess[ed] that undetected smuggling has occurred, although we do not know the extent or magnitude of such thefts. Nonetheless, we are concerned about the total amount of material that could be diverted over the last 10 years." [87] The NIC also reported that security varied widely throughout the nuclear materials complex in Russia.

Echoing such concerns about the security of Russian fissile materials, in March 2003, the GAO found that the key U.S. program for securing fissile materials in Russia, the Material Protection, Control, and Accounting (MPC&A) program of the DOE had made "uneven progress."[88] Summarizing the conclusions of its investigation, the GAO stated:

> DOE's progress in protecting weapons-usable nuclear material has varied widely, depending on the type of site. As of January 2003, DOE had completed security improvements at most of the buildings at civilian sites and naval fuel storage sites. In contrast, DOE has not started work at the majority of the buildings in the nuclear weapons complex, which contains most of the remaining unpro-

tected weapons-usable nuclear material in Russia. Although DOE has now protected 38 percent, or about 228 metric tons, of Russia's weapons-usable nuclear material, the vast majority of the remaining material is at sites in the nuclear weapons complex where, due to Russian national security concerns, DOE has not gained access and begun work. Because DOE has been largely unable to start new work in the weapons complex, most of DOE's new spending for fiscal years 2001 and 2002 was on programs other than installing security improvements at buildings containing weapons-usable nuclear material.[89]

These findings have been accompanied by repeated reports of illicit trafficking in Russian-origin weapons-usable nuclear materials. Although accurate information on such activities is difficult to obtain, and most press stories involve material that cannot be used for nuclear weapons, the IAEA Database on Illicit Trafficking of Nuclear and Other Radioactive Materials lists 18 trafficking incidents involving fissile material between January 1993 and June 2002.[90] The Center for Nonproliferation Studies has found that at least 18 incidents of illicit trafficking in HEU and plutonium from the former Soviet states occurred from 1992 to 2002, although the set of cases do not correspond perfectly to that of the IAEA.[91] Analysts at Stanford University estimate that about 40 kg of weapons-usable material has been stolen from the NIS.[92] Most of the material involved in these reported incidents was recovered, but the total attempts at theft or diversion remains unknown. Commenting on the relatively low amounts of visible illicit trafficking, Rensselaer Lee has argued that "the relatively innocuous visible traffic might conceal a shadow market that is organized on the initiative of the buyer or end-user and oriented toward meeting the latter's specific military requirements."[93] Moreover, other analysts have pointed out that some evidence indicates that criminal organizations are becoming more interested in smuggling nuclear and radioactive material from the Newly Independent States (NIS).[94]

The United States has some half dozen major programs to help Russia secure, consolidate, and eliminate fissile materials. Table 4.6 summarizes these programs, which are described in greater detail in Box 4.1.

While many of these programs have made important progress in reducing the threat posed by these materials, all are far from completion, and the acute dangers posed by Russian HEU and plutonium will continue for much of the remainder of this decade, if not beyond. A particular concern is that the DOE's MPC&A program has yet to provide even rudimentary security improvements for more than half of Russia's fissile materials and has provided comprehensive security upgrades for only 22 percent of this material.[95] The department appears to have made little progress in gaining access to key locations where the largest quantities of these materials are housed: Russia's weapons assembly and disassembly facilities and key locations within that country's nuclear weapons complex.[96]

The U.S. programs to secure, consolidate, and eliminate fissile materials in Russia originated in the early to mid-1990s at a time when the most serious proliferation threat appeared to be that posed by the spread of nuclear weapons to dangerous states, including Iran, Iraq, Libya, and North Korea. However important those threats may have been—and in some cases they remain significant—the most grave and immediate nuclear threat to the United States and its allies today comes from terrorists—that is, from non-state actors seeking weapons of mass destruction. In this context, inadequately secured HEU enriched to 80 percent or more, the material whose loss to terrorists is by far the most likely to lead to a nuclear explosion on U.S. or allied territory, looms as a unique danger.

HEU is doubly dangerous because, unlike plutonium, it is used extensively in Russia in applications other than nuclear weapons and thus is more exposed to potential theft or diversion by terrorist groups.[97] Although the largest stores of HEU and plutonium in Russia outside of weapons are found at nuclear weapon assembly and dismantlement sites and at former fissile material production facilities, and although both are found in some research institutes, high-quality HEU is far more widely dispersed beyond these locations because of its additional uses:

- HEU is used as fuel in some 40 operational research reactors, test reactors, and critical assemblies in Russia.[98] Although the enrichment levels vary depending on the reactor or critical assembly, at least nine reactors rated above 1 MW power (the threshold above which a research reactor is considered to be of relatively high proliferation concern) employ 90 percent enriched HEU. In addition, many of these reactor sites contain stores of fresh HEU fuel or lightly irradiated spent HEU fuel.[99]

- HEU is used in Russian submarine, cruiser, and icebreaker propulsion reactors; a portion of the fuel for these vessels is reportedly enriched to 80 percent or more.[100] Most of the discharged submarine fuel contains enrichment levels between 21 and 45 percent, far below the more easily weapons-usable 80-percent-or-greater enrichment levels; only two classes of Russian submarines (November 645 and Alfa classes) are believed to have used weapons-grade HEU as fuel. While tons of Russian naval spent fuel are stored under highly insecure conditions, in northwest Russia and in the Russian Far East, only a very small portion of this spent fuel contains weapons-grade or near-weapons-grade HEU. However, reportedly the Kirov battle cruiser (now called the Admiral Ushakov) and Russian icebreakers use weapons-grade HEU as fuel.[101] Thus, from the perspective of prevention of nuclear terrorism, the fresh and spent fuel from these vessels deserve the greatest security protection.[102]

- High-quality HEU may also be used in the floating reactors that Russia plans to employ in the Arctic region and potentially sell to other countries. Although the enrichment level of the floating reactors' fuel has not been published, some analysts believe that because the reactor design is based on the design of the icebreakers' reactors, weapons-grade HEU might be employed.[103]

- HEU of varying enrichment levels is also found in large quantities in fuel fabrication facilities—i.e., facilities where marine propulsion and research reactor fuels are manufactured from bulk HEU and at sites where these fuels are designed.

- In addition, weapons-grade HEU is processed in very large quantities under the U.S.-Russia HEU Purchase Agreement. The agreement provides that over the course of twenty years, Russia is to blend down 500 metric tons of HEU from, or intended for, nuclear weapons into low-enriched uranium. The latter material is suitable for use as nuclear power plant fuel but no longer usable for nuclear weapons. The blended-down material is to be purchased by the United States Enrichment Corporation for some $12 billion. As of early 2004, the HEU Purchase Agreement has resulted in the blending down of 201 metric tons of Russian HEU,[104] and each year, 30 metric tons of the material must be taken from four weapon disassembly sites, transported long distances by rail, and introduced into processing plants for blending. Significantly, for the first leg of this journey, the material transported is HEU metal, the form of HEU that could be most readily used by terrorists for an IND.[105]

- As indicated in Table 4.6, the DOE has instituted a number of valuable programs to enhance the security of HEU at many locations in Russia and to reduce the amount of HEU by down-blending the material to non-weapons-usable LEU. It also has sought, with mixed results, to consolidate HEU stocks at fewer civilian nuclear facilities (no progress) and at fewer buildings within those facilities (reductions by about one-third). Significantly, the department's MPC&A program has assisted the Russian Navy to secure almost all fresh HEU submarine fuel.[106]

Despite these initiatives, the unique threat posed by Russian high-quality HEU has not been expressly recognized within the DOE or within the U.S. government, more broadly. As the department seeks access to new sites within the Russian nuclear complex, for example, it has placed neither sites holding high-quality HEU nor sites where it does have access at the top of its list, nor has it given first priority to securing

TABLE 4.6

U.S. PROGRAMS TO SECURE AND REDUCE RUSSIAN FISSILE MATERIALS

Program	Goal	Status	Completion Date
Securing Fissile Materials			
Material protection, control, and accounting (MPC&A)	Secure fissile material outside weapons	Rapid upgrades completed on 43% of material; comprehensive upgrades complete on 22% of material	2008
Mayak Fissile Material Storage Facility	Secure 50 tons of weapons-grade plutonium, but could secure HEU, as well	Loading to begin in 2004 depending on completion of transparency agreement	2020
Eliminating Fissile Materials			
HEU Purchase Agreement	Down-blend 500 metric tons of weapons-grade HEU for sale as commercial nuclear power plant fuel	About 200 tons of HEU rendered unusable for nuclear weapons as of end of 2003; additional conversion at the rate of 30 tons/year	2012
MPC&A HEU consolidation and conversion	Consolidate and down-blend HEU from research centers and reactors in former Soviet Union and Eastern Europe	4.3 tons of HEU rendered unusable for nuclear weapons as of end of 2003; an additional 4 tons to be eliminated by the end of 2005	2005
Plutonium disposition	Use 34 tons of weapons-origin plutonium as power reactor fuel, rendering it very difficult to use for weapons	First use in a Russian reactor scheduled for 2008, depending on resolution of liability agreement and completion of MOX fuel facility	2025

TABLE 4.6 (CONTINUED)
U.S. PROGRAMS TO SECURE AND REDUCE RUSSIAN FISSILE MATERIALS

Program	Goal	Status	Completion Date
Ending Production of Fissile Materials			
Elimination of weapons-grade plutonium production	End production of 1.2 tons/yr of weapons-grade plutonium by providing fossil fuel plants as alternative sources of heat and power for three Russian production reactors	Revised agreement signed between the United States and Russia in 2003; DOE expects to complete design work for fossil fuel plants by end of 2004 and then provide Congress with an updated cost estimate	2011
Elimination of civilian plutonium separation *No U.S. or international program*	End added accumulation of 1+ tons/yr of separated plutonium from Russian VVER nuclear power plants	No program	N/A

high-quality HEU. Similarly, the U.S. government as a whole has failed to establish priorities among the set of U.S. nuclear assistance programs for Russia to make securing high-quality HEU the paramount concern.

Most notably, the DOE and the U.S. government, more generally, are devoting hundreds of millions of dollars and significant diplomatic energies to the program for the eventual elimination of 68 metric tons of excess weapons plutonium (34 tons each of U.S. and Russian material), while devoting only a small fraction of these resources ($25 million in fiscal year 2004) to accelerate the down-blending of HEU beyond the amounts currently covered by the HEU Purchase Agreement.[107] In the latter area, they have achieved very limited results—an increase of only 1.5 tons in the annual blend-down rate for each of the next ten years—even though a large-scale expansion of HEU blend-down activities could be implemented far more rapidly and at much lower cost than the plutonium disposition effort, while eliminating far greater quantities of fissile material.[108] Similarly, the Mayak Fissile Material Storage Facility at Ozersk, constructed under the U.S. Department of Defense CTR Program for a cost of more than $400 million and commissioned in December 2003, is to house 50 tons of Russian weapons-grade plutonium under highly secure conditions. As constructed, however, it could also house 200 tons of weapons-grade HEU—one-third of the fissile material that the DOE is attempting to protect through its MPC&A program, and the material of greatest interest to terrorists. But there does not appear to be a U.S. effort currently under way to persuade Russia to use the facility for this purpose.[109]

The lack of priority given to safeguarding HEU is even more apparent among Russian government officials who, almost without exception, express much greater concern about the terrorist threat posed by "orphaned" radioactive sources. Although it is difficult to explain the lack of urgency about HEU security on the part of both Russian and U.S. officials, a partial explanation may relate to the lingering perception on the part of many senior defense officials and weapons scientists that the difficulty of manufacturing a nuclear weapon is beyond the capability of non-state actors. In the words of the former Russian Deputy Minister of Atomic Energy Alexander Kotelnikov, "we have to bear in mind that even having any nuclear material does not mean that an explosive device can be made [by terrorists]. This is absolutely impossible."[110]

Although high-quality HEU deserves the greatest attention in addressing the danger of terrorist construction of an IND, securing plutonium also remains highly important. As noted in the previous section, it, too, could be used for an IND, although the device would be considerably more difficult to design and construct. In this regard, at a time when the United States is spending hundreds of millions of dollars to secure and eliminate fissile materials, Russia continues to increase its stocks of separated military and civil plutonium at a combined rate of roughly 3 metric tons (360 weapons, using IAEA standards) per year. The Department of Energy has an active program to end production of Russian *military* plutonium, which DOE and the Federal Agency of Atomic Energy expect to complete by 2011, but there is no similar initiative to halt the separation of plutonium from spent fuel produced in certain Russian civil nuclear power plants.[111]

Fissile Material Security Programs in Russia Supported by Other States

Although the United States has given the lion's share of assistance for nuclear material security to Russia, other countries also have provided assistance on a bilateral or multilateral basis since the early 1990s. Of these countries, Canada, France, Germany, Italy, Japan, and the United Kingdom, all members of the G-8, have allocated the largest share of aid in this area. In addition, states such as Finland, the Netherlands, Norway, and Sweden have played an increasing role in cooperative threat reduction efforts. In addition to the contributions of individual states, the European Union (EU) has supported fissile material security and disposition programs.

In 1996 at the G-8 Moscow summit, Canadian Prime Minister Jean Chrétien announced that his country would consider employing American and Russian weapons-grade plutonium as fuel in Canadian reactors. Ongoing MOX studies in Canada at that time were thought to serve as a basis to bring about approval of this tentative plan. Concurrently, a Russian-Canadian study was exploring the capability of manufacturing MOX fuel bundled in Russia for transfer to Canadian nuclear power plants. After the Moscow summit, DOE funded testing of MOX fuel derived from Russian and U.S. plutonium at the research reactor in Chalk River, Ontario. The testing requires several years of reactor operations to determine the effectiveness of the method. From the start, however, the tests sparked opposition to the MOX program. Mostly, opponents are concerned about the potential for adverse environmental and health consequences if there is a reactor accident, but some doubt the efficacy of this plutonium disposition. Regardless of the outcome of any MOX fuel testing, Canadian security analyst John Hay assesses that developments since late 2001 in the plutonium disposition program point toward "a receding probability that Russia would be asking for any long-term MOX commitments from Canada."[112] In other nuclear security work, Canada has contributed the second-largest amount of money as of late 2003—CAN$4 million (about US$3 million)—to the IAEA's Nuclear Security Fund.[113]

France has given funding for weapons dismantlement and material security through its AIDA (*Aide au démantèlement*) program, which began in late 1992. Activities in this program included delivering 100 security containers to help repatriate nuclear weapons from the former Soviet states to Russia, building a facility to store lithium compounds that were used in nuclear weapons, transferring high-precision cutting tools to dismantle weapons, and funding feasibility studies to determine the effectiveness of weapons-plutonium in MOX fuel. Since 1987, France has burned MOX fuel in many of its reactors and has considerable experience in this regard, although it had never used weapons-origin MOX in fuel.[114]

Germany has made available technical and physical protection assistance to several sites in Russia.[115] It has also been involved in several MOX feasibility studies both bilaterally (Germany-Russia) and trilaterally (Germany-France-Russia) to assist the weapons-grade plutonium disposition program.[116] In the critical area of nuclear materials protection, control, and accounting, Germany, as of late 2003, has allocated 40 million euros (about $50 million) to enhance the physical security of nuclear materials at the Kurchatov and Botchvar institutes in Moscow. The funding disbursal may be delayed until the next fiscal year because of the lateness in signing the agreement with Russia during the 2003 funding cycle. It is expected that these two sites will be the start of a broader package of security assistance, ultimately involving 17 facilities in Russia.[117]

In 1999, Italy agreed to participate in the trilateral Germany-France-Russia MOX study. Italian efforts here are mainly focused on nuclear safety research.[118] As of late 2003, Italy had pledged 80 million euros (about $100 million) to the plutonium disposition program.[119]

Japan has provided funds for plutonium storage containers and transportation security equipment.[120] In addition, the Japan Nuclear Cycle Development Institute (JNC) "has collaborated with Russian institutes for the disposition of weapons-grade plutonium using vibro-packed fuel fabrication technology" for potential use as fuel in the BN-600 breeder reactor. "If this option is employed, it is expected that 20 tons of plutonium can be disposed of in [the] BN-600 by 2020."[121] Japan has also funded cleanup of radioactive waste associated with Russia's nuclear submarine fleet in the Russian Far East and has allocated money, as part of a pilot project, for the dismantlement of a decommissioned Victor-III class nuclear-powered submarine.

The United Kingdom has supported nuclear submarine dismantlement, spent fuel storage, transportation security, and other nonproliferation efforts.[122] "The UK, through its Nuclear Materials Accountancy program, provides several Russian facilities with assistance for developing comprehensive accounting capabilities. Sites that have received UK assistance for protection include the Atomflot site at Murmansk. More ambitious plans for protection assistance are in the planning stages, and will receive £1 million per year once a portfolio is developed."[123] The UK has also pledged £70 million for the plutonium disposition program.

Because of its proximity to the submarine complex of northwest Russia and its concern about the environmental impact of nuclear waste from this complex contaminating prime fishing grounds, Norway has focused on helping to address the legacy problem of dozens of decommissioned Russian nuclear submarines. In particular, Norway has allocated 12 million euros (about $15 million) for the dismantlement of two general-purpose nuclear submarines at the Nerpa and Zvezdochka shipyards. "Norway is paying for fuel unloading, cutting of the submarine itself including the reactor compartment, and safe transport of spent nuclear fuel. Norway does not want to pay for spent fuel reprocessing."[124]

Like Norway, Sweden has also been active in addressing nuclear safety issues in northwest Russia. Regarding nuclear materials security, Sweden is involved in assisting with physical protection, safeguards, response to illicit trafficking, and export controls in Russia, Ukraine, and Kazakhstan.[125]

At their summit meeting in Kananaskis, Canada, in June 2002, the G-8 countries announced the Global Partnership Against the Spread of Weapons and Materials of Mass Destruction, also known as the "10

plus 10 over 10" initiative. This program called for the United States to
contribute $10 billion to nonproliferation projects in Russia and in other
countries, and for the remaining states to commit an additional $10 bil-
lion to these programs over the next ten years. In the two years since the
Global Partnership was launched, 13 non-G-8 states have also become
members of the partnership.[126]

At the June 2004 G-8 summit at Sea Island, Georgia, the leaders of
the industrialized democracies reiterated their commitment to combat
the spread of weapons and materials of mass destruction.[127] Although
most of the $20 billion goal for the Global Partnership has been pledged,
including a promised contribution of $2 billion by Russia, many of the
Global Partners have been very slow to translate promises into action.[128]
This lack of action is especially pronounced if one excludes the nonproliferation assistance programs that already were in place prior to the
Kananaskis summit. In short, although some useful new programs are
being developed, there remains a tremendous gap between the progress
that is being made in the realm of nuclear material security and the scope
and urgency of the threat.[129]

Pakistani Fissile Material

Pakistan now produces both HEU and plutonium for weapons, although
the bulk of its arsenal is thought to consist of HEU-based warheads.[130]
The relatively small quantity of fissile material in Pakistan (perhaps
enough to make 30 to 50 weapons, including weapons already assembled,
adding up to perhaps 1 metric ton) would make accounting and control
of these materials significantly easier than is the case in Russia.[131]

The principal danger that Pakistani fissile materials might fall into
the hands of terrorists stems from the presence of extremist Islamic
groups in that country and in the surrounding region, a history of political instability, uncertain loyalties of senior officials in the civilian and
military nuclear chain of command, and a nuclear material security system of questionable efficacy.[132]

Little information has been revealed concerning Pakistani security
measures covering fissile materials. As noted in Chapter 3, an NBC
Nightly News and a press report in January 2004 disclosed that the United

States had been assisting Pakistan with improving the security of Pakistani nuclear material. It has been widely reported that during peacetime, Pakistan keeps the nuclear and non-nuclear components of its nuclear weapons separate. If true, this measure would greatly complicate efforts to seize an intact nuclear device and might also complicate the diversion of fissile material in the form of weapon components, since, presumably, these receive the highest possible security within the Pakistani system.[133] Fissile materials that are in process, however, may be at greater risk. Through manipulation of material balances and other stratagems, insiders might be able to divert small quantities of fissile material from production and/or processing facilities over a period of months and avoid detection. The A.Q. Khan affair and the assistance provided by two Pakistani nuclear scientists to al Qaeda in 2001 demonstrate that the threat of a conspiracy by insiders must remain a significant concern.

Soviet-Origin HEU and U.S.-Origin HEU in Research Reactors

As noted earlier, many civilian nuclear programs use HEU in research reactors, as well as critical and subcritical assemblies.[134] These programs include scientific research and production of radioisotopes for commercial applications. According to a recent IAEA report, "Research Reactors and Security," about 130 research reactors around the world still run on weapons-grade HEU.[135] They may be found in 40 countries. Approximately 100 of the research reactors use (or used) HEU of 90 percent enrichment, and about 20 were designed to use uranium enriched to between 50 and 90 percent.[136] In addition to fresh HEU remaining at many of these reactor sites, the IAEA estimates that about one-third of all spent research reactor fuel also contains HEU.[137] The quantities in question include approximately 12,850 spent fuel assemblies of U.S. origin at research reactors abroad and 24,803 spent fuel assemblies of Soviet origin outside of Russia.[138]

The terrorism risk posed by this material is suggested by a 1993 report of the Office of Technology Assessment. It noted that a "terrorist group would have little difficulty in recovering HEU metal from fresh fuel if it were seized at the reactor site or in transit. Even if the fuel were lightly irradiated, e.g., for a few hours per week at less than 100 kW (e.g., in a typical university research reactor), the small quantities of radioactive fission products it would contain would not prevent recovery of the uranium, especially after waiting a few days or weeks for the fuel's activity to decay to lower levels."[139]

The large number of research reactors using HEU fuel produced and supplied by the Soviet Union and, later, Russia is of particular concern. The U.S. government has identified more than 20 research facilities in 17 countries containing Soviet- or Russian-supplied HEU fuel.[140] These countries are Belarus, Bulgaria, China, Czech Republic, Egypt, Germany, Hungary, Kazakhstan, Latvia, Libya, North Korea, Poland, Romania, Ukraine, Uzbekistan, Vietnam, and the former Yugoslavia. According to the latest available information on research reactors provided by the IAEA and the World Nuclear Association, as of late 2002 14 research reactors or critical assemblies using Soviet-supplied HEU were considered to be operational in the Czech Republic, Germany, Hungary, Kazakhstan, Libya, North Korea, Poland, Ukraine, Uzbekistan, Vietnam, and the former Yugoslavia. However, the HEU fuel at the Libyan facility has since been repatriated to Russia and the only reactor at Vinca that can be considered operational is a small zero-power critical assembly.[141]

Recognizing the potential dangers of dispersing weapons-grade HEU fuel, the Soviet Union began in 1978 to produce and export 36 percent enriched fuel in lieu of more highly enriched material, when the new fuel was compatible with particular research reactor designs of its customers. Almost all of the research and test reactors operating in former client states, such as Hungary, Poland, and Vietnam, have shifted to 36 percent fuel, which they use today.[142] The two that have not yet converted to lower enriched fuel are the Libyan research reactor and the EWG-1 reactor in Kazakhstan—which is believed to no longer receive high-quality HEU from Russia.[143] However, many reactor sites still house unused fresh, previously exported high-quality HEU fuel or spent high-quality HEU fuel, which retains its utility for an IND and is no longer so radioactive as to make handling the fuel difficult. At least nine research reactors in Russia itself also still use weapons-grade HEU as fuel,[144] while nearly 40 research units (reactors and critical and sub-critical assemblies) within Russia employ HEU ranging from 36 percent to 90 percent enrichment.[145]

Given al Qaeda's close connections with the Islamic Movement of Uzbekistan and the well-established smuggling routes between Central Asia and Afghanistan and Pakistan, research reactor sites in Kazakhstan and Uzbekistan may pose special terrorism risks.[146] These sites include the Institute of Nuclear Physics in Ulugbek, near Tashkent; the Institute of Nuclear Physics in Alatau, near Almaty; and the Kurchatov Branch of the Institute of Atomic Energy on the former Semipalatinsk Test Site. Other high grade HEU from the now inactive breeder reactor in Aktau remains inadequately safeguarded in the region as plans for its down-blending have been delayed.

In the past two years, the United States and Russia have begun to work together to bring fresh and/or spent HEU fuel back to Russia, where the material has been blended down into non-weapons-usable low enriched uranium.

- In August 2002, in an operation known as "Project Vinca," approximately 48 kg of unirradiated HEU fuel was removed from a research reactor site at the Vinca Nuclear Institute, near Belgrade, and transported to the Research Institute of Atomic Reactors at Dmitrovgrad, Russia. The operation exemplified international cooperation to secure vulnerable material. Cooperation among the Serbian, Russian, and U.S. governments; the IAEA; and the Nuclear Threat Initiative (a nongovernmental organization that provided $5 million to the institute for environmental cleanup) made the project possible. Nonetheless, the operation took many months to implement. Many bureaucratic hurdles had to be surmounted in several countries,[147] and a large quantity of irradiated HEU remains at Vinca.[148]

- One year later, in September 2003, a similar HEU removal operation occurred in Romania. The Romanian, Russian, and U.S. governments worked together with the IAEA to remove 13.6 kg of fresh Soviet-origin 80 percent enriched uranium from the Pitesti

Institute for Nuclear Research, in Bucharest. Transport and security for the operation cost $400,000. In addition, the United States agreed to help pay for the conversion of the Pitesti reactor from HEU to low-enriched uranium fuel.[149]

- In December 2003, another cooperative repatriation effort airlifted 16.9 kg of unirradiated 36 percent enriched HEU from a decommissioned research reactor at the Institute of Nuclear Research and Nuclear Energetics outside of Sofia, Bulgaria, to secure storage at Dmitrovgrad.[150] The operation took six months of planning by Bulgarian, U.S., Russian, and IAEA officials and cost $440,000, paid by the United States.[151]

- In March 2004, Soviet-origin fresh HEU fuel was repatriated to Russia from Libya. The 88 fuel assemblies contained about 17 kg of 80 percent enriched uranium that had been stored at the Tajoura Nuclear Research Center near Tripoli. DOE provided $700,000 for the airlift operation. The IAEA checked and sealed the HEU cargo and reverified the contents when the material arrived at the All-Russian Scientific Research Institute of Atomic Reactors (VNIIAR) in Dmitrovgrad, Russia.[152]

- On May 26, 2004, Secretary of Energy Spencer Abraham launched the Global Threat Reduction Initiative (GTRI), which has the goal of repatriating all Soviet-origin fresh HEU fuel to Russia by the end of 2005. Moreover, DOE plans to work with Russia to repatriate all Soviet-origin spent nuclear fuel by 2010.[153]

- On May 27, 2004, the Department of Energy press office announced that "preparations are well advanced for the first shipment to Russia of irradiated fuel containing HEU from a research reactor in Tashkent, Uzbekistan."[154]

While the completed repatriation efforts addressed immediate material security concerns at high-risk sites, each project was a complex operation that required many months, and sometimes years, of planning and occasioned much controversy between responsible agencies in the U.S. and other governments.[155] Despite the importance of these initiatives, critics have pointed out that at the current rate of implementation, it could take decades to remove all the weapons-usable nuclear material from high-risk sites.

To codify the relationships that had evolved from the initial ad hoc operations in this sphere, on November 7, 2003, capping almost four years of negotiations, DOE and the Russian Ministry of Atomic Energy (now the Federal Agency for Atomic Energy) signed a formal agreement to repatriate Soviet-origin fresh and spent HEU fuel from Soviet-designed research reactors to Russia. In addition, Russia and the United States pledged to continue to work toward converting a number of these reactors from HEU to low-enriched uranium fuel and to develop jointly new fuels to address cases for which appropriate low-enriched uranium fuel alternatives do not currently exist.[156] As of the end of 2003, "twenty research reactors have been fully converted to LEU fuels outside of the United States," and within the United States, "eleven reactors have been fully converted."[157]

On May 27, 2004, DOE Secretary Abraham and Russian Nuclear Energy Agency head Rumyantsev signed an agreement that provided more specific details and target deadlines to the November 2003 accord. According to Nikolai Shingarev of the Russian Federal Agency for Nuclear Energy, 13 of the 17 countries holding Soviet-origin HEU have given their consent to removal of the HEU fuel, although it is very unlikely that specific plans to repatriate HEU from most of those states have been agreed upon.

One week prior to the launch of the GTRI, and consistent with its intent, the U.S. Senate passed legislation for a "global cleanout" program to focus on removing vulnerable nuclear materials throughout the world. Adopted as an amendment to the fiscal year 2005 Defense Authorization Act, the legislation would permit the president of the United States to establish a task force at DOE, providing it with the authority to secure, remove, and dispose of fissile and radiological materials from vulnerable locations around the globe. The amendment also would require DOE to submit a report to Congress identifying the highest priority sites and developing a comprehensive action plan for securing and/or removing dangerous materials.[158] As of this writing, a Senate and House conference committee is conferring on the 2005 Defense Authorization Act.

Concerning the amount of money devoted to the GTRI, Secretary Abraham stated that the U.S. government plans to dedicate more than $450 million. He specified that this "should be more than sufficient to complete the U.S. Foreign Research Reactor Spent Fuel Return, the Russian Research Reactor Fuel Return efforts and to also fund the conversion of all targeted U.S. and Russian supplied research reactor cores under the Reduced Enrichment for Research and Test Reactors (RERTR) program." However, he then noted that more funds will be needed along with "heightened international cooperation—to finish the job."[159] Despite the promise of substantial funding, it was reported that little of this money will be available soon. "In the coming 18 months, about $20 million will be added to existing programs, an amount likely to reach $60 million in peak years."[160]

Like Russia, the United States has supplied numerous research reactors and test assembly facilities with nuclear fuel over past decades. On November 6, 2003, Secretary of Energy Abraham announced at a press conference that about half of the U.S.-origin HEU supplied to other states has been repatriated, mainly under the auspices of the DOE's Foreign Research Reactor Spent Nuclear Fuel Acceptance Program, which began in 1996 and opened a ten-year window for 41 countries to return to the United States spent nuclear fuel containing HEU. He also said that the United States will continue to supply the remaining facilities with HEU fuel, in accordance with a 1992 U.S. law known as the Schumer Amendment. Under that law, the United States is prohibited from exporting HEU to specific research reactors unless its operators have agreed to convert that reactor to low-enriched uranium once such fuels are available for the specific unit.[161]

The United States is still seeking to repatriate U.S.-origin HEU supplied to dozens of other countries, according to a February 2004 audit by the DOE Inspector General. The audit found, "As of August 2003, the Department [of Energy] was likely to recover only about half of the approximately 5,200 kilograms of HEU covered by the [Foreign Research Reactor Spent Nuclear Fuel] Acceptance Program. Moreover, there was no effort to recover an additional 12,300 kilograms of HEU dispersed to foreign countries which was not included in the Acceptance Program." Identified impediments to recovery of the HEU include the voluntary nature of the program, the view of many countries that the program "was costly and disruptive," and the fact that responsibility for administering the program resides with DOE's Environmental Management office, which is not charged with advancing U.S. nonproliferation goals. The Inspector General recommended that the "Under Secretary, Energy, Science, and Environment work, with the Administrator, NNSA, to determine:

1. Whether aspects of HEU recovery could be more effectively managed by NNSA [the National Nuclear Security Administration, a component of the Department of Energy responsible for implementing DOE nonproliferation programs];
2. Whether the Acceptance Program should be expanded to include all outstanding HEU produced in the U.S. and dispersed to foreign countries;
3. Whether improvements to the program can be made to encourage greater foreign participation; and,
4. Responsibility for the ultimate disposal of HEU in the U.S.

Responding to the Inspector General's report, DOE stated that it "plans to place a priority on accepting eligible material from reactors and countries where the material—whether HEU or low enriched uranium—may pose environmental or proliferation risks."[162] More specifically, on May 26, 2004, Secretary of Energy Abraham stated that as part of the Global Threat Reduction Initiative, DOE "will take all steps necessary to accelerate and complete the repatriation of all U.S.-origin research reactor spent fuel under our existing program from locations around the world within a decade."[163] He also announced that in order to facilitate the implementation of this and other GTRI tasks, he would establish a single organization within DOE's National Nuclear Security Administration to focus exclusively on these efforts.

Fissile Material Security in Other Settings

As suggested earlier, fissile materials are found in hundreds of locations around the globe under varying levels of security. Although the risks posed by these materials are greatest in the settings just described, their presence in many other contexts also creates potential targets for terrorists. Without offering a comprehensive analysis, here, it is worth briefly noting some of these other venues where the materials can be found, and where the need for high security is essential.

Nuclear Weapon Programs outside Russia and Pakistan

All nuclear weapon programs must produce, process, and machine fissile materials, steps that often also involve their transportation among different sites. In many cases, nuclear testing also involves the transportation of fissile materials to test sites, where they are assembled into test devices. In addition, fissile materials are used in nuclear weapon research activities, which may involve still other locations and transportation links. For countries reducing their nuclear arsenals, comparable challenges can arise as materials are removed from weapons and stored, in some cases after additional processing. Each of these settings demands the highest levels of security against theft and diversion. In states with smaller nuclear arsenals—China, France, Great Britain, India, Israel, North Korea, and Pakistan—this challenge is inherently more manageable than for the United States and Russia because of the smaller scale of activities involved. Nonetheless, in less-developed states, underlying weaknesses in national infrastructure—e.g., in rail and highway transportation systems, in communications, and in the level of guard force education and training—may erode security efforts

Even in the United States, where security over fissile materials is generally deemed to be very stringent and where the issue has received added attention since September 11, 2001, evidence has emerged indicating that serious deficiencies may exist at some facilities within the U.S. nuclear weapons complex. In November 2003, *Vanity Fair* magazine quoted Richard Levernier, who had run security intrusion exercises for the U.S. government for six years, regarding pre-9/11 security gaps that have still be to corrected. "In more than 50 percent of our tests of the Los Alamos facility," he stated, "we got in, captured the plutonium, got out again, and in some cases didn't fire a shot because we didn't encounter any guards."[164] In April 2000, responding to internal DOE reports of these findings, then-Secretary of Energy Bill Richardson ordered that "all weapons-grade materials be removed from T.A. 18 [the Technical Area at Los Alamos where the repeated mock attacks occurred] and delivered to the Nevada Test Site by 2003."[165] None of T.A. 18's weapons-grade material had been relocated as of the November 2003 *Vanity Fair* exposé, however. Levernier has also charged that DOE has not factored suicide attacks into its design basis threat planning. DOE issued such a security planning upgrade in May 2003, but "it is not scheduled to take full effect until 2009."[166] The GAO had criticized the new DBT, which the organization found to be less demanding that those assessed by other U.S. government experts.[167]

Doubts have also been raised about lax security at the Y-12 National Security Complex at Oak Ridge National Laboratory, where large quantities of HEU for U.S. nuclear weapons are stored and processed. Representative Christopher Shays (R-Connecticut), Chairman of the House Subcommittee on National Security, Emerging Threats, and International Relations, said in 2003, "My concerns about Los Alamos…pale in comparison to the Y-12 facility at Oak Ridge, Tennessee. This is a very vulnerable site. [It has] too many structures and not enough buffer zone [around it]."[168] Shays' concerns over Y-12 proved well-founded. A DOE report released in January 2004 stated that in several security drills at Y-12, protective forces failed to prevent the theft of more than enough HEU to assemble an IND. The results of other drills were "tainted and unreliable" because protective forces were given access to computer models of simulated attacks before they were carried out.[169] However, three DOE nuclear facilities have received high scores on security. These sites are Argonne National Laboratory-West, the Pantex Plant, and the Savannah River Site.[170]

In May 2004, Secretary of Energy Abraham announced that the fissile material stored at T.A. 18 would be transferred to a highly secure facility, that increased security at Y-12 will be considered, and that the DOE would further refine its DBT to recognize a higher level of potential terrorist capabilities. The implementation of the first and second measures is expected to take many months, and the measures to meet a new DBT may take five years or more.[171]

Naval Propulsion Systems

Several navies power ships with HEU. About 170 nuclear-powered vessels (including submarines, naval surface ships, and civilian vessels) are currently operational, all of which use pressurized-water reactors (PWRs) for propulsion. All U.S. and British nuclear ships, including submarines, use HEU fuel enriched to 93.5 percent U-235. French ballistic missile nuclear-powered submarines and France's single nuclear-powered aircraft carrier use HEU fuel enriched to 90 percent, while French attack nuclear-powered submarines (SSNs) use LEU fuel enriched to 7 percent. China, alone among the world's nuclear navies, uses only LEU fuel for its naval reactors, probably enriched between 3 percent and 5 percent. The nuclear submarine planned by India is likely to use nuclear fuel similar in enrichment to that of many Russian submarines, probably around 20 percent.[172]

Weapons-quality HEU used in the navies noted above is located not only at naval fueling areas, but also at sites where the HEU is produced, in fuel fabrication plants, and in transit to nuclear submarine bases. In addition, spent fuel, which may contain uranium enriched to 80 percent or more, is found at storage sites and in transit to those locations. No cases have been reported outside of Russia involving thefts of, or illicit trafficking in, naval fuel. Nonetheless, Russia's experience—including the concerns of Russian Navy officers that led them to seek U.S. help in securing Russian nuclear submarine fuel—highlight the potential dangers in this sphere.

Plutonium in Civil Nuclear Power Programs and HEU in Non-Military Research Reactors in Industrially Advanced Countries

Until the late 1970s, it was widely assumed among nuclear energy planners that global uranium resources would be rapidly depleted and that it would be necessary to use plutonium, in the form of MOX fuel, as an alternative to LEU fuel in most nuclear power programs. Because of slower-than-expected growth of nuclear power and the continuing discovery of new economically exploitable uranium reserves, however, uranium supplies have remained abundant, while the costs of producing MOX fuel have increased significantly. These economic factors, together with concerns over the proliferation dangers posed by the widespread use of plutonium fuels, have led most nuclear power using states to abandon such separation and "recycling" of plutonium, in favor of the "once-through fuel cycle," in which spent nuclear power plant fuel is stored on an interim basis until emplaced in a permanent storage facility, usually planned for a stable geologic formation.[173]

For a variety of reasons, however, as noted in an earlier section of this chapter, several states continue to pursue plutonium separation for civil nuclear energy purposes, most notably France, Great Britain, Russia, and Japan. Of these, however, only France has a successful recycle program that balances supply (newly separated plutonium) with demand (the fabrication and use of MOX fuel). Great Britain has no domestic program for using MOX fuel, and its plutonium is stored after separation. Russia likewise has no domestic MOX program for civil plutonium. Although it stores spent fuel from its VVER-1000 reactors and RBMK units, it continues to reprocess spent fuel from VVER-440 reactors and store the resulting plutonium.[174] Japan has contracted with France and Great Britain for the reprocessing of Japanese spent fuel; although Japan has a program for using the resulting plutonium as MOX in its nuclear power reactors, that program has been virtually frozen because of domestic opposition and other challenges. As a result, separated Japanese plutonium continues to accumulate in France and Great Britain, without certainty that it will ever be used. Notwithstanding this accumulation of tens of metric tons of separated plutonium awaiting use in these countries, Japan has continued to work on a large-scale plutonium separation facility at Rokkasho-mura, which was scheduled to open in July 2006. However, concerns over the cost of the project have resulted in delays, leading to substantial uncertainty over when the facility will reprocess commercial spent fuel.[175] Once approved for operation, the facility could process about 800 metric tons of spent fuel annually, separating up to 7 tons of plutonium each year.

India also separates plutonium from spent nuclear power plant fuel. Its nuclear industry's plan calls for the use of the plutonium in advanced breeder reactors. Usually powered by fuel containing about 20 percent plutonium, breeder reactors use excess power to irradiate additional uranium, thereby "breeding" new plutonium. Although Russia, India, and Japan still have plans for commercializing this technology, only Russia currently operates a commercial-scale fast neutron reactor, the BN-600, and it has resumed construction of a larger version, the BN-800.

Table 4.3 highlights the impact of these activities. From 1999 through 2002 (the latest year for which complete figures are available from the IAEA), separated plutonium stocks in Great Britain, Japan, and Russia increased by 14 metric tons, from 162.5 metric tons to 176.6 metric tons, enough material to produce about 1,700 weapons (assuming 8 kg of plutonium per weapon and some fabrication losses)—more than the combined arsenals of all of the nuclear weapon states other than Russia and the United States. This sizeable accumulation of separated plutonium, for which in most cases there is no planned use, stands in sharp contrast to extensive and costly Russian, G-8, and U.S. efforts to eliminate fissile materials in other settings.

Regarding HEU use in research reactors in advanced countries, as discussed above, the United States and Russia are working actively to reduce the use of HEU in research reactors they have previously exported (or to which they have provided fuel) and to repatriate and eliminate fresh and spent HEU fuels from these locations. In addition, both countries are gradually reducing the use of HEU fuels at home. Nonetheless, for years to come, more than a dozen major research reactors, located mostly in G-8 countries (including the EU), will continue to use HEU fuels. The list includes several, such as the Petten High Flux Reactor (HFR) in the Netherlands, that have formally agreed to switch to low-enriched fuels once they are available, as well as a number that are likely to use HEU fuels indefinitely because of the unique research and/or isotope production these facilities support. Resisting the trend toward converting research reactors to low-enriched fuel, the German FRM-II reactor in Munich has been designed to use weapons-grade HEU fuel. The reactor owners have agreed to reduce the enrichment to 50 percent by December 2010, but meanwhile, the reactor will use bomb-grade HEU.[176] Table 4.7 lists the reactors of greatest concern in industrially advanced states with respect to the demand for high-quality HEU fuel and the continuance of commerce in this fuel.

Leaving aside whether the continued use of HEU by the group of reactors in Table 4.7 is justified—a matter that has been the subject of considerable debate in many cases—these facilities, which often have substantial inventories of HEU and are sometimes located in relatively open research centers, require the highest levels of security. With these concerns in mind, the United States Nuclear Regulatory Commission has increased security requirements at research reactors in the United States since September 11, 2001.[177] However, as discussed in Chapter 5, concerns remain that more needs to be done to protect these facilities against nuclear terrorist attack or sabotage. It is also noteworthy that the United States is trying to purchase HEU from Russia for use in U.S. research reactors, a two-edged arrangement that reduces HEU stocks in Russia, but facilitates the continued use of such material in U.S. research reactors at a time when both countries are urging other states to convert to less dangerous LEU fuels. The Fiscal Year 2003 Omnibus Bill passed by Congress provided up to $14 million for DOE to direct toward this activity.[178] As of May 2004, negotiations over the potential purchase have not been successful, but there is still interest in the U.S. government to pursue an agreement.[179]

Given the vast quantities of fissile materials in all of the foregoing settings—Russia, Pakistan, Russian- or U.S.-supported research reactors around the globe, the nuclear weapon programs of the other nuclear-armed states, marine propulsion systems, and plutonium and HEU found in civilian nuclear programs—it appears that would-be nuclear terrorists, intent on acquiring material for an IND, enjoy a "target-rich environment."[180]

PREVENTION, ENFORCEMENT, AND RESPONSE MECHANISMS

The foregoing sections have reviewed the potential vulnerabilities of HEU and plutonium worldwide to terrorist acquisition. In doing so, they have highlighted numerous, "nuclear-specific" initiatives to reduce

TABLE 4.7
RESEARCH REACTORS IN INDUSTRIALLY ADVANCED STATES WITH GREATEST DEMAND FOR HEU

State	Reactor	Enrichment (% U-235)	Power (MW)	Fuel Supplier
Australia	HIFAR	60	10	USA, UK
Belgium	BR-2	74-93	100	USA
Canada	MAPLE-1	93	10	USA
Canada	MAPLE-2	93	10	USA
China	HFETR	90	125	China
France	HFR	93	58.3	USA
France	ORPHEE	93	14	USA
Germany	FRM-II	93	20	USA, Russia
Germany	FRJ-2	80-93	23	USA
Netherlands	HFR	20-93	45	USA
Russia	MIR-M1	90	100	Russia
Russia	SM-3	90	100	Russia
Russia	WWR-M	90	18	Russia
Russia	IVV-2M	90	15	Russia
Russia	RBT-10/2	63	10	Russia
South Africa	SAFARI	87-93	20	South Africa
USA	HFIR	93	85	USA
USA	ATR	93	250	USA
USA	MURR	93	10	USA
USA	MITR-2	93	5-10	USA
USA	NBSR	93	20	USA

Source: Alexander Glaser and Frank von Hippel, "On the Importance of Ending the Use of HEU in the Nuclear Fuel Cycle: An Updated Assessment," Paper presented at the 2002 International Meeting on Reduced Enrichment for Research and Test Reactors, November 3-8, 2002; "Research Reactors," World Nuclear Association, August 2003, available at <http://www.world-nuclear.org/info/printable_information_papers/inf61print.htm>, accessed on May 27, 2004; Oleg Bukharin, Christopher Ficek, and Michael Roston, "U.S.-Russian Reduced Enrichment for Research and Test Reactors (RERTR) Cooperation," RANSAC Policy Update, Summer 2002; Robert L. Civiak, *Closing the Gaps: Securing High Enriched Uranium in the Former Soviet Union and Eastern Europe*, Report for the Federation of American Scientists, May 2002; Kenley Butler, "Russia: Research Reactor Table," Center for Nonproliferation Studies, updated on April 11, 2002, available at <http://www.nti.org/db/nisprofs/russia/tables/rurestab.htm>, accessed on January 22, 2004.

this threat, including U.S. programs to help secure, consolidate, and eliminate Russian fissile materials; to secure Pakistani nuclear materials more effectively; and to reduce, by various means, the dangers posed by the dispersion of fissile materials in other diverse areas.

As noted throughout this volume, however, securing, consolidating, and eliminating nuclear assets embody only one dimension of a comprehensive strategy to reduce the threat of nuclear terrorism. Virtually all of the mechanisms noted in Chapter 3 that are being brought to bear to prevent terrorists from acquiring and using an intact nuclear weapon would also contribute to U.S. efforts, and those by other concerned states, to block terrorist manufacture and use of an IND. Consequently, this chapter will not revisit the law enforcement, intelligence capabilities, border security, and consequence management issues covered in Chapter 3. Instead, the discussion will be limited to measures specific to safeguarding fissile material.

International Standards for Protecting Fissile Material

Much work remains to be done in establishing standards for effective physical security over fissile materials. Practices vary significantly from nation to nation, and the voluntary guidelines of the IAEA, known as INFCIRC/225, are so vague that some states have been able to comply without requiring that the guards protecting fissile material be armed.[181] Among other shortcomings, the guidelines do not specify the threat that sites holding fissile materials must protect against. Although those guidelines are incorporated into the 1980 Convention on the Physical Protection of Nuclear Materials (CPPNM), that instrument extends only to nuclear materials in international transit, not to the protection of fissile materials within states. In 1998, the United States proposed that the CPPNM be amended to broaden its scope to require rigorous physical protection standards within states, but the parties to the convention have yet to make much headway. The 44-member Nuclear Suppliers Group (NSG) requires the application of INFCIRC/225 to all items group members export to other states, but the vagueness of the standards undercuts the effectiveness of this rule.[182]

In April 2004, seeking to intensify international controls over activities that could contribute to WMD proliferation and terrorism, the UN Security Council unanimously adopted Resolution 1540. Adopted under Article VII of the UN Charter to address a threat to international peace and security, the resolution is legally binding on all UN member states. The key provisions of the resolution relevant to WMD terrorism state that the UN Security Council

1. Decides that all States shall refrain from providing any form of support to non-State actors that attempt to develop, acquire, manufacture, possess, transport, transfer or use nuclear, chemical or biological weapons and their means of delivery;

2. Decides also that all States, in accordance with their national procedures, shall adopt and enforce appropriate effective laws which prohibit any non-State actor to manufacture, acquire, possess, develop, transport, transfer or use nuclear, chemical or biological weapons and their means of delivery, in particular for terrorist purposes, as well as attempts to engage in any of the foregoing activities, participate in them as an accomplice, assist or finance them;

3. Decides also that all States shall take and enforce effective measures to establish domestic controls to prevent the proliferation of nuclear, chemical, or biological weapons and their means of delivery, including by establishing appropriate controls over related materials and to this end shall:

(a) Develop and maintain appropriate effective measures to account for and secure such items in production, use, storage or transport;

(b) Develop and maintain appropriate effective physical protection measures;

(c) Develop and maintain appropriate effective border controls and law enforcement efforts to detect, deter, prevent and combat, including through international cooperation when necessary, the illicit trafficking and brokering in such items in accordance with their national legal authorities and legislation and consistent with international law....[183]

The resolution goes on to state that member countries will need to implement domestic legislation, if they do not already have this in place, to implement these requirements and provides for a report to be made to the council in two years reviewing the progress that has been made in this regard. Unfortunately, the council's action does not set specific standards, leaving open the possibility that states will adopt weak controls that fall far short of what is needed.

PRIORITY ISSUES

Attempting to manufacture an IND and detonating it in a major city in the United States or elsewhere would pose very difficult challenges for any terrorist organization, and very few would have the motivation, financial and organizational resources, and technical capabilities to do so. Each of the key steps—obtaining fissile material, designing and fabricating the IND, and transporting it or its components to the target—is demanding in its own right, and all the steps together may prove insurmountable for the vast majority of, but not necessarily all, terrorist organizations. At each step, countermeasures are already in place to thwart the attempt, but, as shown, in key instances, these countermeasures remain weak and need to be strengthened. In order to do so, national governments and relevant international organizations should undertake a number of immediate steps designed to (1) pursue an HEU-first strategy with respect to Russia; (2) secure, consolidate, and eliminate HEU globally; (3) focus on the South and Central Asian peril; and (4) promote the adoption of stringent global security standards.

1. *Pursue an HEU-first strategy.* Because of the relative ease of construction of an IND with HEU, U.S. and international nonproliferation assistance programs in Russia should implement an HEU-first strategy that would secure, consolidate, and down-blend all excess stocks of HEU before disposing of weapons-grade plutonium as reactor fuel. Specifically, priority should be given to (1) the acceleration of down-blending of Russian HEU to a non-weapons-usable enrichment level, and (2) the use of the recently opened high-security Mayak Fissile Material Storage Facility for the storage of up to 200 tons of HEU.

2. *Secure, consolidate, and/or eliminate HEU globally.* Significant quantities of fissile materials exist in Russia and globally that are not needed,

are not in use, and in many instances are not subject to adequate safeguards. From the standpoint of nuclear terrorism, the risk is most pronounced with respect to stockpiles of HEU in dozens of countries. It is imperative to secure, consolidate, and, when possible, eliminate these HEU stocks. *The principle should be one in which fewer countries retain HEU, fewer facilities within countries possess HEU, and fewer buildings within those facilities have HEU present.* Important components of a policy guided by this principle include conversion of research reactors to run on low-enriched uranium, rapid repatriation of all U.S.- and Soviet/Russian-origin HEU (both fresh and irradiated), international legal prohibitions of exports of HEU-fueled research and power reactors, and down-blending of existing stocks of HEU to LEU. A policy to accomplish these objectives must be informed by an understanding of the significant bureaucratic, technical, economic, political, and national security impediments to HEU consolidation and elimination, and the development of compelling incentives to overcome these obstacles.

3. *Focus on the South and Central Asian peril.* The international community should be more attentive to the nuclear terrorism danger with respect to INDs in South and Central Asia, a zone where Islamic militant groups are active and where the risk of their gaining access to nuclear materials—especially from unreliable elements within the Pakistani establishment or from certain vulnerable sites in Kazakhstan and Uzbekistan—is highest. It is of urgent importance, therefore, to remove the relatively small, but nuclear terrorism- and proliferation-significant, quantity of fissile material from Central Asia, and to enhance Pakistani fissile material protection, control, and accounting. Means to accomplish the former objective are identified in the preceding paragraph; the latter objective should be pursued by maximizing, consistent with the requirements of the NPT, the sharing of unclassified technology to help Pakistan se-

curely manage its nuclear assets. The United States and other NPT-recognized nuclear weapon states also should develop contingency plans, possibly involving the use of nuclear recovery teams or specialized military forces for recovery of Pakistani fissile materials whose diversion is detected. The fissile material that terrorists might obtain could well require processing and machining before use in an IND, providing time for active recovery operations to succeed. Terrorists would likely set up processing units and related facilities for designing an IND and fabricating its non-nuclear components in advance of the acquisition and completion of a workable IND. Targeted surveillance and intelligence gathering to identify such preparatory activities in their incipiency should be an essential element of the U.S. strategy to disrupt terrorist plans to develop an IND from Pakistani fissile materials. Given limitations of U.S. intelligence, under most circumstances such surveillance, protection, and recovery efforts would require the cooperation of knowledgeable Pakistani authorities.[184]

4. *Promote adoption of stringent, global security standards.* Renewed efforts are required to establish binding international standards for the physical protection of fissile material. An important means to accomplish that objective is to amend the Convention on the Physical Protection of Nuclear Material to make it applicable to civilian nuclear material in domestic storage, use, and transport. Ideally, the amendment would oblige parties to provide protection comparable to that recommended in INFCIRC 225/Rev 4 and to report to the IAEA on the adoption of measures to bring national obligations into conformity with the amendment. However, because amending the convention is likely to require an extended negotiation, it is desirable for as many like-minded states as possible to agree immediately to meet a stringent material protection standard, which should apply to all civilian and military HEU.

Box 4.1

**SUMMARY OF U.S. PROGRAMS IN RUSSIA TO SECURE, CONSOLIDATE, AND
ELIMINATE WEAPONS-USABLE FISSILE MATERIALS**

Two U.S. programs are focused on providing assistance in securing fissile materials: the Material Protection, Control, and Accounting (MPC&A) program, implemented by the U.S. Department of Energy, [185] and the construction of the Mayak Fissile Material Storage Facility, a U.S. Department of Defense program. The former program provides equipment and training to upgrade security at existing sites of the Russian Federal Agency of Atomic Energy housing fissile materials, while the latter is intended to provide a highly secure location for plutonium (and eventually HEU) taken from dismantled Russian nuclear weapons.

Both programs are progressing but will require many years before completion. The MPC&A program has provided at least "rapid upgrades" of security on 43 percent of Russian weapons-grade fissile material and has completed "comprehensive upgrades" on 22 percent of the total stocks. [186] Rapid upgrades include relatively simple measures, such as replacing wooden doors with steel ones, bricking up windows, installing metal detectors for personnel, and hardening guard stations; comprehensive upgrades include more elaborate measures, including perimeter security sensors and material accounting systems. The DOE hopes to complete all of this work by the end of 2008. Much of the remaining work is at defense-related sites, where Russia has been slow to grant access to U.S. security experts, but where the underlying security arrangements are thought to be more effective than at sites performing purely civilian work. The DOD-sponsored Mayak Fissile Material Storage Facility was commissioned at the end of 2003 and is supposed to begin loading weapons-grade plutonium at the rate of two tons per year; thus, more than a decade will be required to complete the securing of 50 tons of plutonium in this installation.

In parallel with these efforts, the United States supports three programs to eliminate Russian fissile material. Under the HEU Purchase Agreement, over the course of twenty years, Russia is to blend down 500 metric tons of weapons-quality highly enriched uranium into LEU suitable for use as nuclear power plant fuel, which will then no longer be usable for nuclear weapons. The blended-down material is to be purchased by the United States Enrichment Corporation (USEC), for some $12 billion. USEC, a private concern, serves as the U.S. government's executive agent for the arrangement. As of early 2004, the HEU Purchase Agreement has resulted in the blending down of about 200 metric tons of Russian HEU, and for each of the next 10 years, an additional 30 metric tons will be transformed into reactor fuel, reducing Russia's total inventory of HEU accordingly.[187] The MPC&A program is undertaking a smaller, parallel effort helping Russia consolidate and then eliminate unneeded HEU fuel from research sites throughout the former Soviet Union and Eastern Europe; the material is brought to two nuclear facilities (Luch and Dimitrovgrad) and blended down to LEU suitable for subsequent use in modified research reactor fuels. By the end of 2003, the program had eliminated 4.3 tons of HEU.

As these programs unfold, Russia continues to produce *new* quantities of fissile material, for which it currently has no obvious need. DOE has taken over as the executive agent for the program on Elimination of Weapons-Grade Plutonium Production, which will assist Russia in shutting down its three remaining plutonium production reactors: one at Zheleznogorsk and two at Seversk, which together produce 1.2 metric tons of weapons plutonium annually, material that must be separated because the spent fuel containing it cannot be stored without corroding.[188] Russia has pledged not to use this plutonium in weapons, and the United States verifies this commitment by periodically sending teams of experts to Russia. The reactors cannot be shut down because they supply essential heat and electricity to the cities where they are located. The United States has agreed to underwrite the refurbishment and construction of fossil fuel plants in these cities to provide an alternative source of heat and power. After this activity has been accomplished, in exchange, Russia has promised to shut down these reactors. As of early 2004, the projected date of final shutdown was 2008 for the Seversk reactors and 2011 for the Zheleznogorsk reactor.[189]

In addition, Russia is accumulating separated plutonium at a rate of more than 1 metric ton annually by reprocessing spent fuel from its VVER-440 nuclear power plants. Russia has no planned use for this plutonium,[190] which though not of the quality used in Russian nuclear weapons, is usable for nuclear arms and could be employed by terrorists to manufacture an improvised nuclear device or a radiological dispersion device. Spent fuel from these reactors could be stored without corrosion, just as Russia stores the spent fuel from its more modern VVER-1000 nuclear power reactors. There is no U.S. or international program aimed at terminating this activity.[191]

DOE also manages the Russian Surplus Fissile Materials Disposition Program, commonly known as the Plutonium Disposition program, to facilitate implementation of the September 2000 Plutonium Management and Disposition Agreement, under which the U.S. and Russia will each dispose of 34 tons of excess weapons-grade plutonium by immobilization or utilization in MOX fuel. Because the Russian Federation considers plutonium to be a valuable fuel resource, it wants to pursue only the MOX fuel disposition option. The plan, as of early 2004, is to burn Russian MOX fuel in Russia's VVER-1000 reactors (the most modern Russian commercial nuclear plants) and possibly in Russia's BN-600 fast-neutron reactor. Moreover, there are possible plans to use some Russian MOX in other countries' nuclear reactors. In January 2002, the Bush administration decided on an all-MOX approach for the U.S. excess weapons-grade plutonium.[192] The estimated costs for the program are $2 billion in Russia and $3.8 billion in the United States. To date, Western donors have not raised the money needed to pay for the Russian part of the program. Another major impediment is the deadlock in reaching a nuclear liability agreement acceptable to both sides. In February 2004, the U.S. government announced another delay when the start of construction of the MOX fuel factory in South Carolina was moved back to May 2005.[193] This program, still in its formative stage and with both sides struggling over a liability agreement, might introduce its first MOX fuel into a Russian nuclear power plant in 2008 and will continue for some 17 years thereafter.

In parallel to pursuing repatriation of HEU to Russia, the DOE has encouraged the development of technologies that would allow an alternate disposition route for research reactor fuel and spent fuel assemblies containing HEU. The alternate path would involve down-blending the HEU at the research reactor site. At least two groups based in the United States are known to have researched portable down-blending systems to accomplish this task. A research team, including Westinghouse Savannah River Company and Argonne National Laboratory-West, has developed the Mobile Melt Dilute (MMD) technique. "The MMD process simply melts the HEU fuel assemblies and dilutes the alloy to less than 20 percent isotopic content using depleted uranium metal or alloy. After processing, the sealed canister containing the solidified non-weapons grade aluminum-uranium ingot can be placed in interim storage pending reprocessing or emplacement into long-term storage using any proven storage technology."[194] Another research group at BWX Technologies has developed the Portable Downblending System (PDS). Like the MMD approach, the PDS can be quickly loaded onto a standard transport container and shipped to almost any part of the world to begin rapid down-blending of HEU at remote sites. BWX Technologies' method can either use a wet or a dry down-blending process.[195]

The U.S. and Russian Federation efforts described above have devoted government resources to both weapons-usable HEU and plutonium security and disposition. Keeping track of the complexity of these programs is a challenging endeavor. Many U.S. government programs have overlapped and at times competed with each other within regions in Russia.[196] A detailed analysis of this management issue is beyond the scope of this book, and only the governments of the United States and Russia have access to the complete set of information needed for such an assessment.

[1] A metric ton is 1,000 kilograms. As detailed elsewhere, Russia dilutes about 30 tons of HEU annually to make it unsuitable for weapons use and separates some 3 metric tons of plutonium each year, while also fabricating large quantities of HEU fuel for marine propulsion reactors.

[2] Under the best of circumstances, facilities handling bulk fissile materials anticipate a measurement uncertainty of 0.5 percent. Thus, for every metric ton of plutonium or HEU (1,000 kg) that a facility processes, its managers would expect to be unable to account for 5 kg of the material and might not detect diversions below this threshold.

[3] William C. Potter and Elena Sokova, "Illicit Nuclear Trafficking in the NIS: What's New? What's True?" *Nonproliferation Review* 9 (Summer 2002), pp. 112-120.

[4] The 20 percent enrichment level was a political decision and was not based on a law of physics that determines what type of uranium is usable in a nuclear bomb. A February 2003 news article (Peter Eisler, "Fuel for Nuclear Weapons is More Widely Available," *USA Today,* February 26, 2003) reminded readers that even uranium enriched to less than 20 percent in uranium-235 could, in principle, be used for weapons. The article reports, "Five years ago, U.S. scientists at Los Alamos National Laboratory secretly designed an atomic bomb with low-enriched uranium....The bomb, which could have fit easily in a small pickup, was weak in nuclear terms but strong enough to destroy a square mile of a city." Bombs can be made with 19 percent, 18 percent, or 17 percent enriched uranium, but these weapons would be more complex and much heavier than a simple gun-type assembly made with much more highly enriched material. Low-enriched uranium, such as material enriched 3-5 percent, employed in commercial light-water reactor fuel cannot be used as is, without further enrichment, in a nuclear weapon. The true physics cutoff is 6.9 percent enrichment, below which the critical mass goes to infinity. Even an IND produced with LEU just below 20 percent enrichment would be massive. For "low-enriched" material at 19.9 percent enrichment, the bare critical mass for a bomb is about 800 kg. Thus, it is extremely unlikely that terrorist groups would obtain enough of this type of material to turn it directly into an IND. Further enrichment would probably be needed.

[5] Some fast breeder reactor designs, such as the Russian BN-600, use HEU. However, only one of these types of reactors is operating as of early 2004, and nearly all commercial power reactors use LEU fuel.

[6] J. Carson Mark, "Explosive Properties of Reactor-Grade Plutonium," *Science & Global Security* 4 (1993), p. 113.

[7] Depleted uranium, by definition, is less enriched in U-235 than is natural uranium, which has an enrichment of 0.7 percent U-235. As a rule, MOX fuel recycles reactor-grade plutonium obtained by reprocessing spent nuclear power reactor fuel. However, the United States and Russia have established a joint program under which they have each declared 34 tons of military plutonium to be in excess of their defense needs and have agreed to dispose of this material by using it to produce MOX fuel, which will be used in nuclear power reactors. Through this process, the military plutonium will be effectively transformed into reactor-grade plutonium, making it unsuitable for use in U.S. and Russian nuclear weapons (which have been designed assuming the use of military plutonium), and the material will be rendered less usable by terrorists because it will be contained in highly radioactive spent fuel.

[8] As noted earlier, the International Atomic Energy Agency defines the significant quantities of fissile material as 25 kg of weapons-grade HEU equivalent and 8 kg of plutonium. These values set the scale for the amounts of fissile material that are needed to form a nuclear weapon roughly equivalent in explosive power to the Hiroshima and Nagasaki bombs. Technically sophisticated nuclear weapon states are able to build nuclear

weapons of this explosive power with less fissile material employing at least as low as 3 to 4 kg of plutonium. According to an analysis by the Natural Resources Defense Council (NRDC), "The IAEA persists in using SQ [significant quantities] values that are outdated, technically erroneous, and even dangerous in light of the recent [early to mid-1990s] seizures of kilogram quantities of stolen Russian nuclear materials for sale on the black market, and the persistent reports of large accounting discrepancies at plutonium production facilities intended for peaceful use." The NRDC called for the IAEA to reduce the significant quantities by eightfold; Thomas B. Cochran and Christopher E. Paine, "The Amount of Plutonium and Highly-Enriched Uranium Needed for Pure Fission Nuclear Weapons," NRDC, April 13, 1995.

[9] It is believed that China stopped producing plutonium for weapons around 1991. David Wright and Lisbeth Gronlund, "Estimating China's Production of Plutonium for Weapons," *Science & Global Security* 11 (2003), pp. 61-80 and references 23 and 31 therein. Wright and Gronlund estimated that China produced between 2 to 5 tons of weapons-grade plutonium.

[10] Russia has pledged not to use this material for nuclear weapons pursuant to an agreement with the United States, under which the United States is to assist Russia in closing down its military plutonium production reactors. See Agreement between the Government of the United States of America and the Government of the Russian Federation Concerning Cooperation Regarding Plutonium Production Reactors, September 23, 1997, Article IV. The U.S. government periodically sends monitoring teams to Russia to ensure that this provision is upheld.

[11] Reprocessing of Japanese nuclear power plant fuel has been performed principally in France and Great Britain. The resulting plutonium is either stored in these countries or is being processed into MOX fuel for shipment back to Japan. In parallel, Japan is constructing its own commercial scale reprocessing facility at Rokkasho-mura.

[12] Israel's possession of a uranium enrichment capability has never been confirmed. North Korea is known to have acquired key technology for uranium enrichment from the A.Q. Khan network, discussed later in the text, but the status of its program and whether it has produced HEU is not known.

[13] U.S. Enrichment Corporation, Press Release, January 14, 2004, "USEC, TENEX Mark 10th Anniversary of Megatons to Megawatts Program," <http://www.usec.com/v2001_02/Content/News/NewsTemplate.asp?page=/v2001_02/Content/News/NewsFiles/01-14-04a.htm>, accessed on April 13, 2004; Charles Yulish, "Status Report on the Megatons to Megawatts Program," comments to the NEI Nuclear Fuel Supply Forum, January 19, 2000, <http://www.usec.com/v2001_02/Content/News/NewsTemplate.asp?page=/v2001_02/Content/News/Speeches/01-19-00.htm>, accessed on April 13, 2004. Since first down-blending under the program in 1995, a total of 201 metric tons of HEU, enough for 8,000 nuclear weapons, have been transformed into LEU. Several observers have called for accelerating the rate of HEU blend-down. See Matthew Bunn and Anthony Wier, "Faster Pace Needed on Uranium Removal," *Boston Globe*, September 23, 2003, p. A19. Bunn and Wier advocate creating an incentives program to encourage the repatriation of HEU from the reactor facilities. In one case, the incentive could be to provide assistance in converting the reactor to low-enriched fuels. In another, the incentive could involve helping to clean up spent fuel and nuclear waste at the reactor site. See also William C. Potter, "Prospects for U.S.-Russian Cooperation to Counter WMD Proliferation and Terrorism," The Aspen Institute Congressional Program, *U.S.-Russian Relations: Opportunities for Cooperation* 18 (2003).

[14] The yield from a fertilizer bomb depends on the percentage of fuel oil used. The estimated yields assume that 1 kg of ANFO (fertilizer bomb using about 5 percent fuel oil) is roughly equivalent to 0.8 kg TNT. Also, the estimates are in metric tons, where 2,200 pounds equal one metric ton.

[15] Matthew Bunn, Anthony Wier, and John P. Holdren discuss in detail the components of this chain of necessary conditions in *Controlling Nuclear Warheads and Materials: A Report Card and Action Plan,* Project on Managing the Atom, Harvard University, March 2003, <http://www.nti.org/e_research/cnwm/threat/global.asp>, accessed on February 6, 2004.

[16] Some variants on this basic model can be imagined, such as the decision to set off the device at a less than optimal site in order to reduce the risk of detection inherent in transporting the device across borders. Collaboration among terrorist organizations is another possibility. See Morten Bremer Maerli, *Crude Nukes on the Loose? Preventing Nuclear Terrorism by Means of Optimum Nuclear Husbandry, Transparency, and Non-Intrusive Fissile Material Verification,* Ph.D. dissertation, Faculty of Mathematics and Natural Sciences, University of Oslo, 2004.

[17] A network of transportation links capable of moving the weapon across land and probably water, for example, would be required in most scenarios. While it is possible that a small team could carry out the transport of the weapon, it appears more likely that a large, well-organized network would be necessary to coordinate the various stages of transport from the original storage site to the end target. Resources would also be needed to sustain a relatively large organization for some period, perhaps comparable to that needed to sustain the four teams of al Qaeda operatives who undertook the September 11, 2001, attacks. To maximize its chances of success, the terrorist organization would also, under most scenarios, require the resources and manpower to study multiple-storage nuclear sites and their vulnerabilities. However, the larger and more complex the organization becomes, the greater the likelihood that it will be discovered before its mission can be accomplished.

[18] See, for example, Carson Mark, Theodore Taylor, Eugene Eyster, William Maraman, and Jacob Wechsler, "Can Terrorists Build Nuclear Weapons?" in Paul Leventhal and Yonah Alexander, eds., *Preventing Nuclear Terrorism: The Report and Papers of the International Task Force on Prevention of Nuclear Terrorism* (Lanham, MD: Lexington Books, 1987), pp. 55-65.

[19] The participation of disaffected Russian nuclear scientists is also a possibility.

[20] The bomb design from Khan is reportedly of an implosion-type weapon, which as discussed in more depth below, is a more sophisticated design than the simplest crude nuclear device. William J. Broad, "Libya 's Crude Bomb Design Eases Western Experts' Fears," *New York Times,* February 9, 2004, p. A7.

[21] Gary Ackerman and Laura Snyder, "Would They If They Could?" *Bulletin of the Atomic Scientists* (May/June 2002), pp. 41-47.

[22] Mike Nartker, "Radiological Weapons: 'Dirty Bomb' Attack is 40 Percent Probability, Expert Says," Global Security Newswire, Nuclear Threat Initiative, November 18, 2002; David Albright and Holly Higgins, "A Bomb for the Ummah," *Bulletin of the Atomic Scientists* (March/April 2003).

[23] Kimberly McCloud and Matthew Osborne, "WMD Terrorism and Usama bin Laden," report for Center for Nonproliferation Studies, 2001, available at <http://cns.miis.edu/pubs/reports/binladen.htm>, accessed on February 18, 2004.

[24] David Albright, "Al Qaeda's Nuclear Program: Through the Window of Seized Documents," Nautilus Institute, Special Forum 47, November 6, 2002.

[25] See Morten Bremer Maerli, "Nuclear Terrorism: Threats, Challenges, and Responses," report for Oxford Research Group, February 2003, p. 3; Bunn, et al., *Controlling Nuclear Warheads and Materials,* p. 226.

[26] The 2002 National Research Council report raised concerns about clandestine production of weapons-usable materials. However, it would be difficult to start with no facilities and build up to a viable program within a few years. Such hidden production is much more likely to occur on the state rather than the non-state level. National Research Council Committee on Science and Technology for Countering Terrorism, *Making the Nation Safer: The Role of Science and Technology in Countering Terrorism* (Washington, DC: National Academy Press, 2002), p. 41.

[27] U.S. General Accounting Office, "Quick and Secret Construction of Plutonium Reprocessing Plants: A Way to Nuclear Weapons Proliferation?" Report by the Comptroller General of the United States, October 6, 1978.

[28] Ibid., p. 2.

[29] It is also possible that the group might employ technicians willing to sacrifice their lives for their cause, but spent fuel can be so radioactive that the individuals involved might become acutely ill before they completed their mission, indicating that some measure of shielding would most likely be employed.

[30] U.S. House of Representatives, Committee on International Relations, Subcommittee on International Security and Scientific Affairs, testimony of Theodore Taylor, October 28, 1975.

[31] Alexander Glaser and Frank von Hippel, "On the Importance of Ending the Use of HEU in the Nuclear Fuel Cycle: An Updated Assessment," paper presented at the 2002 International Meeting on Reduced Enrichment for Research and Test Reactors, San Carlos de Bariloche, Argentina, November 3-8, 2002.

[32] Edwin Lyman and Alan Kuperman, "A Reevaluation of Physical Protection Standards for Irradiated HEU Fuel," 24th International Meeting on Reduced Enrichment for Research and Test Reactors (RERTR-2002), November 2002; Matthew Bunn, "Threat from Research Reactor Fuel," unpublished paper, as of May 2004; and Matthew Bunn and Anthony Wier, *Securing the Bomb: An Agenda for Action,* Project on Managing the Atom, Harvard University, Report Commissioned by the Nuclear Threat Initiative, May 2004, p. 37. Notably, Iraq during its crash program in 1991 to produce a nuclear bomb planned to use both fresh and irradiated

HEU fuel from its research reactors. David Albright, Frans Berkhout, and William Walker, *Plutonium and Highly Enriched Uranium 1996: World Inventories, Capabilities, and Policies,* (SIPRI: Oxford University Press, 1997), pp. 344-349.

[33] Frank Barnaby, "Potential Terrorist Misuses of Plutonium and MOX," edited submission to the UK Government Energy Review, Oxford Research Group, August 2002.

[34] Similar scenarios are discussed in Bunn, et al., *Controlling Nuclear Warheads and Materials.* Concerning the transfer issue, Albright and Higgins, "A Bomb for the Ummah," pp. 49-55, state "Some of Pakistan's nuclear scientists believe that the bomb should be shared with all of the Muslim community, even—or especially—with al Qaeda." Many South Asian experts, however, doubt that radical Islamists are likely to gain power in Pakistan in the near term, and some also question their readiness to transfer nuclear weapons to terrorists. Gaurav Kampani, correspondence with authors, April 6, 2004.

[35] See Chapter 3 and references therein for statements made by Li Gun, Deputy Director of American Affairs in the North Korea Foreign Ministry, in April 2003.

[36] Glenn Kessler, "N. Korea Nuclear Estimate to Rise," *Washington Post,* April 28, 2004, p. A1.

[37] David E. Sanger and William J. Broad, "Evidence is Cited Linking Koreans to Libya Uranium," *New York Times,* May 23, 2004, p. A1; David E. Sanger, "The North Korean Nuclear Challenge," *New York Times,* May 24, 2004, p. A9.

[38] Victor Mallet, "N. Korea Offers US Pledge on Weapons," *Financial Times,* May 3, 2004.

[39] Statements in April 2004 by French President Jacques Chirac, for example, point to a converging view of many leaders in Europe and the United States that Iran is determined to acquire nuclear weapons. Elaine Sciolino, "Speaking for Europe, Chirac Warns Iran on Inspections," *New York Times,* April 22, 2004, p. A10.

[40] Jasen J. Castillo, "Nuclear Terrorism: Why Deterrence Still Matters," *Current History* (December 2003), pp. 426-431.

[41] William C. Potter, "Invade and Unleash?" *Washington Post,* September 22, 2002, p. B7.

[42] Albright and Higgins, "A Bomb for the Ummah."

[43] Center for Nonproliferation Studies, "Confirmed Proliferation-Significant Incidents of Fissile Material Trafficking in the Newly Independent States (NIS), 1991-2001," CNS Reports, November 30, 2001, available at <http://cns.miis.edu/pubs/reports/traff.htm>, accessed on May 27, 2004.

[44] U.S. official, name withheld by request, communication with author, Washington, DC, April 2004. An unspecified quantity of irradiated HEU remains at the site.

[45] Bunn and Wier, *Securing the Bomb: An Agenda for Action,* p. 37.

[46] As noted earlier, weapons-grade HEU is uranium enriched to greater than 90 percent U-235. Highly enriched uranium is defined as uranium enriched to 20 percent or greater in the isotopes U-235 or U-233.

[47] The higher the concentration of uranium, the less the distance the neutrons that cause fission (which is how energy is released in the bomb) have to travel before interacting with a U-235 nucleus in a mass of weapons-grade HEU. Thus, more fissions can occur in a given period of time inside a mass of weapons-grade HEU than in a mass of lower enrichments of HEU.

[48] The critical mass scales inversely to the density squared. Thus, if the density is increased by a factor of two, the critical mass required decreases by a factor of four. In contrast to the gun method, the implosion method significantly changes the density of the fissile material.

[49] David Albright, "South Africa's Secret Nuclear Weapons," ISIS Report, May 1994.

[50] John McPhee, *The Curve of Binding Energy* (New York: Farrar, Straus, and Giroux, 1974), pp. 189-194.

[51] The IAEA's significant quantity for HEU is an amount of uranium containing 25 kg equivalent U-235. However, this amount is based on the assumption that a state could use this material to build the more technically challenging implosion weapon.

[52] See, for example, Mark, et al., "Can Terrorists Build Nuclear Weapons?"; Luis W. Alvarez, *Adventures of a Physicist* (New York: Basic Books, 1988), p.125; Frank Barnaby, "Issues Surrounding Crude Nuclear Explosives," in IPPNW Global Health Watch, *Crude Nuclear Weapons: Proliferation and the Terrorist Threat,* Report Number 1, 1996; Morten Bremer Maerli, "Relearning the ABCs: Terrorists and 'Weapons of Mass Destruction,'" *Nonproliferation Review* 7 (Summer 2000); Frank von Hippel, "Recommendations for Preventing Nuclear Terrorism," Federation of American Scientists Public Interest Report, November/December 2001, p. 1; Matthew L. Wald, "Suicidal Nuclear Threat is Seen at Weapons Plants," *New York Times,* January 23, 2002, p. A9; Robert L. Civiak, *Closing the Gaps: Securing High Enriched Uranium in the Former Soviet Union and Eastern Europe,* Report for the Federation of American Scientists, May 2002; Committee on Science and Technology

for Countering Terrorism, *Making the Nation Safer;* Richard L. Garwin and Georges Charpak, *Megawatts and Megatons: A Turning Point in the Nuclear Age?* (New York: Alfred A. Knopf, 2001); Jeffrey Boutwell, Francesco Calegero, and Jack Harris, "Nuclear Terrorism: The Danger of Highly Enriched Uranium (HEU)," *Pugwash Issue Brief,* September 2002; Union of Concerned Scientists, "Scientists' Letter on Exporting Nuclear Material," to W. J. "Billy" Tauzin, September 25, 2003, available at <http://www.ucsusa.org/global_security/nuclear_terrorism/page.cfm?pageID=1256>, accessed on May 14, 2004; and Gunnar Arbman, Francesco Calogero, Paolo Cotta-Ramusino, Lars van Dessen, Maurizio Martellini, Morten Bremer Maerli, Alexander Nikitin, Jan Prawitz, and Lars Wredberg, "Eliminating Stockpiles of Highly-Enriched Uranium," Swedish Ministry for Foreign Affairs, SKI Report 2004:15, April 2004.

[53] Committee on Science and Technology for Countering Terrorism, *Making the Nation Safer,* p. 45.

[54] Ibid., p. 40.

[55] Union of Concerned Scientists, "Scientists' Letter on Exporting Nuclear Material."

[56] Garwin and Charpak, *Megawatts and Megatons: A Turning Point in the Nuclear Age?,* p. 313.

[57] von Hippel, "Recommendations for Preventing Nuclear Terrorism," p. 1.

[58] Alvarez, *Adventures of a Physicist,* p.125

[59] Wald, "Suicidal Nuclear Threat is Seen at Weapons Plants."

[60] Albert Narath, "The Technical Opportunities for a Sub-National Group to Acquire Nuclear Weapons," XIV Amaldi Conference on Problems of Global Security, April 27, 2002.

[61] Mark et al., "Can Terrorists Build Nuclear Weapons?"

[62] Pugwash Conferences on Science and World Affairs, "The Dangers of Nuclear Terrorism," Statement of the Pugwash Council, November 12, 2001.

[63] John Chalmers, "Nuclear Terror Scenario Exposes Vulnerable World," Reuters, May 4, 2004; Paul Ames, "War Games Give Europeans Glimpse of a Terror Attack," *Boston Globe,* May 5, 2004.

[64] As cited in Richard Rhodes, *The Making of the Atomic Bomb* (New York: Simon and Schuster, 1988), p. 561. Almost all of the scientific thinking and experimentation during the Manhattan Project was devoted to the more technically challenging task of designing and building an implosion bomb. Thus, it did not and would not require a Manhattan Project-like effort to make a gun-type bomb. Moreover, now that the knowledge of an implosion-design is well known, neither would such an effort be required for this method, as discussed later.

[65] David Albright, "South Africa and the Affordable Bomb," *Bulletin of the Atomic Scientists* (July/August 1994).

[66] Plutonium's spontaneous fission rate is much greater than that of uranium. Before the gun-type device would be able to assemble plutonium into a supercritical mass, the neutrons emitted by the spontaneous fission would lead to a dud or a "fizzle" yield. Fizzles result in a small nuclear yield.

[67] Stanislav Rodionov, "Could Terrorists Produce Low-Yield Nuclear Weapons?" in National Research Council, National Academy of Sciences, in Cooperation with the Russian Academy of Sciences, *High-Impact Terrorism: Proceedings of a Russian-American Workshop* (Washington, DC: National Academies Press, 2002), pp. 156-159. The 10- to 20-ton explosive yield estimate is for a relatively fast gun-assembly speed of about 300 meters/second (m/s). For a more modest 100 m/s assembly speed, the yield would be about five times less or a few tons; Rodionov, p. 158.

[68] Ibid., p. 159.

[69] In the original Nagasaki bomb design, it is believed that the designers used "fast" and "slow" explosives arranged in layers or lenses so that when the detonators sent the firing signals to the explosives, a spherical implosion wave was created that would smoothly squeeze the fissile material into a supercritical state.

[70] Mark, et al., "Can Terrorists Build Nuclear Weapons?" The critical mass scales inversely to the density squared. So, if the density of the fissile material is doubled, the critical mass required is decreased by one-fourth. High-energy conventional explosives could squeeze relatively small amounts of fissile material (a few kg of plutonium or several kg of HEU) into a supercritical dense state, thus reducing the amount of fissile material needed for an implosion-type IND. Thus, in principle, if terrorists could acquire these conventional explosives, they could make do with less fissile material. Weapon designers employed by a state would likely be able to use less material. See the next statement in the text about the amount of plutonium used in the Nagasaki bomb.

[71] In 1997, the U.S. government reemphasized earlier pronouncements that reactor-grade plutonium can fuel nuclear weapons. See, U.S. Department of Energy, Office of Arms Control and Nonproliferation, *Final Nonproliferation and Arms Control Assessment of Weapons-Usable Fissile Material Storage and Excess Plutonium Disposition Alternatives,* DOE/NN-0007, Washington, DC, 1997, pp. 37-39. In its report on nuclear terrorism,

the U.S. National Research Council in 2002 stated, "Reactor-grade plutonium can be used to fabricate workable nuclear devices." See National Research Council, Committee on Science and Technology for Countering Terrorism, "Nuclear and Radiological Threats," Chapter 2 in Committee on Science and Technology for Countering Terrorism, *Making the Nation Safer,* p. 40.

[72] Former U.S. nonproliferation official Matthew Bunn, personal communication with authors, November 12, 2003; former Massachusetts Institute of Technology nuclear engineering professor and U.S. arms control consultant Marvin Miller, personal communication with authors, May 5, 2003.

[73] J. Carson Mark, "Reactor-Grade Plutonium's Explosive Properties," paper for Nuclear Control Institute, August 1990, p. 5.

[74] Garwin and Charpak, *Megawatts and Megatons: A Turning Point in the Nuclear Age?,* p. 315.

[75] In its October 8, 1997, report on its inspections in Iraq, the IAEA offered the following conclusions regarding the status of Iraq's weaponization efforts, which began in 1987:
2.6 Summary
1. Iraq's insistence that it had not finalised a nuclear weapon design option at the time of the Gulf War complicates the task of evaluating Iraq's weaponisation capabilities at that time. However, although there are gaps in the documentation of Iraq's weaponization activities, it appears that Iraq's declared progress towards developing practical capabilities, particularly uranium casting and machining and the production of explosive lenses for the implosion package, is consistent with Iraq's resources and the time frame of the programme.
2. Evaluation is further complicated by Iraq's long history of denial of the actual purpose of the Al Atheer nuclear weapons development and production facility and its persistent understatement of the scope and achievements of its weaponisation efforts, even in the post August-1995 era. Nonetheless, Iraqi programme documentation records substantial progress in many important areas of nuclear weapon development, making it prudent to assume that Iraq has developed the capability to design and fabricate a basic fission weapon, based on implosion technology and fuelled by highly enriched uranium. IAEA Report to the UN Security Council, October 8, 1997, UNSC S/97/779, p. 59, <http://www.iaea.org/worldatom/Programmes/ActionTeam/reports/s_1997_779.pdf>, accessed on April 28, 2004. Elsewhere in this document, the IAEA summarized its view: "....Iraq was at, or close to, the threshold of success in such areas as the production of HEU through the EMIS [electromagnetic isotope separation] process, the production and pilot cascading of single-cylinder sub-critical gas centrifuge machines, and the fabrication of the explosive package for a nuclear weapon." Ibid., p. 21.

[76] Dan Stober, "No Experience Necessary," *Bulletin of the Atomic Scientists* (March/April 2003), pp. 57-63.

[77] John Aristotle Philips and David Michaelis, *Mushroom: The Story of the A-Bomb Kid* (New York: William Morrow, 1978).

[78] Garwin and Charpak, *Megawatts and Megatons: A Turning Point in the Nuclear Age?,* p. 349.

[79] Rodionov, "Could Terrorists Produce Low-Yield Nuclear Weapons?" pp. 156-159.

[80] Brian Ross, "How Safe are Our Borders?: Customs Fails to Detect Depleted Uranium Carried from Europe to U.S." ABCNews.com, September 11, 2002, <http://abcnews.go.com/sections/wnt/DailyNews/sept11_uranium020911.html>, accessed on May 1, 2003. Depleted uranium emits a slightly less radioactive signature than does natural uranium or HEU; nonetheless, the ABC News test demonstrated substantial inspection gaps.

[81] Natural Resources Defense Council, "The ABC News Nuclear Smuggling Experiment: The Sequel," September 11, 2003, available at <http://www.nrdc.org/nuclear/furanium.asp>, accessed on September 26, 2003.

[82] Howard Kurtz, "ABC Ships Uranium Overseas for Story," *Washington Post,* September 11, 2003, p. A21.

[83] Wald, "Suicidal Nuclear Threat is Seen at Weapons Plants." Also, as discussed in an earlier section, there is a "good chance" that terrorists could set off a nuclear explosion by dropping one piece of HEU onto another.

[84] U.S. House of Representatives, Subcommittee on Security, Veterans Affairs, and International Relations, *Testimony on Combating Terrorism: Preventing Nuclear Terrorism,* Danielle Brian, Executive Director of the Project on Government Oversight (POGO), September 24, 2002.

[85] U.S. General Accounting Office, "Weapons of Mass Destruction: Additional Russian Cooperation Needed to Facilitate U.S. Efforts to Improve Security at Russian Sites," GAO-03-482, March 2003, p. 15.

[86] The Department of Energy has used the 600-ton figure for many years. It appears that new Russian production of several tons of separated plutonium annually (from military and civilian programs), together with fissile material removed from nuclear weapons and added to Russia's out-of-weapons fissile material

stockpile, roughly balance the 30 tons of HEU per year that is removed from that stockpile through dilution of HEU into non-weapons-usable LEU, pursuant to the U.S.-Russian HEU Purchase Agreement, discussed below. Thus, while the total quantity of Russian fissile material in and out of weapons is declining, the amount outside of weapons appears to be holding relatively constant at the 600-metric-ton level.

[87] National Intelligence Council, "Annual Report to Congress on the Safety and Security of Russian Nuclear Facilities and Military Forces," February 2002.

[88] GAO-03-482, p. 25.

[89] Ibid.

[90] IAEA, "Facts and Figures: IAEA Database on Illicit Trafficking of Nuclear and Other Radioactive Materials: Incidents Involving Nuclear Material," IAEA Web site, <http://www.iaea.org/NewsCenter/Features/RadSources/chart2.html>, accessed on January 30, 2004.

[91] Potter and Sokova, "Illicit Nuclear Trafficking in the NIS."

[92] Lisa Trei, "Database exposes threat from 'lost' nuclear material," Stanford Report, March 6, 2002, <http://news-service.stanford.edu/news/march6/database-36.html>, accessed on March 12, 2002.

[93] Rensselaer Lee, "Nuclear Smuggling: Patterns and Responses," *Parameters* (Spring 2003), p. 96.

[94] Potter and Sokova, "Illicit Nuclear Trafficking in the NIS," pp. 113-116.

[95] Strengthening the Global Partnership, "Global Partnership Scorecard," May/June 2004, available at <http://www.sgpproject.org>. Upon gaining access to a specific site, after conducting a threat and vulnerability assessment, the department initially implements "rapid" security upgrades and then, in a second phase of work, undertakes "comprehensive" improvements. Rapid security improvements include simple steps such as replacing wooden doors with steel ones, bricking up windows, and applying modern tamper-resistant seals. Comprehensive upgrades are tailored to specific sites and incorporate integrated alarm systems and modern material accounting measures. Additionally, the department's National Programs and Sustainability Program have provided hardened trucks and rail cars for transport of nuclear material, supported education and training for nuclear custodians, and undertaken other projects to promote the long-term operation and maintenance of enhanced security systems. The DOE Second Line of Defense program has given equipment and training to customs inspectors and border security forces to improve their ability to detect smuggling of nuclear and radioactive material.

[96] DOE officials respond that within the Russian system, these are the locations that are the most secure, even if they do not meet the level pursued in U.S. assistance programs; that for this reason, terrorists would be least likely to seek fissile materials at these sites; and that the department has had considerable success in enhancing security at the initially more vulnerable facilities in other parts of the Russian nuclear complex. Nonetheless, the stated goal of the MPC&A program is to improve security at these sites and this goal remains far from achievement. Senior DOE official, name withheld by request, interview by author, Washington, DC, April 2004.

[97] This situation would change if MOX fuel were to be widely used, thereby creating significant transportation risks and increasing the processing of plutonium and unirradiated plutonium-bearing MOX fuel. Under the U.S. plutonium disposition program, Russia is to convert 34 tons of weapons plutonium into MOX over a 17-year period and use the fuel in nuclear power reactors, thereby embedding the plutonium in highly radioactive spent fuel, rendering it far less accessible for potential use in nuclear weapons. The transportation and processing activities involved in this program, however, would create potential security risks that would need to be carefully addressed.

[98] Oleg Bukharin, Christopher Ficek, and Michael Roston, "U.S.-Russian Reduced Enrichment for Research and Test Reactors (RERTR) Cooperation," RANSAC Policy Update, Summer 2002, p. 3.

[99] Fresh and lightly irradiated HEU fuels are comparably dangerous because the radiation barrier in the lightly irradiated fuel is generally not great enough to be lethal in the relatively short period of time required to process the fuel to extract HEU and fashion an IND.

[100] Don J. Bradley, *Behind the Nuclear Curtain: Radioactive Waste Management in the Former Soviet Union,* edited by David R. Payson (Richland, Washington: Battelle Press, 1997), p. 283; Oleg Bukharin and William Potter, "Potatoes were Guarded Better," *Bulletin of the Atomic Scientists* (May 1995); Chunyan Ma and Frank Von Hippel, "Ending the Production of Highly Enriched Uranium for Naval Reactors," *Nonproliferation Review* 8 (Spring 2001), p. 91; and Mohini Rawool-Sullivan, Paul D. Moskowitz, and Ludmila N. Shelenkova, "Technical and Proliferation-Related Aspects of the Dismantlement of Russian Alfa-Class Nuclear Submarines," *Nonproliferation Review* 9 (Spring 2002), p. 164.

[101] Calculations by Jungmin Kang and Frank von Hippel indicate that conversion of the Russian icebreakers from HEU to LEU fuel is technically feasible. Jungmin Kang and Frank von Hippel, "Feasibility of Converting Russian Ice-Breaker Reactors from HEU to LEU," Global 2001 International Conference on Back End of the Fuel Cycle: From Research to Solutions, Palais des Congrès, Paris, September 9-13, 2001. Glaser and von Hippel note that conversion of these reactors would reduce civilian HEU demand by 350 to 500 kg per year. Glaser and von Hippel, "On the Importance of Ending the Use of HEU in the Nuclear Fuel Cycle."

[102] Russia has decommissioned about 190 nuclear-powered submarines since the end of the Cold War. Because Russia had not planned for such a massive decommissioning, it was not prepared to handle fully the hundreds of spent fuel assemblies and accompanying radioactive waste.

[103] Glaser and von Hippel, "On the Importance of Ending the Use of HEU in the Nuclear Fuel Cycle."

[104] Data from the United States Enrichment Corporation website, <http://www.USEC.com>; see also, U.S. Embassy Moscow, Russia, Press Release, "Visit to Novouralsk," March 30, 2004, <http://www.usembassy.ru/embassy/release.php?record_id=10>, accessed on April 30, 2004.

[105] A similar HEU blend-down, supported by the European Union, is being implemented at the Elektrostal facility. That blend-down program plans to render 1 ton of HEU per year into LEU form. See Nuclear Threat Initiative, "Reducing Excess Stockpiles: The U.S.-Russia Highly Enriched Uranium Purchase Agreement," <http://www.nti.org/e_research/cnwm/reducing/heudeal.asp?print=true>, accessed on May 28, 2004; Strengthening the Global Partnership, "Global Partnership Scorecard," May/June 2004, available at <http://www.sgpproject.org>.

[106] U.S. Department of Energy, Press Release, "Security Upgrades Completed in Russian Northern Fleet," December 19, 2003.

[107] This measure has been repeatedly identified by outside analysts as an extremely efficient means for reducing the dangers posed by Russian fissile material stocks. To date, studies have focused on developing means to double the rate of eliminating HEU without overloading the blend-down system and without destabilizing the global uranium market. To prevent such destabilization, analysts have recommended down-blending to non-weapons-usable 19.9 percent enrichment, which is undesirable for weapons use, and storing the 19.9-percent output until a time when market conditions are favorable for further down-blending to 3 to 5 percent enriched LEU commercial reactor fuel. See, for example, Civiak, "Closing the Gaps"; Matthew Bunn has also done extensive analysis of the acceleration of HEU down-blending.

[108] For a summary of developments, see Nuclear Threat Initiative, "Reducing Excess Stockpiles."

[109] Tom Z. Collina and John B. Wolfstahl, "Nuclear Terrorism and Warhead Control in Russia," *Arms Control Today* (April 2002).

[110] Russian Central TV, interview of Alexander Kotelnikov, in "Secret Materials," November 29, 2002 (translated by BBC Monitoring Service); also cited by Bunn and Weir, *Securing the Bomb: An Agenda for Action*, p. 17. A similar denial of the possibility that non-state actors have the technical skills to manufacture a nuclear bomb were expressed by the head of the Federal Agency for Atomic Energy. See Robert Serebrennikov, "Russian Minister: No Terrorist Organization Can Manufacture an Atomic Bomb," ITAR-TASS, May 19, 2003. This dangerous myth tends to be grounded in the mistaken assumption that terrorists would seek to meet the same rigorous military specifications of nuclear weapons—including predictable yields, compatibility with delivery systems, and high safety and reliability standards—as do national governments.

[111] This activity takes place at the RT-1 reprocessing plant, at the Mayak Production Complex in Ozersk. The United States has proposed to assist Russia in the construction of spent fuel storage capacity at the site where plutonium separation is now taking place (the RT-1 facility) contingent upon Russia's agreeing to end its nuclear cooperation with Iran, but Russia has not agreed to this arrangement. Cristina Chuen, "Russian Spent Nuclear Fuel," NTI Issue Brief, February 2003, available at: <http://www.nti.org/e_research/e3_25b.html>. In its December 2002 National Strategy to Combat Weapons of Mass Destruction, the Bush administration declared that it "will continue to discourage the worldwide accumulation of separated plutonium...." See The White House, *National Strategy to Combat Weapons of Mass Destruction,* National Security Presidential Directive 17 (unclassified version), December 11, 2002, p. 4, <http://www.whitehouse.gov/news/releases/ 2002/12/ WMDStrategy.pdf>. To date, this prescription will lead to new U.S. initiatives aimed at discouraging Russia to end the separation of plutonium from nuclear power plant fuel.

[112] John B. Hay, "Canada," in Robert J. Einhorn and Michèle A. Flournoy, project directors, *Protecting Against*

the Spread of Nuclear, Biological, and Chemical Weapons: An Action Agenda for the Global Partnership, Volume 3: International Responses, Center for Strategic and International Studies, January 2003, pp. 4-6.

[113] Canada Donor Fact Sheet, Strengthening the Global Partnership Web site, <http://www.sgpproject.org/Donor%20Factsheets/Canada.html>, accessed on May 26, 2004.

[114] Isabelle Facon, "France," in Einhorn and Flournoy, *Protecting Against the Spread of Nuclear, Biological, and Chemical Weapons, Volume 3: International Responses,* pp. 58-60.

[115] "Russia's Cooperation with the Nuclear Summit Participants: the USA, Great Britain, France, Germany, Italy, Canada, and Japan," *International Affairs* 42 (1996), pp. 42-43; and researcher at France's Fondation pour la Recherche Stratégique, as cited in e-mail communication from researcher at the Center for Strategic and International Studies, Washington, DC.

[116] Klaus Arnhold, "Germany," in Einhorn and Flournoy, *Protecting Against the Spread of Nuclear, Biological, and Chemical Weapons, Volume 3: International Responses,* p. 75.

[117] Germany Fact Sheet, Strengthening the Global Partnership Web site, <http://www.sgpproject.org/Donor%20Factsheets/Germany.html>, accessed on May 26, 2004.

[118] Paolo Cotta-Ramusino, Antonino Lantieri, and Maurizio Martellini, "Italy," in Einhorn and Flournoy, *Protecting Against the Spread of Nuclear, Biological, and Chemical Weapons, Volume 3: International Responses,* pp. 103-104.

[119] Italy Fact Sheet, Strengthening the Global Partnership Web site, <http://www.sgpproject.org/Donor%20Factsheets/Italy.html>, accessed on May 26, 2004.

[120] Naoaki Usui, "Japan, Russia Sign Pact," *Nucleonics Week,* October 14, 1993, p. 13, and Takekazu Kawamura, "Japan's Role in Dismantling Russian N-Weapons," *Plutonium* (Spring 1997), p. 6.

[121] Tsutomu Arai and Nobumasa Akiyama, "Japan," in Einhorn and Flournoy, *Protecting Against the Spread of Nuclear, Biological, and Chemical Weapons, Volume 3: International Responses,* p. 110.

[122] Scientific and Technological Options Assessment Programme, Directorate General for Research, European Parliament, "Nuclear Safeguards and Nuclear Safety in the East: Final Report," Luxembourg, November 1996, pp. 23, 45-46, and "Russia's Cooperation with the Nuclear Summit Participants," *International Affairs* (1996).

[123] United Kingdom Fact Sheet, Strengthening the Global Partnership Web site, <http://www.sgpproject.org/Donor%20Factsheets/UK.html>, accessed on May 26, 2004.

[124] Norway Fact Sheet, Strengthening the Global Partnership Web site, <http://www.sgpproject.org/Donor%20Factsheets/Norway.html>, accessed on May 26, 2004. For analysis of Norway's contribution to nonproliferation assistance to Russia, see Morten Bremer Maerli, "Strengthening Cooperative Threat Reduction with Russia: The Norwegian Experience," NUPI Paper No. 633, December 2002.

[125] Sweden Fact Sheet, Strengthening the Global Partnership Web site, <http://www.sgpproject.org/Donor%20Factsheets/Sweden.html>, accessed on May 26, 2004.

[126] As of June 2004, these non-G-8 members included Australia, Belgium, the Czech Republic, Denmark, Finland, Ireland, the Netherlands, New Zealand, Norway, Poland, South Korea, Sweden, and Switzerland.

[127] See "G8 Action Plan on Nonproliferation," The Group of Eight Summit, June 9, 2004.

[128] See "Global Partnership Scorecard," Strengthening the Global Partnership, May/June 2004, available at <http://www.sgpproject.org> and "Russian Hopes that Other Global Partnership Program Signatories Will Translate Promises into Action," RIA Novost, June 9, 2004.

[129] For a clear enunciation of this danger, see Sam Nunn, "G8 Summit Preview: Are G8 Leaders Doing Enough to Prevent Nuke, Chem, Bio Terrorism?" <http://www.nti.org>.

[130] As a more compact fissile material, plutonium could facilitate Pakistan's development of physically smaller warheads for ballistic and cruise missiles, as well as "primaries" to ignite thermonuclear weapons, which would be far more powerful than those now in its arsenal, which are believed to be based on nuclear fission, the principle behind the Hiroshima and Nagasaki bombs.

[131] Robert S. Norris, William M. Arkin, and Joshua Handler, "Pakistan's Nuclear Forces, 2001," *Bulletin of the Atomic Scientists* (January/February 2002).

[132] See Gaurav Kampani, "Nuclear Watch—Pakistan: The Sorry Affairs of the Islamic Republic," NTI Web site, January 2004, <http://nti.org/e_research/e3_38a.html>, accessed on January 30, 2004.

[133] David Albright, "Securing Pakistan's Nuclear Infrastructure," in Carnegie Endowment for International Peace, *A New Equation: U.S. Policy Toward India and Pakistan after September 11,* Working Papers, Number 27, May 2002.

[134] Subcritical and critical assemblies are used for research and nuclear engineering training purposes and typically

contain relatively small amounts of nuclear material compared to cores for research or commercial reactors.

[135] IAEA, "Research Reactors and Security," IAEA Staff Report, March 8, 2004, <http://www.iaea.org/NewsCenter/Features/ResearchReactors/security_20040308.html>.

[136] IAEA, *Nuclear Research Reactors in the World,* Data Series #3, Vienna, 2000.

[137] IAEA, "Research Reactors and Security."

[138] Ibid.

[139] Office of Technology Assessment, *Technologies Underlying Weapons of Mass Destruction,* OTA-BP-ISC-115, Washington, DC, December 1993, p. 136.

[140] T. Dedik, I. Bolshinsky, and A. Krass, "Russian Research Reactor Fuel Return Program Starts Shipping Fuel to Russia," paper presented to the 2003 International Meeting on Reduced Enrichment for Research and Test Reactors, Chicago, Illinois, October 5-10, 2003, available at <http://www.td.anl.gov/Programs/RERTR/RERTR25/PDF/Dedik.pdf>, accessed on February 18, 2004.

[141] IAEA, Research Reactors in the World, last updated in October 2002, available at <http://www.iaea.or.at/worldatom/rrdb/>, accessed on June 30, 2004 and World Nuclear Association, "Research Reactors," August 2003, available at <http://www.world-nuclear.org/info/printable_information_papers/inf61print.htm>, accessed on May 27, 2004.

[142] Ibid., p. 4-5. The bare critical mass for 36 percent enriched HEU is greater than 200 kg, indicating that it might be impracticable for terrorists to acquire such large amounts of this material and be able to fashion it into a workable weapon.

[143] World Nuclear Association, "Research Reactors"; Glaser and von Hippel, "On the Importance of Ending the Use of HEU in the Nuclear Fuel Cycle"; Kenley Butler, Center for Nonproliferation Studies, Monterey Institute of International Studies, e-mail interview with author, May 28, 2004.

[144] Bukharin, et al., "U.S.-Russian Reduced Enrichment for Research and Test Reactors (RERTR) Cooperation"; Civiak, "Closing the Gaps."

[145] World Nuclear Association, "Research Reactors."

[146] See Center for Nonproliferation Studies, "Islamic Movement of Uzbekistan," CNS Web site at <http://cns.miis.edu/research/wtcol/imn.htm>.

[147] Philipp C. Bleek, "Project Vinca: Lessons for Securing Civil Nuclear Material Stockpiles," *Nonproliferation Review* 10 (Fall-Winter 2003), pp. 1-23.

[148] Ibid.

[149] Susan B. Glasser, "Russia Takes Back Uranium from Romania," *Washington Post,* September 22, 2003, p. A16.

[150] U.S. Department of Energy, Press Release, December 24, 2003, "U.S. Nonproliferation Efforts Continue as Nuclear Material is Removed from Bulgaria."

[151] Veselin Toshkov, "U.S., Russian experts remove uranium from Bulgarian reactor to keep it out of terrorists' hands," Associated Press, December 24, 2003.

[152] Center for Nonproliferation Studies, "HEU from Libyan Nuclear Reactor Repatriated to Russia," *NIS Export Control Observer* (April 2004), p. 9; Spencer Abraham, Secretary of Energy, speech before the International Atomic Energy Agency, Vienna, Austria, May 26, 2004.

[153] Abraham, speech before the International Atomic Energy Agency; Matthew L. Wald and Judith Miller, "Energy Department Plans a Push to Retrieve Nuclear Materials," *New York Times,* May 26, 2004, p. A16; Peter Slevin, "Plan Launched to Reclaim Nuclear Fuel," *Washington Post,* May 26, 2004, p. A21.

[154] Jeanne Lopatto, Department of Energy Press Office, "United States and Russian Federation Cooperate on Return of Russian-origin Research Reactor Fuel to Russia," U.S. Newswire, May 27, 2004.

[155] For a discussion of the obstacles to repatriation of Soviet-origin HEU, see Matthew Bunn and Anthony Wier, "Removing Material from Vulnerable Sites," updated January 12, 2004, <http://nti.org/e_research/cnwm/securing/vulnerable.asp>, accessed on February 18, 2004. See also, Bleek, "Project Vinca."

[156] U.S. government policy since 1978 has been to promote conversion of HEU-fueled reactors to low-enriched fuel. Because the Russian effort to reduce fuel enrichment suffered from lack of funds starting in the late 1980s, the United States and Russia formed an initiative in 1994 to develop higher-density low-enriched fuels for Soviet-designed research reactors and to demonstrate the feasibility of fuel conversion in particular reactors. This program has achieved some partial success. See, for example, the work of Armando Travelli at Argonne National Laboratory. One of his papers detailing the successes as of 1996, is Armando Travelli,

"Status and Progress of the RERTR Program," presented to the 1996 International Meeting on Reduced Enrichment for Research and Test Reactors, October 7-10, 1996.

[157] Armando Travelli, "Status and Progress of the RERTR Program in the Year 2003," paper presented to the 2003 International Meeting on Reduced Enrichment for Research and Test Reactors, Chicago, Illinois, October 5-10, 2003.

[158] U.S. Senate, S. Amdt. 3192 to S. 2400 (Fiscal Year 2005 National Defense Authorization Act), May 19, 2004.

[159] Abraham, speech before the International Atomic Energy Agency.

[160] Slevin, "Plan Launched to Reclaim Nuclear Fuel."

[161] Joe Fiorill and Greg Webb, "Russia, U.S. Pledge to Conclude HEU Return Agreement," Global Security Newswire, November 7, 2003. Pursuant to the Schumer Amendment, for example, the United States provides weapons-grade HEU to a Canadian reactor, operated by the company MDS Nordion, to produce radioisotopes for use in commercial radioactive sources. (Chapter 6 discusses the radioactive source market.) In 2003, shipments to this facility in Canada came under increased scrutiny. Earlier that year, Senator Christopher Bond, Republican from Missouri, and Representative Richard Burr, Republican from North Carolina, introduced legislation designed to ease restrictions on shipping HEU to certain countries for use in radioisotope production reactors. (Weapons-grade HEU is used as part of the target material during radioisotope production in some reactors.) Legislation passed into law in 1992 requires the reactor owners to commit to working toward conversion to LEU fuel in order to continue to receive shipments of HEU. The Bond-Burr legislation would lift this requirement. Critics charged that the proposed law would weaken efforts to control nuclear proliferation and to prevent HEU from falling into the hands of terrorists. See, R. Jeffrey Smith, "Measure Would Alter Nuclear Nonproliferation Policy," *Washington Post,* October 4, 2003, p. A2.

[162] U.S. Department of Energy, Office of Inspector General, Office of Audit Services, "Recovery of Highly Enriched Uranium Provided to Foreign Countries," DOE/IG-0638, February 2004.

[163] Abraham, speech before the International Atomic Energy Agency.

[164] Mark Hertsgaard, "Nuclear Insecurity," *Vanity Fair,* November 2003, p. 180; see also Associated Press, "Weapons Lab Security Lax, DOE Whistleblower Charges," *Washington Post,* October 7, 2003, p. A5.

[165] Hertsgaard, "Nuclear Insecurity," p. 188. Critics of Levernier complained that he had always directed his mock terrorists to exploit weak links. His supporters retort that, of course, "red team" members would not be doing their jobs if they did not target weaknesses. Reportedly, in one of the mock attacks, the red team hauled away weapons-grade material in a Home Depot garden cart. Some laboratory authorities charged that this cart was unfairly used because it was not on the list of approved items for the mock attack. In response, Anson Franklin, a National Nuclear Security Administration spokesperson, stated, "Any implication that there is a 50 percent failure rate on security tests at our nuclear-weapons sites cannot be supported by the facts and is not true. The impression has been given that these tests are staged like football games with winners and losers. But the whole idea of these exercises is to test for weaknesses—we want to find them before any adversaries could—and then make adjustments." Ibid., pp. 180-182.

[166] Ibid., p. 188.

[167] Matthew Wald, "Nuclear Weapons Program Could Get Own Police Force," *New York Times,* May 8, 2004, p. A13. In 1997, DOE considered adopting the "stored weapons standard" for protection of U.S. weapons-usable fissile material (in other words, requiring that weapons-usable fissile material should be guarded as strictly as are stored nuclear weapons). At that time, however, the actual requirements for material security were not changed. By analyzing open source U.S. government documents, Stanford University professor George Bunn has pieced together a definition of the stored weapons standard. First, the standard defines the "design basis threat," or DBT, which is a credible threat that authorities must design their storage sites to withstand. The DBT for stored nuclear weapons or weapons-usable material would in rough terms posit "a violent external assault by a group using weapons and vehicles, possibly with inside assistance." To try to defeat this DBT, the stored weapons standard would require, among other safeguarded details, "a strong, secure storage vault with a single entry surrounded by two layers of strong fences and an open, lighted area where no one could hide. Access to the vault should be limited to personnel with a need for access, who are cleared through full-field background investigations and accompanied by another such person (the 'two-person' rule). Such access limitations should be enforced by both armed guards and electronic monitoring devices, supported in case of need by nearby armed backup forces. All of these personnel should be trained to deal with design basis

threats, and their competence checked periodically in exercises like war games." George Bunn, "U.S. Standards for Protecting Weapons-Usable Fissile Material Compared to International Standards," *Nonproliferation Review* 6 (Fall 1998), pp. 137-143; quoted material from p. 138.

[168] Hertsgaard, "Nuclear Insecurity," p. 190.

[169] U.S. Department of Energy, Office of Inspector General, Office of Inspections and Special Inquiries, "Protective Force Performance Test Improprieties," DOE/IG-0636, January 2004.

[170] Ibid.

[171] Wald, "Nuclear Weapons Program"; Ralph Vartabedian, "Security Upgrade for Nation's Nuclear Labs: Energy Secretary's Plan to Lessen the Chance of a Terrorist Attack is Said to Include Closure of Sites, Improved Safeguards and Plutonium Removal," *Los Angeles Times,* May 7, 2004, p. A28.

[172] Ma and von Hippel, "Ending the Production of Highly Enriched Uranium for Naval Reactors." Russia is said to have plans to lease nuclear submarines to other countries. Such transfers to support nonexplosive military uses of nuclear materials are not prohibited under the nuclear Non-Proliferation Treaty. James Clay Moltz, "Closing the Loophole on Exports of Naval Propulsion Reactors," *Nonproliferation Review* 6 (Fall 1998), pp. 108-114

[173] The Netherlands, Germany, Sweden, Spain, and the United States have cancelled domestic plutonium separation plans and/or have reduced or ended contracts for the separation of plutonium abroad and its return in the form of MOX. During the Communist period, Soviet satellite states were obliged to return spent fuel to Russia, where it was reprocessed; the resulting plutonium was not returned, but stored in Russia.

[174] Although, as discussed shortly, under the U.S.-Russia plutonium disposition program, Russia is planning to use MOX fuel in a number of its nuclear power reactors and hopes to build new, more advanced plutonium-fueled reactors. For the foreseeable future, however, all plutonium from these programs will come from stocks originating in the Russian nuclear-weapons sector, not material separated from civilian spent nuclear power reactor fuel.

[175] "Japan N-Fuel Reprocessing Plant Faces Trial Run Delay," Jiji Press English News Service, April 5, 2004, p. 1; Sasaki Masashi, "President of Japan Nuclear Fuel Ltd. To Resign," *Knight Ridder Tribune Business News,* April 30, 2004, p. 1; "Japan to Freeze Testing of Spent Fuel Reprocessing," Jiji Press English News Service, May 13, 2004, p. 1.

[176] Alexander Glaser, "Bavaria Bucks Ban," *Bulletin of the Atomic Scientists* (March/April 2002), pp. 20-22.

[177] U.S. Nuclear Regulatory Commission, "Nuclear Security Enhancements Since September 11, 2001," Fact Sheet, September 2003.

[178] Elaine Hiruo, "Congress Passes Omnibus Bill for FY-03 That Backs Nuclear," *Nucleonics Week,* February 20, 2003, p. 12.

[179] DOE official, name withheld by request, phone interview by author, Washington, DC, May 2004.

[180] With respect to the security issues posed by the civilian nuclear fuel cycle and its possible expansion, see Richard L. Garwin and Georges Charpak, *Megawatts and Megatons: The Future of Nuclear Power and Nuclear Weapons* (Chicago: University of Chicago Press, 2002).

[181] Bunn, "U.S. Standards for Protecting Weapons-Usable Fissile Material," pp. 137-143.

[182] See, George Bunn, "Raising International Standards for Protecting Nuclear Materials from Theft and Sabotage," *Nonproliferation Review* 7 (Summer 2000), p. 146. See also George Bunn and Matthew Bunn, "Strengthening Nuclear Security Against Post-September 11 Threats and Sabotage," *JNMM,* Spring 2002, and George Bunn and Fritz Steinhausler, "An Integrated Approach to Adapt Physical Protection to the New Terrorism Threats," Center for International Security and Cooperation Conference Report, September 2002.

[183] United Nations, UN Security Resolution 1540, April 28, 2004, <http://ods-dds-ny.un.org/doc/UNDOC/GEN/N04/328/43/PDF/N0432843.pdf?OpenElement>, accessed on May 28, 2004.

[184] The authors are grateful to George Perkovich for sharing his perspective on this point; personal correspondence with author, March 31, 2004.

[185] The program also provides assistance in securing Russian nuclear weapons and was recently expanded to provide assistance in securing radioactive sources.

[186] Thus, 21 percent of the total has only received rapid upgrades.

[187] United States Enrichment Corporation, data from Web site, <http://www.USEC.com>.

[188] Michael Roston and David Smigielski, "Accomplishments of Selected Threat Reduction and Nonproliferation Programs in Russia, By Agency," RANSAC Report, May 2002.

[189] Matthew Bunn, "Plutonium Production Reactor Shutdown," updated July 7, 2003, <http://www.nti.org/ e_research/cnwm/ending/plutonium.asp>, accessed on February 19, 2004.

[190] Russia has a stockpile of 30-35 tons of plutonium separated from VVER-440 fuel over the years. All reactors in Russia that might use this material in the form of MOX fuel are already committed, however, to using MOX fuel containing weapons-grade plutonium, pursuant to the plutonium disposition program.

[191] As mentioned earlier, the United States has proposed to assist Russia in the construction of spent fuel storage capacity at the site where plutonium separation is now taking place (the Mayak facility, in Ozersk) contingent upon Russia agreeing to end its nuclear cooperation with Iran, but Russia has not agreed to this arrangement. Cristina Chuen, "Russian Spent Nuclear Fuel." In its December 2002 National Strategy to Combat Weapons of Mass Destruction, the Bush administration declared that it "will continue to discourage the worldwide accumulation of separated plutonium...." See White House, *National Strategy to Combat Weapons of Mass Destruction*. It is not clear whether this prescription will lead to new U.S. initiatives aimed at discouraging Russia to end the separation of plutonium from nuclear power plant fuel.

[192] For a detailed description of the history and projected developments of the plutonium disposition program, see Matthew Bunn, "Reducing Excess Stockpiles: Russian Plutonium Disposition," updated October 3, 2003, <http://www.nti.org/e_research/cnwm/reducing/rpdispose.asp>, accessed on February 19, 2004.

[193] Matthew L. Wald, "U.S.-Russian Plan to Destroy Atom-Arms Plutonium is Delayed," *New York Times*, February 9, 2004.

[194] Thad Adams, Harold Peacock, Don Fisher, Doug Leader, Robert Sindelar, Natraj Iyer, Dave Sell, Ken Allen, Ken Marsden, Joe Mitchell, Mitch Meyer, and Eric Howden, "The Development of Mobile Melt-Dilute Technology for the Treatment of Former Soviet Union Research Reactor Fuel," WSRC-MS-2003-00646, 2003.

[195] As of this writing, additional details of the BWXT technology are considered proprietary information, and those seeking such information should contact BWXT in Lynchburg, VA.

[196] Leonard S. Spector, "Missing the Forest for the Trees: U.S. Non-Proliferation Programs in Russia," *Arms Control Today* (June 2001).

5

RELEASING RADIATION

POWER PLANTS AND OTHER FACILITIES

The terrorist attacks of September 11, 2001, exposed the vulner-ability of certain high-profile U.S. buildings to destruction or severe damage from airplane crashes. Long before September 11th, however, nuclear power plants and other nuclear facilities were recognized as potential targets of terrorism because of their status as symbols of technological advancement and as embodiments of the public's fear of radiation. Although acts of sabotage at a nuclear facility or damage caused from an attack from outside the plant would not lead to a nuclear explosion, the deliberate release of large amounts of radia-tion from such facilities could cause enormous economic losses, social disruption, and grave psychological stress, especially for those near the affected area.[1]

Airplane crashes are just one attack pathway. Depending on the type, location, and security of a nuclear installation, other attack modes might be employed to cause a highly dangerous release of radiation to the en-vironment. Although government officials have known about these vul-nerabilities for decades and have worked to enhance security at these installations, concerns remain that nuclear facilities might be insufficiently protected against devastating terrorist attacks.[2]

The nuclear facilities of greatest concern as potential terrorist tar-gets are those with significant inventories of radioactivity: operating nuclear power reactors; spent fuel storage facilities at these reactor sites; plutonium separation or "reprocessing" plants, and associated facilities for spent fuel storage, liquid high-level radioactive waste storage, and liquid high-level waste processing; and research reactors (which contain considerably smaller inventories of radioactivity than the other types of installations but are more vulnerable to terrorism).

The events of 9/11 spurred many governments to upgrade security around nuclear power plants and other nuclear sites.[3] Considering accomplishments in this area in late 2002, then-Nuclear Regulatory Commission Chairman Richard Meserve stated, "It may not be possible to preclude the possibility of an attack or sabotage event at a plant absolutely, but there are many things that can be done to make such an event extremely unlikely and to ensure that the consequences are reduced."[4] As outlined below, the NRC and the U.S. nuclear industry have taken significant steps to upgrade security around U.S. nuclear power plants.[5] Nonetheless, important vulnerabilities remain. Without discussing plant-specific vulnerabilities or security plans, this chapter will examine the danger of terrorism at U.S. nuclear facilities and means for reducing this threat.

This chapter begins with a review of the chain of events that would be necessary for a terrorist organization to cause a significant release of radiation from a nuclear facility. It then assesses the motivations and capabilities of terrorist groups that might undertake these steps. It next provides an overview of the civilian nuclear power industry, outlines potential vulnerabilities at commercial sites, and discusses the consequences of a successful attempt to damage them, in which a significant release of radioactivity occurred. Finally, the chapter describes preventive, enforcement, and response mechanisms that are currently in place or that are being developed.

THE CHAIN OF CAUSATION

The terrorist route to damaging a nuclear facility and causing a release of radioactivity to the surrounding environment would require the following steps:

1. A terrorist group possessing the desire to cause significant harm to the United States and the necessary technical and financial resources to execute such a scheme by damaging nuclear facilities must organize and begin operations.

2. The group must then choose to engage in an act of nuclear terrorism at a moderately high level of violence by attacking or sabotaging a nuclear facility to cause the release of significant amounts of radioactivity.
3. The terrorist organization must identify a nuclear power plant or other nuclear facility that is vulnerable to attack. To facilitate the success of their mission, the terrorists would likely try to enlist the support of at least one insider.
4. The terrorists must decide how to strike the facility. Attack modes include airplane crashes; commando raids by land, water, or air; or cyberterrorism.
5. The terrorists must overcome the facility's protective measures and disable or destroy vital equipment at the facility or otherwise cause an off-site release of radioactivity.

Terrorist Groups with Motivation and Capabilities to Cause Large-Scale Releases of Radiation

As discussed in Chapter 2, the motives for an attack on a nuclear facility could range from punishment to intimidation to blackmail.[6] Such an attack could factor into a broad range of terrorist objectives from shutting down operations to causing a significant radioactive release. While radioactive fallout could lead to increasing numbers of casualties over a long time period, even a large-scale attack on a nuclear power plant would not embody the horrific spectacle of massive numbers of immediate deaths as pursued by apocalyptic groups.[7] For this reason, while use of a nuclear weapon would probably be contemplated only by a handful of apocalyptic and extreme politico-religious groups, a larger set of organizations, including national-separatist and radical environmental groups, might be motivated to damage a nuclear facility.

From the terrorist's viewpoint, advantages of such action include inflicting potential large-scale psychological stress and social disruption, radioactive contamination, and financial damage, but not a large number of deaths. Terrorist attacks on nuclear facilities, especially commercial nuclear power plants, also offer the additional advantage of striking highly symbolic targets.

The fact that there are potential long-term medical consequences from exposure to ionizing radiation might discourage some terrorists from making contaminated areas uninhabitable. For example, national/separatist terrorists would not want to harm their own bases of support, so they would be less likely to engage in radiological terrorism in their home country. Current international terror organizations, however, might attack a U.S. nuclear facility because their constituencies are at a considerable distance, predominantly in the Islamic world, and they are comprised of mobile, diffuse cells that are not tightly connected to a state or territory.

A 9/11-style strike on a nuclear facility in the United States would have a devastating psychological impact on the public. Beyond the actual damage, such an attack could ignite panic among the nearby population, which knows little about radiation and its effects beyond the haunting images of the Chernobyl accident. A successful attack on a nuclear power or storage facility would also expose the weaknesses of the victim's nuclear security efforts, adding to the fears of those living near a nuclear facility. In addition to causing potentially tens to hundreds of billions of dollars in property damage and hundreds of casualties, the act of striking an apparently secure, high-tech facility within "enemy" territory would provide a symbolic victory for the perpetrators.

Despite these benefits to the attackers, causing a significant radioactive release from a nuclear installation would be a daunting challenge, requiring considerable technical, organizational, and financial resources. Technical skills would be needed to identify relevant buildings and equipment within what are typically large and complex industrial installations; to identify and implement the actions needed to cause a radioactive release; and to defeat all backup safety systems. Organizational requirements would also be very substantial. A ground assault on a nuclear facility would require a sizeable number of assailants, probably divided into teams, a cadre roughly comparable to the 19-man group that executed the 9/11 attacks. Since all U.S. nuclear reactor facilities, except research reactors, are protected by armed guard forces, the assaulting group also would need military-style training to mount a successful attack. Appropriate plant personnel would have to be identified and strategies devised and implemented to gain insider support through ideological indoctrination, bribery, or coercion. Aerial attacks on nuclear facilities would require equally sophisticated planning. If a group of terrorists were to succeed in gaining control of an aircraft, they would also have to be capable of precisely targeting vital plant safety systems, such as the reactor's containment structure, or the spent fuel pools in order to generate substantial off-site release of radioactivity. Significant financial resources would be needed to meet the foregoing technical and organizational requirements. However, the group would not necessarily require the multinational capabilities necessary for nuclear weapon and IND plots involving the transportation of a nuclear weapon or fissile material from locations abroad to the United States.

A relatively small number of terrorist organizations are likely to possess the motivations and capabilities to mount an attack on a nuclear facility. The 9/11 attacks are a strong reminder, however, that these abilities could be within the grasp of a well-organized and well-trained terrorist group.

Several cases offer insights into the behavior of terrorist organizations that might contemplate an attack of this kind. Although they have repeatedly made threats against Russian nuclear facilities,[8] for example, Chechen separatists have yet to carry out such an attack, indicating that they might perceive greater value in the threat than in the act itself. Because most Russian nuclear plants are located hundreds of miles from Chechnya, a release of radiation from these plants would not necessarily harm the base constituency of the Chechens. Their decision to forego an attack on a nuclear facility may derive from the belief that they could not overcome plant defenses or a fear that the Russian government would mete out such severe retribution that they would lose support in the Chechen homeland. They also might be deterred by the likely harsh judgment rendered by international opinion. Even al Qaeda, a politico-religious terrorist organization, has yet to launch an attack against nuclear facilities, although Khaled Sheikh Mohammed and Ramzi Binalshibh, two organizers of the 9/11 attacks, reportedly admitted in 2002 that they contemplated striking nuclear power plants but refrained "for now" for fear that the attack could "get out of control."[9]

Other recent events, though, suggest that a terrorist attack against a nuclear facility remains a serious threat. In March 2003, National Guard troops in Arizona descended on the Palo Verde Nuclear Power Plant—which is about 50 miles west of Phoenix and is the nation's largest nuclear power plant in terms of electric generating capacity—in response to a federal alert that the plant might be in danger from a terrorist attack.[10] DHS Secretary Tom Ridge said that authorities had received threat information that was "serious enough, deemed to be credible enough," but he declined to provide details.[11] He ordered one of the Custom Service's Black Hawk helicopters to the plant's site to increase physical protection measures.[12]

More recently, in August 2003, police in Toronto, Canada, appear to have thwarted a terrorist threat against Canadian nuclear plants, leading to the detention of 19 Pakistani-born men living in Canada, some of whom were arrested on immigration violations. Although as of August 2003 police had not established a definite connection between these men and a terrorist group,[13] their activities were highly suspicious and included surveillance-like acts and airplane lessons that included a flight pattern over a nuclear power plant.[14]

Single-issue anti-nuclear groups have traditionally targeted nuclear facilities in order to bolster popular resistance to the nuclear industry. The Evan Mechan Eco-Terrorist International Conspiracy (EMETIC) represents a classic example of the leftist anti-nuclear terrorist movement. EMETIC first appeared in the late 1980s, operating in the southwest United States. A small group of environmental activists with limited funding and technical ability, EMETIC grew out of the radical environmentalist organization Earth First![15] In May 1989, four EMETIC members were arrested on charges of conspiring to sabotage power lines leading to the Central Arizona Project and Palo Verde nuclear station in Arizona, the Diablo Canyon Nuclear Facility in California, and the Rocky Flats Nuclear Facility in Colorado.[16]

The majority of anti-nuclear attacks has resulted in minor damage that did not threaten to release radioactive material within the facility.[17]

Within the anti-nuclear movement, however, the possibility of an extremist environmental group launching a major offensive against a
nuclear facility cannot be ruled out. "Restoration ecologist" groups believe that an environmental catastrophe could eradicate civilization so
that the environment might renew itself without being polluted by technology and industry.[18] Breaching the containment area of a nuclear facility and releasing radioactive material might appeal to some of these
extremist groups as a means of initiating such an environmental disaster while also increasing public fear and hostility toward nuclear energy.

One of the most serious acts of sabotage against a nuclear power
plant occurred in 1982 in South Africa. It was carried out by the anti-
apartheid movement headed by the African National Congress (ANC)
which, on December 18, 1982, detonated four bombs over a period of
several hours at the nearly commissioned Koeberg nuclear power station. South African authorities at that time had claimed that this facility
was one of the most heavily guarded sites in that country.[19] As the first
nuclear power plant in South Africa, Koeberg represented a highly symbolic target. Because the plant had not yet begun operation, the attack
by the nationalist group intentionally did not result in a massive release
of radiation. The attackers also claimed that they timed the explosions
to take place on a Saturday when few people would be at the site.[20]

The ANC was able to recruit an insider for its operation. Rodney
Wilkinson, a white South African who had embraced radical causes and
the anti-nuclear movement, offered his services to the ANC. As a worker
at the plant, he was able to penetrate the layers of security surrounding
the vital safety areas. He and his ANC handler placed two Soviet-designed
limpet mines near the reactor heads in order to demonstrate the ANC's
ability to breach the tightest layer of security. However, the explosions
were not designed to break the reactor heads themselves, according to a
published interview with Wilkinson.[21] The objective appears to have
been to maximize economic damage to the plant, without discharging
life-threatening releases of radioactivity. This intention underscores nationalist groups' concerns about not harming or alienating their constituency. Due to these explosions and the substantial repair costs, the
plant's commissioning was delayed for 18 months.[22]

In sum, nuclear installations have long been a target of terrorist interest, but to date, for a variety of reasons, no group has possessed both the motivation and capabilities to cause grave harm. The threat of such action, however, has led several governments to implement enhanced security measures at critical nuclear facilities in hopes of deterring any terrorist attacks.

OVERVIEW OF NUCLEAR POWER: NORMAL OPERATIONS AND ACCIDENT PREVENTION

Commercial Nuclear Power Plants

Commercial nuclear power plants generate a significant portion of global electricity production. In 2003, nuclear power produced about 16 percent of the world's electricity and about 20 percent of that of the United States. France leads the world in the proportion of electricity generated by nuclear energy, relying on this source for nearly 80 percent of its electric power, while U.S. nuclear power plants create the largest absolute amount of electricity, about 750 billion kilowatt hours (kWh) in 2003.[23]

About 440 commercial nuclear power reactors operate in 31 countries. The United States possesses the largest fraction of these reactors with 103 operating nuclear reactors at 65 plant sites in 31 states. The next three-largest nuclear power producing nations are France with 59 reactors, Japan with 54, and Russia with 30. Although growth in the nuclear power industry has stagnated in North America and Europe, resurgence in this industry appears set to take place in Asia, notably in China, Japan, the Republic of Korea, and India, which all have plans for constructing several new reactors over the next ten years. The Russian government also projects an expansion of nuclear power in Russia. However, based on past trends in this industry, these ambitious plans are unlikely to be fully realized, at least within the next decade.

In all types of nuclear reactors, fissionable material (mainly uranium and, to a smaller extent, plutonium[24]) fuels the nuclear reaction. Absorption of neutrons by uranium or plutonium nuclei typically results in fission or splitting of these nuclei into two smaller nuclei, or fission products. Additionally, the fission process releases energy and neutrons. These neutrons can cause further fissions, thus sustaining the nuclear chain reaction. The released energy heats up the reactor core. Fluids, such as water, carbon dioxide, or liquid sodium, remove heat from the core and are used to generate steam to drive turbines that produce electricity. Under normal commercial power plant operations, a significant fraction of this energy is ultimately transformed into electricity.

Types of Reactor Technologies

Commercial nuclear power plants use only a relatively small set of reactor technologies. More than three-fourths (almost 350) of the operating reactors employ light water reactor (LWR) technology. In LWRs, ordinary or "light" water both cools and moderates the reactor core. Moderation slows down high-energy neutrons to thermal, or low, energies to be able to sustain the chain reaction. Of the LWRs, the pressurized water reactor (PWR), the most prevalent type, is used primarily in the United States, France, Japan, and Russia. About 250 PWRs are operating in these and other countries. In a PWR, water flows in a primary circuit under high pressure to prevent boiling, and it transfers heat from the reactor core to a secondary circuit of water. This heat transfer is used to generate steam in the secondary circuit, which rotates a turbine to produce electricity. Employed mainly in the United States, Japan, and Sweden, the second-most prevalent type of reactor, the boiling water reactor (BWR), shares many similarities with the PWR, except it uses only a single circuit of water to generate steam for electricity production. The BWR design purposely allows boiling to occur above the reactor core. Both types of reactors use low-enriched uranium dioxide for fuel.[25]

Three other reactor technologies are in widespread use. First, gas-cooled reactors, such as the British-designed MAGNOX reactor, run on natural or enriched-uranium metal fuel and rely on carbon dioxide for cooling and graphite for moderation. Second, pressurized heavy water reactors, such as the Canadian-origin CANDU (Canadian Deuterium) reactors, operate with natural uranium dioxide for fuel and heavy water (in which deuterium, or "heavy hydrogen," substitutes for ordinary hydrogen) for cooling and moderating the core. Third, light-water graphite reactors, such as Chernobyl- or RBMK-type reactors, use enriched uranium dioxide for fuel, light water for cooling, and graphite for moderation.

A few reactors in Japan, France, and Russia are designed not to require moderation of neutrons. Instead, these fast neutron reactors use plutonium, enriched uranium, or both as fuel and liquid sodium as coolant. This type of reactor can be run in a "breeder" mode to generate more fuel than it consumes.

Loss-of-Coolant Accident and Defense-in-Depth Safety Concept

Loss of reactor coolant flow could cause a nuclear accident if safety measures do not restore sufficient cooling. An extremely damaging loss-of-coolant accident (LOCA) would involve the reactor core melting down and releasing highly radioactive fission products to the surrounding environment if these materials are not contained. Inserting control rods, for example, would stop the fission process; however, subsequent radioactive decay of previously produced fission products generates decay heat, which would have to be removed by some cooling mechanism or else the reactor could overheat and melt down. If normal cooling is disrupted, for example by the severing of a pipe used to bring coolant to the core, several backup systems can help ensure continued cooling. For example, the number of coolant pumps in the plant always exceeds the minimum number required to provide needed cooling capacity. Moreover, if electric power is lost to these pumps, the plant can tap into off-site sources of electricity. Furthermore, if these sources are unavailable, emergency diesel generators can supply backup electric power to pumps and other vital plant equipment. Finally, many plants have emergency pumps that are driven by steam turbines. Consequently, in the unlikely event of total loss of electrical power from emergency sources, steam from the plant can be used to pump coolant.

In extraordinary circumstances, coolant piping might break; therefore, nuclear power plants employ added means of emergency core cooling. Most emergency core cooling systems can operate without sources of electric power. (Some very modern reactor designs are "passively safe," meaning that the reactor does not require human intervention to prevent overheating; no reactors using this new approach have been ordered, however.) If these various lines of defense fail, containment structures—which surround the reactor and are made of thick (usually one meter or wider) steel-reinforced concrete—can act to prevent or mitigate the release of radioactivity to the environment. The accident at Three Mile Island (TMI) in 1979 involved loss of coolant and the partial melting of the reactor's core, but only a tiny amount of radioactivity was emitted off-site because the containment at that plant remained intact.[26] Although most power plants use containment structures, some do not, as discussed below.

In general, nuclear power plants rely on these and other defense-in-depth methods to prevent off-site release of radioactivity in the event of an accident or terrorist attack. For most plants, defense-in-depth means employing redundant and separated safety systems to facilitate continued safe plant operation. Of course, accidents or terrorist attacks cannot be absolutely prevented, but defense-in-depth measures can work to reduce the likelihood and consequences of an accident or a successful terrorist attack. Nonetheless, reactor technologies vary in their ability to mitigate such consequences. Even within classes of power plants using the same type of reactor technology, the ability to withstand a terrorist attack also depends on the effectiveness of plant-specific exclusionary and protected zones as obstacles to air, water, or land assault, as well as the readiness and strength of the security force.

Containment Structures and Other Safety Features

Most nuclear power plants worldwide and all U.S. plants employ containment structures as the last line of defense preventing an off-site release of radioactivity. However, many nuclear plants in the former Soviet Union, Eastern Europe, and Great Britain do not use containment structures or employ other safety features that are routine for most Western-designed plants. The risk of a catastrophic accident at these plants, therefore, tends to be greater than at typical Western-designed plants. For example, the Soviet RBMK (Chernobyl-type reactor) lacks a containment structure and has deficiencies in emergency core cooling, fire protection, and reactor control systems.[27]

The main RBMK safety problem linked to the Chernobyl accident was termed "a positive void coefficient." This means that if and when a steam bubble, or void, occurs in the reactor core, the reactor's reactivity increases, which is exactly the opposite effect necessary to control the nuclear reaction.[28] In contrast, light water reactors experience a decrease in reactivity during the production of voids. Another safety problem with RBMKs is that inserting the reactor control rods from their fully withdrawn position increases reactivity—once again, the opposite effect to that desired. During the testing that led up to the Chernobyl accident, the reactor operators had fully withdrawn the control rods. In the aftermath of the accident, this safety defect was removed from RBMKs by altering the control rods.[29] Still, the RBMKs are regarded by Western analysts as inherently less safe than Western-designed reactors.[30] Russia operates eleven RBMKs, and Lithuania has two.

The VVER-440 Model 230, an early-model Soviet-designed PWR, also lacks a number of safety features found in Western PWRs. In particular, it has a "marginal" emergency core cooling system and an inadequate fire protection system.[31] It also does not have a containment structure. This type of power plant is in operation in Bulgaria (four reactors), Slovakia (two), Armenia (one), and Russia (four). The VVER-440 Model 213, which, despite the model number, is a later version of the 440/230, has some safety improvements over the model 230. In particular, the model 213 uses a confinement system to trap radioactivity to prevent escape to the environment; however, this system is not nearly as robust as standard containment structures. Other safety improvements in this design include an emergency core cooling system and a stainless-steel-lined reactor pressure vessel. The VVER-440/213 is in operation in the Czech Republic (four reactors), Hungary (four), Russia (two), Slovakia (two), and Ukraine (two). Despite the inadequacy of some safety features, the VVER-440 has one major safety advantage—that is, the coolant-to-power ratio is about twice that of Western-designed PWRs. Thus, in the event of station blackout as a result of either an accident or terrorist action, the VVER-440 has a greater capacity to keep the reactor core cool.

Not all Western reactors use modern containment structures. In particular, Great Britain operates sixteen MAGNOX reactors without containment buildings. In 2002, British Nuclear Fuel Ltd. (BNFL) announced that it plans to close the four MAGNOX reactors at the Sellafield site soon. Additionally, Britain intends to shut down four other MAGNOX reactors by spring 2005. The graphite used in graphite-moderated reactors, such as the MAGNOX and RBMK designs, presents a radiological safety hazard if the reactor core is breached during an accident or an attack. The graphite could catch fire and burn, spreading radioactive contamination over a huge area. However, the graphite does not burn easily, and measures to block access of air can prevent its combustion.

While containments are mainly intended to guard against radioactivity release caused by internal accidents, most are also designed to withstand severe natural disasters, including earthquakes and tornadoes, depending on the predicted plant exposure to natural hazards. Moreover, in the United States, plants situated near airports or near flight paths have containments that are claimed to be able to withstand many types of airplane crashes. However, post-9/11, statements by the IAEA and the U.S. NRC revealed that containments were not built to prevent penetration by large contemporary aircraft, such as Boeing 757s and 777s. Importantly, plants lacking containments would have little protection against this contingency. The aircraft attack mode is discussed in more depth below.

Although all 103 U.S. nuclear power reactors use containment structures, nine of these reactors employ a relatively weak form of containment. Engineers designed smaller, and therefore weaker, containments for plants using ice-condenser systems because they believed that in the event of a loss of coolant, such systems could absorb enough heat to reduce substantially the pressure buildup inside the containment building. The systems also provided significant construction cost savings at the plants where they are used. However, Sandia National Laboratories analyses showing the inadequacy of ice condensers in some accident scenarios, and the recent discovery of broken screws in the Watts Bar nuclear power plant's ice-condenser system, have raised concern that the ice-condenser plants may not be able to contain radioactivity resulting from accidents or terrorist attacks that resulted in a reactor meltdown.[32]

International Standards for Protecting Nuclear Facilities

Internationally, there are no binding mandates that states meet minimum security standards at research reactors or commercial power plants.[33] The International Atomic Energy Agency has issued voluntary guidelines, however, that have been widely adopted, and the members of the Nuclear Suppliers Group have conditioned the transfer of nuclear equipment and material on recipient state implementation of these guidelines. The IAEA standards, however, are very broad, and this lack of specificity has allowed considerable variance among the national physical security programs that comply with their terms.[34] One widely noted aspect of the guidelines is that they do not require the use of armed guards to protect nuclear power plants, reprocessing plants, or research reactors, and at least one highly advanced nuclear-power-using state is believed not to use them.[35] In 1996, to help less industrially advanced states improve physical security at their facilities, the IAEA established the International Physical Protection Advisory Service (IPPAS).[36] At the request of an IAEA member state, the service assembles a team of international experts in physical protection to assess the state's system, compares it with international standards, and provides recommendations for any improvements that may be needed. The IPPAS has undertaken reviews in Eastern and Central Europe, Latin America, Africa, and Southeast Asia.[37]

Spent Fuel Storage Facilities

Nuclear power plant spent fuel storage facilities contain massive amounts of radioactivity. Most countries store spent fuel adjacent to the nuclear reactor site where it was produced. Worldwide, more than 200,000 metric tons of such spent fuel has accumulated.[38] In the United States, more than 40,000 metric tons of spent fuel is located in underwater cooling pools near power reactors. Roughly, 2,000 tons are added to this inventory every year in the United States. By some estimates, the consequences of a successful terrorist attack on a spent fuel storage area that caused the fuel to ignite could create a radioactive disaster comparable to, if not worse than, one caused by the meltdown of an operating reactor's core and the breaching of its containment, allowing the widespread dispersion of radiation.

Two types of commercial nuclear power plants operate in the United States: boiling water reactors and pressurized water reactors. The spent fuel pools in most BWRs are housed inside reactor buildings and are situated above ground. Those in PWRs are located outside the reactor building (and the containment) and are either partially or fully buried in the ground.[39] At many PWRs the spent fuel pools are largely below the water table, making it very difficult, if not impossible, to drain down the water below the top of the spent fuel rods. Because they are usually raised above ground and thus easier to drain if damaged with explosives, BWR spent fuel pools might appear to be more vulnerable to attack than PWR pools. Once a pool loses its cooling water, residual heat from the spent fuel could lead to a meltdown (depending on the age of the spent fuel, the youngest being the hottest), potentially resulting in a significant off-site release of radioactivity, or even a spent fuel fire, which could spew radioactivity at a considerable distance. Although the NRC requires that all spent fuel pools be constructed to withstand natural disasters such as earthquakes, certain pools may be vulnerable to premeditated man-made attacks. On the other hand, because BWR spent fuel pools are usually inside massive reactor buildings, they appear to be harder to attack than PWR pools, which are located outside of reactor buildings.

Because relatively little spent fuel has been transferred to dry cask storage—the principal alternative at-reactor-site storage system—and because of delays in approving a permanent centralized storage repository, the amount of spent fuel in storage pools at many U.S. power plant sites has increased substantially beyond what was anticipated decades ago. Consequently, plant operators have re-racked storage pools to permit the consolidation of stored spent fuel and to make room for even more. To prevent criticality accidents (that is, unintended heat- and radiation-generating nuclear chain reactions) under these overcrowded, "dense-pack," conditions, neutron-absorbing borated materials are used to separate racks of spent fuel inside the pools.[40]

Although not all spent fuel pools are surrounded by massive, hardened structures such as containments, they are all made of reinforced concrete walls that are four to five feet thick, and most contain a stainless steel liner, which provides added protection against breaches.[41] They also typically contain water several meters (usually about 20 feet) above the top of the spent fuel rods. In addition, the pools are usually designed to prevent drainage of water below the top of the spent fuel. If a terrorist attack or sabotage caused the spent fuel to be uncovered, its zirconium cladding might ignite, which might result in the release of radioactivity.[42] The dense packing in most U.S. spent fuel pools restricts cooling flow, increasing the risk that temperatures could climb to high levels in the event that the spent fuel becomes uncovered.[43]

Transferring spent fuel to dry storage casks could substantially reduce the risks that a terrorist attack might succeed in causing the release of radioactivity from spent fuel into the environment.[44] Rigorous testing of these casks shows that they can withstand crashes, fires, puncture, and water immersion. In addition, the heavy weight of these casks would preclude easy removal by terrorists. Directly addressing the possibility of terrorist attack against the casks, Gail Marcus, former president of the American Nuclear Society, testified to the Senate Committee on Energy and Natural Resources that "the same features that render casks highly resistant to highway and rail accidents tend to make them difficult targets for such attacks."[45] Moreover, these casks would likely be able to store spent fuel safely for at least fifty years, allowing enough time to prepare a national repository for the final disposition of this material.

The National Research Council examined spent fuel pool vulnerabilities in its 2002 report. It found, "[t]he threat of terrorist attacks on spent fuel storage facilities, like reactors, is highly dependent on design characteristics. Moreover, spent fuel generates orders of magnitude less heat than an operating reactor, so that emergency cooling of the fuel in the case of attack could probably be accomplished using low-tech measures that could be implemented without significant exposure of workers to radiation."[46] The Nuclear Regulatory Commission agreed with this assessment. Concerning dry cask storage systems, the National Research Council found that these "systems are very robust and would probably stand up to aircraft attacks as well."[47] The council did not specify how much transferring spent nuclear fuel to storage casks would cost.

In the Fiscal Year 2004 Energy and Water Appropriations Act, Representatives Harold Rogers (R-Kentucky) and David Hobson (R-Ohio) inserted $1 million for a National Academy of Sciences study to examine the vulnerability of spent nuclear fuel stored at commercial nuclear power plants to terrorist attack. As of late 2003, the academy had formed a 10-member panel for a six-month study for Congress. Reportedly, the study will not address whether Yucca Mountain —the anticipated location, in the state of Nevada, of the U.S. national high-level nuclear waste repository —is an appropriate storage site for spent nuclear fuel; it will evaluate safety and security risks of cooling pools versus above ground storage in dry casks at the reactor sites.[48]

The National Research Council also assessed the vulnerability of spent fuel in transit and concluded that "spent fuel transport containers are very robust and appear to offer similar protection against terrorist attack. Studies of the vulnerability of spent fuel transport containers to sabotage suggest that relatively little or no radioactivity would be released in the event of a terrorist attack."[49] Soon after September 11, 2001, the Nuclear Regulatory Commission commenced a review of transport vulnerabilities and has advised licensees to take additional precautions during shipment of highly radioactive materials.

In July 2003, the GAO published a review of "federally sponsored studies that assessed the potential health effects of a terrorist attack or a severe accident on spent fuel, either in transit or in storage." The review also identified "options for DOE to further enhance the security of spent fuel during shipping to Yucca Mountain." The GAO study found,

> The likelihood of widespread harm from a terrorist attack or a severe accident involving commercial spent nuclear fuel is low, according to studies conducted by DOE and NRC. Largely because spent fuel is hard to disperse and is stored in protective containers, these studies found that most terrorist or accident scenarios would cause little or no release of spent fuel, with little harm to public

health. Some assessments found widespread harm is possible under certain severe but extremely unlikely conditions involving spent fuel stored in storage pools.[50]

GAO cautioned that it "did not assess the reliability of data or the methodologies used in the studies that examined potential health effects."[51] Concerning reduction of security risks, GAO identified two major options. First, it recommended consolidating spent fuel into fewer shipments. Under 2003 DOE plans, 175 shipments per year over 24 years would be required to move all spent fuel to the Yucca Mountain repository. If revised contracts between DOE and owners of nuclear plants would allow DOE to remove larger quantities of spent fuel per site, about 300 shipments could be eliminated.[52] Second, GAO advised shipping older, less radioactive spent fuel before transporting younger, more radioactive spent fuel to reduce transportation risks. However, GAO noted that further cost-benefit analysis would be needed to determine whether these options are effective.[53]

Both the NRC and DOE generally approved of this GAO report. Some of the main opponents have been officials and citizens in Nevada, where Yucca Mountain is located. In particular, a study sponsored by the state of Nevada emphasized that past government studies on transportation hazards of spent fuel are inadequate and do not consider the varied range of terrorist attacks that could occur. Consequently, the Nevada study calls for a more comprehensive cost-benefit analysis.[54]

Reprocessing Plants and High-Level Radioactive Waste Storage Sites[55]

Reprocessing plants chemically treat spent nuclear fuel in order to separate its plutonium content (usually about 1 percent by weight) and unused uranium, from highly radioactive fission products. Depending on the intention of the country operating the reprocessing facility, the plutonium can be used either as nuclear power plant fuel, in lieu of uranium, or in nuclear weapons. The fission products within the spent fuel are discharged from the facility and suspended in processing liquids, which are stored in massive tanks nearby as "high-level waste." France, Belgium, and the United Kingdom operate commercial vitrification plants that solidify the liquid high-level waste into a glass matrix. About 1,000 metric tons per year of solidified waste are produced.[56] This amount of vitrification still leaves a backlog of high-level liquid waste remaining in storage tanks, which could be vulnerable to attack or sabotage. Most states with commercial spent nuclear fuel and high-level radioactive waste are planning to place this material into permanent geologic storage, but no state has completed this process. Sweden and Finland appear to be furthest along in siting permanent radioactive waste repositories.

In most nations, reprocessing plants are dedicated either to predominantly civilian or military purposes—that is, to support the plutonium fuel cycle for civilian nuclear power or to provide plutonium for nuclear arms. The civilian reprocessing plants currently in operation are the La Hague facility in France, the Sellafield plant in Great Britain, the Tarapur and Kalpakkam plants in India, and the Mayak facility in Russia. Japan completed a small-scale reprocessing facility at Tokai-mura in 1974 and is currently completing a commercial reprocessing plant at Rokkasho-mura. Most nuclear power-using states do not reprocess spent nuclear power plant fuel but, like the United States, store it at reactor sites pending permanent geologic disposition. Military reprocessing plants are found in Russia, China, India, Israel, Pakistan, and North Korea. Like the United States, France and Great Britain have closed their military reprocessing facilities, but must manage the resulting waste. Russia plans to end its production and separation of weapons-grade plutonium and has already pledged not to use this material for military purposes (as discussed in Chapter 3); however, it will also have the long-term challenge of managing large quantities of high-level liquid waste. China is believed to have stopped producing plutonium for military purposes by the early 1990s.[57] However, as of late 2003, China expressed interest in purchasing the Siemens MOX fuel production plant, which originally was slated to be built in Hanau, Germany. This plant would be situated in Lanzhou, where China has constructed a pilot-scale reprocessing facility for commercial spent nuclear fuel.[58]

As discussed below, in considering potential vulnerabilities of these facilities to terrorist attack, specific targets might include spent fuel pools at the front end of the reprocessing cycle (where fuel from numerous power plants is consolidated awaiting processing, creating very large inventories); the plutonium separation lines (where plutonium and high-level wastes are processed in liquid form); plutonium-oxide powder in high-level waste storage tanks; and high-level waste solidification plants.

Research Reactors

Not only commercial nuclear power plants, but also research reactors, are potential terrorist targets. About 280 of these reactors are operating in 56 countries. According to the compilation of research reactors prepared by the NRC in June 2003, 36 research reactors were operating in the United States, located in 23 states; 12 reactors were being decommissioned; and 7 possessed licenses permitting them only to hold radioactive material.[59] Typically much smaller in size and power output than commercial power reactors, research reactors are primarily employed for scientific research, training, and radioisotope production for medicine and industry, as well as for the testing of materials.[60]

Although the radioactive inventories of research reactors are extremely small in comparison to those at the other types of nuclear installations discussed above, they are typically many times greater than those found in standard radioactive sources that might be used for an RDD. Thus, if the radioactive materials at a research reactor site—most significantly irradiated reactor fuel in the reactor's core or in storage— could be dispersed with explosives, the result would be far less dangerous than a similar act at a nuclear power plant, spent fuel pool, or reprocessing plant, but potentially far more dangerous than most hypothesized RDD incidents.

The NNSA is engaged in assessing the security risks posed by research reactors throughout the world. In particular, the Global Research Reactor Security Initiative Program "is developing a baseline inventory of vulnerable nuclear and radiological materials" at "nuclear research reactors and other such facilities." "Based on this inventory, it will develop a risk-based prioritization of facilities and a strategic plan to effectively mitigate any vulnerability."[61]

POTENTIAL VULNERABILITIES OF NUCLEAR FACILITIES

Considerable information is available in the public domain about vulnerabilities of power plants. This section outlines the ongoing public debate concerning these vulnerabilities, with an eye toward recommending improved security.

A terrorist group that sought to maximize damage to a nuclear power plant or associated facility (e.g., a spent fuel storage pool) would try to harm vital plant systems, such as sources of electric power and cooling. If backup safety systems are inoperable or not available, a prolonged loss of a vital plant system could lead to core damage. As noted above, loss-of-coolant accidents or attacks could damage the reactor core. Similarly, loss-of-heat-sink accidents or attacks in which a plant suffers from insufficient means to remove heat could also result in core damage. Other vital system problems include loss of reactor controls and station blackout in which off-site electric power is lost and on-site backup systems are disabled. Successfully causing large-scale off-site radioactive releases from a spent fuel pool would require breaching the pool walls or floor to cause the loss of cooling water to expose the spent fuel and, most likely, some form of incendiary device to ignite the material. The attack modes outlined below, if successful from the terrorist's perspective, could cause severe harm to a nuclear facility.

Nuclear Power Plants

Nuclear power plant operators have accumulated a vast amount of safety experience through nuclear accident prevention training and planning. In the past several decades, nuclear power has grown into a mature industry. As part of this maturation process, the industry carefully examined the 1979 TMI accident, which resulted in negligible off-site release of radioactivity (as mentioned previously) and the 1986 Chernobyl accident, which resulted in a massive off-site release of radioactivity mainly because the reactor unit was not enclosed inside a containment structure. These accidents provided valuable lessons about nuclear safety. Through study of actual plant operations and numerous computer simulations of plant performance, engineers can predict the likelihood that a particular power plant component would fail due to malfunction. Such failures can occur due to normal wear and tear as well as operator error. To protect against failures arising from equipment malfunction, plant personnel perform preventive maintenance, and to defend against human error, they train thoroughly and frequently. Moreover, the nuclear industry generally has come to embrace a safety culture mentality, which strives to keep safety a high priority.

In contrast to a nuclear accident in which one or perhaps two plant component failures initiate an accident, a terrorist attack could target numerous plant components, thereby potentially damaging more than one vital plant system in a short time period. Thus, defending against a terrorist attack might be more demanding than preventing nuclear accidents. However, because hitting multiple targets simultaneously would challenge terrorist capabilities and because redundant safety systems could further obstruct successful terrorist attacks, most nuclear power plants would likely be resilient to terrorist attack or sabotage.

A terrorist group with access to the detailed layout of a particular nuclear plant and with the technical capability of processing this information to select and strike vital plant systems could cause major damage to the facility. For this reason, this section does not present detailed information on particular plants. However, there is already cause for concern that al Qaeda may have accessed such information. In particular, President Bush stated in the 2002 State of the Union speech that U.S. forces "have found diagrams of American nuclear power plants" in former al Qaeda strongholds in Afghanistan.[62] However, in February 2004, NRC Commissioner Edward McGaffigan said that he doubted that power plant designs were discovered in Afghanistan, but he went on to say he believes that al Qaeda is interested in attacking nuclear facilities. In the same news report, former NRC Chairman Richard Meserve said, "I was very comfortable in putting the nuclear industry at high alert" because of intelligence assessments regarding al Qaeda targets.[63]

Another concern is the spread of nuclear engineering and nuclear power plant operations knowledge throughout a significant fraction of the world—even to so-called rogue states.[64] Thousands of engineers worldwide have received training in nuclear power plant technologies.

However, open-source evidence does not indicate that rogue nuclear engineers are instructing terrorists about how to attack nuclear facilities.

Airplane Crashes

The hijacked commercial airplane attacks of September 11, 2001, raised serious concern that suicidal terrorists flying large airplanes laden with thousands of gallons of jet fuel might strike nuclear facilities. Soon after those attacks, David Kyd, a spokesperson for the IAEA, admitted that nuclear power plants were not designed to protect against crashes of large commercial aircraft. He said, "If you postulate the risk of a jumbo jet full of fuel, it is clear that their [nuclear power plants'] design was not conceived to withstand such an impact."[65] In response to this threat, the U.S. nuclear industry and a few independent analysts have published reports assessing the threats posed by airplanes against power plants and spent fuel pools.

Expressing the Nuclear Regulatory Commission's view about airplane attacks on nuclear power plants, then-NRC Chairman Richard Meserve said in November 2002,

> Many people had asked, understandably, in the period after September 11th about the capacity of nuclear power plants to withstand an aircraft [attack] of the type that occurred in New York and Washington. [The NRC] had not evaluated that matter as a matter of course in the original licensing of the plants. There was an assessment that had been done of the likelihood of an accidental crash into a facility, and if that probability reached a certain level, there was an assessment for the type of aircraft for which that probability rose above the level. ... [The NRC] had not done analysis for large jumbo jets full of aviation fuel."[66] However, post-9/11, the NRC began such an analysis, but the results are classified.

The previous NRC analysis that Meserve referred to assumed an "accidental crash," whereas suicidal terrorists, such as those who flew the planes into the World Trade Center and the Pentagon, would likely be able to strike large targets with great accuracy. There is nothing accidental about hijacked airplanes crashing into power plants. Armed with enough detailed knowledge of a plant, terrorists could conceivably crash planes into the structures that would cause the greatest damage.

Nuclear industry representatives have responded to this threat scenario by pointing out that, in contrast to the World Trade Center, containment buildings present a relatively low profile. Also, they have emphasized that applying maximum force from an airplane to containment structures is difficult because of the round shape of these buildings.[67] Perhaps the focus on containment structures is misplaced because airplane crashes into softer targets, such as auxiliary equipment buildings and other support facilities at the plant, might easily create tremendous damage to the plant and overload emergency response capabilities.[68]

A study sponsored by the Aircraft Owners and Pilots Association concluded that a general aviation aircraft could not penetrate the concrete containment structure surrounding a nuclear reactor. Most general aviation aircraft have payloads of less than 1,000 pounds. (These craft are much smaller than commercial passenger jet airliners.) Because nuclear power plants are designed to prevent a single failure from causing loss of critical safety systems and because support systems are not colocated at a single point, a general aviation aircraft crash could not destroy all safety systems at once. Concerning spent fuel pools, the study pointed out that the pools are deep (filled with some 50 feet of water) and present a low-profile target. Moreover, it calculated that an aircraft would have to ignite a fire that could burn for about 20 hours, which would require some 176,000 gallons of fuel, but general aviation craft carry only about 60 gallons.[69] In comparison, the planes that al Qaeda operatives crashed into the World Trade Center each contained about 22,000 gallons of jet fuel, which had an energy content of 750 billion calories—equivalent to a bomb with an explosive yield of 0.75 kilotons.

In a misleading analysis, the Aircraft Owners and Pilots Association report cites the crash test of an F-4 Phantom fighter jet into a concrete wall as convincing evidence that containment buildings can withstand small airplane crashes. Although the F-4 did not break the wall, this crash test was not intended to demonstrate the integrity of containment structures. More importantly, unlike containment walls, the crash-test wall was allowed to move,[70] thus permitting much of the kinetic energy of the impact to be dissipated rather than channeling this energy into breaching the wall. Nevertheless, in a controversial article in *Science* magazine, 19 authors, who are all members of the National Academy of Engineering and many of whom have close connections to the nuclear industry, continued to draw on the F-4 crash test as evidence that high-speed planes would not penetrate containment structures.[71]

In 2002, the nuclear industry researched the effects of airplane attacks against nuclear facilities. Analysts sponsored by the Electric Power Research Institute (EPRI) and the Nuclear Energy Institute (NEI) wrote the industry report. Using the aircraft ground speed and attack angles associated with the 9/11 Pentagon attack, preliminary results released on June 17, 2002, indicated that containment buildings "can safely protect the reactor against most commercial aircraft," including 757s (the type used in the Pentagon attack) and 777s.[72] For the final report, completed in December 2002, the authors simulated the impact of a Boeing 767-400 into four types of structure: containment buildings, spent fuel storage pools, spent fuel dry storage facilities, and spent fuel transportation containers. Under all scenarios, the simulated airplane crash did not result in release of radioactivity to the environment. The containment buildings suffered "some crushing and spalling (chipping of material at the impact point) of the concrete." The spent storage pools experienced "localized crushing and cracking of the concrete wall," but pools "were not breached," according to the predictions derived from the analysis.[73]

Outside the nuclear industry, John Large, an independent engineering consultant based in the United Kingdom, researched the threat of airplane crashes against British nuclear facilities and completed his report in 2002. Concerning the nuclear facility at Sellafield, his analysis concluded that it is

> ...almost totally ill-prepared for a terrorist attack from the air—the design and construction of the buildings date from a period of over 50 years, many of the older buildings would just not withstand an aircraft crash and subsequent aviation fuel fire, and some of the buildings, now redundant for the original purpose, have been crudely adapted for storage of large quantities of radioactive materials for which they are clearly unsuited.[74]

Although an airplane crash might not cause a complete penetration of the reactor building or other facilities containing radioactive materials,

Large predicted that "even relatively small penetrations will permit the inflow of aviation fuel with the almost certain fire aftermath which would, in itself heighten the release and dispersal of any radioactive materials held within the building structure."[75]

The Nuclear Control Institute (NCI), a nongovernmental organization devoted to research and advocacy on nuclear nonproliferation and nuclear safety, has criticized industry-sponsored analyses that downplay the threat posed to nuclear power plants by airplane crashes. NCI has questioned the assumptions underpinning the industry analysis outlined above. In particular, NCI believes that terrorists such as those that piloted the planes into the World Trade Center and Pentagon could control large commercial planes at much faster speeds and steeper descent angles than considered in the industry studies.[76] Edwin Lyman, a physicist and former president of NCI, calculated whether the engines of a jet could penetrate containment structures. Although for security reasons he did not publish the details of his calculations, he concluded that the engines "would penetrate the containment, leading to a fuel spill within the building and most likely a severe jet fuel fire and/or explosion."[77]

Fires or explosions could cause multiple system, or "common-mode," failures. Although power plants rely on redundant safety systems to prevent or mitigate accidents, common-mode failures are particularly difficult to manage and might easily overwhelm the response capabilities of power plant operators.[78] Furthermore, auxiliary plant buildings are more vulnerable to airplane crashes because, unlike containment buildings, they are not hardened. Tending to the potential damage to auxiliary buildings could severely strain emergency response efforts. One of the most worrisome vulnerabilities is that control rooms are usually not placed inside hardened structures. Destroying or disabling the control room would severely harm the ability to operate the plant. Still, nuclear power reactors can be shut down without use of the control room by using supplementary control stations located outside of the control room proper.

To protect against aircraft attack, NCI has called for "prompt deployment of advanced anti-aircraft weapons to defeat suicidal attacks from the air."[79] After the September 11, 2001, attacks, France, for example, placed anti-aircraft weapons around its reprocessing facility at La Hague, but removed them by early 2002. The NRC, in contrast, does not favor employment of such defensive weapons. Former NRC Chairman Meserve has cautioned that "the operator of the anti-aircraft weapon would need continuous contact with someone who could authorize the downing of a civilian commercial aircraft, with all the attendant implications, and would need to be able to carry out that act in seconds."[80] Other concerns are that "anti-aircraft munitions could impose collateral damage in the surrounding community." The NRC "believes that the best approach to dealing with threats from aircraft is through strengthening airport and airline security measures."[81] In addition, "the NRC has worked with the Federal Aviation Administration and the Transportation Security Administration to put in place a Notice to Airmen advising pilots to not circle or loiter above nuclear power plants or they can expect to be interviewed by law enforcement personnel."[82] Suicidal terrorists flying airplanes would likely not be deterred by the threat of law enforcement interviews. Nonetheless, the main objective of the notice is not to prevent an airborne terrorist attack by itself, but to have a mechanism to determine whether a plant is subject to airborne surveillance or practice runs that could precede an attack.

Soon after 9/11, there was a major restructuring of airline security in the United States. Specifically, the November 2001 Aviation and Transportation Security Act mandated the creation of the Transportation Security Administration (TSA), required explosive-detection systems to screen all bags, demanded that all U.S. airport security be staffed by federal employees, stipulated that cockpit doors be fortified, and called for the hiring of more sky marshals. In addition, all TSA screeners are required to undergo security background checks. Nonetheless, lax enforcement of these checks is reported repeatedly by the press, and great concerns remain about the security at airports abroad that service flights to the United States.[83]

Truck Bombs

Concerns about truck bomb attacks against nuclear facilities date back at least to the 1983 vehicular bombings in Lebanon against American assets. On April 18 of that year, the U.S. Embassy in Beirut experienced a devastating truck bomb attack, and on October 25, the Marine barracks in Lebanon suffered a similar attack. In response to these events, the NRC launched an urgent assessment to determine if it should change its regulations to require licensees to guard against truck bombs. Surprisingly, it decided against the regulation change under consideration after research suggested that this threat was a *greater* security risk than earlier analysis indicated.[84]

Several years later another startling truck bombing spurred the NRC to take action. On February 26, 1993, more than 1,000 pounds of explosive shook the north tower of the World Trade Center. The subsequent federal investigation of this event revealed that Ramzi Yousef, who had ties with al Qaeda, was the mastermind behind this bombing. The NRC issued a requirement for licensees to install truck bomb barriers and incorporated this vulnerability into its design basis threat (DBT) for all U.S. nuclear power plants. In general, the "DBT describes the adversary force composition and characteristics against which licensees design their physical protection systems and response strategies. The DBT applies to power reactors and certain nuclear fuel fabrication facilities."[85] The licensee, such as the nuclear power plant owner, has the responsibility of determining how to defend the licensed facility against the DBT. In particular, the pre-9/11, and presumably the post-9/11, DBT requires defense against a four-wheel-drive vehicle carrying a bomb. The April 1995 Oklahoma City bombing by a domestic terrorist group prompted a renewed review of truck bomb security prevention measures at these plants. By February 1996, the NRC reported that all U.S. nuclear plants had installed adequate vehicular control systems.

Waterborne Attacks

All nuclear power plants require some means of supplying external cooling water. Because of the various backup measures to ensure flow, stopping external cooling water alone would not likely lead to a core meltdown. However, an interruption to this flow for an appreciable time period could force the plant to shut down, and plant managers are concerned about this threat because of the economic impact that could result.

Many power plants are accessible by sea, lake, or river. Thus, a terrorist group in a speedboat, for example, might be able to reach vital water intakes rapidly and attempt to block the water flow. Also, waterborne attacks could take the form of ship-launched cruise missile strikes. Power plant operators at many plants have installed barriers around water intakes. At least in the United States, waterborne attack was not specifically part of the DBT prior to September 11, 2001. Post-9/11, the NRC has reportedly required additional defenses against this means of attack.[86]

Commando-Type Attacks by Land

In the United States, the NRC's DBT prior to 9/11 assumed that a small commando-like group could attack a nuclear power plant. Although the exact size of the group anticipated by this DBT was not openly published, independent assessments had determined that only a handful of attackers was contemplated. As the world witnessed on September 11, 2001, 19 hijackers working in four parallel teams carried out the terrorist attacks in New York and Washington, D.C. (One team, which included four terrorists, failed to carry out its mission, and the hijacked plane was forced to crash into a field in western Pennsylvania.) Nineteen terrorists, a much greater number than a handful of four or five, could form four groups "to drive four vans with large high explosives into the power reactors and spent fuel ponds for a large nuclear facility."[87] Also, such groups could conduct attacks with Katyusha-type rockets (which are Soviet-origin rocket launchers that can fire multiple rockets up to tens of kilometers, for the more advanced variants) or lob mortar shells into the nuclear power plant site. Al Qaeda operatives' firings of Stinger anti-aircraft missiles against commercial passenger planes in Kenya show that terrorist missile attacks against high-value targets are not far-fetched.

The revised U.S. DBT may require defense against relatively large commando groups, but the NRC does not plan to publish the new DBT. While understanding the risks of providing a road map to terrorists if the DBT were publicly available, representatives of nuclear industry watchdog organizations have expressed concern that the NRC did not seek input from such public interest groups when formulating the revised DBT. They have pointed out that prior to September 11, 2001, the NRC was more amenable to considering input from those outside the nuclear industry.[88] According to the NRC, "Meetings to discuss the proposed revisions [to the DBT] have been held with representatives of the nuclear industry cleared to receive such information, and authorized Federal and State agencies."[89]

A post-9/11 event raised concern about the poor state of security at a particular nuclear plant in England. Although this event did not involve commandos, it illustrated how unarmed civilian protestors broke through this plant's defense perimeter. On October 14, 2002, Greenpeace activists easily entered the property of the Sizewell B nuclear power plant in Suffolk, England. About 25 minutes elapsed before two private security guards encountered the encroachers. Although Greenpeace designed this activity as a protest against new nuclear reactors in Great Britain, the breach inadvertently demonstrated the inadequate security at the plant.[90]

Immediately following the terrorist attacks of 9/11, the NRC ordered power plant licensees to increase security at their facilities. An important part of this security enhancement plan was a call for an increase in the number of guards at the plants. Many plant managers, however, were reluctant to spend money on expanding the guard force before knowing how many guards would ultimately be needed. As definitive guidelines from the NRC about guard requirements were not forthcoming for several months, plant managers required guards to work many hours of overtime, leading many guards to experience significant fatigue and stress and raising concerns about their ability to carry out their duties effectively.

Reports[91] about guard disgruntlement eventually prompted the NRC in early 2003 to make improvements, including reducing the amount of overtime allowed, requiring more frequent checks of guards' physical fitness and marksmanship, and generally providing more training to the guard force. Since that time, plant owners have been hiring more security forces. The NRC is also considering how to integrate plant guard forces with those of outside responders, such as state police, to attempt to thwart a large commando-type attack. However, external assistance might not be able to arrive in time to prevent damage to the plant. Some critics of the current guard force structure have called for federalizing the force.[92] In contrast, both NEI and the NRC are opposed to guard force federalization. NEI's report on this issue concluded that "federalizing the security force would weaken coordination with reactor operators" by creating "two separate chains of command for site employees—one for the security force and one for the plant operating staff."[93] NRC's main concern was that federalization could potentially result in conflicting orders being given to the guard force.

For almost two years after September 11, 2001, the NRC did not conduct any force-on-force tests of the guard force. The NRC believed that continuing these drills would have overtaxed an already overworked guard force and was concerned that a drill could create confusion during the high security alert period, thus potentially increasing a plant's vulnerability to attack. In early 2003, the NRC began a pilot program to implement a rigorous testing of the force-on-force program, and in July of that year, the NRC ran its first post-9/11 force-on-force test at the Indian Point Nuclear Power Plant in New York State.

Prior to 9/11, power plant guard forces had failed almost 50 percent of the time to prevent mock terrorist groups from breaching defenses. However, NEI has criticized this characterization of these exercises, which, it argues, were not designed as "pass/fail" tests.[94] In a September 2003 report, the GAO identified many weaknesses of past force on force tests, including "using (1) more personnel to defend the plant during these exercises than during a normal day, (2) attacking forces that are not trained in terrorist tactics, and (3) unrealistic weapons (rubber guns) that do not simulate actual gunfire."[95] The NRC responded that it will add more realism to future exercises by using laser-tag weapons. A June 2003 NEI report stated that guard forces are appropriately trained in terrorist tactics.[96] In general, the NRC felt that the GAO report was "of a historical nature, focusing almost exclusively on NRC's oversight of nuclear power plants prior to September 11, 2001. It thus fails to adequately reflect significant changes [the NRC has] made...to meet the current challenges." NRC Chairman Nils Diaz in his letter to the GAO also noted that "the key issues [GAO] raised are relatively minor and had already been identified by the NRC before [GAO's] review was initiated."[97] GAO replied that it had acknowledged in its report the extensive security improvements made by the NRC after 9/11, and it disagreed that the issues raised in the GAO report were "minor." In particular, GAO underscored that "Sleeping guards, unauthorized access to protected areas, disabled alarms in the vital area, and failure to inspect visitors who set off alarms on metal detectors are all serious security problems that warrant NRC attention and oversight."[98]

To evaluate the risk to the public from a terrorist ground-based assault against a nuclear power plant, the U.S. nuclear industry commissioned a study by EPRI. The EPRI study examined "issues such as the possibility that terrorist threats could inflict damage on reactor fuel; the possibility and magnitude of radiation release from a plant's containment building, which houses the reactor; and the possibility of public health consequences due to potential radiation exposure."[99] In general, the EPRI study found that

> ...risks to public health and safety from a terrorist ground attack on a commercial nuclear power plant are very low.... In more than 90 percent of the scenarios, ground-based terrorist attacks on a nuclear plant would not result in a radiation release severe enough to pose a public health risk.[100]

Essentially, according to the Nuclear Energy Institute's summary of findings, the containment structures and the defense-in-depth safety systems helped to protect the plant and the public during the EPRI study's simulations of terrorist ground-based assaults.[101] Although the NRC believes that quantifying the probability of a terrorist attack against a nuclear plant is impossible, the EPRI study assessed that the qualitative probability of such an attack is "extremely low" due to several factors:

- The low likelihood of a terrorist attack at a nuclear power plant compared with other potential targets

- The high likelihood that an attack force large enough to be successful will be detected and thwarted before an attack can be launched

- The low likelihood that a successful attack could ultimately lead to reactor fuel damage and radiation release due to redundant safety and shutdown features in the plant

- Even in the unlikely event that reactor fuel is damaged, severe public health consequences are unlikely. Even for extreme reactor damage scenarios, the containment building is able to retain a significant percentage of the radiation so that it is not released to the environment. Moreover, damage to the reactor fuel to a point where a substantial release of radiation might occur is a process that takes several hours, allowing time for emergency response measures to be taken.[102]

The first two points above could have been said of the September 11, 2001, terrorist attacks before they occurred. In other words, before 9/11, the United States government did not believe that such attacks had a high probability of occurrence and that such large-scale attacks would succeed undetected. Despite the many opportunities to detect the planning of those attacks, they were not thwarted. However, the EPRI study's conclusions concerning containment of the radiation and the redundant safety systems are security features that buildings such as the September 11, 2001, targets—the World Trade Center and the Pentagon—did not have. The third and fourth points may also be correct as long as containment structures are not breached. As discussed earlier, not all U.S. NPP containments are equally strong. The EPRI analysis apparently factors in a low probability of insider collusion because it credits the nuclear industry with having effective insider threat detection systems in place.[103]

Insider Collusion

Without detailed knowledge of a nuclear power plant's design and operations, terrorists would be hard pressed to carry out a successful attack. Faced with this constraint, a terrorist group might try to enlist the help of plant personnel. Insiders aligned with terrorists pose major threats to nuclear facilities because they can provide knowledge about plant structure, operations, and vital equipment locations during the planning for an attack and can help disable essential plant systems during an attack. In addition, insider collusion represents a grave danger because it can accelerate the terrorist attack, impair timely detection and response, and facilitate simultaneous targeting of vulnerable systems. Disgruntled employees also pose a threat as lone actors. They might sabotage the facility in order to express anger with their superiors or in an attempt to extort funds.

The insider threat has been a concern for decades, since the 1982 attack on South Africa's Koeberg nuclear power plant.[104] In late 2002, then-NRC Chairman Richard Meserve said, "The most difficult [threat] to defend against is the insider."[105] The NRC includes the insider threat in its DBT. Prior to September 11, 2001, the DBT stipulated that a small group of outside attackers could receive assistance from a single insider. Critics have charged that this DBT was inadequate because it assumed that not more than one insider would assist terrorists and that an insider would behave passively—that is, point out vital plant systems, but not actively disable them.[106] Because the revised DBT of April 2003 is considered safeguarded information and not available publicly, it is not possible to determine whether the NRC has addressed these criticisms.

Even before 9/11 the NRC required that background checks on plant personnel be carried out through the FBI's fingerprint database. Because the processing of fingerprints took several months, the NRC had in place a program allowing temporary unescorted access when other checks had been satisfactorily completed. In response to the increased threat environment after 9/11, the NRC moved to tighten access controls by eliminating unescorted access in nearly all circumstances. An expedited three- to five-day turnaround by the FBI of fingerprint checks has made this new policy possible.[107]

The scenario of insider sabotage is particularly problematic in the former Soviet Union, where the prestige of the nuclear industry plunged in the wake of the 1986 Chernobyl accident. In addition, with the breakup of the former Soviet Union, the wages of employees at nuclear facilities plummeted. Underpaid nuclear workers could be easy prey for terrorist groups looking for a contact on the inside.[108]

Cyberterrorism

Although nuclear power plants have experienced few openly reported cyber attacks, the information and control systems of nuclear power plants and other nuclear facilities may be vulnerable to insider sabotage or external hacking. U.S. intelligence officials are believed to be concerned that al Qaeda could launch attacks against computers that control nuclear facilities.[109] Some incidents have underscored that terrorists could exploit this attack mode at least at certain plants. For instance, in 1992, a technician at the Ignalina Nuclear Power Plant, an RBMK-type plant in Lithuania, placed a virus in the computer controlling the plant's auxiliary systems.[110] Allegedly, this worker conducted this act of sabotage in order to call attention to a weakness in the plant's control system and then may have hoped to be rewarded for his service. Instead, Lithuanian authorities arrested him for attempting to damage the facility.[111]

Later reports point to potential cybersecurity weaknesses at U.S. nuclear power plants and other nuclear facilities. Purportedly, a cyberattack penetrated the defenses of a U.S. nuclear facility, but not a commercial power plant, in the recent past.[112] In 2002,

> ...potential terrorists from South Asia and Saudi Arabia were detected surveilling key Web sites nationwide, such as [those of] nuclear power plants and water storage systems. The hackers appeared to be studying, among other things, remote control functions. Strategies on how to manipulate these remote controls have reportedly turned up on al Qaeda computers seized [in 2002].[113]

In January 2003, the Slammer computer worm infested a computer network at the Davis-Besse nuclear power plant in Ohio. This plant was shut down at the time. Because plant computer technicians had not installed a Microsoft security patch, which was available six months prior to the cyberattack, Slammer was able to penetrate the computer network's defenses.[114] Davis-Besse spokesman Richard Wilkins said that, had the plant been running, there would have been little cause for concern because plant operators could have relied on backup analog monitors to ensure safety, thus bypassing the Slammer-infected computer system.[115]

U.S. plants typically use analog control equipment that predates modern computer systems. However, as plants upgrade this analog equipment, they will likely choose more modern computer-based controls that might be vulnerable to software viruses or maliciously damaged hardware.[116] In 2002, the NRC started a research program to examine whether the nuclear facilities it licenses would be vulnerable to cyberattack.[117]

To thwart penetration of computer defenses, computer programmers construct so-called firewalls. Nonetheless, many hackers are adept at breaking through such defenses and would appear to be attractive recruitment targets for terrorists.[118]

Spent Fuel Storage Areas

Several of the modes of attack reviewed above would also be means for attacking spent fuel storage pools at nuclear power plants. These pools could be attacked by airplane crashes, truck bombs, and land-based commando-style raids. Because many of these storage areas are not well hardened against overhead attack, they might be susceptible to attack with stand-off weapons with barrages, such as mortars, which might include explosive shells to breach the pool and drain its water, followed by incendiary shells intended to ignite a spent fuel fire. However, as mentioned previously, spent fuel pools have some inherent protection against attack. For instance, the PWR pools tend to be partially or fully embedded in the ground, making drainage of the pools very challenging or, with some pools, nearly impossible. Moreover, BWR pools tend to be inside massive structures that can provide protection against overhead attack. Furthermore, the pools are built of thick reinforced concrete. Even if a pool is punctured, there might be enough time to restore the cooling water, depending on the intensity of the attack against the nuclear facility. Nevertheless, a substantial release of radiation resulting from an attack on a spent fuel pool cannot be ruled out.

In order to make room for additional spent fuel, pools at U.S. reactor sites have been re-racked to hold more spent fuel than they were originally designed to contain. One of the most effective means for reducing the threat of an attack would be to place spent fuel in highly damage-resistant dry storage casks. A major study by a group of independent analysts in 2003 estimated that $3.5 to $7 billion would be required to transfer some 35,000 metric tons of spent fuel—that is, all spent fuel older than five years stored in pools at reactor sites in the United States as of early 2003—to dry storage casks over the next ten years. (Commercial spent fuel younger than five years would typically require cooling in pools before transfer to dry storage.) This cost estimate is less than one percent of the cost paid by consumers for electricity generated by that fuel.[119] Moreover, short of moving all the fuel to casks, transferring enough spent fuel to dry storage casks to return the pools to a configuration that would allow more effective coolant flow, providing more resistance to ignition even if the pool were drained of water, would significantly reduce the consequences of a terrorist attack.

The NRC and the nuclear industry, however, have criticized this analysis.[120] Because the report is now the focal point of the debate over whether special measures are needed to meet the threat of terrorism at such pools, it is worthwhile to examine the key points at issue in some detail. The NRC staff reviewed the study and found four "significant flaws": (1) "no justification for the postulated probabilities of worst-case spent fuel pool damage," (2) "overestimation of radiation release," (3) "overestimation of consequences and societal costs for the postulated severe event," and (4) "underestimation of the costs of the authors' main recommendation."[121]

Concerning the first objection, in the NRC's view,

> The authors deduce that if there is a 0.7 percent chance in a 30-year period of a terrorist attack leading to a complete release of a spent fuel pool's cesium-137 inventory or an approximately 5 percent chance in a 30-year period of a terrorist attack leading to the release of one tenth of a spent fuel pool's cesium-137 inventory, then the authors' estimated $3.5 to $7 billion cost of relocating the older spent fuel into casks would be justified, but they do not provide any basis for these probabilities.[122]

Alvarez et al. respond that the NRC misquotes the postulated probabilities. In fact, they point out that "the 2001 NRC staff report *Technical study of spent fuel pool accident risk as* [sic] *decommissioning nuclear power plants* (NUREG-1738) estimated a probability for a spent-fuel fire as $0.6\text{-}2.4\times10^{-6}$ per pool per year. Multiplying by 103 pools, this corresponds to a probability of 0.2-0.7 percent in 30 years. Thus the NRC's estimate of the risk of a spent-fuel pool fire caused by accident *alone* would justify the consideration of significant safety improvements. The NRC and Congress must judge how much the urgency is increased by the additional unquantifiable risk of terrorism."[123]

Notably, the United States as of 2004 has accumulated about 3,000 years' worth of commercial reactor power operations, during which time there has not been one accident, including the TMI accident, that has resulted in significant radiation exposure to the public. This laudable operating record is the result of a safety culture that emphasizes defense-in-depth safety systems to protect the public from reactor accidents. In essence, Alvarez et al. are requesting a similar treatment to ensure protection of spent fuel pools. The controversy hinges on whether the nuclear industry has already done enough to guard against radiation release from the pools in the event of a terrorist attack.

Addressing the second point about overestimation of radiation release, the NRC's critique states,

> The assumption of such a large release in NUREG-1738 was a large conservatism which was tolerable for the purpose of that study. However, it is neither a realistic estimate nor an appropriate assumption for a risk assessment of security issues where realism is needed.... Further, preliminary analysis indicates that previous NRC estimates of the quantities of fission products released were high by likely an order of magnitude.[124]

Alvarez et al. respond that the modeling of radiation release during a spent fuel fire is "quite complicated." Moreover, "the range of uncertainty for any serious analysis would be large." They used the range estimates from 10 to 100 percent found in a 1997 study[125] performed for the NRC by Brookhaven National Laboratory (BNL). The NRC's 2001 study employed an estimate of 75 percent. Alvarez et al. argue that if this previous NRC estimate is off by a factor of 10, or "an order of magnitude," then the release fraction of radioactivity is about 7.5 percent, which is not far from the lower bound of 10 percent in the Brookhaven study.[126] Thus, Alvarez et al. imply that even a postulated 7.5 percent release could result in significant radioactive contamination.

Concerning the third critique that the consequences and societal costs are overestimated, the NRC's response states, "The BNL study was performed for a reactor site location that represents an extremely high surrounding population density and that is *not* representative of an industry average.... The use of the BNL study's site characteristics, instead of a mean value considering all sites, biases the economic impacts and societal costs of the postulated worst-case fuel damage event by a factor of 5-10.... When such mitigative site-specific features are taken into account, mean economic impacts and societal costs of the postulated severe fuel damage event would be further reduced."[127] Nonetheless, the NRC did not indicate whether it has done site-specific assessments for all sites. Alvarez et al. counter that once again the NRC misquotes their paper. The authors state that the "assumptions [they] used are standard. The NRC recommended value of $4 million per cancer death is the most important. We used the cancer dose-risk coefficient recommended by the most recent review by the U.N. Committee on Sources and Effects of Atomic Radiation and EPA evacuation criteria." Furthermore, Alvarez et al. state that concerning population density, "the BNL report apparently projected future population growth around U.S. nuclear-power plants," and they chose a value "intermediate between the near and distant population densities used by BNL."[128]

The fourth critique involved an alleged underestimation of the cost of the main recommendation to move the spent fuel from the pools to the dry storage casks. NRC's preliminary estimate is lower than the Alvarez et al. study by "at least a factor of two considering the costs of spent fuel modifications, dry storage facility design and construction, dry storage cask procurement, and cask loading and transfer costs."[129] The NRC also expressed concern that Alvarez et al. did not "address the radiation doses to workers that would result from the removal, disposal, and replacement of the spent fuel pools nor the added risk from these manipulations."[130] Alvarez et al. respond that their own estimate has a factor of two uncertainty already included. In addition, they state that most owners of nuclear facilities are already constructing dry storage facilities; thus that factor need not be included in the overall cost estimate for their recommendation. In general, they accuse the NRC of hiding behind classification restrictions, which block an independent peer review of NRC's analysis. Alvarez et al. recommend that NRC set up a mechanism to allow such a peer review, while taking into consideration how to keep sensitive information outside of the public domain.[131]

Nuclear industry officials interviewed for this book share the assessment of the NRC. As of 2003, they stated that the costs of moving all the spent fuel from the pools into interim dry storage casks outweigh the purported security benefits. In addition, they expressed concern that such transfer would be premature because they would prefer to do just one transfer of spent fuel to transport casks that would then be transported to a permanent repository.[132]

This comment and the several others noted above highlight the need for a comprehensive cost *versus* benefit analysis of whether or not safety and security would be enhanced by the removal of spent fuel from densely packed pools into dry storage casks. Perhaps cost savings and nuclear terrorism risk reduction could come from placing only enough spent fuel into dry storage casks to return the pools to their original design configuration, which would reduce the risk of ignition if a pool were drained, as discussed above. Once a permanent repository for spent fuel is finally approved in the United States, the spent fuel would have to be placed in dry transport casks for removal to the repository. One of the many sticking points involved in the repository decision is the licensing of a cask that would meet this purpose. Depending on the design, such a cask could serve the dual-purpose of acting as dry storage for spent fuel during the interim until the spent fuel were transported to a repository. This issue would require further study. As mentioned above, the National Academy of Sciences formed a task force in late 2003 to conduct a cost/benefit study of pool versus dry cask storage at reactor sites.

Reprocessing Plants

To protect workers, reprocessing takes place behind massive walls, and precautions are taken to prevent unintentional leakage of fission products from the facility. Nonetheless various locations at these plants, including spent fuel pools, processing lines, powered plutonium-oxide storage areas, and high-level liquid waste storage tanks, could be targets for terrorist attacks or sabotage.

Reprocessing sites, therefore, could pose significant nuclear terrorism risks. In Sellafield, for instance, 21 steel tanks contain high-level radioactive waste holding about 211 megacuries (MCi) of cesium-137. In comparison, the Chernobyl accident released approximately 2.4 MCi of cesium-137,[133] although the effects of Chernobyl were greatly intensified because the graphite stack in the reactor burned for ten days and provided a powerful engine for the dispersal of radioactivity. If a large truck bomb of the type employed in the 1995 Oklahoma City bombing were used against a waste tank, it could aerosolize a significant quantity of high-level liquid waste and spew radioactivity over a wide area, while liquid spilling from the damaged tank would cause massive contamination at sites such as Sellafield, including those in the United States. As noted, at operating reprocessing plants, spent fuel storage areas and process lines could also be vulnerable.

Many governments appear to recognize these potential dangers and some, at least, have taken special precautions to protect reprocessing sites. Following the 9/11 attacks in the United States, France, as mentioned, deployed anti-aircraft missiles around the La Hague plant, but removed these by early 2002. Special protective measures at other reprocessing plants have not been publicly disclosed.

Although the United States no longer produces plutonium for nuclear weapons and does not operate reprocessing plants, it continues to maintain storage facilities for extremely radioactive, high-level liquid wastes resulting from prior reprocessing activities. In the United States, two locations are of prime concern: the high-level waste storage tanks at the Savannah River site, in South Carolina, and on the Hanford Reservation, in the state of Washington. Immediately after September 11, 2001, security was strengthened at these sites.[134] However, DOE's inspector general questioned the adequacy of guard training at Hanford, Savannah River, and eight other DOE sites in a March 2004 audit. Specifically, the report revealed that these locations have reduced or eliminated many security training programs. DOE's National Nuclear Security Administration responded that overtime demands have resulted in the training cutback and promised to make improvements.[135]

Research Reactors

Three aspects of research reactors might make them less safe and secure than typical commercial nuclear power reactors.[136] First, many of the low-power (less than 2-megawatt- [MW-] thermal-power output) research reactors in the United States lack containment structures, and even the higher-power research reactors typically use containment structures that are considerably weaker than those used by commercial reactors. Second, most research reactors lack adequate exclusion zones to guard against the potential for truck bombs, and the perimeter protection "is typically a wire fence without anti-vehicle barriers, motion sensors, or electronic/computer-based detection and assessment systems one finds at commercial nuclear power plants."[137] In addition, many research reactors are located on university campuses, where security tends to be less rigorous than at commercial reactor sites. In particular, "many research reactors operated by universities and sometimes by industry are open to visitor specialists (if not to the general public) and have fewer protective security practices than typical nuclear power plants."[138] An added concern is that many university campuses are located in or near cities or high-density suburban population zones. About 50 percent of the high-power operational research reactors in the United States are within 10 miles of population zones containing 500,000 or more people.[139] This group includes reactors in or near Washington, D.C.; Cambridge, Massachusetts; Denver, Colorado; and Austin, Texas. Nuclear power reactors, in contrast, typically are located in more isolated settings, although there are a number of important exceptions to this rule.

In other respects, research reactors generally pose smaller risks than commercial reactors from the nuclear terrorism perspective. Because research reactors generate far less power than commercial power reactors, the inventory of hazardous radioactive materials resident in a research reactor core is considerably less. A typical nuclear power plant has a thermal power output of 2-3 billion watts—2,000-3,000 thermal megawatts (MWth)—while the largest civilian research reactors have outputs of roughly one-hundredth this level, and the majority of research reactors might generate 0.1 to 0.01 percent of this amount. Therefore, in the event of an accident or attack that resulted in a release of radioactivity to the environment, the consequences would be much more limited at a research reactor facility than at a commercial power plant. According to the National Research Council, "Research reactors also generally have fail-safe shutdown systems, and most do not generate sufficient heat to be vulnerable to core accidents, even in the event of a coolant loss."[140] Nonetheless, even a relatively small release of radioactivity could result in actual or perceived harm to the surrounding populace. A February 2003 study on terrorist attacks against research reactors compared to those against power reactors concluded, "The amount and degree of radioactivity of irradiated fuel is likely to be much greater in power reactors, but the vulnerability of irradiated fuel is likely to be greater in research reactors."[141]

After September 11, 2001, the NRC issued advisories to all research and test reactor licensees in order to make them aware of potential terrorist threats to their facilities. The advisories strongly urged licensees to put in place added security measures, including "restricting activities and personnel to those considered essential, reviewing security procedures, enhancing access control, and coordinating with local law enforcement and other federal agencies." The NRC has reported, "All reactors have put measures in place and remain in a heightened state of security awareness."[142] Even with such improvements, however, these units would appear to remain highly vulnerable to an attack with stand-off weapons.

CONSEQUENCES OF EXTREMELY DAMAGING ATTACKS ON NUCLEAR FACILITIES

Some anti-nuclear groups seeking to attack nuclear power plants might seek solely to provoke fear in the surrounding populace and might stop short of attempting to cause an off-site release of radioactivity. Such attacks probably would aim to disrupt the operations of the plant, resulting in financial harm. They also might be designed to increase the public's psychological aversion to nuclear energy.

In contrast, extremist politico-religious terrorist groups such as al Qaeda would likely strive to inflict maximum damage on nuclear facilities and would aim to harm public health through radioactivity release. The analysis below outlines the consequences of extremely damaging nuclear facility attacks. However, the risk assessment data are not sufficient to determine quantitatively the likelihood of such damaging terrorist attacks. A qualitative assessment indicates that—due to the complexity of organizing a successful terrorist assault on a nuclear facility and the defense-in-depth safety and security features at nuclear plants—most attacks would fall short of massive radioactivity release to the environment.

Nuclear Power Plants

An attack targeting a reactor or a spent fuel pool could not ignite an explosive chain reaction—that is, a nuclear bomb-type explosion—and thus the consequences of such an attack will fall far short of a nuclear weapon detonation. Instead, the worst plausible scenario is that terrorists would be able to cause a massive off-site release of radioactivity and substantial damage to the nuclear facility itself. While no such terrorist attacks have occurred, the consequences of the Chernobyl nuclear accident indicate the damage that could result from an extremely damaging terrorist attack.

The 1986 Chernobyl accident directly killed 31 workers who carried out emergency on-site response efforts. They absorbed lethal doses of ionizing radiation. In addition, about 1,800 excess thyroid cancers developed among the surrounding populace exposed to radioactivity from this accident. Although thousands of leukemia cases were predicted, leukemia can require many years to some decades to develop. Richard Garwin and Georges Charpak, two prominent scientists, have estimated that about 24,000 leukemia cases might result from the Chernobyl accident. They point out, however, that because these expected cancer deaths represent a tiny fraction of those that could occur naturally in the population, public health researchers might never be able to determine how many deaths were ultimately a result of this nuclear accident.[143] Bennett Ramberg, an analyst who has written extensively on the accident, offers two reasons why these health effects may have been ambiguously identified:

First, the Chernobyl registry has never been well maintained. Second, mortality across the [former] Soviet Union has increased due to stress, alcoholism, poor diet, etc., all of which will contribute to a decline in Russia's [and the other former Soviet states'] population. This early mortality may mask the impact of the accident.[144]

Despite the uncertainty in the number of cancer deaths, the Chernobyl accident undoubtedly has resulted in tremendous human costs. More than 100,000 people were permanently evacuated because of radioactive contamination in the area surrounding the plant. Varying levels of contamination also spread over large parts of Europe. Substantial areas of Ukraine and Belarus experienced heavy contamination, resulting in exclusion zones where human habitation was strongly discouraged. In addition to being displaced from their homes, many former residents of these zones lost their jobs and suffered from heavy bouts of depression. In Western Europe, contamination made crops and dairy products unfit for consumption, leading to significant economic losses.[145] Worldwide, this accident further deepened the fears and distrust of many individuals regarding nuclear power.

Economic costs stemming from the Chernobyl accident are staggering and result from site cleanup, the contamination of arable land, the closure of dozens of farms, the dislocation of tens of thousands of people, medical care, decommissioning and facility closure, the building of a giant sarcophagus to enclose the destroyed reactor; and the construction of replacement electric generation capacity. Total costs for these activities are upwards of a few hundred billion dollars.[146]

Some 135,000 people were evacuated from the area (approximately 2,700 km^2) about 30 kilometers from the Chernobyl plant in order to prevent acute radiation exposure. The contamination in this exclusion zone exceeded 40 Ci/km^2 of cesium-137. An even larger "affected" area (about 25,000 km^2) had radioactive contamination that exceeded 5 Ci/km^2 of cesium-137. Approximately 825,000 people lived in this area during the late 1980s. The United Nations Scientific Committee on the Effects of Ionizing Radiation (UNSCEAR) has conducted several studies of the health effects in the affected area.

Cesium-137 is the radioisotope of greatest health concern because of its half-life of 30 years, which is on the same order of magnitude as the human life span, and the accident released a large fraction (0.4) of the resident Cs-137 in the Chernobyl reactor core, resulting in about 2.4 MCi emitted to the environment. Cesium-137 also tends to bind to soil and readily enters and contaminates the food chain. Nonetheless, other released radioactive isotopes are of concern, including iodine-131 and strontium-90. Iodine-131 has a half-life of about 8 days and affects the thyroid gland, which strongly absorbs iodine. To prevent this absorption, people would have to have taken potassium iodide to saturate the thyroid gland with non-radioactive iodine (discussed in more detail below). As mentioned above, exposure to I-131 caused some 1,800 people to develop thyroid cancer. Strontium-90 has a half-life (about 29 years) comparable to that of cesium-137, but far less Sr-90 was released (about 0.2 MCi) than that the amount of Cs-137.

In addition, coming seven years after the partial meltdown of a nuclear reactor at the Three Mile Island nuclear power plant in the United States, the Chernobyl accident contributed to the stagnation of the nuclear industry. An often-said aphorism in the nuclear safety field is "a nuclear accident anywhere is a nuclear accident everywhere." To a large extent, the nuclear industry has recovered from the psychological blow, but this recovery took many years of close attention to safety and plant performance. A devastating terrorist attack (or another serious accident) could, once again, hobble the nuclear industry.

Despite fears that most nuclear accidents or even terrorist attacks would result in destruction and harm comparable to the Chernobyl accident, that accident was exceptional. One reason for the extremely severe consequence was the lack of a containment structure. As discussed earlier, all U.S. commercial nuclear power plants use containment structures that would very likely prevent the release of substantial amounts of radioactivity to the environment during an accident or attack, just as the containment protected the public during the 1979 Three Mile Island accident discussed above. Furthermore, U.S. nuclear power plants employ inherently safer designs than that of the Chernobyl plant. Therefore, it is highly improbable that the consequences of a terrorist attack on a U.S. nuclear power plant would approach that of the Chernobyl accident.

Although 13 Chernobyl-style reactors are still operating in Russia and Lithuania, plant operators have made significant safety improvements in these plants to help mitigate the effects of an accident. Consequently, even in the operating RBMK plants, the potential for a Chernobyl-type accident has diminished. Nonetheless, these fixes might not mitigate a terrorist attack that targeted multiple vital safety systems because these plants still do not have containment structures—the last line of defense against release of radioactivity to the environment.

For the foreseeable future, the nuclear power plants with the greatest inherent vulnerability to terrorist attack are the Soviet-designed plants lacking containments. Because many of these are near major population centers, ensuring the security of these facilities remains as one of the highest priority tasks to reduce the risk of a nuclear terrorist attack or sabotage against a nuclear power plant.

Spent Fuel Pool Attacks

By some estimates, an extremely damaging spent fuel pool accident or attack could have more negative health consequences than a worst-case nuclear power plant accident or attack because the inventory of highly radioactive cesium-137 is much greater in the typical spent fuel pool than the 2.4 MCi of cesium-137 released from Chernobyl's reactor core. Calculations by Alvarez et al. show that 400 metric tons of spent fuel from a U.S. PWR and stored in a spent fuel pool would contain about 35 MCi of cesium-137.[147] This amount is significantly greater than the approximately 5 MCi in the core of a 1,000 electric megawatts (MWe) PWR, a typical U.S. PWR. Cesium-137, a radioisotope with a 30 year half-life, decays to barium-137, which emits a penetrating gamma ray, posing a serious external and internal hazard to human health. About half of the fission-product activity in ten-year-old spent fuel comes from these radioisotopes.[148]

As discussed in an earlier section, Alvarez et al. have recently calculated the consequences of a spent fuel pool fire. If 10-100 percent of the cesium-137 were released in a pool containing 35 MCi of cesium-

137, "37,000-150,000 km^2 would be contaminated above 15 Ci/km^2 [curie per square kilometer]; 6,000-50,000 km^2 would be contaminated to greater than 100 Ci/km^2; and 180-6,000 km^2 to a level of greater than 1,000 Ci/km^2."[149] In comparison, the Chernobyl accident contaminated a smaller area, about 10,000 km^2, above 15 Ci/km^2. In 1997, the NRC published a study that estimated the consequences of a spent fuel fire that released 8-80 MCi of Cs-137. It predicted 54,000-143,000 extra cancer deaths; 2,000-7,000 km^2 of condemned farm land; and evacuation costs of $117-$566 billion.[150] Alvarez et al. point out that these consequences are consistent with their independent analysis. (As described in an earlier section, the NRC has published a critique of the Alvarez et al. study.)

Reprocessing Plant/High-Level Waste Storage Facility Attacks

Commercial-scale reprocessing plants, such as Sellafield in the United Kingdom, La Hague in France, and Mayak in Russia, contain greater quantities of highly radioactive materials than a commercial power plant's spent fuel pool. As mentioned above, for example, 21 tanks at Sellafield contain an estimated total of 211 MCi of cesium-137. On average, each tank holds about 10 MCi. This amount is less than one-third the quantity of Cs-137 in a typical spent fuel pool. Thus, if an attack against Sellafield were able to breach and release radioactivity from one tank, the consequences would be somewhat less than the effects from a devastating attack on a spent fuel pool, assuming the same fraction of cesium-137 released in the two scenarios. The amount released depends on the chemical and physical composition of the radioactive material in the tanks. It cannot be ruled out that a terrorist group could breach more than one tank at Sellafield or some other reprocessing plant. In such an event, the consequences could exceed that expected from an attack against a spent fuel pool.

Research Reactor Attacks

Because research reactors contain much less radioactivity than commercial reactors, a devastating attack on a research reactor would not cause nearly as much damage as a similar attack on a commercial reactor, assuming that both reactors were equally distant from population centers. Small research reactors—100 thermal kilowatts (kWth) to 1 MWth—contain a maximum of 0.1 MCi of fission products in their cores, medium-size reactors (1 MWth to 10 MWth) hold about 1 to 10 MCi of radioactivity, and large research reactors (10 MWth to 250 MWth) contain up to 100 MCi. In contrast, the typical commercial PWR's core has several hundred MCi of radioactive fission products. Thus, the consequences of a devastating attack on a typical research reactor would be orders of magnitude less than the effects from an extremely damaging attack on a commercial reactor.

PREVENTION, ENFORCEMENT, AND RESPONSE MECHANISMS

The preceding discussion has examined the steps that a terrorist group would need to take to attack or sabotage a nuclear facility in order to cause a major release of radiation. It has assessed potential vulnerabilities of nuclear facilities, including commercial nuclear power plants, research reactors, spent fuel pools, reprocessing plants, and high-level radioactive waste storage facilities, and it has highlighted some of the efforts undertaken by the United States and other governments to reduce the risk of terrorists causing substantial harm to the public and property through a release of significant amounts of radiation from these facilities. This section will briefly address some activities undertaken by the United States and other nations to reduce the threat of nuclear terrorism against nuclear facilities.

U.S. Efforts

According to a self-assessment in September 2003, "The NRC took security seriously well before the September 11, 2001, terrorist attacks and has redoubled its efforts since then in light of the increased threat [level stemming from 9/11]."[151] Although it has reported "no specific credible threats of a terrorist attack on nuclear power plants since September 11[, 2001],"[152] it acknowledges that, "If a credible threat emerges against a specific nuclear facility, additional protective measures may be mandated even without a change in the overall threat level."[153]

Since 9/11 the NRC's efforts to prevent terrorist attacks against its licensed facilities include:[154]

- Activation of its Emergency Operations Center and its Incident Response Centers.

- Temporary shut down of the NRC Web site to ascertain whether posted material could pose a security threat; subsequently, the NRC has been gradually reposting much, but not all, of the information.

- Initiation of a comprehensive "top-to-bottom review of its security program"; a major part of this effort is to update the design basis threat.

- Integration of security activities within the Commission by forming the Office of Nuclear Security and Incident Response; this office works closely with the Department of Homeland Security, the Federal Bureau of Investigation, the Federal Emergency Management Agency, the Department of Energy, the Federal Aviation Agency (FAA), and any other relevant agencies depending on the required task. (The work with the FAA has focused on notifying pilots to not fly near or loiter next to nuclear facilities.) In addition, as noted earlier, the Transportation Security Administration has acted to tighten security over commercial passenger airlines, measures which, if effectively implemented, would further reduce the risk that passenger jets might be used to as weapons against U.S. nuclear facilities.

- Use of inspections to verify that nuclear facility managers have upgraded security measures; the specific security enhancements are sensitive information that the NRC does not make public. However, these upgrades are known to include greater protection against vehicular bombs and waterborne attacks.

- Renewal of force-on-force exercises in July 2003; subsequently, the NRC intends to require a more frequent three-year instead of the previous eight-year testing cycle for each nuclear power plant.

- Establishment of a five-level threat alert system to reflect the Department of Homeland Security system.

- Issuance on April 29, 2003, of orders "to power reactor licensees to augment additional training and qualifications requirements for security personnel; these orders include more frequent firing of weapons, more realistic training under a broader range of conditions, and firing against moving as well as fixed targets."[155] These licensees were given one year to put in place adequate protection to meet the requirements of the revised design basis threat.

Notwithstanding these new requirements, previously cited reports in the past two years suggest that actual performance under NRC mandates in critical areas has sometimes fallen below acceptable standards, even though licencees may have been technically in compliance with those mandates. These past shortfalls point to the desirability of the commission's adopting rules based on performance rather than on formal compliance with promulgated standards.[156] Performance measures would strengthen protection against terrorist attack if adopted with respect to a wide range of facility security measures, including guard-force capabilities and implementation of access controls, personnel screening, and emergency shut-down/plant protection procedures during the course of terrorist incidents. The resumption of force-on-force exercises in July 2003 is a step in this direction, but the approach needs to be extended to the broadest possible range of NRC directives.

In addition, despite the fact that the NRC in 2003 upgraded the design basis threat against nuclear facilities, it is not clear that the DBT adopted by the commission fully reflects the magnitude of the 9/11 attack—19 motivated and well-trained attackers operating in four separate teams—and it is possible that the NRC has relied too heavily on outside capabilities, such as rapid response forces or the efforts of the Transportation Security Administration to secure commercial air travel against terrorists. It may be recalled that a team of 19 were arrested in Ontario in August 2003 for conspiring to attack a Canadian nuclear power plant and that more than 20 terrorists were alleged to have been involved in the Madrid commuter train bombings of March 11, 2004. This strongly suggests that if the commission's current DBT does not address this threat, it should be reexamined on an urgent basis. Even if a 9/11-type of threat is deemed to go beyond the requirements in a reevaluated DBT, precedents exist to factor such a threat into nuclear plant security planning and testing. Similar to the nuclear industry's preparation for beyond design-basis nuclear accidents, there needs to be expedited preparation for beyond design-basis attacks.

For several years, emergency response plans have been in place in communities surrounding U.S. nuclear power plants. These plans define 10-mile and 50-mile emergency planning zones. For people within the 10-mile zone, upon the event of an emergency, evacuation or sheltering is required. Within the 50-mile zone, officials would continuously monitor radiation levels to determine whether to order residents to evacuate or seek shelter. Consulting with many federal agencies, the Environmental Protection Agency and the NRC determined these zone limits. FEMA has the lead responsibility in emergency response planning beyond a nuclear plant site. The NRC evaluates the performance of each site's biennial exercise of the response plan, and FEMA checks on the surrounding communities' test of the emergency procedures. If a plant does not have an NRC-approved emergency plan, it is not permitted to operate. After September 11, 2001, NRC required plant licensees to review their emergency response plans in light of the potential for terrorist attacks.[157]

Plans are in place for the emergency distribution of potassium iodide (KI) pills to people living within a 10-mile emergency planning zone around a nuclear power plant. Ingesting KI would saturate the thyroid gland and help prevent the absorption of radioactive iodine into that organ, reducing the risk of developing thyroid cancer. Critics have expressed the need for greater stockpiling of KI and implementation of more effective distribution plans.[158] In addition, those immediately outside the 10-mile zone may also need access to KI.

One of the biggest complications that the NRC, FEMA, and other federal and local emergency response officials will have to confront in the event of a real accident or a terrorist attack is the tendency for people to self-evacuate. Such "shadow" evacuations can extend well beyond the zone of potential immediate harm to health. Blocking of roadways could severely complicate emergency response measures.

Improving the effectiveness of emergency response at certain high-risk nuclear plants requires further effort. For example, in a March 2003 review of the emergency preparedness plans for the Indian Point 2 Nuclear Power Plant, which is the closest nuclear plant to New York City, the U.S. GAO found that the NRC itself has discovered that "emergency preparedness weaknesses have continued" at the plant since an earlier review had identified shortcomings.[159] In particular,

> NRC reported that, during an emergency exercise in the fall of 2002, the facility gave out unclear information about the release of radioactive materials, which had also happened during the February 2000 event. Similarly, in terms of communicating with the surrounding jurisdictions, little has changed, according to county officials. County officials told GAO that a videoconference system—promised to ensure prompt meetings and better communication between the plant's technical representatives and the counties—had not been installed.[160]

Illustrative International Efforts

An extended analysis of international developments related to security at nuclear power plants and other facilities is beyond the scope of this study. What follows is a very selective and brief account of recent efforts at several sites outside of the United States to enhance security at commercial power plants and reprocessing facilities. Relevant assistance programs by the IAEA also are noted.

In March 2003, responding to increased perceived threats as a result of the war in Iraq, the Canadian government ordered security enhancements around the Pickering and Darlington nuclear power plants and the waste storage sites at Pickering and Bruce. As discussed above, in August 2003 authorities arrested 19 men on charges of attempting to harm the Pickering plant. In October 2003, the Canadian Nuclear Safety Commission (CNSC) announced new rules to formalize interim security measures that were put into effect after September 11, 2001. The regulations call for an increase in the numbers of guards at Canada's nuclear facilities and the construction of new buildings near the Darlington and Pickering nuclear sites to house the nuclear response force. Members of this force will undergo detailed security screening.

Under the new regulations, Canadian nuclear facilities are required to install explosive detectors and X-ray machines to carry out improved screening of individuals and vehicles seeking to enter the facilities. However, these regulations do not call for reinforcing the facilities against airplane attack. Moreover, the CNSC opposed placing surface-to-air defensive missiles around Canadian nuclear facilities, expressing concern that commercial aircraft could be accidentally shot down.[161]

Soon after 9/11, France developed a plan to increase protection around its nuclear facilities, including the placement of anti-aircraft batteries around the La Hague reprocessing facility. Although by early 2002, these defenses had been removed,[162] France continued to upgrade its nuclear security in other respects, including implementing a strict no-fly zone around its nuclear sites. The December 2002 decree specified a 1,000-meter vertical and 5-km radial zone around each facility. French officials believe that security against terrorism has been especially strong since 1995 when a series of terrorist attacks on French soil prompted France to enact a special security strategy termed "Vigipirate," which remains in place today.[163] However, the trade publication *Nucleonics Week* has reported concerns about the coordination of France's nuclear security efforts and involvement of the public. In June 2003, it stated, "Nuclear safety authorities play essentially no role in defining the design basis threat for nuclear installations in France, with that task falling to the industry ministry's defense division and military authorities. There has been virtually no communication on the subject of aircraft crash protection, in contrast to what has been said about nuclear plant protection in the U.S. and certain other countries, like Switzerland."[164]

In Great Britain, where many nuclear power plants lack containments, the government in July 2002 proposed establishing a Civil Nuclear Constabulary.[165] This agency would act as a stand-alone force with powers to make arrests even at non-nuclear sites, such as ports, and to stop and search individuals and vehicles up to three miles from nuclear sites. Since April 2004, the House of Lords in the British Parliament has had legislative provisions for the nuclear constabulary force included in the energy bill. Unlike French security officials, British authorities decided against arming the reprocessing facility Sellafield with anti-aircraft missiles. In March 2003, Prime Minister Tony Blair announced a high priority review of nuclear material transportation in response to a ninefold increase in the occurrence of safety incidents. Blair also promised to accelerate security enhancements for trains and ships hauling nuclear material.[166] Later in the year, Welsh politicians were reportedly incensed that a train-spotting magazine was publishing the routes of trains carrying nuclear waste. They questioned whether the magazine had breached Britain's 2001 Anti-Terrorism Act. Martin Buck, managing editor of the magazine, reportedly said, "We contacted the Home Office [of the United Kingdom] after September 11 and were told we were okay to keep publishing the times."[167]

Starting in the 1970s, Germany required spent fuel pools to be situated along with nuclear power plant reactors inside hardened containment buildings. When Germany later reevaluated its spent nuclear fuel storage policy, it decided to store spent fuel away from nuclear reactors, but instead of pool storage, it stipulated that spent fuel would have to be stored in dry storage casks, which would be housed inside reinforced-concrete buildings. Tests have shown that these shielded casks and structures can protect the spent fuel even against shaped-charge attacks.[168] According to the December 2002 U.S. nuclear industry-sponsored study conducted by EPRI, such casks can also protect the spent fuel from aircraft crashes.[169]

In Russia, where 17 nuclear power reactors (more than half of the operating commercial Russian reactors) lack containments, the military, emergency responders, and power plant security personnel have conducted training exercises to prevent attacks against nuclear power plants. One scenario involving a group of mock terrorists simulated an attack against the Kalinin nuclear power plant. Expressing confidence about Russia's nuclear plant defense preparations as of 2002, MINATOM Deputy Minister Anatoliy Kotelnikov said, "[Russia's] system for protecting nuclear facilities exists and is sufficiently reliable."[170] In early 2003, however, MINATOM Minister Alexander Rumyantsev called attention to the shortage of funding for physical security at Russian nuclear plants. In particular, he told the Russian Duma, lower house of Parliament, that MINATOM needed $203 million to enhance physical security, including electronic monitors, at all nuclear facilities.[171] Yuri Vishnevsky, former head of the Russian Federal Inspectorate for Nuclear and Radiation Safety, echoed Rumyantsev's concerns. In March 2003, Vishnevsky told the Duma that the level of funding for security "is only 10-15% of what is required."[172] In February 2003, he informed the Interfax news agency that since September 11, 2001, and the October 2002 hostage crisis at the Dubrovka Theater in Moscow, Russian authorities have increased security at nuclear facilities. He stated that Chechen rebel field commander Shamil Basayev occasionally directs threats against nuclear power plants and that the Russian Federal Security Service treats these threats seriously. Vishnevsky said, "We are primarily concerned about nuclear stations in the south—Rostov and Novovoronezh [those nearest to Chechnya]. We pay the greatest attention to these objects, but do not forget about others."[173]

According to a group of Russian sociologists and former workers at nuclear facilities, alcoholism and drug abuse are prevalent at Russia's nuclear power plants and the reprocessing facility at Mayak. Vladimir Lupandin, a researcher with the Institute of Sociology affiliated with the Russian Academy of Sciences, said, "A nuclear power plant does not fight alcoholism, it propagates it. Alcoholics are advantageous for nuclear power plants—they are modest and undemanding." Sergei Kharitonov, who had worked for 27 years at the Leningrad Nuclear Power Plant (an RBMK facility) and who now works for the Norwegian environmental group Bellona, charged that this plant has "a total lack of a culture of security." The news report cited a MINATOM spokesperson as saying that alcohol and drug abuse are less prevalent in cities with nuclear facilities than other Russian cities.[174]

In Lithuania, authorities have expressed concern about the vulnerability of the Ignalina Nuclear Power Plant, which has two RBMK reactors, to terrorist attack. During the twelve months following September 11, 2001, Lithuania spent more than $250,000 to enhance security at Ignalina. In late 2002, the government announced plans to purchase 60 Stinger anti-aircraft missiles from the United States. Reportedly, an unspecified number of the Stingers will be used to help provide protection around Ignalina.[175] However, it is unclear what controls will be in place to prevent downing of non-attacking aircraft that could inadvertently stray into the air space near the plant. Lithuania has agreed to shut down one of its two reactors at the site in 2005; the second is likely to be closed in 2009.

In Japan, information about the security procedures in place at the country's nuclear power plants is not readily available. However, since 9/11, some reports have indicated that security has been enhanced at high-value nuclear facilities. For instance, the Metropolitan Police Department formed a command office to direct some 5,000 security officers to guard critical infrastructure facilities, such as nuclear power plants.[176] Japanese electric utility companies have established anti-terrorism divisions to help analyze security threats against nuclear power plants.[177] Notwithstanding these measures, it often is observed that for cultural reasons Japan employs very different security measures than those used in the United States or Europe. In particular, its guard forces tend to be unarmed.[178] Concerns have also been raised that Japan has not adopted a design-basis threat that reflects today's terrorist threat. Japan's high-level waste facilities at Tokai-mura are not protected by containment structures, and could be especially vulnerable.

China publishes little information about the security of its nuclear facilities. Reportedly, China's Ministry of Health has developed the "Health Ministry's Medical Contingency Plan for Dealing with Nuclear and Radiation Terrorist Attacks," and the government has organized 12-member teams to respond to such attacks and coordinate with security personnel.[179] Informal discussions by the authors with Chinese diplomats and nuclear experts indicate a growing Chinese appreciation of the dangers posed by nuclear terrorism, including the possibility of attacks on nuclear power facilities. It is not yet evident, however, that practical steps will be taken by China to address these threats.

In addition to the measures taken by national governments to improve security at nuclear power installations, the IAEA also has a series of programs to assist member states. They include training programs to help governments raise security standards at nuclear facilities, evaluation missions to assess the physical protection of nuclear material at nuclear power plants and other facilities (the so-called International Physical Protection Advisory Service, or IPPAS), and measures to help states respond to terrorist acts including sabotage.[180] The IAEA, for example, has encouraged all states with a nuclear infrastructure to develop a design basis threat to assess what security enhancements are required. The agency also provides workshops to assist states to define and implement a DBT. According to a March 2004 IAEA report,

> Work continues on the conceptual approaches related to sabotage against nuclear facilities and the protection against an insider threat. In particular, an overview document on protection against sabotage, self-assessment guidelines and facility walk-down procedures have been prepared. Security and safety aspects of sabotage have been considered as complementary in these documents. Work has started to identify a methodology to strengthen information technology security at nuclear installations as a part of sabotage protection.[181]

Further, the IAEA has an Emergency Preparedness Review (EPREV) service for member states to direct reviews of nuclear or radiological emergency preparedness plans. Since 1999, the agency has conducted safety and security assessments of research reactor and spent fuel storage facilities in certain countries of the former Soviet Union as well as Eastern and Central Europe.[182]

In January 2002, the Advisory Group on Nuclear Security (AdSec) was formed to advise the IAEA director general on "the Agency's activities related to preventing, detecting, and responding to terrorist or other malicious acts involving nuclear and other radioactive materials and nuclear facilities."[183] An AdSec Working Group has convened regularly since that date and has prepared research materials for the AdSec. Although detailed information about how much effort AdSec devotes to analyzing the security of nuclear facilities is unavailable, a U.S. government official indicated that he would support the establishment of an IAEA advisory group tasked solely to assess nuclear facilities' security requirements.[184] This action has not yet transpired, but in October 2003 IAEA Director General Mohammed ElBaradei expanded the focus of the International Nuclear Safety Group (INSAG) to include the nuclear security-safety interface. According to Dr. Richard Meserve, a former NRC chairman and the director of INSAG, the group will consider "matters in which safety considerations impact security or in which security demands affect safety."[185]

PRIORITY ISSUES

Under most circumstances, it would be difficult for a terrorist organization to produce a massive radiation release from a U.S. nuclear facility. More terrorists, however, might be prepared to attempt this act than acquire and detonate a nuclear weapon.

At present, all U.S. commercial nuclear power plants employ containment structures and subscribe to defense-in-depth safety and security. The U.S. nuclear industry reportedly is spending significant financial resources to strengthen its nuclear facilities even further. Moreover, the NRC has devoted renewed attention to enhancing the protection of its licensed nuclear facilities. This generally positive picture, however, needs improvement in the following respects:

- *Design basis threat.* It is not clear that the design basis threat adopted by the NRC (or reportedly by other regulatory bodies in other states) fully addresses the magnitude of the 9/11 attacks—19 motivated and well-trained attackers operating in four separate teams. Accordingly, the United States should increase preparedness to address more demanding threats than reportedly incorporated in current regulations. Furthermore, similar to the nuclear industry's preparation for beyond design-basis nuclear accidents, there should be expedited preparation for beyond design-basis terrorist attacks or sabotage of nuclear facilities.

- *Vulnerable systems outside containments.* Certain vital nuclear safety systems and spent fuel pools at certain U.S. nuclear power reactors are potentially vulnerable to attack from the air or from stand-off weapons because they are outside of nuclear power plant containments. A variety of cost-effective measures for hardening these plant elements have been proposed; these should be evaluated on an urgent basis and steps taken rapidly to mitigate these potential vulnerabilities.

- *Ice-condenser containments.* Some U.S. nuclear power plants with ice-condenser containments may be more susceptible to attack from aircraft and stand-off weapons. The NRC should analyze this potential vulnerability on an urgent basis to determine whether long-term compensatory security measures are needed, and, at least for those plants close to large population areas, whether added security measures—including intensified post-attack safe-shut-down drills—should be temporarily required.

- *Nuclear plants without containments.* The United States should also encourage all states to shut down power plants without containment structures. Great Britain's plans to close half of its MAGNOX are welcome, and it would be desirable for all Soviet-designed RBMK reactors also to be phased out as soon as possible.

- *Research reactors.* Research reactors, though containing only a fraction of the radiation inventory of a nuclear power plant, usually do not use containments and are often located in urban settings in the United States. A formal U.S. government assessment of the risks posed by these facilities and of any measures needed to secure them against attack or sabotage is urgently needed.

- *Performance-based security.* The NRC appears to be too dependent on a compliance-based approach for evaluating nuclear power plant security, although in July 2003 it renewed force-on-force performance tests of guard forces. It should continue to take strides toward implementing a performance-based system of evaluation in which security systems and DBTs are continually tested.

[1] The desire to damage sites of symbolic importance to the target country, however, does not necessitate a large-scale attack on a nuclear facility causing a catastrophic release of radiation; sabotage causing limited disruption or damage might suffice.

[2] In 2002, the National Research Council, for example, examined the risks of a terrorist attack on a nuclear power plant (NPP). That study found that an attack "on an NPP could have potentially severe consequences if the attack were large enough. The severity is highly dependent on the specific design configuration of the NPP, including details such as the location of specific safety equipment." National Research Council, "Nuclear and Radiological Threats," Chapter 2 in *Making the Nation Safer: The Role of Science and Technology in Countering Terrorism* (Washington, DC: National Academies Press, 2002), p. 43.

[3] The Progressive Policy Institute in its report, *America at Risk: A Homeland Security Report Card*, Progressive Foundation, July 2003, gave U.S. nuclear power plant security an "A" grade. In particular, the study stated that

"nuclear power plants have always been extremely secure and additional security measures may not be the best use of resources." Overall, PPI gave the Bush administration a "D" grade for homeland security. Unlike many other vulnerable infrastructure sectors in the United States, the nuclear power industry had the benefit soon after 9/11 of a solid foundation of security upon which to make improvements.

[4] Jenny Weil, "NRC Research May Prove to be Key to Improving Security, Meserve Says," *Inside N.R.C.*, November 4, 2002, p. 2.

[5] Maintaining strong security around nuclear power plants could create disincentives for terrorists. Terrorist groups have finite resources and presumably will seek to maximize their chances of success by identifying soft targets. As long as nuclear plants are hardened targets, terrorists are likely to turn their attention to more vulnerable facilities. Moreover, if a terrorist group wants to maximize the body count from an attack, there are easier ways to kill large numbers of people than by attacking nuclear plants.

[6] Oleg Bukharin, "Upgrading Security at Nuclear Power Plants in the Newly Independent States," *Nonproliferation Review* 4 (Winter 1997), p. 31.

[7] Gavin Cameron, *Nuclear Terrorism: A Threat Assessment for the 21st Century* (London: Palgrave MacMillan, 1999).

[8] Center for Nonproliferation Studies, "Chechen separatists threatened attacks on various Russian military and industrial facilities, including nuclear power plants." CNS WMD Terrorism Database, Entry #1000, July 22, 2000; Ibid., "Russian security reported credible threat that Chechen rebels were threatening to terrorize Russian nuclear facilities. It was reported that Chechen gunmen stated that they planned to 'take advantage of Russian laxity and give Russia a second Chernobyl.'" Entry #810, February 3, 2000.

[9] Quoted from a documentary film by Yosri Fouda, the chief investigative reporter for the Arab television station Al-Jazeera, as reported in Alaa Shahine, "Al Qaeda is Said to Have Weighed Nuclear Targets," *Washington Post*, September 9, 2002, p. A13.

[10] News reports from that period illustrate the uncertainties plaguing the intelligence addressing the threat against the Palo Verde nuclear power plant. One report indicated that al Qaeda might target the plant. Chitra Ragavan, Douglas Pasternak, Betsy Streisand, and Stephen Sawicki, "Alert and Anxious: There are still lots of holes in the U.S. security blanket," *U.S. News and World Report*, March 31, 2003, pp. 35-37. Another report said that government officials were concerned that Iraqi sleeper cells might launch an attack against the plant. "Possible Nuclear Plant Threat Probed: U.S. Investigation is Underway as Security is Bolstered at the Arizona Palo Verde Facility," *Los Angeles Times*, March 21, 2003, p. A35. The reported threat to the plant developed as the U.S.-led war against Iraq was starting. Finally, an unnamed government official was quoted as saying that the threat came from "uncorroborated information." Melanie Tatum, "Energy Sector Vital to Security, but Question of Financing Remains," *Inside F.E.R.C.'s Gas Market Report*, March 28, 2003, p. 10.

[11] Gary Fields, Ann Davis, and Jacob M. Schlesinger, "U.S. is Pressed to Boost Role in Private-Sector Security," *Wall Street Journal*, March 21, 2003, p. A4.

[12] Tatum, "Energy Sector Vital to Security."

[13] "Police Detain 19 Men, Some for Possible Terrorist Links," Agence France Presse, August 22, 2003.

[14] DeNeen L. Brown, "Canada Arrests 19 As Security Threats," *Washington Post*, August 23, 2003, p. A20.

[15] Melanie Axelrod, "When Activism is Regarded as an Act of Eco-Terrorism," Earth Times News Service, October 1997, <http://www.guardiannewsltr.com/subscribers/environews/october97.htm>.

[16] U.S. House of Representatives, House Resources Committee, Subcommittee on Forests and Forest Health, Statement of James F. Jarboe, Domestic Terrorism Section Chief, Counterterrorism Division, Federal Bureau of Investigation, on the Threat of Eco-Terrorism, February 12, 2002.

[17] Gavin Cameron, *Nuclear Terrorism: A Threat Assessment for the 21st Century* (New York: Palgrave MacMillan, 1999), pp. 117-118.

[18] Walter Laquer, "Postmodern Terrorism," *Foreign Affairs* 75 (September/October 1996).

[19] Joseph Lelyveld, "Bombs Damage Atom Plant Site in South Africa," *New York Times*, December 20, 1982, p. A1.

[20] David Beresford, "Man Who Spiked Apartheid's Bomb," *Guardian* (London), January 2, 1996, p. 9.

[21] Ibid.

[22] Ibid.

[23] U.S. Energy Information Agency, "U.S. Nuclear Generation of Electricity," <http://www.eia.doe.gov/cneaf/nuclear/page/nuc_generation/gensum.html>, accessed on April 7, 2004.

[24] Even in uranium-fueled reactors, plutonium eventually provides a significant portion of the energy pro-

duced because of the nuclear transformation of uranium-238 into plutonium during reactor operations. However, most reactors are initially fueled with uranium (with uranium-235 being the fissile isotope), not plutonium.

[25] Some pressurized water reactors in operation today are certified by regulatory authorities to use plutonium as fuel. Such fuel takes the form of mixed oxide (MOX) fuel, combining uranium dioxide with plutonium dioxide. Some critics of MOX fuel have claimed that the use of MOX increases the potential consequences of accidents. Proponents counter this criticism by pointing out that strict licensing requirements are in place. Should an accident or terrorist attack result in off-site release of radioactivity from MOX-fueled reactors, the number of cancer deaths in the surrounding populace could be greater than such deaths resulting from similar accidents in or attacks on uranium-fueled reactors because plutonium is a greater health hazard than is uranium; E. S. Lyman, "Public Health Risks of Mixed Oxide Fuels," *Science & Global Security* 9 (2001), pp. 33-79. While the intention here is not to settle the controversies over using MOX fuel in pressurized water reactors, it is worth noting that nuclear terrorists seeking to maximize harm to public health might specifically decide to strike PWRs using MOX. At a minimum, public fears would likely be further stimulated once people are made aware that the attacked nuclear plants use plutonium for fuel.

[26] Of the more than 1 million curies of iodine-131 in the Three Mile Island reactor core, only an estimated 15 curies were released. The health effects from the accident were deemed to be below the detectable level. David Bodansky, *Nuclear Energy: Principles, Practices, and Prospects* (Woodbury, New York: AIP Press, 1996), pp. 217-218.

[27] Office of International Nuclear Safety and Cooperation, "Soviet-Designed Nuclear Power Plant Profiles," U.S. Department of Energy, October 2000, <http://insp.pnl.gov/?profiles/introduction>.

[28] For more technical details about this phenomenon, see, for example, Bodansky, *Nuclear Energy*, p. 221.

[29] The increase in reactivity arose from the displacement of water by the control rods. In the RBMKs, water acted as a reactivity "poison" such that it absorbed neutrons, thus decreasing the reactivity of the reactor. In the initial design of the RBMK, inserting control rods would displace water away from the fuel during the first 1.25 meters of insertion of the rods, thus, in effect, increasing the number of neutrons and increasing the reactivity. Bodansky, *Nuclear Energy*, p. 221.

[30] G7 Officials' Statement, "Lisbon Initiative on Multilateral Nuclear Safety," G7 Summit, Lisbon, Portugal, May 1992; U.S. General Accounting Office (GAO), "Nuclear Safety: Concerns with the Continuing Operation of Soviet-Designed Nuclear Power Reactors," GAO/RCED-00-97, April 2000.

[31] Office of International Nuclear Safety and Cooperation, "Soviet-Designed Nuclear Power Plant Profiles, pp. 5-6.

[32] Kenneth D. Bergeron, *Tritium on Ice: The Dangerous New Alliance of Nuclear Weapons and Nuclear Power* (Cambridge, MA: MIT Press, 2002), p. 72. Specifying some of the major technical concerns about ice-condenser reactors, Bergeron writes, "The problem with these reactors is that the volume of the containment building is small compared to large dry containments, but the reactor core is about the same size. The ice suspended in the massive banks of wire baskets…would certainly be effective in absorbing the steam from a pipe break accident, but severe accidents tend to overwhelm the ice. Buildup of hydrogen is a particular problem, since removing steam from a steam-hydrogen-air mixture increases the concentration of hydrogen, making the gas more combustible, even detonable."

[33] George Bunn, Chaim Braun, Alexander Glaser, Ed Lyman, and Fritz Steinhausler, "Research Reactor Vulnerability to Sabotage by Terrorists," *Science & Global Security* 11 (2003), p. 86.

[34] IAEA, *The Physical Protection of Nuclear Material and Nuclear Facilities*, INFCIRC/225/Rev.4 (Corrected), October 1998.

[35] Ibid. Section 7.2.14 of INFCIRC/225 states: "A 24-hour guarding service should be provided. The guard force or the central alarm station personnel should report at scheduled intervals to the off-site response forces during non-working hours. Guards should be trained and adequately equipped for their function in accordance with national laws and regulations. When guards are not armed, compensating measures should be considered. The objective should be the arrival of adequately armed guards and/or response forces before an act of sabotage begins or while the act is in progress so that they may prevent its successful completion."

[36] IAEA, "Guidelines for IAEA International Physical Protection Advisory Service (IPPAS)," <http:// www.iaea.org/worldatom/Programmes/Safeguards/Protection/guideline.html>.

[37] IAEA, "Promoting Nuclear Security: What the IAEA is Doing," IAEA Information Series, Division of Public Information, 03-01610/FS/Series 1/03/E, <http://www.iaea.org/NewsCenter/Features/NuclearSecurity/iaea20040601.html>.

[38] George Bunn, Fritz Steinhausler, and Lyudmila Zaitseva, "Strengthening Nuclear Security Against Terrorists and Thieves Through Better Training," *Nonproliferation Review* 8 (Fall-Winter 2001), p. 139.

[39] U.S. GAO, "Spent Nuclear Fuel: Options Exist to Further Enhance Security," GAO-03-426, July 2003, p. 4.

[40] Robert Alvarez, Jan Beyea, Klaus Janberg, Jungmin Kang, Ed Lyman, Allison MacFarlane, Gordon Thompson, and Frank von Hippel, "Reducing the Hazards from Stored Spent Power-Reactor Fuel in the United States," *Science & Global Security* 11(2003), pp. 1-51.

[41] Robert Alvarez, "What about the Spent Fuel?" *Bulletin of the Atomic Scientists* (January/February 2002), p. 45.

[42] U.S. Nuclear Regulatory Commission, *Technical Study of Spent Fuel Pool Accident Risk at Decommissioning Nuclear Power Plants*, Report NUREG-1738, NRC, 2001, executive summary p. xi.

[43] Alvarez et al., "Reducing the Hazards from Stored Spent Power-Reactor Fuel."

[44] Ibid.

[45] U.S. Senate, Committee on Energy and Natural Resources, written testimony by Gail H. Marcus, May 22, 2002.

[46] National Research Council, "Nuclear and Radiological Threats," p. 47.

[47] Ibid., p. 47.

[48] Associated Press, "Security of Stored Nuke Waste at Reactors to Get New Study," *Las Vegas Journal Review*, December 4, 2003.

[49] Ibid., p. 48.

[50] U.S. GAO, "Spent Nuclear Fuel: Options Exist to Further Enhance Security," executive summary.

[51] Ibid., p. 2.

[52] Ibid., pp. 2-3.

[53] Ibid., p. 3.

[54] Nuclear Waste Project Office, State of Nevada, "Terrorism Considerations in the Transportation of Spent Nuclear Fuel and High-Level Radioactive Waste," Fact Sheet, available at: <http://www.state.nv.us/nucwaste/yucca/terrfact.htm>, accessed on November 3, 2003.

[55] Globally, in addition to operational power and research reactors, as of late 2001—the date of the most recent compilation by the International Atomic Energy Agency—there were 89 uranium mills and uranium conversion plants, 22 uranium enrichment plants, 59 nuclear fuel fabrication plants, 67 interim radioactive waste storage sites, and 13 reprocessing facilities. Anita Nilsson, "The Threat of Nuclear Terrorism: Assessment and Preventive Action," paper delivered to Symposium on Terrorism and Disarmament, United Nations, New York, October 25, 2001. Of these, reprocessing plants and certain waste storage sites are the only ones whose sabotage or attack could result in extensive off-site radiological contamination.

[56] Uranium Information Centre, "Radioactive Waste Management," July 2002, <http://www.uic.com.au/wast.htm>, accessed on April 7, 2004.

[57] David Wright and Lisbeth Gronlund, "Estimating China's Production of Plutonium for Weapons," paper for Union of Concerned Scientists, January 16, 2003.

[58] Stephanie Lieggi, "Controversy in Germany: Siemens Sale of MOX Plant to China," CNS Research Story of the Week, December 12, 2003, <http://www.cns.miis.edu/pubs/week/031212.htm>, accessed on April 15, 2004.

[59] U.S. Nuclear Regulatory Commission, "Research and Test Reactors," Fact Sheet, June 2003, available at <http://www.nrc.gov/reading-rm/doc-collections/fact-sheets/research-reactors.pdf>, accessed on December 5, 2003.

[60] For the different types of research reactors in each country see IAEA, "Nuclear Research Reactors in the World,"<http://www.iaea.or.at/worldatom/rrdb/>.

[61] National Nuclear Security Administration, Global Research Reactor Security Initiative, <http://www.nnsa.doe.gov/na-20/nrtr_grrsip.shtml>, accessed on June 4, 2004.

[62] Bill Gertz, "Nuclear Plants Targeted," *Washington Times*, January 31, 2002.

[63] Matthew L. Wald, "Panel Member Says that Bush Erred on Details of Threat to Reactors," *New York Times*, February 10, 2004.

[64] John H. Bickel, "The Threat to US Licensed Nuclear Power Plants from Terrorism," paper prepared for CNS, "Different Faces of Nuclear Terrorism Project," November 2002.

[65] William J. Kole, "Global Atomic Agency Confesses Little can be done to Safeguard Nuclear Plants," Associated Press, September 19, 2001.

[66] Richard A. Meserve, "Nuclear Terror Threats," remarks delivered during panel discussion, Carnegie International Non-Proliferation Conference, Washington, DC, November 15, 2002.

[67] Officials at the Nuclear Energy Institute (names withheld by request), interview by authors, Washington, DC, February 2003.

[68] Brett Lieberman, "Experts Question Nuclear Plants' Strength Under Assault," Newhouse.com, September 14, 2001.

[69] Robert M. Jefferson, "Nuclear Security: General Aviation is Not a Threat," report for Aircraft Owners and Pilots Association, May 16, 2002.

[70] Sandia National Laboratories, which conducted the crash test, has stated, "The test was not intended to demonstrate the performance (survivability) of any particular type of concrete structure to aircraft impact." Sandia Science Photo Gallery, Sandia National Laboratories, <http://www.sandia.gov/media/NRgallery00-03.htm>, accessed on June 4, 2004.

[71] Douglas M. Chapin, Karl P. Cohen, W. Kenneth Davis, Edwin E. Kintner, Leonard J. Koch, John W. Landis, Milton Levenson, I. Harry Mandil, Zack T. Pate, Theodore Rockwell, Alan Schriesheim, John W. Simpson, Alexander Squire, Chauncey Starr, Henry E. Stone, John J. Taylor, Neil E. Todreas, Bertram Wolfe, and Edwin L. Zebroski, "Nuclear Power Plants and Their Fuel as Terrorist Targets," *Science*, September 20, 2002, p. 1997. This article generated much controversy as evidenced by the critical press coverage and critiques by independent analysts, including letters to *Science* by Frank von Hippel and Richard Garwin, who expressed strong disagreement with the Chapin et al. article.

[72] "Nuclear plant damage from air attacks not likely," *Nuclear News*, August 2002, p. 21.

[73] Electric Power Research Institute, "Deterring Terrorism: Aircraft Crash Impact Analyses Demonstrate Nuclear Power Plant's Structural Strength," Nuclear Energy Institute, December 2002.

[74] John H. Large, "The Implications of 11 September for the Nuclear Industry," *Disarmament Forum*, May 2003, p. 30.

[75] Ibid, p. 33.

[76] John Mintz, "Nuclear Plants are Secure, Study Says: Industry Critics Dismiss the Report as Flawed," *Washington Post*, December 26, 2002, p. A2.

[77] Nuclear Control Institute, National Press Club Briefing, September 25, 2001, statement by Edwin Lyman in "Security of the Nation's 103 Nuclear Reactors."

[78] Ibid.

[79] U.S. House of Representatives, House Committee on Energy and Commerce, Subcommittee on Oversight and Investigations, *A Review of Security Issues at Nuclear Power Plants*, statement of Paul Leventhal on Behalf of the Nuclear Control Institute and Committee to Bridge the Gap, "Nuclear Power Reactors are Inadequately Protected Against Terrorist Attack," December 5, 2001.

[80] U.S. House of Representatives, House Committee on Energy and Commerce, Concerning Nuclear Power Plant Security, statement by Richard A. Meserve submitted by the United States Nuclear Regulatory Commission to the Subcommittee on Oversight and Investigations, April 11, 2002.

[81] U.S. Senate, Concerning Nuclear Power Plant Security, statement by Richard A. Meserve, submitted by the United States Nuclear Regulatory Commission to the Committee on Environment and Public Works, June 5, 2002.

[82] U.S. Nuclear Regulatory Commission, "Nuclear Security Enhancements Since Sept. 11, 2001," Fact Sheet, September 2003.

[83] See Jennifer Oldham, "Baggage Checkers Breach Security at LAX," *Los Angeles Times*, June 12, 2003, p. B1; Denise Marois, "Congress Wants Answers to Box Cutter Security Breach," *Aviation Daily*, October 23, 2003, p. 4; and Karen Lee Scrivo, "Carry On?" *Government Executive*, December 2003, p. 24. As of March 2004, more than one million ground employees at U.S. airports are still allowed to bypass security checkpoints that screen for weapons. David Stone, the acting chief of the TSA, said that TSA's security emphasis is on background checks, and the cost of employee screening at all 445 major airports in the United States would be cost

prohibitive. Critics contend that by not requiring these employees to pass through security checkpoints, one of them could easily hand a gun or other weapon to a terrorist who had already been cleared through the checkpoint. Another concern is that TSA has yet to conduct deeper background checks, although it has plans to do so. Jonathan Kim, "TSA Defends Its Scrutiny of Airport Workers," *Washington Post*, March 18, 2004, p. A14.

[84] Daniel Hirsch, "The Truck Bomb and Insider Threats to Nuclear Facilities," in Paul Leventhal and Yonah Alexander, eds., *Preventing Nuclear Terrorism: Report and Papers of the International Task Force on Prevention of Nuclear Terrorism* (Lanham, Maryland: Rowan & Littlefield, 1987).

[85] U.S. NRC, "Nuclear Security Enhancements Since Sept. 11, 2001," p. 3.

[86] Ibid., p. 3.

[87] George Bunn and Lyudmila Zaitseva, "Guarding Nuclear Reactors and Materials from Terrorists and Thieves," paper presented to the plenary session, "Combating Nuclear Terrorism," IAEA Symposium, November 2, 2001.

[88] Bennett Ramberg, "Safety or Secrecy?" *New York Times*, May 20, 2003.

[89] U.S. NRC, "Nuclear Security Enhancements Since Sept. 11, 2001."

[90] Catherine Auer, "Greenpeace to Sizewell B: D'oh!," *Bulletin of the Atomic Scientists* (January/February 2003), pp. 6-7; "Protesters Invade British Nuclear Plant," *New York Times*, January 14, 2003.

[91] Project on Government Oversight (POGO), "Nuclear Power Plant Security: Voices from Inside the Fence," Report, September 2002; U.S. Senate, House Subcommittee on National Security, testimony of Danielle Brian, Executive Director of POGO, "Combating Terrorism: Preventing Nuclear Terrorism," September 24, 2002; Matthew L. Wald, "Surveyed Reactor Guards Feel Vulnerable," *New York Times*, September 12, 2002; Matthew L. Wald, "Guards at Nuclear Plants Say They Feel Swamped by a Deluge of Overtime," *New York Times*, October 20, 2002.

[92] For example, Democratic Massachusetts congressman Edward Markey favors federalizing the guard force; Matthew L. Wald, "Security at U.S. Reactors Criticized by Congressman," *New York Times*, March 25, 2002.

[93] Nuclear Energy Institute, "Implications of Security Force Federalization on Nuclear Power Plant Security: An Evaluation by the Nuclear Energy Institute," December 2001.

[94] According to the Nuclear Energy Institute, "The results of past force-on-force exercises conducted by the NRC have been mischaracterized by some NRC staff members and anti-nuclear activists. In past exercises, an adversary's simply touching a piece of plant equipment was falsely characterized as a 'failure' of security—even though it would not have jeopardized plant safety or security. In addition, to artificially increase the percentage of what they describe as 'failures,' critics compare the number of touches to the number of plant exercises, rather than to the total number of simulated drills conducted in each exercise (four simulations per exercise). For example, while 37 deficiencies were identified by the NRC in 81 force-on-force plant exercises conducted between 1991 and 2001, the total number of simulated drills in that period was 324. Thus, deficiencies were identified, and immediately fixed, in 11 percent of the simulations." NEI, "The NRC's 'Force-on-Force' Exercises for Nuclear Plant Security," Public Policy Issues Paper, June 2003.

[95] U.S. GAO, "Nuclear Regulatory Commission: Oversight of Security at Commercial Nuclear Power Plants Needs to be Strengthened," GAO-03-752, September, 2003.

[96] NEI, "The NRC's 'Force-on-Force' Exercises for Nuclear Plant Security."

[97] Letter from NRC Chairman Nils Diaz to James Wells, director, Natural Resources and Environment Division, U.S. General Accounting Office, August 7, 2003, published in GAO, September 2003, GAO-03-752, pp. 33-34.

[98] GAO, GAO-03-752, September 2003, pp. 25-26.

[99] Nuclear Energy Institute, "Public Health Risk Low in Unlikely Event of Terrorism at Nuclear Plant, EPRI Study Finds," Public Policy Issues Paper, March 2003.

[100] Ibid.

[101] Ibid.

[102] Ibid.

[103] Ibid.

[104] Hirsch, "The Truck Bomb and Insider Threats to Nuclear Facilities."

[105] Richard A. Meserve, "Nuclear Terror Threats," remarks for panel discussion at the Carnegie International Non-Proliferation Conference, Washington, DC, November 15, 2002.

[106] Union of Concerned Scientists backgrounder, "Nuclear Reactor Safety," available at <http://www.ucsusa.org/clean_energy/nuclear_safety/page.cfm?pageID=176>, accessed on October 7, 2003.

[107] Two NRC officials, names withheld by request, interviews by authors, Rockville, MD, February 3, 2003.

[108] Bukharin, "Upgrading Security at Nuclear Power Plants in the Newly Independent States," pp. 31-32.

[109] Eric Lichtblau, "Warning on Iraqi Hackers and U.S. Safety," *New York Times*, January 17, 2003.

[110] Bukharin, "Upgrading Security at Nuclear Power Plants in the Newly Independent States," p. 32.

[111] William Potter, "Less Well-Known Cases of Nuclear Terrorism and Nuclear Diversion in the Former Soviet Union," August 1997, <http:www.nti.org/db/nisprofs/over/nuccases.htm>.

[112] U.S. government official (name withheld by request), personal communication with authors, Washington, DC, January 2003.

[113] Editorial, "A Virtual Arsenal," *Washington Times*, February 15, 2003, p. A12. Corroborating information was published in A. Oppenheimer, "Terrorism Threats to Infrastructure Security," *Jane's Terrorism & Security Monitor*, January 1, 2003.

[114] Kevin Poulsen, "Slammer Worm Crashed Ohio Nuke Plant Network," *SecurityFocus*, August 19, 2003, available at <http://www.securityfocus.com/news/6767>, accessed on October 11, 2003.

[115] Daniel Horner, "Cyber-Security Lapse at Davis-Besse Prompts Markey Letter to NRC," *Nucleonics Week*, August 28, 2003, p. 13.

[116] NRC official (name withheld by request), interview by authors, Rockville, MD, February 3, 2003.

[117] Weil, "NRC Research May Prove to be Key to Improving Security, Meserve Says," p. 2.

[118] Council on Foreign Relations, "Q&A on Cyberterrorism," <http://www.terrorismanswers.com/terrorism/cyberterrorism2.html>, accessed on February 9, 2003.

[119] Alvarez et al., "Reducing the Hazards from Stored Spent Power-Reactor Fuel in the United States."

[120] NRC and Nuclear Energy Institute officials (names withheld by request), interviews with authors, Washington, DC, February 2003; U.S. Nuclear Regulatory Commission, "NRC Review of Paper on Reducing Hazards from Stored Spent Nuclear Fuel," Fact Sheet, available at: <http://www.nrc.gov/reading-rm/doc-collections/fact-sheets/reducing-hazards-spent-fuel.html>, accessed on October 13, 2003.

[121] Ibid.

[122] Ibid.

[123] Robert Alvarez, Jan Beyea, Klaus Janberg, Jungmin Kang, Ed Lyman, Allison MacFarlane, Gordon Thompson, and Frank von Hippel, "Response by the authors to the NRC review of 'Reducing the Hazards from Stored Spent Power-Reactor Fuel in the United States,'" *Science & Global Security* 11 (2003). Emphasis was in the original.

[124] U.S. Nuclear Regulatory Commission, "NRC Review of Paper on Reducing Hazards from Stored Spent Nuclear Fuel," (Hereafter cited as NRC Response). Even long before the Alvarez et al. study was published, the NUREG-1738 report was considered controversial at the NRC.

[125] Brookhaven National Laboratory, *A Safety and Regulatory Assessment of Generic BWR and PWR Permanently Shutdown Nuclear Power Plants*, NUREG/CR-4982, 1997.

[126] Alvarez et al., "Response by the authors to the NRC."

[127] NRC response

[128] Alvarez et al., "Response by the authors to the NRC."

[129] NRC response

[130] Ibid.

[131] Alvarez et al., "Response by the authors to the NRC."

[132] Nuclear Energy Institute officials, names withheld by request, interviews with authors, Washington, DC, February 2003. Research at Oak Ridge National Laboratory is leading toward potential development of a multifunctional cask that can be used for spent nuclear fuel (SNF) "storage, transport, and disposal. The SNF is handled only once—when the cask is loaded—minimizing handling of SNF and allowing the cask to be welded shut after loading." Charles Forsberg, "A Multi-Functional Cermet Spent-Nuclear-Fuel Super Cask," Proceedings of the Institute of Nuclear Materials Management 44th Annual Meeting, Phoenix, Arizona, July 13-17, 2003.

[133] Zackary Moss, "The Vulnerability of the UK's Nuclear Facilities to Terrorism," Bellona Position Paper, November 11, 2002.

[134] John Stang, "Hanford, nuclear plant boosting security," *Tri-City Herald*, September 12, 2001, and John Bankston, "August-Ga.-Area Industrial Sites Boost Security after Sept. 11 Attacks," *Knight Ridder Tribune Business News*, September 8, 2002.

[135] U.S. Department of Energy, Office of Inspector General, "The Department's Basic Protective Force Training Program," Audit Report, DOE/IG-0641, March 2004, and "Nuclear Security Training Lacking; Plants Eliminated or Reduced Drills Designed to Repel Attacks, U.S. Says," *Washington Post*, March 18, 2004, p. A29.

[136] Paul Levental and Yonah Alexander, "Preventing Nuclear Terrorism," in Paul Leventhal and Yonah Alexander, eds., *Preventing Nuclear Terrorism: Report and Papers of the International Task Force on Prevention of Nuclear Terrorism* (Lanham, Maryland: Rowan & Littlefield, 1987).

[137] George Bunn et al., "Research Reactor Vulnerability to Sabotage by Terrorists," p. 89

[138] Ibid., p. 88.

[139] In February 2004, CNS surveyed all 52 operational research reactors and zero-power critical assembly facilities in the United States. Of these, 20 had power ratings of 1 MW or greater; 23 had power ratings less than 1 MW, but greater than "zero-power" critical assemblies; and the remaining 9 were zero-power critical assemblies. Ten of the high-power research reactors were near or in high-density population zones of 500,000 or more people; five of these reactors were near (within 10 miles) or in intermediate zones containing 100,000 to 499,999 people; and five were near or in low zones containing less than 100,000 people.

[140] National Research Council, "Nuclear and Radiological Threats," p. 45.

[141] George Bunn and Chaim Braun, "Terrorism Potential for Research Reactors Compared With Power Reactors," *American Behavioral Scientist* 46 (February 2003), p. 714.

[142] U.S. NRC, "Research and Test Reactors," Fact Sheet, p. 5.

[143] Richard L. Garwin and Georges Charpak, *Megatons and Megawatts: A Turning Point in the Nuclear Age?* (New York: Knopf, 2001), pp. 189-195.

[144] Bennett Ramberg, e-mail correspondence with authors, November 13, 2003.

[145] For example, see the U.N. Science Committee on the Effects of Atomic Radiation (UNSCEAR) reports on the Chernobyl accident, available at <http://www.unscear.org/chernobyl.html>, accessed on November 3, 2003.

[146] Although it is very difficult, if not impossible, to add up the total costs, Belarus has estimated that "losses over the 30 years following the accident will amount to $235 billion." Ukraine has estimated "the loss as $148 billion over the period from 1986 to 2000." *The Human Consequences of the Chernobyl Nuclear Accident: A Strategy for Recovery*, A Report Commissioned by UNDP and UNICEF with the support of UN-OCHA and WHO, January 25, 2002, p. 63. Belarus and Ukraine experienced the most radioactive contamination and economic damage compared to all other nations affected by the accident.

[147] Alvarez et al., "Reducing the Hazards from Stored Spent Power-Reactor Fuel in the United States."

[148] Manson Benedict, Thomas H. Pigford, and Hans Wolfgang Levi, *Nuclear Chemical Engineering*, 2nd Edition, (New York: McGraw-Hill Book Company, 1981), Table 8.1.

[149] Alvarez et al. "Reducing the Hazards from Stored Spent Power-Reactor Fuel in the United States."

[150] Ibid.

[151] U.S. NRC, "Nuclear Security Enhancements Since Sept. 11, 2001."

[152] Richard A. Meserve, Chairman, U.S. Nuclear Regulatory Commission, "One Year After—Reflections on Nuclear Security," INFOCAST Conference: The Nuclear Renaissance: Maximizing the Value of Nuclear Assets, Washington, DC, September 11, 2002.

[153] NRC, "Nuclear Security Enhancements Since Sept. 11, 2001."

[154] This material comes from U.S. NRC, "Nuclear Security—Before and After September 11," <http://www.nrc.gov/what-we-do/safeguards/response-911.html>, accessed on November 27, 2002; and U.S. NRC, "Nuclear Security Enhancements Since Sept. 11, 2001."

[155] U.S. NRC, "Nuclear Security Enhancements Since Sept. 11, 2001." Similar to the NRC's assessment, the U.S. nuclear power industry's view is that it "has always had the highest security standards of any American industry." Nevertheless, the industry reports that it has significantly strengthened security since September 11, 2001. In particular, it points to the additional 2,000 security officers at nuclear power plants and the $370 million increase in security expenditures. Nuclear power plants now also have tighter access requirements. To access vital areas of a plant, an attacker would have to pass through many guarded and controlled entry points. Key-card access is required to gain admission into vital areas. This security mechanism would also allow plant

managers and security staff to track the whereabouts of employees, thereby helping to prevent the insider threat. Further protection against insider attack comes from a "fitness-for-duty" program, which includes drug and alcohol abuse prevention programs and behavioral observation. Employees are required to pass extensive background checks. Moreover, plant owners have installed more vehicle barriers and intrusion detection equipment. The Nuclear Energy Institute emphasizes that the nuclear industry is "one of the few industries whose security program is regulated by the federal government." See Nuclear Energy Institute, "Nuclear Plant Security," Fact Sheet, May 2003.

Although the dominant security paradigm is that more security forces provide more overall security, not all observers accept this view. Stanford University professor Scott Sagan challenged this conventional wisdom in a 2003 paper titled, "The Problem of Redundancy Problem: Why More Nuclear Security Forces May Produce Less Nuclear Security." This paper will be published in *Risk Analysis: An International Journal* (August 2004) and won the Columbia University's Institute for War and Peace Studies 2003 best paper in Political Violence prize. In this analysis, Sagan identifies three ways in which more security forces could lead to less nuclear security. First, the insider threat could increase with the addition of more guards. Although there is a very small probability that a particular guard could act as a subversive force, he notes, adding more guards would undoubtedly raise the likelihood that a rogue guard is included in the guard contingent. The nuclear industry, of course, conducts background checks of its guards. However, Sagan cautions, "Unfortunately, organizations that pride themselves on high degrees of personnel loyalty can be biased against accurately assessing and even discussing the risk of insider threats and unauthorized acts." Once background checks are completed on a particular guard, that person could become the target of foreign or domestic terrorist cooption through extortion or other means of influence. The possibility that a guard could become an insider threat needs to be factored into the NRC's design basis threat.

Second, Sagan warns that guard "redundancy can backfire … when diffusion of responsibility leads to 'social shirking.'" It is common human nature that individuals in a group tend to assume that others "will take up the slack." Sagan cites examples of social shirking even within elite military units. Alarmingly, there appears to be little awareness of this phenomenon in the nuclear industry or the NRC.

Third, increasing the number of guards can lead to overconfidence that the security system is stronger than it actually is. Sagan specifies the unintended consequence is that "improvements in safety and security … [can] lead individuals to engage in inherently risky behavior—driving faster, flying higher, producing more nuclear energy, etc." In this scenario, the "expected increases in system reliability could be reduced or even eliminated." Sagan cautions, "Predicted increases in nuclear security forces should not be used as a justification of maintaining inherently insecure facilities or increasing the numbers of nuclear power plants, storage sites, or weapons facilities."

Sagan does not imply that "redundancy never works in efforts to improve reliability and security." Instead, he recommends that the nuclear industry and federal agencies be cognizant of the potential shortfalls of simply adding more security forces. Finally, he warns that "low probability events happen all the time." It requires increased vigilance to protect against the tendency to assume that improbable events are essentially impossible events.

[156] Danielle Brian, Speech by Project on Government Oversight's Executive Director to the Nuclear Regulatory Commission's 2004 Regulatory Information Conference, Marh 11, 2004, available at <http://www.pogo.org/p/environment/et-040301-nukepower.html>, accessed on June 15, 2004.

[157] Nuclear Energy Institute, "Emergency Preparedness near Nuclear Power Plants," Fact Sheet, August 2003.

[158] Carl E. Behrens, "Nuclear Power Plants: Vulnerability to Terrorist Attack," Congressional Research Service Report for Congress, RS21131, July 28, 2003.

[159] Jim Wells, Director, Natural Resources and Environment, U.S. General Accounting Office, "Nuclear Regulation: Emergency Preparedness Issues at the Indian Point 2 Nuclear Power Plant," GAO-03-528T, March 10, 2003.

[160] Ibid.

[161] Bill Curry, "Reactors Won't be Protected by Missiles: Risking of Shooting down Airliners Outweighs Benefit of More Security," *Ottawa Citizen*, October 28, 2003.

[162] "European Commission Unable to Monitor Nuclear Industry," *WISE/NIRS Nuclear Monitor*, May 3, 2002, available at <http://www.antenna.nl/wise/567/5399.html>, accessed on October 29, 2003.

[163] Nathalie Schuck, "France Increasing Security to Prevent Terrorist Attacks," Associated Press, March 20, 2003.

[164] Ann MacLachlan, "Two Unknown Aircraft Overfly France's Civaux Nuclear Plant," *Nucleonics Week*, June 12, 2003, p. 3.

[165] Angela Jameson and James Bone, "Nuclear Sites Get Armed Police: 600 Strong Force to Guard Against Terror," *Times* (London), July 5, 2002.

[166] Mark Townsend, "Nuclear Fuel Transport Fears Force Security Review," *Observer*, March 16, 2003.

[167] Gareth Bicknell, "Nuclear Timetable Could be Used for Terrorism," icNorthWales.co.uk News, September 29, 2003, <http://www.icnorthwales.co.uk>.

[168] See Alvarez et al., "Reducing the Hazards from Stored Spent Power-Reactor Fuel in the United States," p. 15 and Ref. 42.

[169] Electric Power Research Institute, "Deterring Terrorism: Aircraft Crash Impact Analyses Demonstrate Nuclear Power Plant's Structural Strength."

[170] "Russian Response: Defenders Thwart Mock Nuclear Plant Terrorists," Global Security Newswire, August 16, 2002.

[171] "Nuclear Security Needs More Funds, Aide Says," *International Herald Tribune*, March 6, 2003.

[172] "Minatom is Alarmed by the State of Security in the Russian Federation's Nuclear Complex," Moscow Grani.ru, March 5, 2003, in FBIS Document ID: CEP20030320000391.

[173] "Russian Nuclear Inspectorate Tightens Control over Physical Security of Nuclear Facility," Interfax, February 25, 2003.

[174] Steve Gutterman, "Activists Say Drinking and Drugs a Major Problem at Russian Nuclear Facilities," Associated Press, March 17, 2003.

[175] "NATO-bound Lithuania Buys U.S. Anti-Aircraft Missiles," *AP World Politics*, November 14, 2002.

[176] Han Jianjun, "Japan Works to Tighten Security and Stabilize Economy," Xinhua News Agency, March 20, 2003; "Japan Police Tighten Guard at U.S. Bases, N-Plants," Jiji Press Ticker Service, March 18, 2003.

[177] "Worried Firms Hunker down to Wait Out Uncertainty," *Nikkei Weekly*, March 24, 2003.

[178] See, for example, Hiroyoshi Kurihara, "The Protection of Fissile Materials in Japan," in James Goodby, Ronald Lehman, and William Potter, eds., *A Comparative Analysis of Approaches to the Protection of Fissile Materials* (Livermore, CA: Lawrence Livermore National Laboratory, 1998), pp. 103-109.

[179] "China Formulates Medical Contingency Plan on Prevention of Nuclear Terrorism," Global News Wire, April 12, 2003.

[180] See "Promoting Nuclear Security: IAEA Action Plan Against Terrorism," Staff Report, June 1, 2004, <http://www.iaea.org>.

[181] IAEA, "Nuclear Security – Measures to Protect Against Nuclear Terrorism," GOV/INF/2004/1, March 3, 2004, p. 4.

[182] Ibid.

[183] IAEA, "Nuclear Security – Measures to Protect Against Nuclear Terrorism," GC(47)/17, August 20, 2003, p. 3.

[184] U.S. government official (name withheld by request), author's telephone interview, May 2004.

[185] Richard Meserve, email correspondence with author, May 12, 2004.

6

DISPERSING RADIATION
THE DIRTY BOMB AND OTHER DEVICES

Terrorists seeking to tap into the public's nuclear fear can readily exploit radioactive materials to make a "dirty bomb"—a conventional explosive coupled with radioactive material—or other devices to release radiation. Regardless of the fact that, as of this writing, no dirty bombs have been detonated, the image of a dirty bomb has seized the imagination of the news media and the public since September 11, 2001. Although the haunting vision that has been seared into the public's consciousness is literally of commercial passenger airliners slamming into buildings, this event and the anthrax attacks of October 2001 have primed people to imagine other forms of unconventional terrorism, such as dirty bombs. A dirty bomb, however, represents only one way to release radiation. Radiological dispersion devices, which may or may not use explosives, are designed to spread radioactivity over a wide area, and radiation emission devices, which do not use explosives, emanate radiation over a localized area.

Because radioactive materials are much more widely available than nuclear weapons-usable fissile material and because conventional explosives (if this method is chosen for dispersal) are also relatively easy to acquire, it is more likely that terrorists would construct and use an RDD or RED than an improvised nuclear device. Unlike an IND, neither an RDD nor an RED would typically cause destruction on the scale associated with weapons of mass destruction. However, radiological devices could result in mass *disruption,* potentially sparking widespread panic and contamination of property.

Al Qaeda has expressed interest in acquiring radiological weapons. In June 2002, the U.S. government announced the arrest of José Padilla— a.k.a. Abdullah Al-Mujahir, who was allegedly an al Qaeda operative planning a dirty bomb attack in the United States.[2] In January 2003, British officials reportedly uncovered evidence that al Qaeda may have already built a dirty bomb in Afghanistan.[3] Later that year in December—during the elevated "orange" threat level in response to concerns that al Qaeda was about to launch attacks against the U.S. homeland— Department of Energy scientists fanned out across five American cities (Baltimore, Las Vegas, Los Angeles, New York, and Washington, DC) searching for radiological devices. Reportedly, this search did not discover any radiological weapons.[4]

This chapter will describe the high-risk radioactive materials, including commercial radioactive sources, used and stored throughout the world. After discussing the consequences of a radiological attack, the chapter will examine the chain of events necessary for a terrorist organization to unleash this sinister act. It will then review security methods applied to commercial radioactive sources and highlight areas where enhancements are urgently needed. This discussion will provide a foundation for identifying the primary means of reducing the risk of a terrorist radiological attack. Because securing all high-risk radioactive materials in the United States alone will remain a daunting challenge for years to come,[5] a comprehensive risk-reduction strategy will require effective measures for mitigating the consequences of such an attack. Accordingly, this chapter will examine the role of public education and preparedness as well as urgently needed improvements in emergency response efforts.

HIGH-RISK RADIOACTIVE MATERIALS

Radioactive materials in the form of commercial radioactive sources[6] are used in virtually every nation in various applications, such as cancer treatment, industrial radiography, oil well logging, and scientific research. Although some naturally occurring radioactive substances such as radium are employed, most commercial applications use radioactive materials that are produced in particle accelerators and nuclear reactors.

The accelerator-produced materials tend to be short-lived and generally do not last long enough to present an RDD threat. In addition, accelerators do not typically generate bulk quantities of radioactive materials, further reducing the risk that materials from this production method would be used in an RDD. In contrast, nuclear reactors are the main workhorses for making commercial, long-lived, bulk quantities of radioactive material. Both accelerators and reactors create unstable isotopes,[7] or radioisotopes, which try to become stable by emitting radioactivity. Of the dozens in use, only a small number of these radioisotopes pose a high security concern, as discussed in detail below.

Other categories of radioactive material could be hazardous from the security perspective. For instance, commercial nuclear reactors generate high-level waste, such as spent nuclear fuel. Unshielded, this material could cause a lethal dose in a bystander in a short period of time. Even suicidal terrorists would need to consider using proper equipment and handling since they would likely be killed long before they could deliver an RDD attack. On the other hand, if the spent fuel has been out of the reactor for a long period of time and the amount of radioactive fission products contained within the spent fuel is relatively small, then it might be safely handled without highly specialized equipment. In this scenario, terrorists might be able to manipulate the fuel without suffering a lethal dose and transform it into a potent radiological weapon. In April 2004, for example, the Nuclear Regulatory Commission announced that two small pieces of spent fuel from the Vermont Yankee Nuclear Power Plant were missing. Although it is likely that the pieces might be at the bottom of a spent fuel pool, Vermont state officials have expressed concern that these materials could end up in a dirty bomb.[8]

Although spent fuel from commercial nuclear power plants is usually too radioactive for terrorists to handle, spent fuel produced by research reactors may be more vulnerable to terrorist use. The physical security surrounding research reactors tends to be lighter than that for power plants. Moreover, the research reactor spent fuel typically contains fewer fission products than does commercial power spent fuel because of the lower power levels in most research reactors. Thus, research reactor spent fuel may not require as many special precautions to prevent a lethal dose. Because research reactor spent fuel assemblies tend to weigh much less than commercial assemblies, hauling away the former would be easier than the latter.

Low-level waste is even more abundant than high-activity spent fuel and may, in certain cases, pose a security concern. Although very-low-level waste would not have sufficient radioactivity for an effective RDD, a 2002 U.S. National Research Council report pointed out that

> Low-level waste may be a particularly attractive terrorist target: It is produced by many companies, universities, and hospitals, it is not always stored or shipped under tight security, and it is routinely shipped across the country. Although labeled "low-level," some of this waste has high levels of radioactivity and could potentially be used to make an effective terrorism device.[9]

A substantial part of this form of low-level waste comes from disused and unwanted commercial radioactive sources.

In a 2003 study,[10] the Center for Nonproliferation Studies identified seven reactor-produced radioisotopes as posing the greatest security concern. These radioisotopes are americium-241 (Am-241), californium-252 (Cf-252), cesium-137 (Cs-137), cobalt-60 (Co-60), iridium-192 (Ir-192), plutonium-238 (Pu-238), and strontium-90 (Sr-90). The naturally occurring radium-226 (Ra-226) also poses a high security risk in large amounts.[11] All of these radioisotopes are present in commercial radioactive sources. In spent nuclear fuel, cesium-137 is usually the greatest radiological safety hazard.

These isotopes have half-lives ranging from months to decades.[12] This observation is important from a security standpoint because radioisotopes that emit most or essentially all of their radioactivity during a typical human lifespan pose the greatest risk to human health. Very short half-life isotopes would not last long enough to allow terrorists to create potent RDDs that could contaminate an area for an appreciable time period. Very long half-life isotopes, such as uranium-235, emit their radiation more slowly than those isotopes with half-lives on the human timescale. Table 6.1 lists relevant properties (half-life, specific activity in curies per gram,[13] and types of ionizing radiation[14] emitted) for the seven reactor-produced radioisotopes that present the highest security risks.

TABLE 6.1
RADIOISOTOPES THAT POSE THE GREATEST SECURITY RISK

Radio-isotope	Half-Life	Specific Activity (Ci/g[i])	High Energy Alpha Emissions	High Energy Beta Emissions	High Energy Gamma Emissions
Cobalt-60	5.3 years	1,100	N/A	Low energy	Yes
Cesium-137 (Barium-137m)[ii]	30 years (2.6 min)	88 (540 million)	N/A	Low energy (Low energy)	N/A (Yes)
Iridium-192	74 days	>450 (std) >1,000 (high)	N/A	Yes	Yes
Strontium-90 (Yttrium-90)	29 years (64 hours)	140 (550,000)	N/A	Yes (Yes)	N/A (Low energy)
Americum-241	433 years	3.4	Yes	No	Low energy
Californium-252	2.7 years	536	Yes	No	Low energy
Plutonium-238	88 years	17.2	Yes	No	Low energy
Radium-226	1,600 years	1	Yes	No	Low energy

---

[i] Curies per gram.
[ii] Quantities within parentheses refer to daughter isotopes that have short half-lives. For example, the decay of cesium-137 produces the daughter barium-137m.

Source: Charles D. Ferguson, Tahseen Kazi, and Judith Perera, *Commercial Radioactive Sources: Surveying the Security Risks,* Occasional Paper No. 11 (Monterey, CA: Center for Nonproliferation Studies, Monterey Institute of International Studies, January 2003), Table 5, p. 16.

Aside from half-life, several other characteristics of radioisotopes determine the relative security risk of a particular type of source. Sources containing a large amount of radioactivity obviously have the potential to create a more harmful RDD than a source with a small amount. High-activity sources include radioisotope thermoelectric generators (RTGs), teletherapy machines, blood irradiators, industrial radiography equipment, food irradiators, and irradiators used in research applications. These sources belong to the highest category of security concern, according to the IAEA.[15]

Sources that are easily transportable are vulnerable to theft from a legitimate user. For example, high-dose-rate brachytherapy devices, used to treat cancer, are easy to carry and could contain sufficient radioactivity to raise security concerns. Industrial radiography sources are another example of portable sources housing relatively high amounts of radioactivity. Gauging sources, used to measure the density and thickness of a substance, are also small and transportable, but because they usually contain small amounts of radioactivity, they would not generally pose a major security risk. The amount of radioactivity in smoke detectors is also too small to be a threat.

Sources containing radioactive material that is readily dispersible present a greater RDD risk than sources using solid, less dispersible materials. For instance, cesium-137 in large radioactive sources—that is, containing large quantities of radioactive material—tends to be in the form of powdered cesium chloride, which can be easily dispersed. In contrast, many cobalt-60 sources use solid metal pellets, which are less easily dispersed.

Another important factor that raises a source's risk profile is how prevalently it is used. Sources employing the seven reactor-produced radioisotopes appear in many devices and equipment around the world. Data on illicit radiological trafficking indicate that traffickers are typically caught with radioactive sources containing many of these isotopes. In particular, the IAEA illicit trafficking database highlights cobalt-60, cesium-137, iridium-192, and strontium-90 as isotopes frequently found in illegal transactions. Although uranium tops the list of radioactive materials detected in illicit trafficking,[16] cesium-137 is the second-most common with 53 seizures between 1993 and 1998, which contributed to 22.6 percent of all radioactive material seizures.[17] Interestingly, the above-mentioned isotopes are all gamma and beta emitters, which are easier to detect than alpha emitters, such as americium-241 or plutonium-238. This observation suggests than many illicitly transported alpha emitters might be escaping detection.

An analysis of the half-life, radioactivity, portability, dispersibility, and prevalence of sources actually employed or in storage leads to the conclusion that only a small fraction of the existing millions of sources pose a high security risk. Although this finding provides some comfort concerning the management of the security task, the challenge is still daunting because, in absolute terms, this high-risk group includes up to tens of thousands of sources throughout the world.[18] Because most countries, including the United States, do not have accurate national inventories of radioactive sources, the actual number of high-risk sources is unknown. In 1998, Lubenau and Yusko estimated that about two million devices containing licensed sources were located in the United States.[19] While most devices only had one source, others contained multiple sources. Most of the devices are not considered high risk. In particular, roughly one-quarter require a specific license, and the remaining three-quarters need only general licenses. Specific licenses typically are for higher-risk sources. However, not all specific-licensed sources pose high-security risks, nor do all general-licensed sources present low security risks.[20] To illustrate the latter point, in early 2001, the NRC increased the regulatory rigor of certain classes of general-licensed sources that have raised concerns. Table 6.2 lists the commonly used high-risk sources along with the radioisotopes contained within each type of source and the typical radioactivity content in curies.[21]

EFFECTS AND CONSEQUENCES OF A RADIOLOGICAL ATTACK

Both RDDs and nuclear weapons use radioactive materials, but an RDD is not a nuclear weapon. Unlike a nuclear weapon explosion, use of an RDD would not involve a nuclear chain reaction or a massive release of energy. A typical RDD would kill few, if any, people in the near term from the ionizing radiation. If conventional explosives are used to disperse the radioactive material, the bomb blast, depending on the location and population density, might kill hundreds of people, at most. Although the consequences of an RDD attack in lives lost would be many orders of magnitude fewer than a nuclear weapon detonation, an RDD could be an effective terror weapon. In addition, RDDs might be used in conjunction with more destructive attacks to impede rescue

TABLE 6.2
HIGH-RISK RADIOACTIVE SOURCES

Practice or Application	Radioisotope	Typical Radioactivity Level (Curies)
Radioisotope thermoelectric generators (RTGs)	Strontium-90 Plutonium-238	20,000 280
Sterilization and food irradiation	Cobalt-60 Cesium-137	Up to 4,000,000 Up to 3,000,000
Self-contained and blood irradiators	Cobalt-60 Cesium-137	2,400-25,000 7,000-15,000
Single-beam teletherapy	Cobalt-60 Cesium-137	4,000 500
Multi-beam teletherapy	Cobalt-60	7,000
Industrial radiography	Cobalt-60 Iridium-192	60 100
Calibration	Cobalt-60 Cesium-137 Americium-241	20 60 10
High- and medium-dose-rate brachytherapy	Cobalt-60 Cesium-137 Iridium-192	10 3 6
Well logging	Cesium-137 Americium-241/beryllium Californium-252	2 20 0.03
Level and conveyor gauges	Cobalt-60 Cesium-137	5 3-5

Source: International Atomic Energy Agency, *Categorization of Radioactive Sources*, IAEA-TECDOC-1344, July 2003.

work and multiply the real, physical effects of those attacks. For these reasons, RDDs are generally not considered weapons of mass destruction, but because of the potential for mass panic, they could be termed weapons of mass *disruption*.[22] "It is also generally believed that even a very large RDD is unlikely to cause many human casualties, either immediately or over the long term."[23]

Ionizing radiation can damage human cells through external exposure (absorbed from outside the body) or internal exposure (by inhalation or ingestion). Radioactive material that could potentially be used in RDDs emits three types of ionizing radiation—alpha beta, and gamma–that could produce adverse health effects.[24] Because alpha radiation, which consists of fast moving helium nuclei (two protons and two neutrons bound together), can be stopped by the dead layer of skin, it does not represent an external health threat. However, inhalation or ingestion of radioactive materials emitting alpha radiation could result in significant internal exposure, depending on the quantity of radioactivity present in the body. Unlike alpha radiation, beta and gamma radiation could cause both internal and external health effects. Beta radiation, which consists of high-energy electrons or positrons, is not as penetrating as gamma radiation, which consists of high-energy particles of light. Thus, gamma radiation poses the greatest external health threat.

Health effects from ionizing radiation fall into two different categories. First, large doses of radiation received in a short period of time cause health effects that have a direct link to the dose; these effects are called "deterministic" because knowing the dose, a physician can predict the near-term harm to health. These deterministic effects include organ function loss, nausea, damage to blood-forming organs, hair loss, and skin burns. In contrast to these certain effects of high doses are the less definite effects of low doses, which can differ depending on the individual. Low-radiation doses could result in development of cancers in some members of an affected population from several years to decades after exposure. Because of their probabilistic (random) nature, these low-dose effects are termed "stochastic." A person who develops a cancer from the ionizing radiation of an RDD would probably not know that the RDD itself caused the cancer because of the probabilistic nature of the cancer-triggering mechanism for low doses and because about 20 percent of the population will die from cancers triggered by many different factors. Though cancers arising from an RDD would likely add a tiny fractional increase to the 20 percent trend, people who are exposed would have to live with the uncertainty of whether they will be a victim of RDD-induced cancer in the long term. In sum, the typical RDD could cause some deterministic and stochastic effects, but it is likely that few deterministic effects would result from the typical radiological attack. The extent of these effects depends on the size of the exposed population and the doses received. Given comparable populations, the radiation health effects of an RDD are expected to be far less than those from an IND or nuclear weapon.

Aside from causing health effects, RDDs have the potential for spreading massive contamination. Such contamination could create delays for first responders tending to the injured. Depending on the location of the contamination, clean-up costs could climb into the billions of dollars. If buildings could not be decontaminated to acceptable limits, tearing down and rebuilding these structures could cause economic damage to soar upwards of tens of billions of dollars.[25] Furthermore, the ripple effects on the economy at large could be immense.

Many people greatly fear radioactivity. Much of this fear stems from ignorance about radiation and its effects.[26] Although radioactivity in very low levels from many sources constantly surrounds and impinges on people, it can spark concern because it is invisible and cannot be detected in low doses by human sensory organs. While public fear may not be proportional to the threat, radiological terrorists would attempt to prey on this fear to spur panic. Evacuation of a radioactively contaminated area could result in chaos if emergency responders and authorities are not prepared to direct people away in an orderly manner and promptly provide accurate information about any hazards associated with an RDD attack. After decontamination, even though the affected area might meet the strictest public health standards, many people still might not want to return to the area for fear of residual contamination.[27]

THE CHAIN OF CAUSATION

The principal elements that would have to combine for a terrorist group to launch a radiological attack at a high-value target, such as an American city, include the following steps:

1. A terrorist group with extreme objectives must form.
2. The group must decide to engage in nuclear terrorism, such as use of a radiological dispersion device.

3. The terrorist organization must acquire radioactive materials through theft, purchase, gift, diversion, or discovery of a lost radioactive source.

4. The terrorists must then use these materials to construct a device to release radiation.

5. The terrorists must be able to deliver the radiological weapon to a high-value target.

6. Finally, they must detonate the RDD or disperse the radioactive material through some other mechanism to complete their plan.

Terrorist Groups with Motivation and Capabilities to Acquire and Use Radiological Weapons

As discussed in Chapter 2, the number of terrorist organizations that are highly motivated to employ radiological weapons, such as radiological dispersion devices, is small but much larger than the number of groups that would seek to detonate nuclear weapons. For example, al Qaeda, a politico-religious group, and Chechen rebels, a nationalist/separatist group, have both expressed interest in acquiring materials for radiological dispersion devices. In addition, right-wing domestic terrorists might be inclined to engage in radiological terrorism. Because a substantial number of groups might have the motivation to carry out such an attack, focusing intelligence assets on identifying these terrorists would be very challenging. The intelligence community could benefit from tapping the expertise of regulatory officials who have extensive experience in licensing radioactive sources and in spotting licensing fraud.

The financial and technical resources required to unleash a radiological attack are modest in comparison to those necessary to implement a nuclear terror act using an intact nuclear weapon or an improvised nuclear device. A terrorist group possessing a few tens of thousands of dollars could conceivably obtain potent radioactive sources and devise an effective means of dispersal. The group in question could be small in size—a few individuals, or possibly one or two, might be all that are needed to acquire the radioactive materials, build a dispersal device, and

Box 6.1
Case Study of a Radiological Accident at Goiania, Brazil

Because terrorists have not detonated or unleashed RDDs to date, the uncertainties about the actual extent of the damage are many. However, an examination of the 1987 radiological incident in Goiania, Brazil, as a case study indicates the order-of-magnitude effects of an RDD.[30] In September 1987, scavengers looking for scrap metal to sell broke into an abandoned medical clinic in Goiania. Inside, they found a teletherapy machine that contained a canister filled with 1,375 curies of cesium-137 in powdered form. They breached the canister and distributed the components to a junkyard as well as to family and friends. Because the radioactive material was in an easily dispersible form, the contamination spread quickly. The four people who died from exposure and the 28 people who had radiation burns clearly received deterministic doses. More than 200 people suffered contamination, with at least half of them experiencing significant internal doses due to inhalation or ingestion of the powdered material.

This incident sparked panic among the local population, resulting in more than 110,000 people demanding to be monitored for contamination. This large number of so-called "worried well" demonstrates the widespread psychological and social effects that can grip a populace. Further inflaming fears, the press printed stories that water supplies were contaminated, although there was no clear evidence of substantial contamination in reservoirs. Nonetheless, about one square kilometer (roughly 40 city blocks) of land was contaminated and required a massive cleanup effort. Several homes and buildings had to be destroyed because they could not be decontaminated below acceptable limits. In total, some 3,500 cubic meters of radioactive waste were generated. Costing about $20 million, this cleanup captured most (about 1,200 curies) of the contamination. These costs were only a small fraction of the total economic damage. Goiania had relied on tourism and agriculture to earn much of its revenue. Following this radiation safety accident, tourism plummeted, and people fled the region. Prices on agricultural goods fell even though they were found not to be contaminated. In effect, Goiania became a pariah city. Although the scavengers did not set out to spread radioactivity, the end result demonstrated many of the consequences expected in an actual RDD event.

plan the attack. Moreover, obtaining the expertise to handle radioactive sources would be relatively easy to attain. A group wanting to make a dirty bomb would require a basic understanding of explosives, a characteristic common to most terrorist organizations. A radiological terror attack involving simple exposure, rather than actual dispersal, would require even less technical ability than a dirty bomb. A radioactive source hidden in a suitcase and placed in a public area would appear harmless yet potentially affect hundreds of passersby. This "passive" type of weapon is also known as a radiation emission device. If a terrorist organization intends to disperse the radioactive material through means other than a dirty bomb or an RED, a greater degree of technical sophistication could be necessary. Contamination of water or food supplies, or even airborne dispersal, would require scientific skills in addition to a large supply of radioactive material in order to prevent too much dilution given the effectiveness of most modern city water filtration systems, protection of food sources, and environmental effects.

Acquisition of Radioactive Materials

In the chain of causation outlined above, acquiring radioactive materials for an RDD or RED would be the most difficult step for a terrorist group to accomplish. Yet many scenarios offer pathways for terrorists to obtain potent radioactive materials. A state might give these materials to a terrorist organization, or government officials with access to such materials could transfer them to terrorists for ideological or mercenary reasons. Licensees, including owners of businesses possessing radioactive sources, or custodians at these facilities could provide sources to terrorists. Motives could involve monetary gain, blackmail, or ideological alignment with the terrorist group's objectives. Radioactive materials could fall into terrorist hands during times of political chaos. For example, in April 2003, rampant looting in Iraq raised concern that radioactive materials could advertently or inadvertently be stolen and acquired by terrorists or other malicious individuals.

Appropriation of vulnerable radioactive sources could transpire through other methods. For instance, terrorists could try to pose as le-

gitimate buyers of radioactive sources by obtaining or forging fraudulent licenses. They might collude with organized crime or less sophisticated criminal gangs to seize radioactive materials. In addition, they could
also steal from facilities containing radioactive materials. Such facilities
include hospitals, universities, and oil production sites where commercial radioactive sources are used. In addition, research reactor sites often house radioactive sources as well as spent nuclear fuel assemblies,
which are more readily portable and safer to handle than those for commercial reactors, as discussed above. Moreover, terrorist groups could
target shipments of radioactive sources. They could try to track down
orphan sources (sources that have been lost or abandoned), but doing
this would require using radiation detection gear, or looking for other
telltale signs, such as copious heat emission from large sources, or hiring others to find the orphan sources for the terrorist organization.

Deliberate Transfer by a National Government

While there is no evidence that states have deliberately transferred radioactive materials to terrorists groups, all state sponsors of terrorism,
as designated by the U.S. State Department, possess high-risk radioactive sources. In addition, Iran and North Korea are believed to have the
capability to produce cobalt-60 sources.[29] As discussed in Chapter 3 in
the context of transferring an intact nuclear weapon, a state that provided radioactive material to terrorists would have to be extraordinarily
reckless, desperate, or inordinately confident in the recipient group given
the risk that the material could be traced back to the state. Because the
United States would most likely retaliate against a state that had provided radioactive materials to terrorists, states will likely be deterred
from doing so.

Unauthorized Insider Assistance: Government Official or Facility Custodian

Although a state's political leadership may not desire to give radioactive
materials to terrorists, government officials with access to these materials might decide to effect such transactions. These officials might be
motivated to do so because they are ideologically aligned with the ter-

rorist organization, seek monetary gain, or are confronted with black-mail. As of this writing, there have been no reports that such transfers have occurred.

Similarly, a licensee or custodian of a facility containing radioactive sources could be persuaded by ideology, monetary payment, or black-mail to facilitate access to potent radioactive materials. In addition to "opening the doors to the vault," so to speak, insiders could share knowl-edge about how to handle highly radioactive materials safely, thus re-ducing the likelihood that the terrorists would receive lethal doses—even suicidal terrorists would have to consider their surviving long enough to build and deliver a radiological weapon.

Exploiting this route would present formidable challenges. Terror-ists would have to devote sufficient time and resources to identify sym-pathetic, corruptible, or vulnerable insiders. Nevertheless, in contrast to the security personnel sworn to protect nuclear weapons or weap-ons-usable fissile material, those with access to radioactive sources do not generally undergo rigorous personnel reliability programs to moni-tor their commitment to protect such materials. Thus, it is more likely that the insider route to radioactive sources poses a greater risk than that to intact nuclear weapons or fissile material for improvised nuclear devices.

Looting During Times of Political or Societal Unrest

In contrast to the above two unlikely scenarios for illicit acquisition of radioactive material is one in which terrorists could exploit times of political unrest and chaos within a state at war or a failing state that is losing control over high-risk radioactive sources. For example, in 2003 after the fall of Baghdad, looting of Iraqi facilities containing radioac-tive materials raised concerns that U.S. security at these critical sites was inadequate. Reports surfaced that the nuclear site at Tuwaitha, Iraq, had been ransacked. Reportedly, American soldiers who had been guard-ing this site were too few in number and allowed many Iraqis access to the site. Looters carried away office supplies and other equipment as well as barrels that had once contained low-enriched uranium. These acts stirred fears that the estimated 200 radioactive sources at Tuwaitha may have been stolen. Some of the sources may be powerful enough to fuel a potent RDD. According to the IAEA, Iraq possessed some 1,000 radioactive sources before the recent war.

IAEA Director General Mohammed ElBaradei petitioned the United States and the Coalition Provisional Authority in charge of Iraq to allow IAEA inspectors access to the Tuwaitha site to check on the condition of the safeguarded nuclear material.[30] The IAEA inspection occurred from June 7 to 23, 2003, at Location C Nuclear Material Storage Facility in the Tuwaitha complex and was limited to this facility. According to the Director General's report, "The inspection team found that some safeguards seals…had been removed." Uranium compounds had been dumped onto the floor of the buildings, and several containers were missing. The IAEA report noted, however, "Many of the containers that were initially missing have been subsequently recovered." While the inspection team estimated "that at least 10 kg of uranium compounds could have been dispersed…, [t]he quantity and type of uranium compounds dispersed are not sensitive from a proliferation point of view."[31] However, the number of missing radioactive sources in Iraq remains uncertain, and many could be at high risk for use in RDDs.

Licensing Fraud

Even in the regulatory systems of developed countries, such as the United States, people can misrepresent themselves and obtain fraudulent licenses. One case involved Stuart Lee Adelman, also known as Stuart von Adelman, who over several years from the 1980s through the 1990s acquired radioactive materials through illegitimate means, including fraudulent use of licenses.[32] In at least one instance, he engaged in this fraud by posing as a university professor. Although no definite evidence connects Adelman to terrorism, an assistant U.S. District Attorney stated that radioactive material Adelman had in Canada may have been used in a scam to earn money from terrorists. In 1992, he was arrested in Toronto, Canada, on a U.S. fugitive warrant. Radioactive materials he illegally acquired were discovered in a public storage locker. In 1996, he was arrested in the United States, where he pleaded guilty to a federal felony of fraudulently obtaining radioactive material. He was sentenced to a five-year prison term.[33]

Malicious individuals can also pose as legitimately licensed buyers in order to purchase used sources on the secondhand market.[34] Once a licensee no longer wants a source, he or she has three options: storage, disposal, or resale. Long-term storage at a licensee's premises can create safety and security hazards. Disposal, as discussed in detail below, can be expensive. Resale offers a way to off-load a potentially hazardous substance or recoup some of the costs from the original purchase. A potential problem is that resale could transpire with essentially no regulatory oversight. Although the buyer and the seller are required to exchange licensing information prior to shipment of the source, the buyer could attempt to pawn off a fraudulent license. If the doctored license appears legitimate, the seller would have no reason to question it or deny the sale. Even if the document raises suspicions, the seller may be unscrupulous or anxious to complete the sale and thus accept the document as legitimate. Buyers and sellers can initiate a proposed sale through openly available Internet servers. Thus, this route would appear to be easy to monitor by regulatory officials; however, completion of the transaction could occur offline or through exchange of personal e-mail messages. In addition, non-licensees can arrange such transfers, making it more difficult for regulating agencies to track such activity. A requirement for the seller to obtain a copy of the license from the regulatory agency, not the buyer, could reduce the likelihood that the secondhand market would be exploited for malicious uses.[35] A way to provide this licensing information could be to allow access to it on a secure Web site maintained by the Nuclear Regulatory Commission.[36]

Fraudulent licenses could also be used to import radioactive sources into the United States. For instance, in May 2003, a regulatory official in Argentina investigated what at first appeared to be a suspicious request from someone in Texas for a shipment of cobalt-60 to be used in a teletherapy machine. (A source of this size is considered high risk.) The "license" raised suspicions because it was a dental X-ray registration certificate. Although the FBI investigation of this incident reportedly has not uncovered terrorist activity, it points to a need for improvements in import and export controls, as discussed in detail below, because if not for alert regulatory officials, export/import licensing fraud can readily occur.[37]

Organized Crime

While links between terrorists seeking radioactive materials and organized crime have not been proven, the potential for terrorist acquisition of illicit materials through criminal activity was underscored by the theft and ransom of five radioactive sources in Ecuador in December 2002. A criminal gang stole iridium-192 sources from the Technint company's site in Quininde in the northern oil-producing region of Esmeraldas, Ecuador. After paying the ransom, the company received only three of the sources from the criminals. As of this writing, the other two sources remain missing.[38] According to the *Washington Post*, this "was the first known case of successful blackmail involving radiological material, and U.S. and UN experts fear the pattern could be repeated."[39]

Theft from Facilities

Many sites containing high-risk radioactive materials remain vulnerable to theft. Alarmingly, in 2003, thieves ransacked three Russian lighthouses, in the Arctic region, housing powerful RTGs—potent sources that could fuel devastating RDDs. Because the actual radioactive cores of the RTGs were found stripped of their metal casings, it is believed that the thieves wanted the scrap metal to sell for money.[40] However, these thefts underscore the relative ease with which certain powerful sources can be accessed and taken away to make RDDs.

Materials at unsecured radioactive-waste disposal facilities could be vulnerable to theft by terrorists. For example, Chechnya reportedly has 26 facilities storing radioactive waste. Of special concern is the Radon Special Combine in Grozny, containing an estimated 1,250 curies of radioactivity as of the mid-1990s. In 1995, a Russian government commission began an investigation of security at this site. Because of combat operations in the region, the commission was unable to complete its assignment in a timely fashion. Finally, in 2000, the Russian government reported that it had control of the Radon facility. A large number of radioactive sources are reportedly unaccounted for in Chechnya.[41]

Transportation Links

While incidents of terrorist sabotage of radioactive material shipments have not been reported, sources outside the control of facilities and in transit may pose greater susceptibility of being targeted by terrorists than in-facility materials. According to the IAEA, more than 10 million packages containing radioactive material are transported annually throughout the world.[42] However, most of these shipments hold small amounts of radioactivity whose use would not result in potent RDDs. As discussed below, shipments containing large quantities of radioactive materials tend to be continuously monitored. Nonetheless, a Sandia National Laboratories report cautions that "during transfer, SRSs [sealed radioactive sources] are particularly susceptible to theft since the sources are in a shielded and mobile configuration, transportation routes are predictable, and shipments may not be adequately guarded."[43]

Orphan Sources

An estimated several thousand radioactive sources are orphaned—that is, they are outside of regulatory controls through theft, abandonment, or lax accounting.[44] Although only a small fraction of these sources are truly high risk, many of the most dangerous orphan sources are located in regions experiencing terrorist activity or accessible to terrorists, such as the Newly Independent States.[45] To acquire orphan sources, terrorists could either use radiation detectors to track them down or look for other telltale signs, such as heat emission. In the former case, the terrorist organization would need to have a member who knew how to operate detection equipment or hire someone to do that job. The group would also have to have an idea of where to look in order to increase the effectiveness of the search. But such expertise is not always necessary. In a notorious incident in late December 2001 in the Republic of Georgia, three lumberjacks discovered two potent strontium-90 sources that were abandoned and used to power RTGs.[46] These men, who were not equipped with radiation detectors, made this find because the sources had melted snow. The woodsmen received severe radiation exposures because they had gathered around the RTG sources to warm themselves. From the mid-1990s through June 2002, according to the IAEA, almost three hundred orphan radioactive sources have been recovered in Georgia.[47]

Transporting the Weapon or Device to Its Target

Should a terrorist group actually acquire radioactive materials and make a radiological weapon, it would still confront the task of delivering the device to the group's intended target. To actualize the worst-case scenarios of greatest threat to the United States or its allies, terrorists would not have to transport the radiological device over a large distance or even cross any borders. Because, as discussed earlier, high-risk radioactive materials are prevalent in the United States and practically all other nations, a terrorist organization would not necessarily require a multinational capability. A domestic terrorist group, for example, could acquire radioactive sources in the United States and launch a radiological attack against an American city. Alternatively, a terrorist sleeper cell in the United States with connections to a multinational network could be directed to obtain U.S. radioactive materials for an attack against the American homeland.

Other plausible scenarios, however, would require multinational capabilities. For instance, some of the most potent radioactive sources, such as RTGs, were manufactured in the former Soviet Union and still reside there. If a terrorist group wanted to attack the United States with one of these sources, it would have to cross borders to actualize the attack.

Radioactive materials can be detected during transport, but the range and effectiveness of detection depend on the quantity and type of radiation emitted and the presence of any shielding.[48] Underscoring the difficulty of detecting shielded devices, Duane Sewell, a former Assistant Secretary of Energy, said: "You have to have very sensitive instrumentation, and you have to be essentially right on top of it if they shield it pretty well."[49] High-risk radioactive materials, which emit significant amounts of radiation, are, of course, more easily detected than lower-risk materials. Many types of radiation detection instruments have been developed and are in the process of being developed. However, a critical requirement for maximum chance of detection is ensuring that the detectors are in place at border crossings and around high-value targets. For example, as discussed in more depth below, U.S. Customs officials are equipped with handheld radiation detectors, which can be used to sense quantities of radioactivity in high-risk sources.

Detonation or Dispersion of Radiation

Detonating a crude dirty bomb would not require much technical competence. Such a weapon would need conventional explosives, which can be readily acquired or made by reasonably capable terrorists, and radioactive materials, which can be obtained via the routes outlined above. Placing an RED in a public area would also require minimum technical competence. A high-value target would pose a major challenge because of the need to escape detection by radiation sensors in place near these targets. Efficient contamination of a large area through dispersal of radioactive materials would be the most technically demanding type of radiological attack. However, relative to detonating an intact nuclear weapon or improvised nuclear device, building and using an effective RDD would be easy.

RADIOACTIVE MATERIALS SECURITY

The analysis above of the steps required for terrorist use of an RDD or RED demonstrates that this mode of nuclear terrorism is highly likely as long as terrorists are motivated to launch this type of attack. Before 9/11, securing radioactive sources took a backseat to ensuring that these materials were used safely, although in the 1990s the IAEA had begun to take steps toward highlighting the need for better security.[50] While the emphasis on safety still makes sense given the numerous radiation safety accidents over several decades and the lack of successful uses of RDDs, as of this writing, the post-9/11 paradigm has underscored the need for improvements in the security of radioactive sources and other radioactive materials that could fuel potent radiological weapons.[51] This section outlines the security measures that tend to be in place for each step in the life-cycle of radioactive sources.[52]

Every part of the life-cycle presents potential security risks. Reducing these risks depends on ensuring adequate layered security at each stage of the life-cycle. Figure 6.1 depicts the life-cycle. Paths in this diagram traveling along the solid lines represent recommended practices. In contrast, the dashed lines show where sources can leave safe and secure environments and potentially end up in malicious hands. The discussion below walks through the stages and points out general security practices that are in place and pitfalls where sources can become orphaned, i.e., left outside of regulatory control because of theft, loss, abandonment, or improper accounting.

The radioisotopes that pose the greatest security concern tend to be long-lived and are generally produced in reactors, as mentioned previously. This production begins the life-cycle. Most radioisotope production reactors are owned and operated by governments. These reactors, and the few that are not government owned and operated, are all required to have adequate security in place according to government regulations. Security at the reactor sites includes fences, truck barriers, guards, and access control points. Workers at these sites may also undergo criminal background checks. Such checks, however, are typically not a mandatory regulatory requirement.

After their production in a reactor, radioisotopes are processed into radioactive sources. Because processing occurs at reactor sites, adequate security generally surrounds this stage. From here, sources can be shipped directly to end users or to subsidiary manufacturers who produce equipment, such as teletherapy devices, that employ radioactive sources. Often, because of the significant vertical integration in the radioactive source industry, the same corporation generates the radioisotopes and manufactures the equipment holding the source. Only about a half dozen major corporations around the world manufacture most of the commercial radioisotopes. These companies then globally distribute their products to dozens of subsidiaries and thousands of users.[53]

Transportation of a radioactive source takes the material from the relatively secure haven of the reactor site or the major manufacturer. Thus, shipment can raise the security risk profile. Typically, large shipments of highly radioactive material involve layers of physical protec-

FIGURE 6.1
LIFE-CYCLE OF A RADIOACTIVE SOURCE

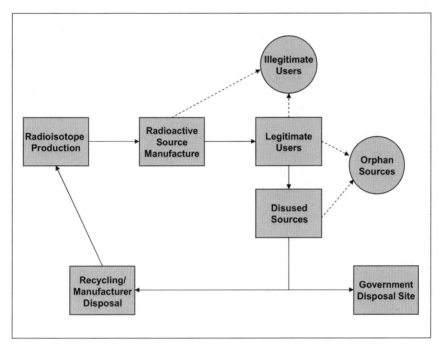

tion. For instance, such shipments are continuously monitored and are coordinated with law-enforcement authorities.[54]

The security practices at users' facilities vary depending on the application and type of source. Facilities containing very highly radioactive materials (millions of curies of radioactivity)— for example, at food irradiation and medical instrument sterilization centers—generally have in place strict physical security, although typically not as strong as that for nuclear power plants. Other facilities with lower activity sources, such as hospitals and universities, tend to guard these materials as they would high-value items. Adequate security methods at the user stage include restricted access, guards, procedures to lock up materials when not in use, and personnel training. Nonetheless, in the United States, regulations do not currently specify required security practices; the regulations state in full that for radioactive sources in storage, "The licensee shall secure from authorized removal or access licensed materials that are stored in controlled or unrestricted areas,"[55] and that for sources not in storage, "The licensee shall control and maintain constant surveillance of licensed material that is in a controlled or unrestricted area and that is not in storage."[56]

Some facilities by their very nature can present security challenges. For instance, hospitals and universities, by design, are accessible to the public.[57] This situation has to be factored into security planning. Although other facilities, such as well-logging sites, are in remote locations and are, therefore, less accessible to the public, the transnational nature of the oil well–logging industry may increase the likelihood that a source may be lost or stolen. Illustrating this concern, in the first half of 2003, well-logging sources were stolen in Nigeria.[58] These sources eventually ended up in a scrap yard in Germany.[59] Radiation safety experts have observed for years that well-logging and radiography sources imported into developing countries are susceptible to abandonment and theft.[60]

Well-functioning regulatory systems require users to obtain a license in order to own a source. The type of license depends on the radioactive content and usage of a source. Possession of higher-activity and higher-risk sources within the United States requires specific licenses. In contrast, licensees of lower-activity sources usually have to acquire only a general license, which does not have to be filed because it is a license granted by regulation. The regulatory requirements for specific licenses are stricter than those for general licenses. Inspections of specific licensees occur more frequently, for instance, within an effective regulatory system. Regulatory checks of licensees help ensure that the purchase of a source is valid and that safety and security practices are being followed.

Assuming that legitimate users beneficially employ sources, the next stage in a source's life-cycle occurs when a source is no longer needed by the user. Such unwanted sources are known as disused sources. Ideally, a disused source would either be returned to a manufacturer for disposal or sent to a government-sponsored disposal site.

Another option is to sell the source to another user, as discussed above. This secondhand market flows mainly from the developed to the developing world. Because many countries in the developing world do not have effective regulatory systems, the practice of transferring sources to these regions can, in general, raise the security risk of a source becoming orphaned. Many developing nations are aware of this issue and are working indigenously and through the IAEA to improve regulatory controls, but these efforts will require significant investment of time and resources to create lasting positive change.

Most major manufacturers offer the service of disposal or recycling of sources containing radioisotopes, such as cobalt-60, that can be recycled. At least two problems can derail this preferred pathway back to the producer. First, manufacturers can, and do, go out of business. For instance, General Electric and Westinghouse, once major suppliers of teletherapy machines, no longer produce these devices nor do they dispose of disused teletherapy sources.[61] Second, the accounting trail back to the manufacturer can be broken if the source is transferred to a secondhand user. Although some major manufacturers try to track these transfers, there is no requirement for this to occur.

Users, in principle, have the option of disposing of an unwanted source in a government-run disposal facility. Here again problems arise. Disposal costs are generally expensive. Many governments, including the United States, have not installed comprehensive source disposal systems. For instance, some classes of low-level-activity disused sources have disposal pathways, while higher-activity sources do not. The disposal problems faced by the United States are discussed in more detail below.

PREVENTION, ENFORCEMENT, AND RESPONSE MECHANISMS

The foregoing analysis has highlighted the steps that a terrorist group would need to complete in order to implement a radiological attack. It has also examined potential vulnerabilities of radioactive materials to terrorist seizure. This section will explore a number of efforts under way to reduce the risk of terrorism involving radiological dispersion devices or other terrorist radiological weapons.

International Efforts Involving the IAEA

Since September 11, 2001, the United States, many other states, and the IAEA have been trying to improve the security of high-risk radioactive sources. Even before 9/11, the IAEA and several member states recognized the threat posed by unsecured radioactive material. For example, the first international conference devoted to both safety and security of radioactive sources took place in Dijon, France, in September 1998. One of the major results of this conference was the start of the Code of Conduct on the Safety and Security of Radioactive Sources. The Code of Conduct, a nonbinding document, serves as a guide to governments to point them to better safety and security practices. It describes the components of an effective regulatory system. Recognizing that most radioactive sources would not cause great harm to human health if used in an RDD, the code urges nations to prioritize security measures on those sources that pose the greatest risk.

In addition to the Code of Conduct, the IAEA created an Action Plan mapping out the way to implement the findings of the Dijon conference.[62] One year after the conference, the IAEA Board of Governors approved this plan, which outlined improvements in regulatory infrastructures, management of disused radioactive sources, response to radiological events, education and training, and information exchange.

The second major international conference devoted to safety and security of radioactive sources occurred in Buenos Aires, Argentina, in December 2000.[63] Representatives from 75 member states participated. Their governments were asked to pledge to follow the Code of Conduct.

The events of September 11, 2001, prompted a renewed effort to evaluate the security of radioactive materials. This review highlighted that the Code of Conduct and the companion document on Categorization of Radiation Sources focused more on safety rather than security. To make sure security received proper attention in these documents, the IAEA and representatives of 17 member states formed an intergovernmental working group in August 2002 to change the code and the categorization to reflect the increased perceived threat of radiological attack. In July 2003, the working group finished the revisions, and in September 2003, the IAEA Board of Governors approved the revised code. In early 2004, the U.S. State Department launched a major initiative to encourage states to pledge to uphold the code; Secretary of State Colin Powell wrote and sent a letter to all embassies to jumpstart this effort. Important recommendations in the code include:

- Ensure that those who seek to possess radioactive sources are authorized to do so by competent regulatory authorities.

- Conduct regular announced and unannounced inspections of licensees' facilities where radioactive sources reside.

- Require adequate safety and security of radioactive sources throughout their life-cycles from production to use to disposal.

- Ensure that inventory controls are conducted periodically by licensees of the radioactive sources.

- Establish confidential, national registries of holders of sources.

- Make sure that exports of high-risk sources occur, other than in exceptional circumstances, only to recipients who are authorized to safely and securely possess these sources.

Years before work commenced on the Code of Conduct, the IAEA established in 1995 the Model Project, which is designed to offer assistance to governments seeking to improve regulatory infrastructures. The IAEA assistance team provided radiation safety experts, radiation detection equipment, and documents showing how to set up legislation and regulations. Without an adequate regulatory system, radioactive sources are particularly vulnerable to becoming orphaned. The IAEA has determined that about 110 nations, the majority of the world, have inadequate regulatory systems.[64]

In September 2001, the IAEA issued a report describing the progress during the first six years of the Model Project. By then, 52 nations had participated, and another 29 requested assistance from the project. As the September 2001 report documented:

about 77 percent of the participating countries had promulgated laws, about 77 percent had established a regulatory authority, more than 42 percent had adopted regulations, about 80 percent had an inventory system in place and operational, and about 50 percent had a system for the notification, authorization, and control of radiation sources in place and operational.[65]

While these statistics describe the success stories, the report also discussed the roadblocks to further progress. These barriers included lengthy legislative procedures, dysfunctional governmental institutions, funding shortfalls, overlapping responsibilities within the government, inadequate technical resources, and insufficient staff. In sum, the Model Project has achieved and continues to achieve much success; however, years of effort are typically required to establish functional and sustainable regulatory systems in which safety and security cultures have become ingrained.

The IAEA has also been active in securing orphan sources. For instance, on several occasions, it has assisted the Republic of Georgia in finding and securing high-risk discarded sources.[66] After September 11, 2001, the IAEA stepped up its orphan source recovery efforts. In February 2002, for example, it helped secure two large unshielded Sr-90 sources in Georgia, as described above. The next month, the IAEA worked with Afghan officials to secure radioactive sources discovered during a UN environmental monitoring mission. One of the Afghan sources contained Co-60 and came from a radiotherapy machine located in a former hospital in Kabul. While recovery efforts such as these are essential, creating a sustainable system requires providing governments with information that would allow them to safely and securely recover their own orphan sources. To foster this necessary effort, the IAEA is working on a technical document (TECDOC) on National Strategies for Detection and Location of Orphan Sources and their Subsequent Management. The IAEA intends to hold regional workshops to encourage member states to form effective national action plans to detect and secure orphan sources.

To help member states in their development of effective radioactive source security systems, the IAEA published interim guidance in

June 2003, and the agency plans to update this information as needed, factoring in feedback from member states. This document defines how to assess a design basis threat—that is, "the attributes and characteristics of potential insider and/or external adversaries, who might attempt damage to, or unauthorized removal of, radioactive sources, against which a physical protection system is designed and evaluated."[67] It also walks through how to assign radioactive sources at certain premises within a state to four security groups, from Group A, which includes highest-risk sources requiring the most rigorous security and quickest detection of an attempt at unauthorized acquisition to Group D, which includes the lowest-risk sources that need periodic verification of their presence at set intervals.

The United States government has been one of the most active governments involved in revising the Code of Conduct and in supporting the other efforts of the IAEA, such as the Model Project, in enhancing the security of radioactive materials. In June 2002, the U.S. Department of Energy formed a Tripartite Initiative with the Russian Ministry of Atomic Energy (MINATOM) and the IAEA. The initiative is geared toward locating, recovering, and securing high-risk orphan radioactive sources in the former Soviet Union. In March 2003, the United States and Russia continued their cooperation in reducing the risk of RDDs by sponsoring the third international conference devoted to the safety and security of radioactive sources. This conference gathered together the largest governmental group to date—more than 700 delegates from over 100 nations (most of the IAEA member states)—to meet the urgent task of improving the security of high-risk radioactive sources. Several officials from the Newly Independent States participated. The conference fostered greater collaboration between government officials and international organizations by including representatives of the European Police Office (EUROPOL), the International Criminal Police Organization (ICPO-INTERPOL), and the World Customs Organization (WCO).

This collaborative effort among IAEA member states and key international organizations such as the IAEA, EUROPOL, Interpol, and the WCO came through in the conference findings. The first major finding focused on tracking down, recovering, and securing high-risk orphan sources. The other major finding emphasized encouraging and helping governments develop effective national regulatory infrastructures to control radioactive sources. The IAEA intends to hold the next international conference on radioactive source security in 2005.[68]

During the March conference, U.S. Secretary of Energy Spencer Abraham unveiled a new initiative called the Radiological Security Partnership, which is a three-pronged plan. First, the United States has committed to assist "countries accelerate and expand national initiatives to keep track of and better secure national inventories of high-risk radioactive sources." Second, he requested that nations "draw on international resources" to obtain "practical advice and assistance" for securing high-risk orphan sources. The United States will implement part of this element of the plan by expanding the aforementioned tripartite initiative. The expansion will bring more countries, especially those in the developing world, into the work begun by DOE and MINATOM. Abraham emphasized that the United States is "prepared to work with other countries to locate, consolidate, secure, and dispose of high-risk orphan" radioactive sources. The third prong of the plan would ensure that major transit and shipping hubs have adequate radiation detection capabilities. During the week immediately following the conference, U.S. officials met with their IAEA counterparts to determine how to implement this part of the partnership. Abraham announced that, to initiate the Radiological Security Partnership, the United States has contributed $3 million.[69] In April 2003, Ambassador Linton Brooks of the Department of Energy testified before Congress that the Bush administration requested an additional $19.7 million to increase efforts to track down and secure high-risk radioactive sources in the Newly Independent States.[70]

Also during the conference, Russian Atomic Energy Minister Aleksander Rumyantsev highlighted the need for an international education campaign to better inform the public about radiation safety and radiological security. He called on the assembled officials to develop "a large-scale civilized informational system for the society on all range of issues on safe use of ionizing radiation sources" to prevent "their unauthorized use." His educational program would enlist the "mass media, i.e., press, radio, and TV," involve "specialized educational programs in schools," and bring together "community representatives, scientists, industry people" and government officials in roundtable discussions. Furthermore, he encouraged the IAEA, the World Health Organization, and the national academies of sciences to work together to develop a radiation safety and security education plan.[71]

Should an actual RDD detonation occur, nations would be able to receive assistance through the IAEA if they had joined the Convention on Assistance in the Case of Nuclear Accident or Radiological Emergency. As an outgrowth of the 1986 Chernobyl accident, this convention serves as a mechanism to foster cooperation among parties to it and to grant aid in the event of nuclear accidents or radiological emergencies. Developing countries, depending on their need, may receive assistance without cost. As of January 2004 (the latest published update, as of this writing), the convention included 89 parties and 68 signatories.[72] Thus, less than half the world's nations are parties to this convention. In contrast, virtually every nation possesses radioactive sources.

Industry and G-8 Security Efforts

Industry officials have recognized that a radiological attack could have a chilling effect on the health of the commercial radioactive source industry. Consequently, since 9/11, the major source manufacturers have begun to meet regularly to discuss outstanding issues involving the safety and security of their products. For instance, in April 2003, a month after the governmental conference on radioactive source security, the IAEA sponsored the Technical Meeting to Enhance the Safe and Secure Design, Manufacture, and Supply of Radioactive Sources. This meeting brought together representatives of the major corporations that produce and distribute radioactive sources. In addition, regulatory officials, IAEA radiological safety and security experts, and U.S. government officials from the Department of Energy's Office of International Materials Protection and Cooperation participated. In addition to serving as a means for information exchange, the meeting mainly strived for consensus on industry efforts to enhance security and reduce the risk of RDDs. The meeting concentrated on the safe and secure management of radioactive sources. Industry participants generally agreed that finding replacements for cesium-chloride, which in a pow-dered form poses a high risk for radioactivity dispersal, is an important goal. For example, the Los Alamos National Laboratory has been work-ing on developing alternatives to powered cesium-chloride and is inter-ested in working with industry to develop commercial substitutes. A public-private partnership could provide an effective conduit to direct this type of laboratory research to the marketplace.

The conference also addressed disposition of disused sources. Most major manufacturers provide recycling and disposal services. However, at times companies go out of business or discontinue these services. To resolve some of these problems, industry representatives appeared to agree that regulatory agencies should maintain records on sources for at least 30 years. One of the greatest concerns of the industry is that regulations could differ among nations, leading to an uneven playing field in which some companies would be at a competitive disadvantage. This first IAEA-sponsored industry meeting pointed toward consensus in some important security areas, but more meetings are needed to solidify higher standards and address continuing concerns of the industry.[73]

In June 2003, the heads of state of the Group of Eight (G-8) in-dustrialized nations and the representatives of the European Union de-voted a substantial part of their agenda to improving the security of radioactive sources throughout the world.[74] The June 2004 summit at Sea Island, Georgia, also called for increased controls over radioactive sources, as discussed in detail below. Because most of the major pro-ducers and distributors of radioactive sources are located in G-8 states,[75] the G-8 initiative could lead to ramped-up security standards in the states that make most of the high-risk radioactive sources. These states could require that purchasing states would have to meet these standards in order to receive the sources. If all the major producing states banded together, they could create a level playing field that would prevent a state from undercutting the others. In an August 2003 interview, an of-ficial with a leading radioisotope producing corporation headquartered in a G-8 nation indicated that the major corporations are moving to-ward forming a coalition to promote best security practices.[76]

Orphan and Disused Source Initiatives in the United States

On the international level, the United States took the lead in formulating the G-8's statement and action plan on radiological security. On the national level, the United States has been trying to secure orphan and high-risk disused sources through a couple of different programs. Disused sources that exceed the Nuclear Regulatory Commission's limits for low-level radioactive waste are considered Greater-Than-Class-C (GTCC) waste—usually considered to pose relatively high security risks—and therefore fall under the purview of the Department of Energy.[77] Such sources would typically pose a high security risk from the RDD perspective. To manage GTCC waste, DOE established the Off-Site Source Recovery (OSR) Project. The OSR Project has provided safe and secure interim storage for several thousand GTCC sources. In October 2002, Congress stemmed the shrinking budgets of the OSR Project by issuing a $10 million supplement. On May 18, 2004, DOE announced that OSR personnel have secured more than 9,500 sources.[78] However, several thousand other disused sources are awaiting collection or are anticipated to become unwanted within the coming years. Beyond interim storage, DOE has a mandate to provide for permanent storage of these sources. According to a GAO audit in April 2003, DOE has not made this activity a priority, and development of a permanent repository will be delayed beyond 2007.[79] The GAO also expressed concern that the current DOE headquarters' management of the OSR Project is inadequate. Subsequent to publication of the GAO report, the DOE shifted management in November 2003 of the OSR Project from its Environmental Management division to the National Nuclear Security Administration's leadership under the Materials Protection, Control, and Accounting program. In Fiscal Year 2005, NNSA will assume full responsibility for the OSR Project, and it has requested $5.6 million for that year. The projected cost for OSR activities over the next five years is about $40 million.[80]

Within the United States, about one radioactive source is reported as orphaned every day. Most of these sources are not powerful enough to pose a high security risk. Nonetheless, the fact that sources are becoming orphaned at this rate points out that even an advanced, industrialized country such as the United States has gaps in its radioactive source regulatory system. To help alleviate this problem, the Environmental Protection Agency (EPA) is funding the Orphan Source Initiative, which is the first national program in the United States designed to control orphan sources. EPA is working in cooperation with the Conference of Radiation Control Program Directors (CRCPD), which is a coalition of members of state radiation control agencies. Recognizing that facilities such as steel mills and scrap yards are destinations for orphan sources, the initiative has focused on addressing the orphan source problem at these sites. EPA and CRCPD are striving to build a nationwide program that would identify, remove, and safely and securely dispose of orphan sources. EPA is also coordinating this effort with the NRC and DOE.

In addition, CRCPD operated a pilot program in Colorado to implement a risk-based ranking system for disposal of orphan sources. The pilot program, which finished in April 2001, resulted in the collection of 30 orphan sources containing a total of 3.16 curies of Cs-137. These sources would not be considered high-risk under the IAEA's current guidelines.[81] In October 2001, the CRCPD Board of Directors began the National Orphan Radioactive Material Disposition Program. The goal is "to financially assist, and provide technical guidance to, state radiation control programs in the disposition of discrete orphan radioactive material."[82] The NRC has helped fund this program.

Nuclear Regulatory Commission's Security Efforts

The NRC has also played an active role in trying to improve the security of radioactive sources. In October 2001, the NRC issued a limited-distribution "safeguards advisory" that called on licensees holding radioactive sources to enhance security efforts. The following month, the NRC promulgated a more detailed advisory, specifying certain security measures at sites containing radioactive sources and in the transportation of these materials. The specific measures are not publicly available because they are considered "safeguards" information. Publishing the details could aid terrorists who are probing security loopholes. Nevertheless, giving the public adequate information to assess the general security status would promote the democratic process and could provide confidence in the work that the NRC and the rest of the government have done. To its credit, the NRC has issued general security information on its Web site and through other mechanisms such as congressional testimonies and public speeches given by NRC officials.

The NRC advisories are not binding on licensees; however, the NRC's staff has been confirming voluntary compliance by conducting spot checks. NRC uses a risk-based assessment scheme that ranks the sources on their potential to cause harm. Consequently, security measures differ by the type of source. For instance, food irradiation facilities and large shipments of highly radioactive sources would deserve the highest security measures. In other settings, such as hospitals, universities, and oil well logging sites, the NRC advisories likely call for security commensurate with industrial practices to guard high-value items. Radioactive materials would have to be locked up when not in use, for example.

Most of the states (33 out of 50) in the United States belong to the Agreement States system, which regulates about three-quarters of the licensees and thus is the first line of responsibility for regulating most radioactive sources in these states, with the NRC providing an oversight role. The Agreement States adopted the NRC advisories and have also conducted spot checks to verify compliance. Since issuance of the advisories, the NRC is deciding on what additional mandatory regulations are necessary to protect sources.

In June 2002, the NRC formed a joint task force with DOE to examine the issue of changes in the regulatory structure. In May 2003, the task force published a report that addressed outstanding regulatory issues and made the following recommendations:[83]

- Establish a national RDD protection level in coordination with the Department of Homeland Security and other agencies.

- Develop a national threat policy. Define threat characteristics that could impact use of radioactive material in an RDD in coordination with the Department of Homeland Security. Continue assessing vulnerabilities of specific facilities or licensees or classes of licensees.

- Initiate development of a national source tracking system to better understand and monitor the location and movement of sources of interest.

- Develop an integrated national response strategy for rapid recovery of unsecured sources in coordination with the Department of Homeland Security.

- Develop an integrated national strategy for disposition of unsecured sources.

- Enhance coordination and communication with other federal agencies, including the Department of Homeland Security (including its Transition Management Office), and the Department of Defense, that have RDD prevention and mitigation activities under way.

- Continue U.S. coordination with the IAEA.

In July 2003, the NRC announced that it is considering new regulations to improve the security of a class of sources that are susceptible to theft. The proposed new rule would require two independent physical security controls, such as locks, on portable radioactive gauges.[84] According to an NRC staff memo, about 50 gauges are reported stolen each year out of more than 22,000 licensed gauges.[85] Such gauges would be considered low risk from the standpoint of fueling an RDD. Interviews with NRC officials confirmed that the July 2003 announcement had been in development before 9/11 and was not specifically tied to concerns about radiological terrorism.

However, a month prior to the news about the gauges, the NRC issued an order that was clearly connected to concerns about terrorist use of radioactive materials. The June 2003 order tasks licensees of two types of high-risk radioactive sources—panoramic and underwater irradiators authorized to possess greater than 10,000 curies—to increase security at their facilities.[86] The details of the ordered enhancements are considered safeguards information and will not be publicly released. While this order will most likely make these irradiators more secure, the reason that the NRC ordered more security over these types of irradiators than other types of high-risk sources was not the result of a systematic vulnerability assessment. Rather, it was because there are relatively small numbers of the panoramic and underwater irradiators in the United States and enhancing their security appeared easy to accomplish because they are not readily portable and would prove difficult for terrorists to transport without suffering a lethal dose of radiation. According to interviews with NRC officials, the commission is considering issuing orders for other types of high-risk sources.[87]

Emergency Planning and Response Exercises

Emergency response exercises involving simulated chemical, biological, radiological, and nuclear attacks occurred in the United States long before 9/11. The 1995 Aum Shinrikyo sarin gas attack on the Tokyo subway system spurred the U.S. Congress to enact a law in 1998 that mandated the federal government to work with state and local officials in a series of exercises termed TOPOFF for "top officials." TOPOFF is mainly focused on training high-level federal officials or their surrogates to respond effectively to crises such as RDD attacks. The first TOPOFFs took place in May 2000 in Denver, Colorado, and Portsmouth, New Hampshire, where there were simulated chemical and biological attacks, respectively.

Planning for TOPOFF 2 began before 9/11. In May 2003, Seattle hosted the radiological attack scenario for TOPOFF 2. (Chicago was the site for the companion TOPOFF 2 simulated bioterrorism attack.) According to the U.S. government, the objectives for TOPOFF 2 were to respond to the impact on critical infrastructure and quickly restore essential services, including communications, utilities, transportation, business operations, and medical, law enforcement and fire services; maintain local and state leadership and preserve critical government operations; operate a unified command with multiple levels of government; demonstrate short- and long-term recovery efforts; exercise mutual aid agreements between various governments; and demonstrate an ability to conduct joint public information operations.[88]

Government officials were quick to praise the TOPOFF 2 exercise, but months later, in October 2003, a FEMA report surfaced that underscored major problems during the test. The report cited agencies' inability to share information, unclear government procedures, and conflicts across the chain of command. In particular, the shortage of secure phone lines hampered communications, and many participants did not have security clearances.[89] A follow-on government report in December 2003 pointed out additional problems with TOPOFF 2. One of the most startling conclusions was that

> a continuing lack of preparedness by federal and local governments would result in unnecessary deaths in the event of a major terrorist attack. But [officials] insisted that many of the communications and logistical problems identified in the exercise had been corrected in the seven months since the $16 million exercise was conducted.[90]

Another problem was that the government was not able to provide consistent and accurate information about the path of radiological plumes despite the fact that the exercise was heavily scripted. Critics have argued that a real dirty bomb attack would come as a surprise.[91]

Other major U.S. metropolitan areas have also conducted planning exercises for possible RDD attacks. For instance, in June 2003, officials held a mock radiological attack in Montgomery County near Washington, DC. The simulated event involved hundreds of emergency responders from Maryland and Virginia. The main lessons learned were how to assess a contaminated area, how to tend to casualties, and how to evacuate people from the affected region effectively. Moreover, drills such as these can contribute to reassuring the public that authorities are equipped to respond to an RDD attack.[92]

Government scientists have been installing sensors that can measure wind currents and ionizing radiation and, thus, provide needed information to officials in the event of an RDD attack. By June 2003, the prototypical DCNet sensor network had been established in the Washington, DC, metropolitan area. As of April 2004, seven towers containing the sensors had been erected on government buildings.[93] Three more towers are planned to be installed near critical locations, such as Capitol Hill, the Pentagon, and the White House. New York City has two operational sensor sites. Ultimately, the planners have requested to build a DCNet system consisting of 75 to 175 towers, which could cost up to $10 million. Reportedly, the Department of Homeland Security is weighing this expansion proposal in coordination with the National Oceanic and Atmospheric Administration, which is the lead federal agency for DCNet. Sensing and then analyzing data generated by this network in real time could give authorities the necessary information to be able to direct people away from the paths of radioactive plumes.[94] While this network would provide enhanced monitoring capabilities for gamma-emitting radioactive materials, it is unclear whether the detection system would be able to track alpha emitters, which are much harder to detect than gamma emitters.

Radiation Treatment Drugs

As part of its planning to mitigate the effects of RDDs and ionizing radiation, the U.S. government is trying to develop radiation treatment drugs. On January 31, 2003, the U.S. Food and Drug Administration (FDA) called on companies to create marketing plans for Prussian blue. The FDA news release stated, "After a review of cases in published literature, FDA determined that 500-mg Prussian blue capsules would be safe and effective for the treatment of patients with known or suspected internal contamination with radioactive thallium, nonradioactive thallium, or radioactive cesium."[95] On October 1, 2003, the FDA approved Heyl Pharmaceuticals, a German company, to sell its brand of Prussian blue, Radiogardase®.

Prussian blue works by combining with thallium or cesium in the intestines, from where the material is excreted. In effect, Prussian blue can help rapidly flush radioactive cesium or thallium from the systems of people who are suffering from internal contamination. Perpetrators of an RDD attack would be more likely to use radioactive cesium than radioactive thallium because thallium is used only in low doses in medical treatment and diagnostics, but cesium is often employed in larger amounts in many applications, as discussed in an earlier section. Although this drug shows promise, it is not a panacea in that it cannot treat internal contamination from all radioactive substances. Treatments for internal contamination are essential because this contamination pathway could trigger health effects in large enough doses.

For several years, a radiation prevention drug for nuclear accidents has received attention. Potassium iodide, known also by the chemical formula KI, has been shown to be effective in preventing thyroid cancer if it is administered shortly before or within a short period of time after exposure to radioactive iodine. The thyroid gland preferentially absorbs iodine, especially in growing children. Saturating the thyroid with KI would help to block the adsorption of radioactive iodine. Similar to Prussian blue, KI specifically targets a particular radioactive element. The FDA cautions that "the use of KI should be as an adjunct to evacuation, sheltering and control of contaminated foods, such as milk."[96] KI can have serious side effects in fetuses or in adults who are susceptible to thyroid disease. However, the potential use of iodine-131 or other radioisotopes of iodine in RDDs, while possible, is considered a less significant risk than other radioactive materials. Thus, while stockpiling KI in communities near nuclear power plants with potential releases of radioactive iodine might offset risks of developing thyroid cancer in the affected population, storing KI in anticipation of such an RDD attack would likely result in more costs than benefits. Nonetheless, officials should anticipate demands from the public at large for KI treatment, regardless of the efficacy, because of the perception that this drug could offer protection in the event of a radiological attack. This concern is another reason for a concerted public education campaign to teach Americans about the real versus the perceived risks of RDDs.

The United States is also searching for drugs that can be administered to first responders to protect them from the effects of ionizing radiation. In May 2003, the U.S. military announced the results of preliminary tests of the drug HE-2100, developed by Hollis-Eden Pharmaceuticals, Inc., of San Diego, California. Reportedly, this drug is the first of thousands examined since the 1950s that show promise of protecting against some health effects of ionizing radiation. HE-2100 works by strengthening the part of the immune system resident in bone marrow. The drug allows the bone marrow to continue to manufacture neutrophils, infection-fighting cells, even when being bombarded by ionizing radiation. Further tests are required before approval for human use. The U.S. military and the FDA are reportedly striving to fast-track the readiness of such drugs.[97]

Radiation Detection and Border Protection

On March 1, 2003, the new Bureau of Customs and Border Protection in the Department of Homeland Security began using radiation detection devices to screen every person who enters the United States at border security checkpoints. Every border security inspector is expected to be equipped with the pager-size radiation detectors, which cost $2,500 apiece. Other radiation detection tools include handheld "radiation isotope identifiers," which in essence can measure the radioactive "fingerprint" of a material and, therefore, determine the exact type of radioactive material that is being detected. Inspectors also can employ X-ray machines to determine if heavy shielding, such as lead, is being used to prevent detection of radioactive materials by the handheld detectors. The bureau is trying to bring to bear new detection tools such as portal monitors, which were added in October 2002.[98] Portal monitors are used to detect radiation inside cargo carried by trucks.

This new bureau brings together 9,000 former Customs Service inspectors, 6,000 former Immigration and Naturalization Service (INS) inspectors, 3,000 former Agriculture Department inspectors, and 10,000 officials from the former Border Patrol. At the level of personnel, the new bureau is a step forward in achieving an integrated and unified border security agency. At the level of radioactive materials detection at U.S. borders, the bureau has acknowledged that the new handheld radiation detectors are only one aspect of a defense-in-depth system. However, the administration's plans for a multilayered and integrated border defense system to prevent the inflow of potentially dangerous radioactive and nuclear materials remain unclear.

In addition, the Department of Homeland Security has been trying to work with its counterparts in other countries to detect nuclear and radioactive materials in ships in foreign ports before embarkation to the United States. The Container Security Initiative has focused on the so-called megaports, those ports that are involved in about 90 percent of the world's shipping. Because detection capabilities are limited and inadequate for checking all containers, officials have relied on profiling techniques, such as detailed checks of a ship's manifest, to determine whether containers require scrutiny with radiation detectors. Even if this detection capability were fully in place, there would still be the need to recheck ships and cargo before entering U.S. ports. For instance, a determined terrorist could shield the radioactive contents of the potentially deadly cargo or could transfer nuclear or radiological materials onto ships at sea that had received a "clean" detection sweep in a foreign port.

PRIORITY ISSUES

Acquiring high-risk radioactive materials and constructing a radiological dispersion device, such as a dirty bomb, would not pose nearly as daunting a challenge to a terrorist group as obtaining and detonating an intact nuclear weapon or improvised nuclear device. Consequently, the prospects for terrorist success are relatively high for a radiological attack. Because commercial radioactive sources are very prevalent and will continue to have lower physical protection around them than nuclear weapons or nuclear-weapons-usable materials, a radiological attack appears to be all but certain within the coming years. To reduce the risks of this face of terrorism, efforts must be made to close the gaps in prevention by working diligently to improve regulatory controls over high-risk radioactive materials and to devote adequate resources toward educating the public and preparing to manage the consequences of such an attack.

Export Controls and Licensing Fraud

In January 2003, CNS identified a gap in the U.S. export licensing rules that permits shipments of most high-risk radioactive sources under a general license without any requirements for a U.S. governmental license review to confirm the credentials of the recipient.[99] While embargoed countries, including Cuba, Iran, Iraq, Libya, North Korea, and Sudan, would not receive these materials, nations where terrorist activity has frequently occurred, such as Syria,[100] which is on the State

Department's list of state sponsors of terrorism, as well as Afghanistan, Algeria, Columbia, India, Indonesia, Israel, the Philippines, Pakistan, and Saudi Arabia can receive unlimited shipments of most types of radioactive sources, including many considered high risk, without a U.S. government license review.

The U.S. government has stepped up efforts to plug this gap by coordinating with other governments, especially through the G-8 and the IAEA. Moreover, the NRC issued a voluntary advisory in March 2003 to licensees requesting that they report to the NRC any shipments containing large quantities of radioactivity at least ten days in advance of the transport. While this advisory moves in the direction of increased security, the NRC has yet to issue, as of this writing, a mandatory order to work toward permanently correcting the loophole. Meanwhile, the NRC has been working closely with U.S. Customs to track large shipments of radioactive materials and to develop a database of these transfers.[101] Encouragingly, at the June 2004 summit, the G-8 agreed to implement specific licensing requirements, which will mandate government checks on the credentials of importers and exporters of the highest risk sources.[102] The G-8 called for IAEA "approval of the guidance to ensure that effective controls are operational by the end of 2005 and applied in a harmonized and consistent manner."[103] Sustained leadership, through the United States, the G-8, and other partner states, will be required to encourage all states to adopt stricter import and export licensing rules. A major struggle is coordinating with international partners to ensure that changes in the export licensing system are harmonized. Mismatched systems would tend to block commerce and shipment of beneficial radioactive sources to legitimate users.[104]

Other nations involved in exporting significant quantities of highly radioactive sources are not conducting end-user checks. For instance, in an October 2003 report, Sandia National Laboratories pointed out that Canada and Russia, which are both major exporters, are exporting highly radioactive sources "without first determining if the recipient is authorized by the receiving country to own and use" the sources and recommended "stronger controls on the export and import of highly radioactive" sources.[105] However, if the aforementioned G-8 proposal is adopted, both Canada and Russia, as G-8 member states, will commit to enforcing stricter import and export rules.

As discussed above, in 2003 a high-risk radioactive source was almost shipped from Argentina to Texas without proper documentation. An Argentine regulatory official was able to contact his counterpart through the Internet. While the Texas radiation control office was listed on the Web, not all such offices for the United States and counterpart offices in other countries are available at a centralized location on the Internet. For instance, an IAEA-hosted Web site listing all such offices could facilitate expeditious communication. Furthermore, this incident points to the need for rapid information exchange among radiation safety and security officials to share lessons learned.[106]

Weak Regulatory Controls

Probably the biggest impediment to establishing effective export controls over radioactive sources is the weak or essentially nonexistent regulatory controls in more than half the world's nations—approximately 100 states. While the IAEA is currently assisting more than 80 member states to develop more effective regulatory systems through the Model Project, more member states need regulatory assistance. Even if all IAEA member states had adequate controls over radioactive sources, about 50 non-member states would be in need of assistance that the IAEA could not provide because of their membership status. Perhaps the major radioactive-source producing states can find a way to offer regulatory help. Creating a sustainable regulatory infrastructure that nurtures a safety-and-security culture takes time and commitment from governments.

Illicit Trafficking

While governments have increased efforts to detect illicit trafficking through programs such as the DOE's Second Line of Defense, more work is needed to stem the flow of radioactive materials smuggling. Borders in many countries, including the United States, are porous enough to allow passage of radioactive substances without being detected. Effectively reducing the amount of trafficking requires understanding whether a demand-side model or a supply-side model is primarily at work. That is, is the smuggling occurring mainly as a result of opportunistic thieves who are stealing sources and hoping to sell them for a profit, or is it principally due to organized crime or terrorist networks who are targeting these substances? The latter case obviously presents a greater risk of an RDD attack. Further research and data are required to understand the dynamics and motivations behind illicit trafficking of radioactive materials.

Disused Radioactive Source Disposal

Even in developed states, such as the United States, security over all aspects of a source's life-cycle is lacking. One crucial area involves ensuring that safe and secure disposal facilities are available for disused sources. As discussed above, the DOE is in charge of providing a permanent disposal site for higher-activity disused sources, most of which are categorized as Greater Than Class C radioactive waste. Funding shortages and insufficient prioritization by upper level management had indefinitely delayed establishment of this disposal site and the security of disused sources through the Off-Site Source Recovery Project. But in November 2003, DOE reprioritized this program as coming under the National Nuclear Security Administration's mandate. While it is anticipated that the OSR Project will receive adequate funding to round up thousands of disused high-risk sources, in the not-so-distant future, money will be required to ensure that a permanent depository for these sources is built.

Many lower-activity sources below the GTCC threshold also pose high security risks. For instance, disused sources containing high-risk radioisotopes such as cobalt-60 and iridium-192 are not categorized as GTCC waste. Under the 1985 Low Level Radioactive Waste Policy Amendments Act (LLRWPAA), the states assumed the responsibility for disposal of most low-level waste, and the federal government was tasked with disposing of higher-activity waste. The states were directed to form compacts. Each compact was to contain a low-level-waste disposal site. As of this writing, almost 19 years after passage of the LLRWPAA, the compacts have not established any new disposal sites.[107] The one disposal site that did open operates outside the compact system and is intended only for the lowest-activity waste.[108] Starting in 2008, when the Barnwell, South Carolina, disposal facility shuts its doors to states outside its compact, 35 states will be left without a disposal site for most of their low-level radioactive waste. Without such a facility, disused sources, some of which could pose a security threat, will accumulate at relatively unsecured locations, such as hospitals and universities.

Other countries are in need of safe and secure disused source depositories. States lacking the funds to finance these facilities should consider pooling resources to create regional depositories. The United States should determine how to direct seed money or other forms of assistance to these states to facilitate developing secure depositories where needed.

In addition, for future purchases of sources, imposing a disposal fee, for example, to be paid when sources are acquired, could create an incentive for prompt and proper disposal of disused sources. The fee would be partially refunded once proper disposition occurs.

High-Risk Orphan Sources

The IAEA, United States, and Russia, as well as other nations in the former Soviet Union (FSU), are working toward securing high-risk orphan sources in the region, as discussed above. Because this program is relatively new, however, gaps remain to be addressed. In May 2003, the GAO published an audit of the United States and international assistance efforts to control radioactive sources. The GAO found that "the department [DOE] has not fully coordinated its efforts with NRC and the Department of State to ensure that a government wide strategy is established."[109] Although DOE is correctly concerned about securing high-risk orphan sources in the FSU and is working to expand this program to states outside of the FSU that need assistance, a focus on working with the IAEA and other international partners to develop functioning regulatory systems in countries with chronic orphan source problems would ultimately create a sustainable solution. In other words, simply locking up high-risk orphan sources is a Band-Aid approach; stopping the flow of such sources requires healing ailing regulatory systems.

Port and Border Security

About one year after September 11, 2001, the Council on Foreign Relations published a report that assessed American ports as more vulnerable to terrorist attacks than the aviation system.[110] According to the General Accounting Office, programs designed to detect radioactive material or nuclear weapons at border crossings also "are limited in a number of respects."[111] Only a small portion of the total land- and sea-based shipments are screened. Moreover, insufficient and inadequate radiation detection is available for this task. In particular, there are not enough detectors in operation that can screen the entire contents of all cargo containers. Customs officials primarily use small, handheld detectors that are incapable of screening large containers.

Alternative Technologies

Looking to the future, security risks could be reduced by replacing radioactive sources with nonradioactive alternative technologies, where appropriate. The basis for this substitution can rest on solidly founded scientific analysis of radiation protection. The International Commission on Radiological Protection (ICRP) and the U.S. National Council on Radiation Protection and Measurements (NCRP) have developed a radiation protection framework. Under this framework, the principle of justification asks if the benefits of a radioactive source outweigh the risks of use. Waste disposal considerations are recommended to be factored into the decision process. If alternative technologies can provide comparable benefit at lower risk than a radioactive source, users are advised to choose the alternative nonradioactive source. For instance, in the great majority of cases, hospitals in the United States have switched from using radioactive sources in teletherapy machines to employing particle accelerator technology to deliver comparable treatment. However, some hospitals still use radioactive sources because the beam profile from the source is better for certain types of treatment. Similarly, the U.S. steel industry has been replacing radioactive source gauges located on continuous casters with alternative nonradioactive materials. The concern here was that molten metal accidentally striking the radioactive gauges could lead to significant contamination and costly cleanup.

Despite the acceptance of alternatives to radioactive sources in certain applications, the NRC has neither endorsed the principle of justification, nor has it embraced the consideration of alternative technologies in licensing reviews.[112] Although NRC licensing policy prohibits "frivolous" uses for radioactive material, the user bears responsibility for making the decision about whether or not to purchase a source. The NRC has contended that encouraging alternative technologies is not part of its mission. However, Congress has tasked the commission with protecting public health, safety, and property from radiation exposure and to provide for the common defense and security. Such responsibilities could give reason for the NRC to make licensees aware of alternative technologies.[113] Recommendations to consider alternatives to radioactive sources have come from the IAEA, the National Academy of Sciences, the NCRP, and the Health Physics Society.

Security Risks from Future Radioactive Sources

Even when users choose to continue to use radioactive sources, there are ways to reduce the inherent security risks of the source itself. For instance, manufacturers, by and large, have produced sources with the minimum amount of radioactivity needed to perform the necessary beneficial task. In addition, producers should strive to move toward less easily dispersible source material. For instance, as mentioned above, major manufacturers are reportedly considering phasing out powdered cesium chloride, which is readily dispersible if the source's seal is breached. Research at U.S. national laboratories is under way to find chemical substitutes for cesium chloride. Governments should foster public-private partnerships to convert this research into viable commercial products, which would reduce the security risks of future radioactive sources.

Consequence Management

As noted above, the TOPOFF 2 exercise in 2003 highlighted some major flaws in the ability of local, state, and federal agencies to communicate vital information and to coordinate their activities during a simulated radiological attack. Another lesson learned was the need for a radiological decontamination standard. Existing regulations for site cleanup were not developed with radiological terrorism in mind. In the summer of 2003, the DHS formed an advisory group to determine a standard that could help to achieve effective decontamination in balance with keeping the cleanup costs to a manageable level.[114] Reportedly, DHS is planning to issue a document for public comment in the summer of 2004.[115] While involving the public is needed, it is unclear whether DHS sought out public input during the earlier stages of review. It is important that all stakeholders are involved in the decision-making process. Developing new decontamination standards behind closed doors risks creating a public backlash and could worsen government credibility.

In addition to formulating decontamination standards, there is a pressing need to develop effective decontamination technologies.[116] Moreover, regional stockpiles of decontamination equipment throughout the United States are urgently required in order to rapidly deliver decontamination capabilities to the scene of a radiological attack.[117] However, it is not sufficient that decontamination methods and equipment are available; first responders must train to learn how to decontaminate effectively after a radiological attack.[118]

First responders require training about how to operate in a radioactively contaminated environment.[119] They will need to know how to minimize radiation exposures while continuing to save lives and protect property.[120] Training exercises have often shown that medical personnel tend to want to decontaminate injured people before administering treatment for wounds. However, medical personnel should be taught that in almost all cases of public contamination resulting from an RDD attack, life-threatening injuries should be treated before attempting decontamination of the injured person. The level of expected contamination from a radiological attack would typically not pose a significant health risk to medical personnel during the time required to treat an injury.[121]

Public Education

The psychological effects from a radiological attack could pose the greatest short-term health effects. Consequently, the public's reaction can be one of the best defenses or one of the greatest weaknesses in responding to radiological terrorism. If Americans are given accurate, credible information about the real risks of radiological attack and how to protect themselves in the event of such attack, they will be less likely to panic. In contrast, keeping Americans in the dark about the reality of this threat would probably result in a terrorized public if an RDD were used, thus serving one of the terrorists' prime objectives. Therefore, a high priority in preparing for radiological attack is to educate the public beforehand.[122] The U.S. National Academy of Sciences in 2002 concluded that "Education and training can serve as an effective counter to future RDD attacks."[123] At its best, this education can help to "psychologically immunize" the public against a radiological attack, making citizens less likely to panic.[124] Press reports, however, continue to raise concern that Americans are ill-prepared for an act of terrorism.[125]

Educating the public about radiation and its effects is very challenging. For example, even after numerous public hearings about the cleanup of the Rocky Flats site in Colorado, which was heavily contaminated with plutonium waste from the U.S. nuclear weapons program, many Coloradoans were very skeptical that the site could ever be made safe or that their health would not be in jeopardy. Thus, it is important to draw upon past experiences and difficulties in communicating with the public when developing a credible, effective education campaign.[126]

During a radiological attack, people need rapid delivery of accurate information to know whether they should shelter or flee and what additional measures they can use to protect themselves. Self-directed evacuations when not necessary for saving life could block first responders and other emergency personnel from arriving at the actual scene of attack. Police do not have the authority to prevent people from fleeing. Thus, a rapid, reliable means of communicating with the public is urgently needed. The existing Emergency Alert System, which replaced the Emergency Broadcast System, is a vital means of communication from authorities to the public. In addition, officials need to be able to assess quickly the locations of greatest danger and communicate that information to the public in a timely manner.

Equally important to informing the public is teaching the news media, first responders, and federal, state, and local officials about the effects of radiation, radioactive materials, and RDDs and how to communicate credibly and effectively with the public. The U.S. National Academy of Sciences in 2002 recommended developing and disseminating "prepackaged kits" of instructional material for the news media and national, state, and local leaders. These kits should be distributed long before an actual radiological attack, and officials should rehearse their message to the public. Identifying and training spokespeople, such as the surgeon general, whom Americans would trust, is also essential.[127] While the Department of Homeland Security's public education campaign launched in early 2003 through the Ready.gov Web site is laudable, much more needs to be urgently done to teach Americans about the real risks of radiological weapons.

[1] This chapter draws heavily upon Charles D. Ferguson, Tahseen Kazi, and Judith Perera, *Commercial Radioactive Sources: Surveying the Security Risks*, Occasional Paper No. 11 (Monterey, CA: Center for Nonproliferation Studies, Monterey Institute of International Studies, January 2003).

[2] Some have questioned whether Padilla, acting alone, had the organizational and technical skills to find and acquire radioactive materials and then construct a dirty bomb. See, for example, Lewis Z. Koch, "Dirty Bomber? Dirty Justice," *Bulletin of the Atomic Scientists* (January/February 2004), pp. 59-68. Moreover, information provided by the U.S. Justice Department on June 1, 2004 also casts doubt on the effectiveness of Padilla's alleged plans to detonate a dirty bomb. Allegedly, Padilla was directed by Abu Zubaida, a top al Qaeda operative, to attack the United States with a uranium-based dirty bomb. However, uranium is not very radioactive and would cause little or no actual harm if used in an RDD although it could cause a psychological effect. Charles J. Hanley, "Much Less to Padilla 'Dirty Bomb' Than Meets Feds' Eyes, Scientists Say," Associated Press, June 9, 2004.

[3] As reported by the Associated Press, unidentified British government officials said that they found documents indicating that al Qaeda built a small dirty bomb near Herat in western Afghanistan. In that same news report, however, an unnamed American official states that there is no evidence to substantiate that al Qaeda operatives made such a device. Associated Press, "BBC Says Al Qaeda Produced a 'Dirty Bomb' in Afghanistan," *New York Times*, January 31, 2003.

[4] Sara Kehaulani and Susan Schmidt, "U.S. Checking Foreign Airlines for Terror Risks," *Washington Post*, December 24, 2003, p. A1; Greg Krikorian, "L.A. Checked as Possible 'Dirty Bomb' Attack Target," *Los Angeles Times*, January 7, 2004, p. A12.

[5] The Progressive Policy Institute in its report, *America at Risk: A Homeland Security Report Card,* Progressive Foundation, July 2003, gave radioactive material security in the United States a "D" grade. The report cited the large number of radioactive sources and the lax security at many facilities containing such sources.

[6] According to the revised *Code of Conduct on the Safety and Security of Radioactive Sources,* IAEA report IAEA/CODEOC/2004, January 2004, a radioactive source is radioactive material that is permanently sealed in a capsule or closely bonded or in a solid form and not exempt from regulatory control. It excludes material in the nuclear fuel cycles of research and power reactors.

[7] Each chemical element, such as hydrogen, cobalt, or uranium, has different isotopes. All of the isotopes of a given element family have the same number of protons in their nuclei, resulting in the same chemical properties. However, they differ in the number of neutrons, and the number of neutrons determines whether the isotope is stable or unstable and undergoing radioactive decay. In this book, the convention for labeling isotopes will be to place the total number of protons and neutrons within the isotope's nucleus after the name of the element family, for example, cobalt-59, cobalt-60, uranium-235, or uranium-238.

[8] One piece is reportedly about the length of a pencil, and the other is as thick as a pencil, but about 17 inches long. "In 2002, a Connecticut nuclear power plant was fined $288,000 after a similar loss." That fuel was never found. Wilson Ring, "Vermont Nuclear Plant Searching for Missing Fuel Rods," Associated Press, April 21, 2004.

[9] Committee on Science and Technology for Countering Terrorism, National Research Council, "Nuclear and Radiological Threats," Chapter 2 in *Making the Nation Safer: The Role of Science and Technology in Countering Terrorism* (Washington, DC: National Academy Press, 2002), pp. 48-49.

[10] Charles D. Ferguson, et al., *Commercial Radioactive Sources.*

[11] Long before scientists had the capability to make radioisotopes, they extracted radium from uranium ore for use in radioactive sources. The use of radium in the United States peaked around 1950 at about 5,500 users and has been steadily declining since then. Many radium sources have been swept up and disposed of, but because for many decades radium was not regulated, old sources continue to surface. For a discussion of the history of radium sources in the United States, see Joel O. Lubenau, "A Century's Challenges: Historical Overview of Radiation Sources in the USA," *IAEA Bulletin* 41 (March 1999), pp. 49-54.

[12] Half-life is the amount of time it takes for half the amount of a radioactive substance to decay. After two half-lives, one fourth of the original material is left; after three half-lives, one-eighth; and so on. After seven half-lives, only about 1 percent of the initial amount remains.

[13] Curies measure the number of nuclear transformations per unit time occurring in a radioactive material. Specifically, a curie equals 3.7×10^{10} transformations per second, which is approximately equivalent to the amount of radioactivity emitted by one gram of radium-226. In most of the world, the scientific unit Becquerel has replaced the curie. One Becquerel equals one nuclear transformation per second. This book uses curie because it is still widely used in the United States and radiation safety experts throughout the world are familiar with it.

[14] The three types of ionizing radiation of concern are alpha, beta, and gamma radiation. Alpha radiation consists of a helium nucleus (two protons and two neutrons bound together). It is the least penetrating of the three types and can be stopped by a piece of paper or the dead outer layer of human skin. Beta radiation consists of a high-speed electron or positron (positively charged electron) and can be typically blocked by a few millimeters of aluminum. Gamma radiation is composed of high-energy electromagnetic radiation (which has a higher energy than X-rays) and is the most penetrating type of ionizing radiation; generally speaking, only thick pieces of lead or concrete can block gamma radiation.

[15] IAEA, *Categorization of Radiation Sources,* IAEA report IAEA-TECDOC-1344, July 2003.

[16] Although uranium in a highly enriched form can be useful for an IND, this weakly radioactive element would not be useful for a potent RDD.

[17] Abel J. Gonzalez, "Strengthening the Safety of Radiation Sources and the Security of Radioactive Materials: Timely Action," *IAEA Bulletin* 41 (March 1999), p. 4.

[18] The *Code of Conduct on Safety and Security of Radioactive Sources* defines categories of high-risk sources. "Category 1 sources, if not safely managed or securely protected would be likely to cause permanent injury to a person who handled them, or were otherwise in contact with them, for more than a few minutes. It would probably be fatal to be close to this amount of unshielded material for a period of a few minutes to an hour. These sources are typically used in practices such as radiothermal generators, irradiators and radiation tele-

therapy. Category 2 sources, if not safely managed or securely protected, could cause permanent injury to a person who handled them, or were otherwise in contact with them, for a short time (minutes to hours). It could possibly be fatal to be close to this amount of unshielded material for a period of hours to days. These sources are typically used in practices such as industrial gamma radiography, high dose rate brachytherapy and medium dose rate brachytherapy. Category 3 sources, if not safely managed or securely protected, could cause permanent injury to a person who handled them, or were otherwise in contact with them, for some hours. It could possibly—although it is unlikely—be fatal to be close to this amount of unshielded radioactive material for a period of days to weeks. These sources are typically used in practices such as fixed industrial gauges involving high activity sources (for example, level gauges, dredger gauges, conveyor gauges, and spinning pipe gauges) and well logging…. In addition to these categories, States should give appropriate attention to radioactive sources considered by them to have the potential to cause unacceptable consequences if employed for malicious purposes, and to aggregations of lower activity sources." IAEA, *Code of Conduct on Safety and Security of Radioactive Sources,* p. 15. In the United States, the Nuclear Regulatory Commission considers high-risk sources to be those in the first two categories. Notably, the above categorization of high-risk sources depends solely on their potential harm to human health. Critics of this scheme, such as certified health physicist Joel O. Lubenau, believe that this definition is too restrictive. Even so-called low-risk sources, i.e., those with lower amounts of radioactivity than the "high-risk" sources above, could provoke serious psychological and social effects depending on the terrorism scenario. An upcoming section examines health and psychosocial effects.

[19] Joel O. Lubenau and James G. Yusko, "Radioactive Material in Recycled Metals—An Update," *Health Physics* 74 (March 1998), pp. 293-299.

[20] The use of two distinctive licensing systems, specific and general, appears to be unique to the United States.

[21] According to the IAEA, the curie levels that would trigger placing the radioisotopes of greatest security concern into categories 1, 2, and 3 of high-risk sources are: Am-241: 2,000, 20, 2; Cf-252: 500, 5, 0.5; Co-60: 800, 8, 0.8; Cs-137: 3,000, 30, 3; Ir-192: 2,000, 20, 2; Pu-238: 2,000, 20, 2; Ra-226: 1,000, 10, 1; and Sr-90 (Y-90): 30,000, 300, 30. IAEA, *Code of Conduct on Safety and Security of Radioactive Sources,* p. 16.

[22] Henry C. Kelly, president of the Federation of American Scientists, and Steven Koonin, a physics professor and provost of the California Institute of Technology, were among the first analysts after September 11, 2001, to draw attention to the massively disruptive effects of RDDs. U.S. Senate, Committee on Foreign Relations, testimony by Henry C. Kelly, March 6, 2002, available at <http://www.fas.org/ssp/docs/kelly_testimony_030602.pdf>, accessed on April 23, 2004; U.S. Senate, Committee on Foreign Relations, "Radiological Terrorism," testimony by Steven E. Koonin, March 6, 2002, published in *Physics & Society* (April 2002), pp. 12-13.

[23] Peter D. Zimmerman with Cheryl Loeb, "Dirty Bombs: The Threat Revisited," *Defense Horizons* 38 (January 2004), p. 1.

[24] Neutron exposure is significant in an IND or a nuclear weapon, but of minimal significance in RDDs.

[25] Michael A. Levi and Henry C. Kelly, "Weapons of Mass Disruption," *Scientific American* (November 2002), pp. 76-81. Kelly has also testified to Congress about these effects. U.S. Senate, Henry C. Kelly testimony, March 6, 2002.

[26] According to the U.S. National Academy of Sciences, "In general, public fear of radiation and radioactive materials appears to be disproportionate to the actual hazards." Committee on Science and Technology for Countering Terrorism, *Making the Nation Safer,* p. 61.

[27] National Council on Radiation Protection and Measurements (NCRP) has published an extensive analysis of psychological and social effects of radiological attack in *Management of Terrorist Events Involving Radioactive Material,* NCRP Report No. 138, October 2001, Chapter 5. In addition, the Department of Homeland Security has developed guidance through a medical working group to aid in treating psychological effects. In particular, this group has advised physicians and other health-care providers to follow the "Principles of Psychological First Aid," in *Department of Homeland Security Working Group on Radiological Dispersal Device (RDD) Preparedness, Medical Preparedness and Response Sub-Group,* Working Document, May 1, 2003 Version, p. 36, available at <http://www1.va.gov/emshg/docs/Radiologic_Medical_Countermeasures_051403.pdf>, accessed on April 23, 2004.

[28] "A careful examination of the tragic accident in Goiania, Brazil, however, shows that some forms of radiological attack could kill tens or hundreds of people and sicken hundreds or thousands." Zimmerman with Loeb, "Dirty Bombs: The Threat Revisited," p. 1.

[29] It is uncertain how much cobalt-60 Iran or North Korea could produce. However, a September 2003 Los Alamos National Laboratory report lists the Atomic Energy Organization of Iran and the Center for Atomic Energy in North Korea as possible third-tier producers. Gregory J. van Tuyle, Tiffany L. Strub, Harold A. O 'Brien, Caroline F. V. Mason, and Steven J. Gitomer, Reducing RDD Concerns Related to Large Radiological Source Applications, Los Alamos National Laboratory report LA-UR-03-6664, September 2003, pp. 36-37.

[30] Ian Traynor, "Nuclear Watchdog Fears Terrorist Dirty Bomb after Looting at al-Tuwaitha," *The Guardian*, May 14, 2003.

[31] IAEA, *Implementation of the Safeguards Agreement between the Republic of Iraq and the International Atomic Energy Agency pursuant to the Treaty on the Non-Proliferation of Nuclear Weapons*, IAEA Report by the Director General, July 14, 2003.

[32] Louis J. Freeh, "Chapter 2: FBI Leadership in National Security," in *A Report to the American People on the Work of the FBI: 1993-1998*, <http://digilander.libero.it/supcomandante/attaccoagliusa/report5.htm>, accessed on August 25, 2003.

[33] Charles D. Ferguson and Joel O. Lubenau, "Securing U.S. Radioactive Sources," *Issues in Science and Technology* (Fall 2003), p. 71.

[34] Joel O. Lubenau, "Street Smarts," *Health Physics Society Newsletter* (February 2004).

[35] Andrew Karam, Radiation Safety Officer, Rochester Institute of Technology, e-mail communication with author, April 6, 2004.

[36] Joel O. Lubenau, "Sources of Radioactive Isotopes for Dirty Bombs," paper delivered to the American Physical Society, Annual Meeting, Denver, Colorado, May 3, 2004.

[37] Ferguson and Lubenau, "Securing U.S. Radioactive Sources," p. 71.

[38] Center for Nonproliferation Studies, "Missing Iridium Partly Recovered in Ecuador," *NIS Export Control Observer* (September 2003), pp. 11-12.

[39] Joby Warrick, "Smugglers Enticed by Dirty Bomb Components: Radioactive Materials are Sought Worldwide," *Washington Post*, November 30, 2003, p. A1.

[40] Center for Nonproliferation Studies, *NIS Export Control Observer* (December 2003/January 2004), pp. 18-24. Two RTG sources were reported found on November 17, 2003, and the other was discovered on April 17, 2003.

[41] Yevgeny Vladimirovich Antonov, "Threat of Terrorist Act Using Weapons of Mass Destruction from Chechnya," *Yaderny Kontrol* (March/April 2001), in FBIS CEP20010610000001, February 20, 2001.

[42] Eileen M. Supko, "Using Friendly Instruments for Enhancing Communications," paper delivered to the IAEA International Conference on the Safety of Transport of Radioactive Materials, Vienna, Austria, July 7-11, 2003.

[43] John R. Cochran, Susan W. Longley, Laura L. Price, and Kendra J. Lipinski, *The Adequacy of Current Import and Export Controls on Sealed Radioactive Sources*, Sandia National Laboratories SAND Report, SAND2003-3767, October 2003, p. 3.

[44] Charles D. Ferguson et al., *Commercial Radioactive Sources*, p. 16.

[45] IAEA, Press Release, June 24, 2002, "Inadequate Control of World's Radioactive Sources"; Joby Warrick, "Makings of a 'Dirty Bomb': Devices Left by Soviets Could Attract Terrorists," *Washington Post*, March 18, 2002, p. A1; Joby Warrick, "Hunting a Deadly Soviet Legacy: Concerns about 'Dirty Bomb' Drive Efforts to Find Radioactive Cesium," *Washington Post*, November 11, 2002, p. A1; Richard Stone, "The Hunt for Hot Stuff," *Smithsonian* (March 2003).

[46] "IAEA Aids Recovery of Sources Found in Georgian Mountains," *Nucleonics Week*, February 7, 2002, p. 16.

[47] IAEA, Press Release, June 10, 2002, "Search Begins for Missing Radiation Sources in the Republic of Georgia."

[48] While penetrating gamma radiation would be easiest to detect, alpha radiation would be the most difficult to spot. However, many alpha sources also emit some gamma radiation, which although are often low energy, might still be detected depending on the sensitivity of the radiation sensor. In addition, alpha-emitting radioisotopes that decay into daughter isotopes that emit gamma radiation might give a large enough radiation signal to be detected.

[49] Christopher Lee, "DOE Bomb Squads' Exacting Mission: Team Hunting for Radioactive Explosives Faces Aging Equipment, Talent Shortage, Analysts Say," *Washington Post*, March 9, 2004, p. A21.

[50] For example, the *International Basic Safety Standards for Protection against Ionizing Radiation and for the Safety of*

Radiation Sources, IAEA Safety Series No. 115, 1996, para. 2.34, requires that: "Sources shall be kept secure so as to prevent theft or damage…a source not be transferred unless the receiver possesses a valid authorization; and…a periodic inventory of movable sources be conducted at appropriate intervals to confirm that they are in their assigned locations and are secure." In addition, the IAEA Board of Governors, resolution GC(42)/RES/12, September 25, 1998, states in part that all governments are encouraged "to take steps to ensure the safety of radiation sources and the security of radioactive materials."

[51] Safety and security are intertwined. "To ensure security of sources requires that measures be applied to prevent unauthorized access to radioactive sources at all stages of their life cycle, as well as loss, theft, and unauthorized transfer of sources. To ensure the safety of radioactive sources requires controlling exposure to radiation from sources, both directly and as a consequence of incidents, so that the likelihood of harm attributable to such exposure is very low. Security is therefore a prerequisite for safety." *Security of Radioactive Sources: Interim Guidance for Comment,* IAEA-TECDOC-1355, June 2003, p. 2.

[52] Most of this section is adapted from Charles D. Ferguson, "Reducing the Threat of RDDs," *IAEA Bulletin* 45 (2003), pp. 37-40; and Charles D. Ferguson, et al., *Commercial Radioactive Sources.*

[53] Charles D. Ferguson et al., *Commercial Radioactive Sources,* pp. 26-40; Gregory van Tuyle et al., *Reducing RDD Concerns,* pp. 33-43.

[54] Industry officials, names withheld by request, interview by author, Washington, DC, September 2002; Washington State official, name withheld by request, interview by author, Monterey, CA, March 2004.

[55] Nuclear Regulatory Commission (NRC), NRC Regulations, Part 20: Standards for protection against radiation, 10 CFR 20.1801: Security of stored material.

[56] Ibid., 10 CFR 20.1802: Control of material not in storage.

[57] For example, in 1998, officials at the Moses Cone Hospital in Greensboro, North Carolina, reported that 19 vials of radioactive cesium were missing. An extensive search never uncovered the missing radioactive material. Reportedly, this incident, which is believed to have been a theft, served as a wake-up call for hospitals in North Carolina to improve their security practices. As a result, doctors and other personnel at these hospitals are instructed to follow tighter security methods, including locking up radioactive material when it is not in use, limiting access to keys that unlock radioactive source storage lockers, and using layers of locks to protect the material from unauthorized access. Danielle Deaver, "North Carolina Hospitals Boost Security to Handle Radioactive-Material Threats," *Knight Ridder Tribune Business News,* June 12, 2002, p. 1.

[58] Bret Baier, "Radioactive Material Stolen in Nigeria," Fox News, February 28, 2003.

[59] Joby Warrick, "Smugglers Enticed by Dirty Bomb Components," *Washington Post,* November 30, 2003, p. A1.

[60] For example, Abel Gonzalez, the lead radiation safety official at the IAEA, has spoken often about this concern.

[61] Ferguson and Lubenau, "Securing U.S. Radioactive Sources," pp. 71-72.

[62] IAEA Board of Governors General Conference, "The Action Plan for the Safety of Radiation Sources and the Security of Radioactive Materials," IAEA/GOV/2000/34-GC(44)/7, August 7, 2000.

[63] *Proceedings of the National Regulatory Authorities with Competence in the Safety of Radiation Sources and the Security of Radioactive Materials,* Buenos Aires, Argentina, December 11-15, 2000.

[64] As cited in U.S. General Accounting Office, "Nuclear Nonproliferation: U.S. and International Assistance Efforts to Control Sealed Radioactive Sources Need Strengthening," GAO-03-638, June 2003.

[65] *Report on the Implementation of Model Projects for Upgrading Radiation Protection Infrastructure,* IAEA Board of Governors report GOV/2001/48, November 8, 2001, p. 4.

[66] IAEA, Press Release, May 19, 2000, "IAEA Searches for Discarded Radioactive Sources in Republic of Georgia."

[67] IAEA, *Security of Radioactive Sources: Interim Guidance for Comment,* IAEA report IAEA-TECDOC-1355, June 2003.

[68] For more information on the findings and speeches given at the conference, see the conference Web site at <http://www.iaea.org/worldatom/Press/Focus/RadSources/index.shtml>.

[69] U.S. Secretary of Energy Spencer Abraham, remarks at the IAEA Conference on the Security of Radioactive Sources, Vienna, Austria, March 11, 2003.

[70] U.S. Senate, Committee on Appropriations, prepared statement of Ambassador Linton F. Brooks before the Subcommittee on Energy and Water Development, April 10, 2003.

[71] Aleksandr Rumyantsev, Russian Atomic Energy Minister, remarks at the Conference on the Security of Radioactive Sources, Vienna, Austria, March 11, 2003.

[72] For further information on this convention, see <http://www.iaea.org/Publications/Documents/Conventions/cacnare_status.pdf>.

[73] Center for Nonproliferation Studies, "IAEA Conference for the Radioactive Source Industry," *NIS Export Control Observer* (June 2003), pp. 16-17.

[74] G-8, "Non Proliferation of Weapons of Mass Destruction: Securing Radioactive Sources - A G8 Action Plan," G-8 Summit document, June 2003, available at <http://www.g8.fr/evian/english/navigation/2003_g8_summit/summit_documents/non_proliferation_of_weapons_of_mass_destruction_securing_radioactive_sources_-_a_g8_action_plan.html>.

[75] The G-8 states are Canada, France, Germany, Italy, Japan, Russia, the United Kingdom, and the United States. Five of these states are in the group of major manufacturers and distributors of commercial radioactive sources. That group includes Argentina, Belgium, Canada, France, the Netherlands, Russia, South Africa, the United Kingdom, and the United States.

[76] Industry official, name withheld by request, interview by author, Washington, DC, August 19, 2003.

[77] As discussed in more detail later, a 1985 U.S. law mandated that the federal government is in charge of disposing of the higher-activity GTCC waste, whereas the states are responsible for forming compacts to create disposal sites for the lower-activity waste: Classes A, B, and C, as defined by the U.S. Code of Federal Regulations 10 CFR 61.55 and 61.56. Although the waste categorization scheme is not centered on security, from the perspective of this book, the security risks tend to increase from Class A to GTCC because the radioactivity levels generally increase from Class A to GTCC. Typically, the more highly radioactive disused sources with relatively long half-lives would be considered GTCC waste. In particular, radioisotopes with half-lives of less than five years would not exceed the GTCC threshold. Thus, Cf-252, Co-60, and Ir-192, the three radioisotopes with the shortest half-lives of the eight isotopes identified earlier, would usually not fall into the GTCC category.

[78] U.S. Department of Energy, "DOE Surpasses Congressional Target of Recovering Radioactive Sources," Press Release, May 18, 2004. The Los Alamos National Laboratory, Off-Site Source Recovery Project Web site, <http://osrp.lanl.gov/>, accessed on July 7, 2004, states that the Project has "recovered over 7,500 sealed sources."

[79] GAO, *Nuclear Nonproliferation: DOE Action Needed to Ensure Continued Recovery of Unwanted Sealed Radioactive Sources,* General Accounting Office report GAO-03-483, April 2003.

[80] U.S. Senate, Armed Services Committee, Statement of Paul M. Longsworth, Deputy Administrator for Defense Nuclear Nonproliferation, National Nuclear Security Administration, U.S. Department of Energy, March 10, 2004.

[81] IAEA, *Code of Conduct on the Safety and Security of Radioactive Sources,* p. 16.

[82] Conference of Radiation Control Program Directors, Inc., "Announcement: A National Orphan Radioactive Material Disposition Program," October 2001, <http://www.crcpd.org/SpecialServices&Projects/Orphan_Rad_Mat_Pgm/Announcement.pdf>.

[83] DOE/NRC Interagency Working Group on Radiological Dispersal Devices, *Radiological Dispersal Devices: An Initial Study to Identify Radioactive Materials of Greatest Concern and Approaches to Their Tracking, Tagging, and Disposition,* report to the Nuclear Regulatory Commission and the Secretary of Energy, May 2003.

[84] These gauges typically contain an 8-10 millicurie Cs-137 source and a 40-50 millicurie Am-241/beryllium source.

[85] Global Security Newswire, "Radiological Weapons: NRC Proposes Increased Security for Industrial Gauges," July 22, 2003.

[86] Office of the Federal Register, National Archives and Records Administration (NARA), *Federal Register* 68 (June 13, 2003), Notices, p. 35458.

[87] NRC officials, names withheld by request, interviews by the author, conducted at NRC Headquarters, Rockville, MD, November 2003.

[88] James Hagey, "New test of our terrorism defenses," *News Tribune,* Tacoma, WA, April 22, 2003.

[89] Robert Block, "FEMA Points to Flaws, Flubs in Terror Drill," *Wall Street Journal,* October 31, 2003, p. B1.

[90] Philip Shenon, "Terrorism Drills Showed Lack of Preparedness, Report Says," *New York Times,* December 19, 2003, p. A32.

[91] Jaime Yassif, "How Well did TOPOFF 2 Prepare Us for Mitigating the Effects of a Dirty Bomb Attack," *FAS Public Interest Report,* Summer 2003.

92 Susan Levine, "Area Crews Drill for a Day of Disaster," *Washington Post,* June 11, 2003, p. B3.

93 U.S. Senate, Committee on Commerce, Science, and Transportation, Subcommittee on Oceans, Fisheries, and Coast Guard, written statement by Under Secretary of Commerce for Oceans and Atmosphere, Conrad C. Lautenbacher, Jr., Vice Admiral, U.S. Navy (Ret.), on the National Oceanic and Atmospheric Administration's FY 2005 Budget, April 29, 2004, <http://www.legislative.noaa.gov/Testimony/042904lautenbacher.htm>, accessed on May 18, 2004.

94 Spencer S. Hsu, "Sensors May Track Terror's Fallout," *Washington Post,* June 2, 2003, p. A1.

95 U.S. Food and Drug Administration, "FDA Encourages New Drug Application Submissions for Prussian Blue as a Treatment for Thallium or Radioactive Cesium Contamination," *FDA News,* January 31, 2003.

96 Marilyn Chase and Rachel Zimmerman, "If 'Dirty Bomb' Hits, Hospitals Must Improvise," *Wall Street Journal,* June 12, 2002, p. B1.

97 John Mintz, "Radiation Sickness Drug Developed," *Washington Post,* May 19, 2003, p. A2.

98 Seth Schiesel, "Their Mission: Intercepting Deadly Cargo," *New York Times,* March 20, 2003, p. G1.

99 Charles D. Ferguson et al., *Commercial Radioactive Sources,* pp. 60-62; Leonard S. Spector made major contributions to that finding in the January 2003 report.

100 However, with respect to Syria, President Bush, on December 12, 2003, signed the Syria Accountability and Lebanese Sovereignty Restoration Act of 2003, which authorizes economic and diplomatic sanctions against Syria. The act calls on Syria to "halt Syrian support for terrorism, end its occupation of Lebanon, stop its development of weapons of mass destruction, cease its illegal importation of Iraqi oil and illegal shipments of weapons and other military items to Iraq." It requires the president to impose two out of six of the following sanctions: reducing diplomatic contacts; banning U.S. exports to Syria; prohibiting U.S. businesses from investing or operating in Syria; restricting travel of Syrian diplomats to Washington and the UN; banning Syrian aircraft from taking off, landing in, or flying over the United States; and freezing Syrian assets in the United States. The law, however, allows President Bush to waive the sanctions for periods of one to six months if he decides that it is in the security interests of the United States. During the signing ceremony for the act, President Bush pointedly said that the policy statements in the act are not binding. "Bush Signs Syria Sanctions Bill," CNN.com, December 13, 2003, http://www.cnn.com/2003/US/12/12/bush.syria/, accessed on June 4, 2004. Thus, in principle, the act could result in blocking U.S. exports of radioactive sources to Syria, but the Code of Federal Regulations still lists Syria as eligible to receive such shipments.

101 NRC officials, names withheld by request, interviews by author, Washington, DC, June and July 2003.

102 As discussed earlier, these sources belong to categories 1 and 2 of the IAEA's risk categorization system.

103 G8 Action Plan on Nonproliferation, June 9, 2004, available at <http://www.g8usa.gov/d_060904d.htm>, accessed on June 15, 2004.

104 Charles D. Ferguson and Leonard S. Spector, "Closing the Gap in Export Licensing Rules of High-Risk Radioactive Sources" *Proceedings of the 44th INMM Meeting,* July 2003.

105 John R. Cochran et al., *The Adequacy of Current Import and Export Controls on Sealed Radioactive Sources,* p. 3.

106 Ferguson and Lubenau, "Securing U.S. Radioactive Sources," p. 71.

107 The three existing low-level radioactive waste disposal sites are Barnwell, located in Barnwell, South Carolina; Hanford, located in Hanford, Washington; and Envirocare, located in Clive, Utah. Envirocare can accept waste from all regions, but it is limited to only Class A waste. Barnwell and Hanford can dispose of Classes A through C, but are restricted in the states that they can serve. See, also, the June 2004 analysis by the GAO. U.S. General Accounting Office, "Low-Level Radioactive Waste: Disposal Availability Adequate in the Short Term, but Oversight Needed to Identify Any Future Shortfalls," GAO-04-604, June 2004.

108 Joel O. Lubenau, "Security Risks of Radioactive Material," paper delivered to the Eighth International Symposium on the Synthesis of Isotopes and Isotopically Labeled Compounds, Boston, MA, June 2, 2003.

109 GAO-03-638.

110 Independent Task Force Sponsored by the Council on Foreign Relations, *America Still Unprepared – America Still in Danger,* October 2002.

111 JayEtta Z. Hecker, Director, Physical Infrastructure Issues, *Container Security: Current Efforts to Detect Nuclear Materials, New Initiatives, and Challenges,* GAO report GAO-03-297T, November 2002.

112 According to NRC Chairman Nils Diaz, "the NRC does not have regulatory authority to evaluate non-nuclear technologies or, as a general matter, to require applicants to propose and evaluate alternatives to radioactive material. Moreover, the evaluation may be significantly outside the scope of existing NRC exper-

tise, given that the evaluation would need to consider, on a case-specific basis, not only the relative risks of the various non-nuclear technologies that could be applied, but also the potential benefits, including consideration of the societal benefits of using each technology." Nils J. Diaz, Chairman, Nuclear Regulatory Commission, "Radiological terrorism," Letter-to-the-Editor, *Issues in Science and Technology* (Winter 2004), p. 13.

[113] Joel O. Lubenau, "Security Risks of Radioactive Material," CNS Report, May 27, 2003, available at <http:///www.cns.miis.edu/pubs/reports/lubenau.htm>.

[114] Harvey Simon, "Ridge Wants DHS to Develop Single Radiological Contamination Standard," *Aviation Week's Homeland Security & Defense,* July 2, 2003, p. 4.

[115] Philip Ball, "US Unprepared for Dirty-Bomb Attack," *Nature,* April 26, 2004.

[116] The Los Alamos National Laboratory held a decontamination workshop in September 2003 which recommended, "Based on the determination of gap analyses and science needs, enabling science must be invested in to realize a new generation of revolutionary decontamination technology capable of addressing the variety of radionuclides and substrates that will inevitably require decontamination to publicly acceptable limits." Tammy P. Taylor, David E. Morris, Thomasin C. Miller, and Sandra L. Gogol, *Radionuclide Decontamination Science and Technology Workshop: Workshop Summary and Findings,* Los Alamos National Laboratory report LA_UR-03-8215, September 16-17, 2003, p. 1.

[117] The Los Alamos National Laboratory decontamination workshop recommended, "Immediately develop and implement a plan to stockpile decontamination supplies based on existing decontamination technologies so that, in the event of an RDD incident, it will be possible to respond using best existing methods to mitigate the contamination." Ibid., p. 1.

[118] "The Department [of Homeland Security] would begin requiring annual certification of first responder preparedness to handle and decontaminate any hazard. This certification process would also verify the ability of state and local first responders to work effectively with related federal support assets." Warren B. Rudman, Chair, Richard A. Clarke, Senior Adviser, Jamie F. Metzl, Project Director, *Emergency Responders: Drastically Underfunded, Dangerously Unprepared,* Report of an Independent Task Force Sponsored by the Council on Foreign Relations, July 2003. In addition, the Los Alamos National Laboratory workshop in September 2003 recommended that "Emergency response playbooks should be developed to guide first responders. The playbooks should serve as a living database and be continuously updated based on the latest response and technology development available for responders." Tammy P. Taylor, et al., *Radionuclide Decontamination Science and Technology Workshop,* p. 1.

[119] A March 2002 workshop by the Center for Strategic and International Studies (CSIS) prepared for the Metropolitan Washington Council of Governments concluded that "police and fire agencies must develop plans to protect initial responders from radiation, stagger rescue crews to prevent overexposure and ensure that protective gear and equipment can be rushed in from regional sources," as reported by Spencer S. Hsu, "Plan Urged for 'Dirty' Explosive: Radioactivity Could Spur Panic, Report Cautions," *Washington Post,* May 4, 2002, p. B1. See, also, Philip Anderson, "Greater Washington, DC Crisis Planning," Report for CSIS, March 21, 2002.

[120] The Health Physics Society has published a set of recommendations for decision makers and first responders to guide their actions during a radiological attack. Health Physics Society, Position Statement, "Guidance for Protective Actions Following a Radiological Terrorist Event," January 2004. One of the major recommendations is that "Lifesaving actions and actions to secure the area of a radiological terrorist event from further terrorist activities should take precedence over radiological considerations following a radiological terrorist event, with the possible exception of the area near ground zero soon after detonation of a nuclear weapon." The position paper also spells out when sheltering or evacuation is recommended.

[121] According to the September 2003 Los Alamos National Laboratory decontamination workshop's findings, "National guidelines and legislation (if necessary) should be enacted to ensure that radiologically contaminated victims of an RDD incident receive necessary medical treatment despite the added danger of the radioactive contamination." Taylor et al., *Radionuclide Decontamination Science and Technology Workshop,* p. 1.

[122] CSIS, in its March 2002 study, also made this recommendation. RAND in 2003 published a book-length study of how to prepare individuals to respond to a chemical, biological, radiological, or nuclear attack. The RAND study underscored that "because ordinary citizens are a primary target of terrorism, being informed, prepared, and ready to respond is likely to provide an individual with a sense of empowerment and confidence to combat the feelings of violation and despair that are the aims of terrorism. Moreover, if terrorists believe

that they are less likely to be successful because of individual preparedness, then that preparedness could also serve to deflect terrorists from attacks against Americans." Lynn E. Davis, Tom LaTourrette, David E. Mosher, Lois M. Davis, and David R. Howell, *Individual Preparedness and Response to Chemical, Radiological, Nuclear, and Biological Terrorist Attacks,* RAND, 2003, p. 1. Concerning RDD preparedness, this study recommended that an individual's highest priority during such an attack is to avoid breathing in radioactive dust.

[123] Committee on Science and Technology for Countering Terrorism, *Making the Nation Safer,* p. 62.

[124] Charles Ferguson and Kaleb Redden, "Facing the Inevitable: Arm Public with Facts on Dirty Bomb Defense," *Defense News,* February 9, 2004, p. 53. Gary Ackerman of the Monterey Institute's Center for Nonproliferation Studies was among the first counterterrorism experts to use the phrase "psychological immunization."

[125] See, for example, Mimi Hall, "Most Aren't Prepared for Attack," *USA Today,* March 31, 2004.

[126] "The messages need to be repeated often, along with the kind of education about potential threats (a dirty bomb is not the same as a nuclear bomb) that can hold down fear." Editorial, "Preparing for Trouble," *Washington Post,* June 24, 2002, p. A18.

[127] Committee on Science and Technology for Countering Terrorism, *Making the Nation Safer,* p. 62. NCRP, *Management of Terrorist Events Involving Radioactive Material,* NCRP Report No. 138, October 2001, contains an examination of public communication issues; see Chapter 7 "Public Communication." Regarding the issue of identifying credible spokespeople, a post-9/11 study conducted by Steven M. Becker at the University of Alabama at Birmingham found that test audiences trusted television meteorologists to present unbiased scientific information and felt that they could rely on the guidance presented by this group of professionals in an emergency. Steven M. Becker, "Psychological and Communication Issues in Radiological Terrorism Situations," Presentation at the Advances in Consequence Management for Radiological Terrorism Events meeting, National Council on Radiation Protection and Measurements, Crystal City, Virginia, April 14, 2004.

7

MEETING THE CHALLENGE
A PLAN FOR URGENT ACTION AGAINST NUCLEAR TERRORISM

The foregoing chapters have reviewed the dangers posed by the four faces of nuclear terrorism: the theft and detonation of an intact nuclear weapon, the theft or purchase of fissile material leading to the fabrication and detonation of a crude nuclear weapon, the attack on or sabotage of nuclear installations, and the dispersal of highly radioactive material by conventional explosives or other means. This analysis, while describing many initiatives under way to meet these growing dangers, also revealed significant gaps in these efforts. This chapter will distill these findings and highlight the most critical priorities in need of immediate attention by the United States and other concerned nations.

The foremost requirement, which underpins all of the specific recommendations made below, is the need for the United States to alter dramatically its ranking of threats to its national security and to that of its friends and allies. American thinking about nuclear dangers was forged during the tensions of the Cold War confrontation with another nuclear superpower and in the face of the disturbing, though relatively slow, spread of nuclear arms to additional nations. Today, the nuclear threat posed by other nuclear-armed states is being eclipsed by a new type of threat, that of nuclear instruments in the hands of non-state, terrorist organizations. This reality requires a profound change in the way the United States thinks about nuclear policy.

It is fair to conclude that at this point in history, certain terrorist organizations are the *only* entities that are seeking to rain nuclear destruction on the United States without regard to the potential consequences to themselves or to the innumerable innocent victims of such action. Moreover, even in those instances where nuclear assets in the hands of states cause U.S. policy makers deep concern, in virtually all cases the foremost source of their apprehension is not the possibility that the states, themselves, will use these assets against the United States, but that these assets may come into the hands of terrorist groups who are all too eager to do so.

Russia, President Bush has declared, is a partner, not an enemy; it is highly unlikely to use its nuclear capabilities against the United States. Rather, the principal U.S. concern in this setting is that because of poor security terrorists might gain access to Russian nuclear weapons, weapons-usable material, or extremely powerful radioactive sources and use these capabilities against U.S. targets.

Pakistani nuclear weapons and weapons material pose a danger not because Pakistan's current government might threaten the United States. Rather they constitute a grave threat because figures in Pakistan's nuclear or military establishment who are sympathetic to radical Islam may offer nuclear materials or assistance to terrorist organizations espousing an intensely anti-Western ideology—and because a coup or political instability in Pakistan may bring to power radical Islamists, who would inherit Pakistan's nuclear assets and who would be closely tied to terrorist groups.

Iran's acquisition of nuclear arms and of weapons-usable uranium, similarly, is particularly threatening because of the Iranian Revolutionary Government's links to terrorist organizations. Even North Korea, whose long-range nuclear missile program could well threaten the U.S. homeland in the future, is likely to be deterred from ever using such weapons against the United States. North Korea poses a more serious danger to the United States because of its possible sale of nuclear assets to state sponsors of terrorism or to terrorists themselves, who might act independently to wreak destruction in the U.S. homeland.

The new salience of the nuclear terrorist threat must transform the way the United States thinks about and responds to a range of nuclear dangers. During the Cold War, Russia's enormous intercontinental ballistic missile warheads were perceived to pose the gravest danger to the

United States. Today, however, Russia's *smallest* nuclear weapons pose the greatest threat. Deployed in part on Russia's front lines, often under questionable security, and sometimes lacking internal locks to prevent unauthorized use, Russia's tactical nuclear weapons are far more attractive to terrorists than less portable strategic warheads attached to long-range missiles in secure silos or well-protected mobile missile bases.

Similarly, during the Cold War, the knowledge that Russian nuclear-armed missiles could obliterate hundreds of U.S. cities overshadowed the lesser threats of sabotage of U.S. nuclear facilities and the use of radiological weapons. But when terrorism is the leading concern, what were once "lesser included threats" need to be appreciated as significant dangers in their own right. As noted in Chapters 5 and 6, the destruction of a nuclear power plant or the use of a potent RDD could make large areas uninhabitable and cause massive economic dislocation. Although such incidents would cause only a small fraction of the destruction of a single nuclear detonation, if repeated at multiple locations, they could cause widespread panic and, potentially, loss of confidence in the ability of the U.S. government to protect its citizens.

Despite the recognition of the dangers of nuclear terrorism by President Bush and other U.S. leaders, numerous U.S. nuclear policies remain mired in the past and are impeding measures to reduce the nuclear terror dangers of today. Thinking about U.S.-Russian nuclear arms control arrangements, for example, requires extensive restructuring to give heightened prominence to the terrorist threat. The 2002 Moscow Treaty, which reduces nuclear deployments of strategic nuclear warheads by two-thirds, for example, will lessen the scale of an increasingly unlikely future nuclear exchange between Washington and Moscow. Its most important and most immediate contribution to U.S. national security, however, will more likely come from a factor that none of the negotiators gave thought to: the fact that the treaty will significantly reduce the number of warheads transported annually to and from Russian deployment sites on vulnerable rail links and through vulnerable rail transfer centers, thereby reducing the number of attractive targets for would-be nuclear terrorists. However, a shortcoming of this treaty is that it does not require any irreversible removal or destruction of nuclear warheads.

Each side is allowed to keep as many strategic nuclear warheads as it wants in storage, potentially raising the risk of terrorist acquisition of any portable strategic warheads kept in reserve.

In contrast, central features of the nonbinding 1991-1992 Presidential Nuclear Initiatives were specifically intended to reduce the proliferation dangers posed by U.S. and Russian tactical nuclear weapons, the weapons most attractive to terrorists. These understandings have led to the complete elimination in both the United States and Russia of certain classes of tactical nuclear weapons and provide that most categories retained in Russia will be placed in central storage, although this undertaking has yet to be fully implemented. If terrorism using nuclear weapons is, indeed, the paramount U.S. national security concern, future U.S.-Russian arms control agreements will need to follow the example of the 1991-1992 initiatives and incorporate measures aimed directly at reducing this danger—such as arrangements for the elimination of nuclear warheads—rather than leaving progress toward nuclear terror dangers to happenstance.

Multilateral arms control measures must also be reevaluated in terms of their potential contribution to reducing the nuclear terror threats. A global Fissile Material Cut-Off Treaty (FMCT), for example, which would prohibit the further production of fissile materials for nuclear weapons, was first envisioned nearly a decade ago as a nonproliferation measure that would cap the fissile material stocks of the nuclear-armed states and, thus, indirectly, the size of their nuclear arsenals. Although this goal is highly worthwhile in itself, today it is clear that such a treaty would serve a second, equally important objective: capping certain classes of fissile material and reducing the number of processing facilities that might be targets of terrorists seeking to develop an improvised nuclear device.[1] This crucially important, but heretofore overlooked, benefit of the treaty should spur the member states of the Conference on Disarmament in Geneva, where the treaty is to be negotiated, to put aside disputes over unrelated issues which have stalled negotiations and to begin this process in earnest.

Numerous additional U.S. nuclear policies of today that are discussed throughout this book and highlighted in the remainder of this chapter are similarly tied too closely to past thinking and need revision based on the recognition that non-state actors seeking to cause nuclear mayhem represent the paramount threat facing the United States today. Among the policies that need reexamination are U.S. nuclear material security programs that do not give priority to the fissile material of greatest interest to terrorists—that is, highly enriched uranium; U.S. nuclear-weapon-security assistance programs that restrict aid for fear of supporting Russian nuclear weapon deployments and operations; the continued Cold War-era deployments of nuclear weapons in Western Europe; and the failure of any U.S. agency or international organization to champion alternative technologies that could reduce the use of hard-to-secure radioactive sources worldwide.

The United States is not the only state pursuing shortsighted nuclear policies, however. Russia, too, is a potential target of nuclear terror, but despite its growing hard currency reserves and budget surpluses it continues to spend only a pittance on securing its own nuclear resources, leaving the United States to provide the lion's share of the costs of multi-billion-dollar security upgrades.[2] In these circumstances, Russia's support for the recently adopted UN Security Council Resolution 1540, creating a legally binding requirement for all UN member states to provide for the security of their nuclear assets, is somewhat ironic.

Equally out of step with the new realities of international security are the decisions of a number of foreign governments to continue separating weapons-usable plutonium from spent nuclear power plant fuel when they have no practical program for using the separated material—reprocessing without a purpose. Although a number of states have responsibly abandoned this practice, it continues in the United Kingdom, which has no domestic plutonium use program. Japan, similarly, is paying to have civil plutonium separated in Great Britain and France; the separated material continues to accumulate there because domestic opposition, among other factors, has brought Japan's plutonium use program to a virtual standstill. Notwithstanding such reverses, Japan is also completing a massive plutonium separation plant at home. As for Russia, even as it accepts billions of dollars in foreign assistance to improve the protection of its nuclear-weapon-usable materials, it continues to add to the nuclear terror danger by separating fresh plutonium from spent nuclear power plant fuel, with no current plans for its use.

In sum, virtually the entire spectrum of nuclear policy—including arms control, deployments, threat reduction assistance, civilian nuclear energy, and even medical and industrial uses of potent radioactive sources—needs reshaping in the United States and in many other countries to give full recognition to the paramount dangers of nuclear terrorism. Sadly, there is still far to go before, in each of these policy areas, countering nuclear terrorism becomes an aim point, not an afterthought.

Although such a new strategic vision lags far behind the dramatic shift in the threat environment, as earlier chapters have noted, numerous U.S. and international programs have been initiated to alleviate terrorist threats. The global war on terror has disrupted some terrorist organizations, removed certain safe havens, and interfered with some terrorist financing activities. The United States is also improving port and border detection of illicit trafficking of nuclear and radioactive materials into this country, work that will require years of additional effort to complete. New radiation sensors are being installed around certain cities considered likely terrorist targets, and commercial air travel security has been significantly tightened to reduce the risk that a commercial aircraft might be used as an instrument of a terrorist attack.

During 2004, a number of notable initiatives are likely to strengthen these efforts further. The adoption of Security Council Resolution 1540, noted above, requiring all UN member states to adopt measures to secure their nuclear assets, to adopt effective export controls on WMD material, and to criminalize actions by non-state actors to develop WMD is a major step forward, although its contribution to reducing nuclear terror dangers will be felt only once states fully implement its requirements. The Department of Energy's May 2004 Global Threat Reduction Initiative to sweep up all stocks of U.S. and Soviet/Russian-origin highly enriched uranium at vulnerable research centers around the globe is another signal development. Although this very positive initiative established an ambitious and laudable deadline for completion of repatriation of Soviet- and Russian-origin fresh fuel (end of 2005) and for spent fuel (end of 2010), it is far from clear whether the U.S. government has crafted a workable plan with the necessary high-level institutional champions and financial resources to overcome the many bureaucratic obstacles that have long impeded implementation of less ambitious HEU initiatives in the past within both the United States and Russia. Moreover, the deadline for repatriating irradiated fuel containing HEU needs to be significantly shortened. The IAEA's increasing high-level attention to high-consequence nuclear terror threats, observed in new programs and in major addresses by IAEA Director General Mohammed ElBaradei, are also to be applauded. The agency, however, needs to reconcile these very prudent programs and pronouncements with an institutional culture that continues to support the export and use by member states of HEU-fueled reactors.

The benefits from these initiatives, both those directed at countering terrorism and those directed more specifically at protecting nuclear assets, are cumulative and mutually reinforcing, and in time, they will develop into a "defense in depth" that will reduce the overall danger of nuclear terrorism to acceptable levels. In this respect, it is worth reemphasizing that very few terrorist organizations known today have the capabilities to execute the most complex nuclear terror scenarios, those involving the theft of nuclear weapons or materials in the former Soviet Union or South Asia and the subsequent detonation of a nuclear explosive in the United States. Thus, locating and obstructing terrorist groups can have a significant impact on thwarting the gravest nuclear terror dangers, and further enhancements of this and all elements of the layered defense approach to this threat deserve strong support. However, the United States and its international partners can make the most rapid advances by taking specific, urgent actions to secure nuclear weapons, fissile material, nuclear facilities, and high-risk radioactive sources.

The crucial first step, however, is to recognize the preeminence of nuclear terrorism, in all of its manifestations, as the leading national security challenge facing the United States and its friends and allies.

URGENT PRIORITIES

Our fundamental conclusion is that the United States must work immediately to reduce the probability of nuclear terror acts with the highest consequences and mitigate the consequences of the nuclear terror acts that are the most probable.

Because terrorist attacks with nuclear explosives would have devastating consequences, urgent and immediate changes are needed in U.S. efforts to secure nuclear weapons and materials abroad. At the same time, because we conclude that terrorism involving radioactive materials is virtually inevitable, it is crucial that the United States prepare now to deal with such an event and its aftermath, even as efforts to control and secure high-risk radioactive sources are intensified. Steady progress must also continue in protecting nuclear facilities against attack or sabotage. With this in mind, we have identified the most urgent practical steps toward these twin objectives, measures that could make a significant difference in the next year to 18 months. Without abandoning other valuable efforts, these need to become the focal point of U.S. and international action in the immediate future—the leading edge of global efforts to reduce the nuclear terror danger.

Reducing the Probability of Nuclear Terrorism with Nuclear Weapons or Improvised Nuclear Devices

We believe the United States must reprioritize its efforts to prevent the terrorist detonation of a nuclear device by dramatically intensifying its focus on three key policies: putting HEU first; reducing nuclear terror risks in South and Central Asia; and securing vulnerable Russian nuclear weapons.

Put HEU First

The United States must dramatically revise U.S. efforts to protect fissile materials abroad so as to make securing, consolidating, and eliminating highly enriched uranium the leading and most urgent task, taking clear precedence over addressing the dangers posed by plutonium, which must, nonetheless, remain an important priority. The overarching principle guiding policy should be to move toward a world in which fewer countries retain HEU, fewer facilities within countries possess HEU, and fewer locations within those facilities have HEU present. Specifically, we urge that the following steps be implemented as rapidly as possible.

- *Put HEU at the head of the queue, when securing nuclear materials.* The Department of Energy must establish clear priorities in its extensive Material Protection, Control, and Accounting (MPC&A) program in Russia that unambiguously place sites containing HEU at the top of its list, and it must aggressively pursue the completion of security upgrades at these locations, with the goal of finishing the implementation of "rapid upgrades" within one year.

- *Renew the U.S. initiative to accelerate down-blending of Russian HEU.* The United States should redouble its efforts to accelerate the down-blending of Russian HEU to the non-weapons-usable enrichment level, as recommended by the U.S. National Academy of Sciences. In 2003, the United States gained Russian agreement to increase the down-blending of HEU by 1.5 tons annually, with the resulting low-enriched uranium to be placed in a strategic reserve in the United States. The U.S. Congress refused to fund the initiative, however. The president should make this an urgent priority in the current budget cycle, citing the need to reduce the threat of nuclear terrorism, while also pressing Russia to enlarge further the annual amount of down-blended HEU. The costs would be modest in the context of the overall budget for material protection, consolidation, and elimination and could be partially recouped at some point in the future when the material might be gradually sold off in a way that did not perturb the commercial low-enriched uranium market.

- *Accelerate repatriation of Soviet/Russian- and-U.S.-origin HEU.* The Department of Energy must implement its new Global Threat Reduction Initiative at an accelerated schedule, especially with respect to HEU in the form of spent fuel. Highest priority should be given to removing HEU from Belarus, Kazakhstan, Ukraine, Uzbekistan, and the former Yugoslavia.[3] Repatriation of all U.S.-origin HEU must be completed well in advance of the current target date, which is 2014. A policy to accomplish these objectives must be informed by an understanding of the significant bureaucratic, technical, economic, political, and national security impediments to HEU consolidation and elimination, and the development of compelling incentives to overcome these obstacles on a site-by-site basis.

- *Accelerate conversion of research reactors.* All civilian research reactors currently reliant on HEU should be converted to use low-enriched uranium fuel. In addition, efforts should be undertaken immediately to adopt legally binding prohibitions on the export of HEU-fueled research (and power) reactors.

- *Encourage Japan to build a strategic low-enriched uranium reserve, using material from Russian HEU, to increase the rate of HEU elimination.* The United States, through the G-8 Global Partnership to Combat the Proliferation of Weapons and Materials of Mass Destruction, should encourage Japan to build a strategic low-enriched uranium reserve composed of material down-blended from Russian weapons HEU, with the goal of increasing significantly beyond current levels the total amount of Russian HEU eliminated annually. Japan has long justified its plutonium separation program on the grounds that it will guarantee that country energy independence by providing a domestic source of nuclear power plant fuel. The strategic low-enriched uranium would achieve this result far more rapidly.[4] Equally important, it would permit Japan to defer the start-up of the Rokkasho-Mura reprocessing plant and avoid the terrorist risks associated with the accumulation of additional, currently unneeded stocks of plutonium.

- *Use the Mayak Fissile Material Storage Facility to secure HEU.* Simultaneously, the United States should press Russia to place 200 tons of HEU within the high-security Mayak facility, which was designed to accept this quantity of this material, until additional down-blending capabilities are available. If necessary, the United States should pay for the costs of transporting the HEU to the Mayak facility, an expense that would be offset by the reduced costs of securing the material elsewhere, under the MPC&A program,[5] and by the savings from postponing the plutonium disposition program, discussed below.

- *Subordinate the Plutonium Disposition Program to focus diplomatic and financial resources more intensively on HEU.* With the opening of the Mayak Fissile Material Storage Facility, 25 tons of Russian weapons plutonium will be placed in highly secure storage over the next four years, greatly reducing the risk of terrorism involving this material and simultaneously reducing the urgency of the longer-term program to work with Russia to eliminate this material.[6] Accordingly, we recommend that the United States temporarily subordinate the latter program, which has made minimal progress in the face of numerous bureaucratic and technical problems, to efforts to address the HEU danger. Rather than continuing to expend high-level political capital on this initiative with little result, the United States should concentrate its efforts on implementing the next phases of the HEU security, consolidation, and elimination program, which will have a far greater short-term impact in reducing the danger of nuclear terrorism. If new funding for such HEU efforts, to include the costs of transporting HEU to Mayak, cannot be added to the federal budget, it would be a wise investment to shift monies from the Plutonium Disposition Program for this purpose.

We would also recommend that the premises underlying the Plutonium Disposition Program be carefully reexamined in light of heightened concerns regarding nuclear terrorism. While the long-term goal of eliminating separated weapons plutonium is laudable, the program as currently envisioned entails greatly increased shorter-term risks by removing plutonium from secure storage, introducing it into numerous additional facilities, and transporting it over considerable distances within Russia.

Reduce Nuclear Risks in South and Central Asia

The United States and its allies must recognize that for the moment, the locus of greatest nuclear terror danger is South and Central Asia, a zone where Islamic militant terrorist groups are very active and where the risk of their gaining access to nuclear materials—especially from unreliable elements within the Pakistan establishment or from certain vulnerable sites in Kazakhstan and Uzbekistan—is highest. Accordingly,

- It is of urgent importance to remove the relatively small but nuclear-terrorism-significant quantity of fissile material from Central Asia.

- The United States must implement a strategy of promoting internal and regional stability, while maximizing—consistent with the dictates of the Non-Proliferation Treaty—the sharing of unclassified technology to help Pakistan securely manage its nuclear assets.

- It is also critically important for the United States to develop contingency plans, potentially involving the use of American nuclear recovery teams or specialized military forces, to help secure Pakistani nuclear assets in the event of instability in that country, to ensure that these assets do not fall into the hands of terrorist organizations or their sponsors.

Secure Vulnerable Russian Nuclear Weapons

The last area that must be addressed to reduce the likelihood of highest-consequence nuclear terrorism is securing Russia's most vulnerable nuclear weapons, in particular those tactical nuclear weapons that are forward deployed and portable and that may lack permissive action links.

- Specifically, the United States must encourage Russia to implement fully its pledges under the 1991-1992 Presidential Nuclear Initiatives, including the removal to central storage of all but one category of tactical nuclear weapons. Ideally, all tactical nuclear weapons should be stored at exceptionally secure facilities far from populated regions. In parallel, the United States should declare its intention to return to U.S. territory the small number of air-launched tactical nuclear weapons currently deployed in Europe. Although probably less at risk to terrorist seizure than tactical nuclear weapons forward deployed in Russia, there no longer is a military justification for their presence in Europe. The U.S. action, while valuable in its own right, might be linked to Russian agreement to move its tactical nuclear arms to more secure locations.

- In the meantime, the Bush administration must revamp its current policy prohibiting security assistance for Russian nuclear weapons that are operationally deployed and/or where such assistance might indirectly contribute to Russian nuclear operational capabilities. As President Bush has stressed, the greatest danger to the United States today comes from weapons of mass destruction in the hands of terrorists, not from Russia, which we no longer treat as an enemy. Protecting those sites where tactical nuclear weapons remain against terrorist access must be a priority goal.

Mitigating the Consequences of the Most Likely Nuclear Terror Acts

The use of radioactive materials to cause massive disruption and economic loss is by far the most likely nuclear terror act. Although loss of life and destruction of property would not begin to rival that from a nuclear detonation, the harm caused would be grievous, particularly if radiological attacks were launched in multiple locations. Given the significant quantities of radioactive material currently outside regulatory control around the world, the unambiguous evidence of terrorist interest in using these materials to cause harm, and the ease of carrying out a radiological attack, we believe that such an attack is all but inevitable. Thus, even as the United States pursues measures to reduce the availability of radioactive materials, it should greatly increase its preparations for a radiological terror event through the following measures.

Train Officials and Responders

Federal, state, and local governments need to plan and train extensively to cope with a radiological attack.

- These efforts must include: preparing public communications strategies, readying evacuation plans and escape routes, coordinating the deployment and application of monitoring and detection capabilities, stockpiling and preparing distribution plans for specialized emergency equipment, training first responders and law enforcement/traffic officials to operate in a radioactive environment, and preparing medical facilities to cope with injured individuals contaminated by radioactive materials and those, likely rarer, cases of illness due to radiation exposure.

Develop Decontamination Technologies, Post-Attack Therapies, and a New Consensus on Standards

The most damaging impact from most radiological attacks will be the contamination of property, destroying property values and disrupting employment patterns. If decontamination technologies were available and rapidly put to use, such impacts could be significantly reduced. Similarly, if therapies were available for purging radioactive materials from the body, short- and long-term health effects from a radiation incident could be minimized. In both of these areas, much research is under way, but much remains to be done. The public must also have confidence in government pronouncements regarding the safety of decontaminated areas if they are to be restored to their prior economic uses.

- Research on and the development of decontamination technologies and post-event therapies must be greatly accelerated. They are the linchpin for meeting the threat of radiological attack because they not only mitigate the consequences of such attacks, but, if widely publicized beforehand, would reduce panic and assist in emergency management. Perhaps even more important, if these technologies are developed, they could reduce the likelihood of such attacks by making them less attractive to terrorists seeking massive disruption of our society.

- No less important is the need to develop workable standards for decontamination that effectively and credibly protect public health, while providing greater flexibility in the continued use of economic resources than would be allowed under current standards. A new consensus on this issue is urgently needed before an actual incident so that the public can be confident that the standards are based on scientific principles, not on expediency in the wake of a terrorist attack.

Control Radioactive Materials

We have emphasized the need to prepare for a radiological attack because we fear that such an attack could occur at any time and is all but inevitable in coming years. Nonetheless, even as we prepare for this eventuality, it is essential to improve controls over radioactive materials so that over time, the likelihood of a radiological attack can be reduced. A comprehensive program requires positive regulation over radioactive materials throughout their "life cycle" —from production, to use, to ultimate disposition. Currently, extensive efforts are under way in the United States, among the G-8 industrialized states (including the European Union), and at the IAEA to establish such comprehensive controls, but major gaps remain. For the near term, the following initiatives can have the greatest impact and deserve the most urgent attention.

- Locate and secure remaining radio-thermal generators in the former Soviet Union, arranging for substitute technologies in remote locations requiring electricity.

- In the United States and within the G-8 (including the EU), impose mandatory physical security and accounting controls over the most dangerous classes of radioactive sources, beginning with the most potent; use U.S.-G-8 regulations as a model to encourage comparable regulations globally.

- Impose rigorous domestic licensing and import and export controls over high-risk radioactive sources that include prelicensing determinations of credentials of end users; use U.S.-G-8 regulations as a model to encourage comparable regulations globally.

- In the United States and within the G-8 (including the EU), develop or accelerate programs to sweep up and store securely unwanted (disused) radioactive sources and provide for their ultimate safe and secure disposition, at interim sites if necessary, until permanent repositories are available. In the United States, fully fund and implement the U.S. Department of Energy Off-Site Source Recovery Program and extend it to all high-risk unwanted sources in this country. Encourage parallel programs globally.

- Actively promote the use of alternative technologies to radioactive sources, where appropriate. Subsidize substitution alternatives in states lacking adequate regulatory controls over radioactive materials. Ensure that any radioactive sources and related equipment that are displaced by substitution are not introduced into a secondary market that may lead to their acquisition by states with inadequate regulatory controls.

Improve Protection of Nuclear Facilities against Attack or Sabotage

With certain qualifications, U.S. nuclear power plants pose considerable obstacles to successful terrorism leading to a major release of radioactivity. These facilities are built to withstand many physical challenges through the use of containment structures as well as redundant safety systems. The U.S. Nuclear Regulatory Commission required intensified security measures at U.S nuclear power plants after September 11, 2001, and it has gradually formalized these requirements, which, we understand, are adjusted according to the level of terror threat identified by the U.S. Department of Homeland Security. The United States and other Western states are also reported to have enhanced security at other nuclear facilities with large inventories of radioactivity, including plutonium extraction plants and high-level nuclear waste facilities.

Important gaps in this improved security situation remain to be addressed, but we believe that these fixes, while important, do not require the extremely urgent priority that we would attach to our recommendations to improve the security of fissile materials and nuclear weapons and to address the dangers of a radiological attack. In this context, we recommend the following measures be implemented.

- We are not confident that the "design basis threat" adopted by the NRC (or reportedly by other regulatory bodies in other states) fully reflects the magnitude of the September 11 attack—19 motivated and well-trained attackers operating in four separate teams. Accordingly, we believe the United States should increase preparedness to address more demanding threats than incorporated in current regulations. Moreover, similar to the nuclear industry's preparation for beyond design-basis accidents, the NRC and the nuclear industry must expedite preparedness for beyond design-basis attacks or sabotage of nuclear facilities.

- Certain vital nuclear safety systems, such as reactor control rooms and some types of spent fuel pools, are potentially vulnerable to attack from the air or from stand-off weapons because they are outside of nuclear power plant containments. A variety of cost-effective measures for hardening these plant elements have been proposed; these should be evaluated on an urgent basis and steps taken rapidly to mitigate these potential vulnerabilities. The United States should also encourage Great Britain and Russia to maintain high security at nuclear power plants without containments.

- The NRC currently is too dependent on a compliance-based approach for evaluating nuclear power plant security. It must implement a performance-based system of evaluation in which design basis threats are continually tested.

- Research reactors, though containing only a fraction of the radiation inventory of a nuclear power plant, are often located in urban settings. Many of the low-power research reactors do not use containment buildings, and even the high-power research reactors that do, have much weaker containment structures than found at commercial power plants. A formal U.S. government assessment of the risks posed by these facilities and of any measures needed to secure them against attack or sabotage is urgently needed.

Educate the Public

One of the most dangerous elements of a radiological attack is the panic that it can spur, which would likely lead to more immediate casualties than the ionizing radiation itself triggered by the attack.

- It is imperative that the public be *psychologically immunized* against the radiological attack threat, through an extensive public education campaign that leads citizens to understand (1) that such attacks rarely pose immediate threats to life, (2) that the decision to shelter or flee will depend on the circumstances of the event and that minimizing risk to personal health will depend on rapidly receiving and adhering to guidance from governmental authorities, and (3) that proper treatment can greatly reduce long-term health effects in many cases.

Sustaining the Effort

The action plan enumerated above provides a blueprint for significantly reducing the most salient risks stemming from the four faces of nuclear terrorism. However, neither these urgent steps nor the more comprehensive measures listed in previous chapters will eliminate these risks completely. The dangers of nuclear terrorism will continue to confront the United States and other nations as long as nuclear weapons, weapons-useable nuclear material, and high-risk radioactive sources continue to exist. Recognizing this, the United States allies must develop a sustained defense-in-depth against nuclear terrorism. At the global level, states and international organizations must consistently weigh the risks of nuclear terrorism in making decisions on the development and use of nuclear assets and radioactive materials. At the national level, deployment patterns and storage arrangements for nuclear weapons, decisions to produce nuclear weapons materials for civilian purposes, choices regarding nuclear power plant designs, and decisions to use radioactive sources or substitutes, must all take the risks of nuclear terrorism into account.

Nuclear weapons offer terrorists the ultimate means of inflicting mass destruction. A combined strategy of enhanced intelligence, disruption of terrorist organizations, protection of nuclear weapons and material, and emergency preparedness is required to combat this threat. The United States and its allies must therefore give high priority to a coordinated and sustained effort to reduce the risks of nuclear terrorism as an essential element of the worldwide struggle against terror.

回

[1] Under the FMCT, as many now envision it, states would be required to place under IAEA inspection any fissile material they produce to ensure it will not be used for nuclear weapons; fissile material production under such IAEA safeguards for peaceful purposes could continue. With one important use for fissile materials eliminated, it is assumed that total stocks would grow at a slower rate than would otherwise be the case and, presumably, certain production facilities would be closed, reducing potential terrorist targets. It may be noted, however, that in a number of countries, the treaty, as a practical matter, might end the production of certain forms of particularly dangerous fissile material altogether—for example, weapons-grade HEU and weapons-grade plutonium. HEU enriched to lower levels and reactor-grade plutonium would present added challenges to terrorists seeking to use them for improvised nuclear devices.

[2] Matthew Bunn and Anthony Wier, *Securing the Bomb: An Agenda for Action*, Project on Managing the Atom, Harvard University, Report Commissioned by the Nuclear Threat Initiative, May 2004.

[3] Although nearly 50kg of fresh HEU fuel was removed from Vinca (outside of Belgrade) in 2002, a large quantity of equally dangerous HEU in spent fuel remains on site.

[4] Paul Leventhal and Steven Dolley, "A Japanese Strategic Uranium Reserve: A Safe and Economic Alternative to Plutonium," *Science & Global Security* 5 (1994), pp. 1-31.

[5] It may be noted that much of the HEU in question appears to be located currently at highly classified Russian sites where the United States has had difficulty gaining access and implementing MPC&A measures. The Mayak option would have the added benefit of removing the HEU from locations where security is of uncertain quality to one where it is known to be very high.

[6] The Mayak facility would hold 25 tons of the 34 intended for ultimate disposition and could be expanded to hold additional quantities if Russia chose to make them available.

Selected Bibliography

Ackerman, Gary, and Laura Snyder, "Would They If They Could?" *Bulletin of the Atomic Scientists* (May/June 2002).

Acronym Institute, "News Review: Chilling Rhetoric, Ongoing Nuclearisation in South Asia," *Disarmament Diplomacy* (February/March 2003).

Adams, Thad et al., "The Development of Mobile Melt-Dilute Technology for the Treatment of Former Soviet Union Research Reactor Fuel," WSRC-MS-2003-00646 (2003), <http://sti.srs.gov/fulltext/ms2003646/ms2003646.pdf>.

Agreement between the Government of the United States of America and the Government of the Russian Federation Concerning Cooperation Regarding Plutonium Production Reactors, Article IV, September 23, 1997.

Albright, David, "Securing Pakistan's Nuclear Infrastructure," in Lee Feinstein, James C. Clad, Lewis A. Dunn, and David Albright, *A New Equation: U.S. Policy Toward India and Pakistan after September 11*, Working Paper Number 27, Carnegie Endowment for International Peace, May 2002.

Albright, David, *Separated Civil Plutonium Inventories: Current and Future Directions* (Washington, D.C.: Institute for Science and International Security, June 2000).

Albright, David, "South Africa and the Affordable Bomb," *Bulletin of the Atomic Scientists* (July/August 1994).

Albright, David, Frans Berkhout, and William Walker, *Plutonium and Highly Enriched Uranium 1996: World Inventories, Capabilities, and Policies* (Oxford: Oxford University Press, 1997).

Albright, David, and Holly Higgins, "A Bomb for the Ummah," *Bulletin of the Atomic Scientists* (March/April 2003).

Alexander, Yonah, and Paul A. Leventhal, eds., *Preventing Nuclear Terrorism: The Report and Papers of the International Task Force on Prevention of Nuclear Terrorism* (Lanham, MD: Rowman & Littlefield, 1987).

Allison, Graham, "How to Stop Nuclear Terror," *Foreign Affairs* (January/February 2004).

Allison, Graham, *Nuclear Terrorism: The Ultimate Preventable Catastrophe* (New York: Times Books, 2004).

Allison, Graham and Andrei Kokoshin, "The New Containment: An Alliance against Nuclear Terrorism," *National Interest* (Fall 2002), <http://articles.findarticles.com/p/articles/mi_m2751/is_2002_Fall/ai_92042419>.

Alvarez, Luis W., *Adventures of a Physicist* (New York: Basic Books, 1988).

Alvarez, Robert, "What about the Spent Fuel?" *Bulletin of the Atomic Scientists* (January/February 2002).

Alvarez, Robert, Jan Beyea, Klaus Janberg, Jungmin Kang, Ed Lyman, Allison MacFarlane, Gordon Thompson, and Frank von Hippel, "Reducing the Hazards from Stored Spent Power-Reactor Fuel in the United States," *Science & Global Security* 11 (2003).

Alvarez, Robert, et. al., "Response by the authors to the NRC review of 'Reducing the Hazards from Stored Spent Power-Reactor Fuel in the United States,'" *Science & Global Security* 11 (2003).

Anet, Bernard, "Nuclear Terrorism: How Serious a Threat to Switzerland?," *Spiez Laboratory Report* (November 2001), <http://www.vbs.admin.ch/ls/e/current/fact_sheet/nuklearterrorismus/pronto/pronto_e.pdf>.

Anonymous, *Through Our Enemies' Eyes: Osama bin Laden, Radical Islam, and the Future of America* (Washington, D.C.: Brassey's Inc., 2002).

Arai, Tsutomu, and Nobumasa Akiyama, "Japan," Chapter 9 in Robert J. Einhorn and Michèle Fournoy, eds., *Protecting Against the Spread of Nuclear, Biological, and Chemical Weapons: An Action Agenda for the Global Partnership*, Vol. 3 (Washington, D.C.: Center for Strategic and International Studies, January 2003).

Arbman, Gunnar, Francesco Calogero, Paolo Cotta-Ramusino, Lars van Dessen, Maurizio Martellini, Morten Bremer Maerli, Alexander Nikitin, Jan Prawitz, and Lars Wredberg, "Eliminating Stockpiles of Highly-Enriched Uranium," Report submitted to the Swedish Ministry for Foreign Affairs, *SKI Report* 15 (April 2004).

Arnhold, Klaus, "Germany," Chapter 5 in Robert J. Einhorn and Michèle Fournoy, eds., *Protecting Against the Spread of Nuclear, Biological, and Chemical Weapons: An Action Agenda for the Global Partnership*, Vol. 3 (Washington, D.C.: Center for Strategic and International Studies, January 2003).

Auer, Catherine, "Greenpeace to Sizewell B: D'oh!," *Bulletin of the Atomic Scientists* (January/February 2003).

Ball, Philip, "US Unprepared for Dirty-Bomb Attack," *Nature* (April 26, 2004).

Barnaby, Frank, "Issues Surrounding Crude Nuclear Explosives," in *Crude Nuclear Weapons: Proliferation and the Terrorist Threat*, IPPNW Global Health Watch Report Number 1, 1996.

Basrur, Rajesh M., and Hasan-Askari Rizvi, *Nuclear Terrorism and South Asia*, Occasional Paper 25, Cooperative Monitoring Center, Sandia National Laboratories (Albuquerque, NM: Sandia National Laboratories, February 2003).

Benedict, Manson, Thomas H. Pigford, and Hans Wolfgang Levi, *Nuclear Chemical Engineering*, 2nd Edition (New York: McGraw-Hill Book Company, 1981).

Bergeron, Kenneth D., *Tritium on Ice: The Dangerous New Alliance of Nuclear Weapons and Nuclear Power* (Cambridge, MA: MIT Press, 2002).

Blair, Bruce G., *Global Zero Alert for Nuclear Forces*, Brookings Occasional Papers (Washington, D.C.: Brookings Institution Press, 1995).

Blair, Bruce G., *Strategic Command and Control* (Washington, D.C.: Brookings Institution Press, 1985).

Blair, Bruce G., John E. Pike, and Stephen I. Schwartz, "Targeting and Controlling the Bomb," in Stephen I. Schwartz, ed., *Atomic Audit: The*

Costs and Consequences of U.S. Nuclear Weapons Since 1940 (Washington, D.C.: Brookings Institution Press, 1998).

Bleek, Philipp C., "Project Vinca: Lessons for Securing Civil Nuclear Material Stockpiles," *Nonproliferation Review* 10 (Fall/Winter 2003).

Bodansky, David, *Nuclear Energy: Principles, Practices, and Prospects* (Woodbury, NY: AIP Press, 1996).

Bradley, Donald J., and David R. Payson, *Behind the Nuclear Curtain: Radioactive Waste Management in the Former Soviet Union* (Columbus, OH: Battelle Press, 1997).

Brookhaven National Laboratory, *A Safety and Regulatory Assessment of Generic BWR and PWR Permanently Shutdown Nuclear Power Plants*, NUREG/CR-4982, 1997.

Bukharin, Oleg, "Upgrading Security at Nuclear Power Plants in the Newly Independent States," *Nonproliferation Review* 4 (Winter 1997).

Bukharin, Oleg, *The Threat of Nuclear Terrorism and the Physical Security of Nuclear Installations and Materials in the former Soviet Union* (Monterey, CA: Center for Russian and Eurasian Studies, Monterey Institute of International Studies, 1992).

Bukharin, Oleg, and William Potter, "Potatoes were Guarded Better," *Bulletin of the Atomic Scientists* (May 1995).

Bunn, George, "Raising International Standards for Protecting Nuclear Materials from Theft and Sabotage," *Nonproliferation Review* 7 (Summer 2000).

Bunn, George, "U.S. Standards for Protecting Weapons-Usable Fissile Material Compared to International Standards," *Nonproliferation Review* 6 (Fall 1998).

Bunn, George, and Chaim Braun, "Terrorism Potential for Research Reactors Compared With Power Reactors," *American Behavioral Scientist* 46 (February 2003).

Bunn, George, and Fritz Steinhausler, "Guarding Nuclear Reactors and Material from Terrorists and Thieves," *Arms Control Today* (October 2001).

Bunn, George, Fritz Steinhausler, and Lyudmila Zaitseva, "Strengthening Nuclear Security Against Terrorists and Thieves Through Better Training," *Nonproliferation Review* 8 (Fall/Winter 2001).

Bunn, George, Chaim Braun, Alexander Glaser, Ed Lyman, and Fritz Steinhausler, "Research Reactor Vulnerability to Sabotage by Terrorists," *Science & Global Security* 11 (2003).

Bunn, Matthew, *Preventing Nuclear Terrorism: A Progress Update* (Cambridge, MA: Project on Managing the Atom, Harvard University, and the Nuclear Threat Initiative, October 22, 2003), <http://www.nti.org/c_press/analysis_cnwmupdate_102203.pdf>.

Bunn, Matthew, and Anthony Weir, *Securing the Bomb: An Agenda For Action* (Washington, D.C.: Nuclear Threat Initiative and the Project on Managing the Atom, Harvard University, May 2004), <http://www.nti.org/e_research/analysis_cnwmupdate_052404.pdf>.

Bunn, Matthew, and George Bunn, "Strengthening Nuclear Security Against Post September 11 Threats of Theft and Sabotage," *JNMM* (Spring 2002).

Bunn, Matthew, Anthony Wier, and John P. Holdren, *Controlling Nuclear Warheads and Materials: A Report Card and Action Plan* (Cambridge, MA: Project on Managing the Atom, Harvard University, and the Nuclear Threat Initiative, March 2003), <http://www.nti.org/e_research/cnwm/cnwm.pdf>.

Bunn, Matthew, John P. Holdren, and Anthony Wier, *Securing Nuclear Weapons and Materials: Seven Steps for Immediate Action* (Cambridge, MA: Project on Managing the Atom, Harvard University, and the Nuclear Threat Initiative, May 2002), <http://www.nti.org/e_research/securing_nuclear_weapons_and_materials_May2002.pdf>.

Busch, Nathan, "China's Fissile Material Protection Control, and Accounting: The Case for Renewed Collaboration," *Nonproliferation Review* 9 (Fall-Winter 2002).

Caldwell, Dan, and Peter Zimmerman, "Reducing the Risk of Nuclear War with Permissive Action Links," in Barry M. Blechman, ed., *Technology and the Limitation of International Conflict* (Washington, D.C.: SAIS, 1989).

Cameron, Gavin, "Nuclear Terrorism Reconsidered," *Current History* (April 2000).

Cameron, Gavin, *Nuclear Terrorism: A Threat Assessment for the 21st Century* (New York: Palgrave Macmillan, 1999).

Cameron, Gavin, "WMD Terrorism in the United States: The Threat and Possible Countermeasures," *Nonproliferation Review* 7 (Spring 2000).

Canadian Security Intelligence Service, *Chemical, Biological, Radiological, and Nuclear (CBRN) Terrorism*, Report #2000/02, December 18, 1999, <http://www.csis-scrs.gc.ca/eng/miscdocs/20000d2_e.html>.

Carter, Ashton B., "The Architecture of Government in the Face of Terrorism," *International Security* (Winter 2001/2002).

Carter, Ashton B., "Catastrophic Terrorism: Imagining the Transforming Event," *Foreign Affairs* (November/December 1998).

Carter, Ashton B., John D. Steinbruner, and Charles A. Araket, eds., *Managing Nuclear Operations* (Washington, D.C.: Brookings Institution Press, 1987).

Castillo, Jasen J., "Nuclear Terrorism: Why Deterrence Still Matters," *Current History* (December 2003).

Center for Nonproliferation Studies, "HEU from Libyan Nuclear Reactor Repatriated to Russia," *NIS Export Control Observer* (April 2004).

Center for Nonproliferation Studies, "IAEA Conference for the Radioactive Source Industry," *NIS Export Control Observer* (June 2003).

Center for Nonproliferation Studies, "Missing Iridium Partly Recovered in Ecuador," *NIS Export Control Observer* (September 2003).

Center for Nonproliferation Studies, *WMD Terrorism Database*, Monterey Institute of International Studies, <http://cns.miis.edu/dbinfo/about.htm#wmdt>.

Center for Nonproliferation Studies, "WMD Terrorism Database Annual Review," *Nonproliferation Review* 7 (Summer 2000).

Center for Strategic International Studies, *Wild Atom: Nuclear Terrorism*, Global Organized Crime Project, 1998.

Chapin, Douglas M., et al., "Nuclear Power Plants and Their Fuel as Terrorist Targets," *Science* (September 20, 2002).

Cirincione, Joseph, Jon B. Wolfsthal, and Miriam Rajkumar, *Deadly Arsenals: Tracking Weapons of Mass Destruction* (Washington, DC: Carnegie Endowment for International Peace, 2002).

Civiak, Robert L., *Closing the Gaps: Securing High Enriched Uranium in the Former Soviet Union and Eastern Europe*, Report for the Federation of American Scientists, May 2002.

Cochran, John R., Susan W. Longley, Laura L. Price, and Kendra J. Lipinski, *The Adequacy of Current Import and Export Controls on Sealed Radioactive Sources*, SAND Report, Sandia National Laboratories, SAND2003-3767, October 2003.

Collina, Tom Z., and Jon B. Wolfstahl, "Nuclear Terrorism and Warhead Control in Russia," *Arms Control Today* (April 2002).

Cotta-Ramusino, Paolo, Antonino Lantieri, and Maurizio Martellini, "Italy," Chapter 8 in *Protecting Against the Spread of Nuclear, Biological, and Chemical Weapons: An Action Agenda for the Global Partnership*, Vol. 3 (Washington, D.C.: Center for Strategic and International Studies, January 2003).

Davis, Lynn E., Tom LaTourrette, David E. Mosher, Lois M. Davis, and David R. Howell, *Individual Preparedness and Response to Chemical, Radiological, Nuclear, and Biological Terrorist Attacks: A Quick Guide* (Santa Monica: RAND, 2003).

"Department of Transportation, Research and Special Programs Administration: International Standards on the Transport of Dangerous Goods; Public Meetings," *Federal Register* 68 (May 30, 2003), <http://www.unreports.com/public/DOT%20notice%20(23rd%20UNSCOE).pdf>.

Diaz, Nils J., Chairman Nuclear Regulatory Commission, "Radiological terrorism," Letter-to-the-Editor, *Issues in Science and Technology* (Winter 2004).

DOE/NRC Interagency Working Group on Radiological Dispersal Devices, *Radiological Dispersal Devices: An Initial Study to Identify Radioac-*

tive Materials of Greatest Concern and Approaches to Their Tracking, Tagging, and Disposition, Report to the Nuclear Regulatory Commission and the Secretary of Energy, May 2003.

Eden, Lynn, "City on Fire," *Bulletin of the Atomic Scientists* (January/ February 2004).

Eden, Lynn, *Whole World on Fire: Organizations, Knowledge, & Nuclear Weapons Devastation* (Ithica, NY: Cornell University Press, 2004).

Facon, Isabelle, "France," Chapter 4 in Robert J. Einhorn and Michèle Flournoy, eds., *Protecting Against the Spread of Nuclear, Biological, and Chemical Weapons: An Action Agenda for the Global Partnership*, Vol. 3 (Washington, D.C.: Center for Strategic and International Studies, January 2003).

Falkenrath, Richard A., "Confronting Nuclear, Biological, and Chemical Terrorism," *Survival* (Autumn 1998).

Falkenrath, Richard A., "Problems of Preparedness: U.S. Readiness for a Domestic Terrorist Attack," *International Security* (Spring 2001).

Falkenrath, Richard A., Robert D. Newman, and Bradley A. Thayer, *America's Achilles Heel: Nuclear, Biological, and Chemical Terrorism and Covert Attack*, BCSIA Studies in International Security (Cambridge, MA: MIT Press, 1998).

Ferguson, Charles D., "Reducing the Threat of RDDs," *IAEA Bulletin* 45 (2003).

Ferguson, Charles D., and Joel O. Lubenau, "Securing U.S. Radioactive Sources," *Issues in Science and Technology* (Fall 2003).

Ferguson, Charles D., Tahseen Kazi, and Judith Perrera, *Commercial Radioactive Sources: Surveying the Security Risks*, Occasional Paper No. 11, Center for Nonproliferation Studies (Monterey, CA: Monterey Institute of International Studies, January 2003).

Flakus, Franz-Nikolaus, "Radiation in Perspective: Improving Comprehension of Risks," *IAEA Bulletin* 37 (June 1995).

Flynn, Stephen E., "America the Vulnerable," *Foreign Affairs* (January/ February 2002).

Flynn, Stephen E., "Beyond Border Control," *Foreign Affairs* (November/ December 2000).

Freeh, Louis J., "Chapter 2: FBI Leadership in National Security," in *A Report to the American People on the Work of the FBI: 1993-1998*, <http:// digilander.libero.it/supcomandante/attaccoagliusa/report5.htm>.

French Atomic Energy Commission (CEA), "Contributing to National Defence," in *CEA Annual Report* (2001), <http://www.cea.fr/gb/publications/AnnualReport>.

Garwin, Richard L., and Georges Charpak, *Megawatts and Megatons: The Future of Nuclear Power and Nuclear Weapons* (Chicago: University of Chicago Press, 2002).

Glaser, Alexander, "Bavaria Bucks Ban," *Bulletin of the Atomic Scientists* (March/April 2002).

Glasstone, Samuel, and Philip J. Dolan, *Effects of Nuclear Weapons* (Washington, D.C.: U.S. Government Printing Office, 1977).

Gonzalez, Abel J., "Strengthening the Safety of Radiation Sources and the Security of Radioactive Materials: Timely Action," *IAEA Bulletin* 41 (March 1999).

Guinnessy, Paul, "Nations Tackle Nuclear Terrorist Threat: Lax Controls on Nuclear Materials and a Thriving Black Market are Alarming Officials," *Physics Today* (July 2001).

Gurr, Nadine, and Benjamin Cole, *The New Faces of Terrorism: Threats from Weapons of Mass Destruction* (London and New York: I.B. Taurus, 2000).

Hart, Gary, Warren B. Rudman, and Stephen E. Flynn, *America Still Unprepared – America Still in Danger*, Report of an Independent Task Force Sponsored by the Council on Foreign Relations, October 2002.

Hay, John B., "Canada," Chapter 1 in Robert J. Einhorn and Michèle Flournoy, eds., *Protecting Against the Spread of Nuclear, Biological, and Chemical Weapons: An Action Agenda for the Global Partnership*, Vol. 3 (Washington, D.C.: Center for Strategic and International Studies, January 2003).

Hecker, Jay Etta Z., "Container Security: Current Efforts to Detect Nuclear Materials, New Initiatives, and Challenges," U.S. General Accounting Office, GAO-03-297T, November 2002.

Hecker, Siegfried S., "Nuclear Terrorism" in Committee on Confronting Terrorism in Russia, Office for Central Europe and Eurasia Development, Security, and Cooperation, National Research Council in Cooperation with the Russian Academy of Sciences, *High-Impact Terrorism: Proceedings of a Russian-American Workshop* (Washington, D.C.: The National Academies Press, 2002).

Hirsch, Daniel, "The Truck Bomb and Insider Threats to Nuclear Facilities," in Paul Leventhal and Yonah Alexander, eds., *Preventing Nuclear Terrorism: Report and Papers of the International Task Force on Prevention of Nuclear Terrorism* (Lanham, MD: Rowan & Littlefield, 1987).

Hirsch, Daniel, Stephanie Murphy, and Bennett Ramberg, "Protecting Reactors from Terrorists," *Bulletin of the Atomic Scientists* (March 1986).

Hitz, Frederick P., and Brian J. Weiss, "Helping the CIA and FBI Connect the Dots in the War on Terror," *International Journal of Intelligence and CounterIntelligence* 17 (Spring 2004).

Hoffman, Bruce, *Inside Terrorism* (New York: Columbia University Press, 1998).

Hoffman, Bruce, "Terrorism Trends and Prospects," in Ian Lesser, ed., *Countering the New Terrorism*, Document MR-989-AF (Santa Monica: RAND, 1999).

Hoffman, Bruce, *Terrorism in the United States and the Potential Threat to Nuclear Facilities*, Report R-3351-DOE (Santa Monica: RAND, April 1986).

Hoffman, Bruce, "Terrorism and WMD: Some Preliminary Hypotheses," *Nonproliferation Review* 4 (Spring/Summer 1997).

Hyams, Kenneth, et al., "Responses to Chemical, Biological or Nuclear Terrorism: The Indirect and Long-Term Health Effects May Present the Greatest Challenge," *Journal of Health Politics, Policy and Law* 27 (April 2002).

International Atomic Energy Agency, *The Action Plan for the Safety of*

Radiation Sources and the Security of Radioactive Materials, Board of Governors General Conference, IAEA/GOV/2000/34-GC(44)/7, August 7, 2000.

International Atomic Energy Agency, *Categorization of Radiation Sources,* IAEA Report, IAEA-TECDOC-1344, July 2003.

International Atomic Energy Agency, *Code of Conduct on the Safety and Security of Radioactive Sources,* IAEA Report, IAEA/CODEOC/2004, January 2004.

International Atomic Energy Agency, *Convention on Assistance in the Case of a Nuclear Accident or Radiological Emergency,* Registration No: 1534, <http://www.iaea.org/Publications/Documents/Conventions/cacnare_status.pdf>.

International Atomic Energy Agency, *Implementation of the Safeguards Agreement between the Republic of Iraq and the International Atomic Energy Agency pursuant to the Treaty on the Non-Proliferation of Nuclear Weapons,* Report of the Director General, July 14, 2003.

International Atomic Energy Agency, *International Basic Safety Standards for Protection against Ionizing Radiation and for the Safety of Radiation Sources,* IAEA Safety Series No. 115 (1996).

International Atomic Energy Agency, *Nuclear Security—Measures To Protect Against Nuclear Terrorism,* Report by the Director General, General Conference document GC(47)/17, August 20, 2003.

International Atomic Energy Agency, *Nuclear Security—Measures To Protect Against Nuclear Terrorism,* Report by the Director General, General Conference document GOV/INF/2004/1, March 3, 2004.

International Atomic Energy Agency, *Measures to Strengthen International Cooperation in Nuclear, Radiation, and Waste Safety: The Action Plan for the Safety of Radiation Sources and the Security of Radioactive Material,* Board of Governors General Conference, GOV/2000/34-GC(44)7, August 9, 2000.

International Atomic Energy Agency, *Nuclear Security—Progress on Measures to Protect against Terrorism,* Report of the Director General, GOV/INF/2002/11-GC(46)/14, August 12, 2002.

International Atomic Energy Agency, *The Physical Protection of Nuclear Material and Nuclear Facilities,* INFCIRC/225/Rev.4, October 1998.

International Atomic Energy Agency, *Promoting Nuclear Security: IAEA Action Plan Against Terrorism*, Staff Report, June 1, 2004.

International Atomic Energy Agency, *Promoting Nuclear Security: What the IAEA is Doing,* IAEA Information Series, Division of Public Information, 03-01610/FS/Series 1/03/E.

International Atomic Energy Agency, *Report on the Implementation of Model Projects for Upgrading Radiation Protection Infrastructure,* Board of Governors, Report GOV/2001/48, November 8, 2001.

International Atomic Energy Agency, *Security of Radioactive Sources: Interim Guidance for Comment,* IAEA-TECDOC-1355, June 2003.

International Institute for Strategic Studies, *The Military Balance, 2003-2004* (Oxford: Oxford University Press, 2003).

Joseph, Jofi, "The Proliferation Security Initiative: Can Interdiction Stop Proliferation?" *Arms Control Today* (June 2004).

Kaplan, David, "Aum Shinrikyo," in Jonathan B. Tucker, ed., *Toxic Terror: Assessing Terrorist Use of Chemical and Biological Weapons* (Cambridge, MA: MIT Press, 2000).

Kanwal, Gurmeet, "Command and Control of Nuclear Weapons in India," *Strategic Analysis* 23 (January 2000), Columbia International Affairs Online, <http://www.ciaonet.org/olj/sa/sa_00kag01.html>.

Kaplan, David, *The Cult At the End of the World* (New York: Crown Publishers, 1996).

Kawamura, Takekazu, "Japan's Role in Dismantling Russian N-Weapons," *Plutonium* (Spring 1997).

Kennedy, Harold, "U.S. Coast Guard Ratchets Up Port Security," *National Defense* (June 2003).

Khan, Feroz Hassan, "Challenges to Nuclear Stability in South Asia," *Nonproliferation Review* 10 (Spring 2003).

Koch, Lewis Z., "Dirty Bomber? Dirty Justice," *Bulletin of the Atomic Scientists* (January/February 2004).

Kurihara, Hiroyoshi, "The Protection of Fissile Materials in Japan," in James Goodby, Ronald Lehman, and William Potter, eds., *A Comparative Analysis of Approaches to the Protection of Fissile Materials* (Livermore, CA: Lawrence Livermore National Laboratory, 1998).

Kutsenko, Vladimir M., and A.P. Morozov, "Problems of Preventing Acts of Nuclear and Radiological Terrorism," in Committee on Confronting Terrorism in Russia, Office for Central Europe and Eurasia Development, Security, and Cooperation, National Research Council in Cooperation with the Russian Academy of Sciences, *High Impact Terrorism: Proceedings of a Russian-American Workshop* (Washington, D.C.: The National Academies Press, 2002).

Lambert, Stephen, and David Miller, *Russia's Crumbling Tactical Nuclear Weapons Complex: An Opportunity for Arms Control*, Occasional Paper 12, Institute for National Security Studies (Colorado Springs: USAF Academy, April 1997).

Laquer, Walter, "Postmodern Terrorism," *Foreign Affairs* 75 (September/October 1996).

Laquer, Walter, *The New Terrorism: Fanaticism and the Arms of Mass Destruction* (Oxford: Oxford University Press, 1999).

Large, John H., "The Implications of 11 September for the Nuclear Industry," *Disarmament Forum* May 2003.

Larsen, Jeffrey A., and Kurt J. Klingenberger, eds., *Controlling Non-Strategic Nuclear Weapons* (Colorado Springs: U.S. Air Force Institute for National Security Studies, 2001).

Lee, Rensselaer, "Nuclear Smuggling: Patterns and Responses," *Parameters* (Spring 2003).

Lefebvre, Stephane, "The Difficulties and Dilemmas of International Intelligence Cooperation," *International Journal of Intelligence and CounterIntelligence* 16 (Winter 2003).

Leventhal, Paul, ed., *Nuclear Terrorism: Defining the Threat* (Washington, D.C.: Brassey's, Inc., 1986).

Levental, Paul, and Yonah Alexander, "Preventing Nuclear Terrorism," in Paul Leventhal and Yonah Alexander, eds., *Preventing Nuclear Terrorism: Report and Papers of the International Task Force on Prevention of Nuclear Terrorism* (Lanham, MD: Rowan & Littlefield, 1987).

Leventhal, Paul and Steven Dolley, "A Japanese Strategic Uranium Reserve: A Safe and Economic Alternative to Plutonium," *Science& Global Security* 5 (1994).

Levi, Michael A., and Henry C. Kelly, "Weapons of Mass Disruption," *Scientific American* (November 2002).

Lubenau, Joel O., "A Century's Challenges: Historical Overview of Radiation Sources in the USA," *IAEA Bulletin* 41 (March 1999).

Lubenau, Joel O., and James G. Yusko, "Radioactive Material in Recycled Metals—An Update," *Health Physics* 74 (March 1998).

Lugar, Richard G., "The Next Steps in U.S. Nonproliferation Policy," *Arms Control Today* (December 2002).

Lyman, Edwin S., "Public Health Risks of Mixed Oxide Fuels," *Science and Global Security* 9 (2001).

Ma, Chunyan, and Frank Von Hippel, "Ending the Production of Highly Enriched Uranium for Naval Reactors," *Nonproliferation Review* 8 (Spring 2001).

Maerli, Morten Bremer, *Crude Nukes on the Loose? Preventing Nuclear Terrorism by Means of Optimum Nuclear Husbandry, Transparency, and Non-Intrusive Fissile Material Verification*, Ph.D. dissertation, Faculty of Mathematics and Natural Sciences, University of Oslo, 2004.

Maerli, Morten Bremer, "Relearning the ABCs: Terrorists and 'Weapons of Mass Destruction,'" *Nonproliferation Review* 7 (Summer 2000).

Mark, J. Carson, "Explosive Properties of Reactor-Grade Plutonium," *Science & Global Security* 4 (1993).

Mark, J. Carson, Theodore Taylor, Eugene Eyster, William Maraman, and Jacob Wechsler, "Can Terrorists Build Nuclear Weapons?" in Paul Leventhal and Yonah Alexander, eds., *Preventing Nuclear Terrorism: Report and Papers of the International Task Force on Prevention of Nuclear Terrorism* (Lanham, MD: Rowan & Littlefield, 1987).

Matthews, Jim, "A Tale of 2 Fire Departments," *Homeland Security* (March 2004).

McPhee, John, *The Curve of Binding Energy* (New York: Farrar, Straus, & Giroux, 1974).

Milhollin, Gary, "Can Terrorists Get the Bomb?" *Commentary* (February 2002).

Millar, Alistair, "Russia, NATO, and Tactical Nuclear Weapons after 11 September," in Brian Alexander and Alistair Millar, eds., *Tactical Nuclear Weapons: Emergent Threat in an Evolving Security Environment* (Washington, D.C.: Brassey's Inc., 2003).

Moltz, James Clay, "Closing the NPT Loophole on Exports of Naval Propulsion Reactors," *Nonproliferation Review* 6 (Fall 1998).

Moody, R. Adam, "The International Science Center Initiative," in John M. Shields and William C. Potter, eds., *Dismantling the Cold War* (Cambridge, MA: MIT Press, 1997).

National Council on Radiation Protection and Measurements (NCRP), *Management of Terrorist Events Involving Radioactive Material,* NCRP Report No. 138, October 2001.

National Intelligence Council, "Annual Report to Congress on the Safety and Security of Russian Nuclear Facilities and Military Forces," Central Intelligence Agency, February 2002.

National Intelligence Council, "Foreign Missile Developments and the Ballistic Missile Threat Through 2015," National Intelligence Estimate, Central Intelligence Agency, December 2001.

Natural Resources Defense Council Nuclear Notebook, *Bulletin of the Atomic Scientists,* <http://www.thebulletin.org/issues/nukenotes/nukenote.html>.

Nilsson, Anita, "Security of Material: The Changing Context of the IAEA's Programme," *IAEA Bulletin* 43 (2001).

Norris, Robert S., Andrew S. Burrows, and Richard W. Fieldhouse, *Nuclear Weapons Databook, Volume V: British, French, and Chinese Nuclear Weapons* (Boulder, CO: Westview Press, 1994).

Norton, Augustus R., and Martin H. Greenberg, *Studies in Nuclear Terrorism* (Boston: G.K. Hall & Co., 1979).

"Nuclear and Radiological Threats," Chapter 2 in Committee on Science and Technology for Countering Terrorism, National Research Council, *Making the Nation Safer: The Role of Science and Technology in Countering Terrorism* (Washington, D.C.: National Academy Press, 2002).

Office of the Federal Register, National Archives and Records Administration (NARA), *Federal Register* 68 (June 13, 2003).

Office of International Nuclear Safety and Cooperation, "Soviet-Designed Nuclear Power Plant Profiles," U.S. Department of Energy, October 2000.

Office of Technology Assessment, *Technologies Underlying Weapons of Mass Destruction*, OTA-BP-ISC-115, December 1993.

Oppenheimer, A., "Terrorism Threats to Infrastructure Security," *Jane's Terrorism & Security Monitor* (January 1, 2003).

Philips, John Aristotle, and David Michaelis, *Mushroom: The Story of the A-Bomb Kid* (New York: William Morrow, 1978).

Posen, Barry R., "The Struggle Against Terrorism: Grand Strategy, Strategy, and Tactics," *International Security* (Winter 2001/2002).

Potter, William C., "Practical Steps for Addressing the Problem of Non-Strategic Nuclear Weapons," in Jeffrey A. Larsen and Kurt J. Klingenberger, eds., *Controlling Non-Strategic Nuclear Weapons* (Colorado Springs: U.S. Air Force Institute for National Security Studies, 2001).

Potter, William C., "Prospects for U.S.-Russian Cooperation to Counter WMD Proliferation and Terrorism," The Aspen Institute Congressional Program, *U.S.-Russian Relations: Opportunities for Cooperation* 18 (2003).

Potter, William C., and Elena Sokova, "Illicit Nuclear Trafficking in the NIS: What's New? What's True?" *Nonproliferation Review* 9 (Summer 2002).

Potter, William C., Nikolai Sokov, Harold Müller, and Annette Schaper, *Tactical Nuclear Weapons: Options for Control* (Geneva: United Nations Institute for Disarmament Research, 2002).

Potter, William C., Charles D. Ferguson, and Leonard S. Spector, "The Four Faces of Nuclear Terror and the Need for a Prioritized Response," *Foreign Affairs* (May/June 2004).

Progressive Policy Institute, *America at Risk: A Homeland Security Report Card,* Progressive Foundation, July 2003.

Project on Managing the Atom, Harvard University, "Controlling Nuclear Warheads and Materials," Nuclear Threat Initiative website, <http://www.nti.org/e_research/cnwm/overview/cnwm_home.asp>.

Project on Government Oversight, *Nuclear Power Plant Security: Voices from Inside the Fence*, POGO Report, September 2002.

Project on Government Oversight, *U.S. Nuclear Weapons Complex: Security at Risk*, POGO Report, October 2001.

"The Proliferation Security Initiative: An Interview With John Bolton," *Arms Control Today* (December 2003).

Pry, Peter Vincent, *War Scare: Russia and America on the Nuclear Brink* (Westport, CT: Praeger, 1999).

Ramberg, Bennett, *Nuclear Power Plants as Weapons for the Enemy: An Unrecognized Military Peril* (Berkeley: University of California Press, 1984).

Rawool-Sullivan, Mohini, Paul D. Moskowitz, and Ludmila N. Shelenkova, "Technical and Proliferation-Related Aspects of the Dismantlement of Russian Alfa-Class Nuclear Submarines," *Nonproliferation Review* (Spring 2002).

Rhodes, Richard, *The Making of the Atomic Bomb* (New York: Simon and Schuster, 1988).

Richardson, Michael, *A Time Bomb for Global Trade: Maritime-related Terrorism in an Age of Weapons of Mass Destruction* (Singapore: Institute of Southeast Asian Studies, 2004).

Richelson, Jeffrey T., "Defusing Nuclear Terror," *Bulletin of the Atomic Scientists* (March/April 2002).

Rodionov, Stanislav, "Could Terrorists Produce Low-Yield Nuclear Weapons?" in Committee on Confronting Terrorism in Russia, Office for Central Europe and Eurasia Development, Security, and Cooperation, National Research Council in Cooperation with the Russian Academy of Sciences, *High-Impact Terrorism: Proceedings of a Russian-American Workshop* (Washington, D.C.: The National Academies Press, 2002).

"Russia's Cooperation with the Nuclear Summit Participants: the USA, Great Britain, France, Germany, Italy, Canada, and Japan," *International Affairs* 42 (1996).

Sagan, Scott D., *The Limits of Safety: Organizations, Accidents, and Nuclear Weapons* (Princeton, NJ: Princeton University Press, 1993).

Sagan, Scott D., "The Problem of Redundancy Problem: Why More Nuclear Security Forces May Produce Less Nuclear Security," *Risk Analysis: An International Journal* (August 2004).

Sanz, Timothy L., "Nuclear Terrorism: Selected Research Materials," *Low Intensity Conflict & Law Enforcement* 1 (Winter 1992).

Schroeer, Dietrich, *Science, Technology, and the Nuclear Arms Race* (Ontario: John Wiley & Sons Canada Ltd., 1984).

Simon, Jeffrey D., "The Alphabet Bomber," in Jonathan B. Tucker, ed., *Toxic Terror: Assessing Terrorist Use of Chemical and Biological Weapons* (Cambridge, MA: MIT Press, 2000).

Smith, Brent L., *Terrorism in America: Pipe Bombs and Pipe Dreams* (New York: State University of New York Press, 1994).

Spector, Leonard S., *Going Nuclear* (Cambridge, MA: Ballinger Publishing Company, 1987).

Spector, Leonard S., "Interview: Ambassador Linton Brooks on U.S. Nuclear Policy," *Nonproliferation Review* 9 (Fall-Winter 2002).

Spector, Leonard S., "Missing the Forest for the Trees: U.S. Non-Proliferation Programs in Russia," *Arms Control Today* (June 2001).

Spector, Leonard S., "The New Landscape of Nuclear Terrorism," in Michael Barletta, ed., *After 9/11: Preventing Mass-Destruction Terrorism and Weapons Proliferation*, Occasional Paper No. 8, Center for Nonproliferation Studies (Monterey, CA: Monterey Institute of International Studies, May 2002).

Stana, Richard M., Director Homeland Security and Justice, "Homeland Security: Preliminary Observations on Efforts to Target Security Inspections of Cargo Containers," U.S. General Accounting Office, GAO-04-325T, December 16, 2003.

Stein, Peter, and Peter Feaver, *Assuring Control of Nuclear Weapons*, CSIA Occasional Paper #2, Center for Science and International Affairs (Cambridge, MA: Harvard University Press, 1987).

Steinhausler, Friedrich, "What It Takes to Become a Nuclear Terrorist," *American Behavioral Scientist* (February 2003).

Stern, Jessica, *The Ultimate Terrorists* (Cambridge, MA: Harvard University Press, 2001).

Stern, Jessica, *Terror In the Name of God: Why Religious Militants Kill* (New York: Harper Collins Publishers, 2003).

Stober, Dan, "No Experience Necessary," *Bulletin of the Atomic Scientists* (March/April 2003).

Stone, Richard, "The Hunt for Hot Stuff," *Smithsonian* (March 2003).

"Strategic Partnership aims to secure the future of global supply chains," *ISO Bulletin*, International Organization for Standardization, June 2003, <http://www.iso.ch/iso/en/commcentre/isobulletin/articles/2003/pdf/ships03-06.pdf>.

Taylor, Tammy P., David E. Morris, Thomasin C. Miller, and Sandra L. Gogol, *Radionuclide Decontamination Science and Technology Workshop: Workshop Summary and Findings,* Los Alamos National Laboratory Report LA_UR-03-8215, September 16-17, 2003.

U.S. Department of Defense, *Proliferation: Threat and Response* (Washington, D.C: U.S. Government Printing Office, 2001).

U.S. Department of Energy, National Nuclear Security Administration, *Global Research Reactor Security Initiative*, <http://www.nnsa.doe.gov/na-20/nrtr_grrsip.shtml>.

U.S. Department of Energy, National Nuclear Security Administration, Office of Defense Nuclear Nonproliferation (NA-24), *Russian Research Reactor Fuel Return*, <http://www.nnsa.doe.gov/na-20/rrrfr.shtml>.

U.S. Department of Energy, Office of Arms Control and Nonproliferation, *Final Nonproliferation and Arms Control Assessment of Weapons-Usable Fissile Material Storage and Excess Plutonium Disposition Alternatives*, DOE/NN-0007, 1997.

U.S. Department of Energy, Office of Inspector General, Office of Inspections and Special Inquiries, *Protective Force Performance Test Improprieties*, DOE/IG-0636, January 2004.

U.S. Department of Energy, Office of Inspector General, *The Department's Basic Protective Force Training Program*, Audit Report, DOE/IG-0641, March 2004.

U.S. Department of Energy, Office of Inspector General, Office of Audit Services, *Recovery of Highly Enriched Uranium Provided to Foreign Countries*, DOE/IG-0638, February 2004.

U.S. Department of Energy, Office of Inspector General, Office of Inspections and Special Inquiries, *Protective Force Performance Test Improprieties*, Inspection Report, DOE/IG-0636, January 2004.

U.S. Department of Energy's Office of Nonproliferation and International Security website, *Programs*, <http://www.nnsa.doe.gov>.

U.S. Department of State, Arms Control and Disarmament, *Glossary of Terms*, <http://usinfo.state.gov/topical/pol/arms/stories/pt11.htm>.

U.S. Energy Information Agency, *U.S. Nuclear Generation of Electricity*, <http://www.eia.doe.gov/cneaf/nuclear/page/nuc_generation/gensum.html>.

U.S. General Accounting Office, *Low-Level Radioactive Waste: Disposal Availability Adequate in the Short Term, but Oversight Needed to Identify Any Future Shortfalls*, GAO-04-604, June 2004.

U.S. General Accounting Office, Testimony of William O. Jenkins, Jr. Director Homeland Security and Justice Issues, *Homeland Security: Challenges in Achieving Interoperable Communications for First Responders*, GAO-04-231T, November 6, 2003.

U.S. General Accounting Office, Jim Wells, Director Natural Resources and Environment, *Nuclear Regulation: Emergency Preparedness Issues at the Indian Point 2 Nuclear Power Plant*, GAO-03-528T, March 10, 2003.

U.S. General Accounting Office, *Letter from NRC Chairman Nils Diaz to James Wells, Director Natural Resources and Environment Division, August 7, 2003*, GAO-03-752, September 2003.

U.S. General Accounting Office, Testimony of Randall A. Yim Managing Director National Preparedness, *National Preparedness: Integration of Federal, State, Local, and Private Sector Efforts if Critical to an Effective National Strategy for Homeland Security*, GAO-02-621T, April 11, 2002.

U.S. General Accounting Office, *Nuclear Nonproliferation: DOE Action Needed to Ensure Continued Recovery of Unwanted Sealed Radioactive Sources*, GAO-03-483, April 2003.

U.S. General Accounting Office, *Nuclear Nonproliferation: U.S. and International Assistance Efforts to Control Sealed Radioactive Sources Need Strengthening*, GAO-03-638, June 2003.

U.S. General Accounting Office, *Nuclear Regulatory Commission: Oversight of Security at Commercial Nuclear Power Plants Needs to be Strengthened*, GAO-03-752, September 2003.

U.S. General Accounting Office, *Nuclear Safety: Concerns with the Continuing Operation of Soviet-Designed Nuclear Power Reactors*, GAO/RCED-00-97, April 2000.

U.S. General Accounting Office, *Nuclear Security: Lessons to be Learned from Implementing NNSA's Security Enhancements*, GAO-02-358, March 2002.

U.S. General Accounting Office, *Spent Nuclear Fuel: Options Exist to Further Enhance Security*, GAO-03-426, July 2003.

U.S. General Accounting Office, *Quick and Secret Construction of Pluto-nium Reprocessing Plants: A Way to Nuclear Weapons Proliferation?* Report by the Comptroller General of the United States, October 6, 1978.

U.S. General Accounting Office, *Weapons of Mass Destruction: Additional Russian Cooperation Needed to Facilitate U.S. Efforts to Improve Security at Russian Sites,* GAO-03-482, March 2003.

U.S. General Accounting Office, *Weapons of Mass Destruction: Defense Threat Reduction Agency Addresses Broad Range of Threats, but Performance Reporting Can Be Improved,* GAO-04-330, February 2004.

U.S. Government, *National Strategy for Combating Terrorism,* February 2003.

U.S. Government, *National Security Strategy of the United States of America,* September 2002.

U.S. Government, *National Strategy to Combat Weapons of Mass Destruc-tion,* National Security Presidential Directive 17 (unclassified version), December 11, 2002.

U.S. House of Representatives, Armed Services Committee, Testimony of J. D. Crouch II Assistant Secretary of Defense for International Security Policy, March 4, 2003.

U.S. House of Representatives, Energy and Commerce Committee, Sub-committee on Oversight and Investigations, Statement of Paul Leventhal President of the Nuclear Control Institute and on behalf of the Com-mittee to Bridge the Gap, *A Review of Security Issues at Nuclear Power Plants,* December 5, 2001.

U.S. House of Representatives, Energy and Commerce Committee, Sub-committee on Oversight and Investigations, Statement by Richard A. Meserve submitted on behalf of the United States Nuclear Regulatory Commission, *Nuclear Power Plant Security,* April 11, 2002.

U.S. House of Representatives, Government Reform Committee, Subcom-mittee on National Security, Veterans Affairs, and International Relations, Testimony of Christopher E. Paine, *Preventing Nuclear Terrorism,* September 24, 2002.

U.S. House of Representatives, Government Reform Committee, Subcommittee on National Security, Veterans Affairs, and International Relations, Testimony of Danielle Brian Executive Director of the Project on Government Oversight (POGO), *Combating Terrorism: Preventing Nuclear Terrorism*, September 24, 2002.

U.S. House of Representatives, Government Reform Committee, Subcommittee on National Security, Veterans Affairs, and International Relations, Rose Gottemoeller, *Statement of Rose Gottemoeller*, September 24, 2002.

U.S. House of Representatives, Government Reform Committee, Subcommittee on National Security, Emerging Threats, and International Relations, Testimony of Robin M. Nazzaro, Director Natural Resources and Environment Team, *Nuclear Weapons Security*, June 24, 2003.

U.S. House of Representatives, International Relations Committee, John R. Bolton, *The Bush Administration and Nonproliferation: A New Strategy Emerges*, March 30, 2004.

U.S. House of Representatives, International Relations Committee, Subcommittee on International Security and Scientific Affairs, Testimony of Theodore Taylor, October 28, 1975.

U.S. House of Representatives, Resources Committee, Subcommittee on Forests and Forest Health, Statement of James F. Jarboe, Domestic Terrorism Section Chief, Counterterrorism Division, Federal Bureau of Investigation, *Eco-Terrorism*, February 12, 2002.

U.S. National Academies Committee and Russian Academy of Sciences, Committee on U.S.-Russian Cooperation on Nuclear Non-Proliferation, *Overcoming Impediments to U.S.-Russian Cooperation on Nuclear Non-Proliferation: Report of a Joint Workshop* (Washington, D.C.: The National Academies Press, 2004).

U.S. Nuclear Regulatory Commission, *NRC Regulations, Part 20: Standards for protection against radiation*, 10 CFR 20.1801: Security of stored material; 10 CFR 20. 1802: Control of material not in storage.

U.S. Nuclear Regulatory Commission, "NRC Review of Paper on Reducing Hazards from Stored Spent Nuclear Fuel," Fact Sheet, <http://

www.nrc.gov/reading-rm/doc-collections/fact-sheets/reducing-haz-ards-spent-fuel.html>.

U.S. Nuclear Regulatory Commission, "Nuclear Security Enhancements Since Sept. 11, 2001," Fact Sheet, September 2003.

U.S. Nuclear Regulatory Commission, "Research and Test Reactors," Fact Sheet, June 2003.

U.S. Nuclear Regulatory Commission, *Technical Study of Spent Fuel Pool Accident Risk at Decommissioning Nuclear Power Plants*, Report NUREG-1738, NRC, 2001.

U.S. Office of Technology Assessment, "The Non-State Adversary," in *Nuclear Proliferation and Safeguards*, U.S. Congress (Washington, D.C.: U.S. Government Printing Office, 1977).

U.S. Senate, Appropriations Committee, Subcommittee on Energy and Water Development, Prepared statement of Ambassador Linton F. Brooks, April 10, 2003.

U.S. Senate, Appropriations Committee, Testimony of Tom Ridge Secretary Department of Homeland Security on FY05 Budget, February 10, 2004.

U.S. Senate, Armed Services Committee, Testimony by Paul M. Longsworth Deputy Administrator for Defense Nuclear Nonproliferation, National Nuclear Security Administration, March 10, 2004.

U.S. Senate, Armed Services Committee, Subcommittee on Emerging Threats and Capabilities, Testimony of Lisa Bronson Deputy Under Secretary of Defense for Technology, Security Policy and Counterproliferation, March 10, 2004.

U.S. Senate, Commerce, Science, and Transportation Committee, Subcommittee on Oceans, Fisheries, and Coast Guard, Written statement by Conrad C. Lautenbacher, Jr., Vice Admiral, U.S. Navy (Ret.), Under Secretary of Commerce for Oceans and Atmosphere, *National Oceanic and Atmospheric Administration's FY 2005 Budget*, April 29, 2004.

U.S. Senate, Energy and Natural Resources Committee, Written Testimony by Gail H. Marcus, May 22, 2002.

U.S. Senate, Environment and Public Works Committee, Statement by Richard A. Meserve submitted by the United States Nuclear Regulatory Commission, June 5, 2002.

U.S. Senate, Foreign Relations Committee, Testimony by Henry C. Kelly President of the Federation of American Scientists, March 6, 2002.

U.S. Senate, Foreign Relations Committee, Testimony by Steven E. Koonin, *Radiological Terrorism,* March 6, 2002, published in *Physics & Society* (April 2002).

U.S. Senate, Foreign Relations Committee, Testimony of Sam Nunn Co-chairman of the Nuclear Threat Initiative, *The Treaty Between the United States of America and the Russian Federation on Strategic Offensive Reductions,* July 23, 2002.

U.S. Senate, Governmental Affairs Committee, Written Testimony of Stephen E. Flynn, *The Fragile State of Container Security,* March 20, 2003.

Van Dyke, Jon M., "The Legal Regime Governing Sea Transport of Ultrahazardous Radioactive Materials," *Ocean Development & International Law* 33 (2002).

Van Leeuwen, Marianne, "Netherlands," Chapter 10 in Robert J. Einhorn and Michèle Flournoy, eds., *Protecting Against the Spread of Nuclear, Biological, and Chemical Weapons: An Action Agenda for the Global Partnership,* Vol. 3 (Washington, D.C.: Center for Strategic and International Studies, January 2003).

Van Tuyle, Gregory J., Tiffany L. Strub, Harold A. O'Brien, Caroline F. V. Mason, and Steven J. Gitomer, *Reducing RDD Concerns Related to Large Radiological Source Applications,* Los Alamos National Laboratory, Report LA-UR-03-6664, September 2003

Vignard, Kerstin, ed., "Nuclear Terrorism," United Nations Institute for Disarmament Research, *Special Issue of Disarmament Forum,* No. 2 (2003).

Von Hippel, Frank, "Recommendations for Preventing Nuclear Terrorism," *Federation of American Scientists Public Interest Report* (November/December 2001).

Webster, William H., Arnaud de Borchgrave, and Linnea P. Raine, eds., *Wild Atom: Nuclear Terrorism*, CSIS Task Force Report (Washington, D.C.: Center for Strategic and International Security, 1998).

Whittaker, David J., *Terrorism: Understanding the Global Threat* (New York: Longman, 2002).

Woolf, Amy F., "Nuclear Weapons in Russia: Safety, Security, and Control Issues," CRS Report, April 11, 2003.

Wright, David, and Lisbeth Gronlund, "Estimating China's Production of Plutonium for Weapons," *Science & Global Security* 11 (2003).

Zimmerman, Peter D., and Cheryl Loeb, "Dirty Bombs: The Threat Revisited," *Defense Horizons* 38 (January 2004).

Index

A

Abkhazia, Georgia 130
Abraham, Spencer 158, 159, 160, 161, 163, 288
Adelman, Stuart Lee (a.k.a. Stuart von Adelman) 274
Advisory Group on Nuclear Security 247
African National Congress (ANC) 196
AIDA (Aide au démantèlement) 152
air launched cruise missile 48
al Qaeda 2, 8-9, 16-17, 19, 22, 27, 31-32, 37, 42, 47, 56, 81-82,
    95, 116-118, 125, 127, 133, 155, 157, 194, 211, 213, 217-218,
    224, 232, 260, 270
Al-Fadl, Jamal Ahmed 116
Algeria 21, 301
Alphabet Bomber 25
Alvarez, Luis 132
Alvarez, Robert 226, 227, 228, 236
americium-241 262, 264
apocalyptic terrorist group 16, 54, 192
Argentina 275, 284, 302
Argonne National Laboratory-West 163, 176
Arlington County Fire Department (ACFD) 92
Armed Forces Radiobiological Research Institute 93
Armenia 201
Asahara, Shoko 16, 28
Atomic Energy Commission (CEA; France) 68
Aum Shinrikyo 16, 17, 28, 29, 31, 54, 119, 295
Australia 82, 119
Aviation and Transportation Security Act 216

B

Basque terrorist group ETA 24, 42
Belarus 156, 234, 326
Bhabha Atomic Research Centre (BARC) 79
bin Laden, Osama 19, 31, 47, 64, 116, 117
Binalshibh, Ramzi 194
Black Dawn 134
British Nuclear Fuel Ltd. (BNFL) 202

boiling water reactor (BWR) 198, 204, 225
breeder reactor 153, 157, 166, 199
Britain (see Great Britain, United Kingdom)
Bronson, Lisa 73
Brookhaven National Laboratory (BNL) 227
Brooks, Linton 288
Bulgaria 156, 158, 201
Bureau of Customs and Border Protection 83, 141, 299
Bush, President George W. 4, 8, 55, 73, 81, 95, 124, 176, 211, 288, 319-320, 330

C

Canada 2, 151, 153, 195, 242, 274, 301
CANDU (Canadian Deuterium) reactors 198
Central Industrial Security Force (CISF) 79
Central Intelligence Agency (CIA) 80
cesium chloride 264, 306
cesium-137 226, 230, 234-237, 262, 264
Chaghai Hills, Pakistan 78
Charpak, Georges 132, 136, 233
Chechen rebels 29, 270
Chechnya 23, 42, 194, 245, 276
Cheney, Vice President Richard B. 4
Chernobyl 27, 193, 201, 210, 223, 230, 233-237, 289
China 47, 60, 62, 66, 68, 69, 110, 156, 162, 164, 197, 208, 246
Chinese Communist Party 69
Chirac, Jaques 69
Chrétien, Jean 151
Christian Identity movement 18
Clinton, William Jefferson 81
Coast Guard, U.S. 83, 104
cobalt-60 262, 264, 272, 275, 283, 303
Code of Conduct 284, 285, 287
Columbia 301
Conant, James Bryant 134
Conference of Radiation Control Program Directors (CRCPD) 292
Congress, United States 67, 73, 83, 92, 122, 159, 167, 206, 227, 288, 291, 293, 295, 306, 326
consequence management 169
Consequence Management Advisory Team (CMAT) 93
Container Security Initiative 83, 299
Convention on Assistance in the Case of Nuclear Accident or Radiological Emergency 289
Convention on Physical Protection of Nuclear Material (CPPNM) 12, 169

Cooperative Threat Reduction (CTR) program 66, 71, 73, 75, 94, 150
Coulport submarine base 68
Council on Foreign Relations 305
Crouch II, J.D. 73
Cuba 300
Customs, U.S. 141, 279, 299, 301, 305
cyberterrorism 192, 224
Czech Republic 156, 201

D

DCNet 296
Defense Threat Reduction Agency (DTRA) 71, 92, 93
Department of Defense (DOD) 57, 72-75, 80, 83, 94, 150, 174, 294
Department of Energy (DOE) 67, 72-75, 80, 83-84, 94, 119, 143, 145,
    147, 149, 151, 158-161, 163, 167, 174-176, 206-207, 230, 239,
    260, 287-289, 291, 293, 302-304, 323, 326, 332
Department of Homeland Security (DHS) 81, 83-84, 91-92, 195, 239,
    293-294, 297, 299, 307, 309, 333
depleted uranium 108, 123, 141, 176
design basis threat (DBT) 10, 67, 163, 217, 239-240, 243, 247-
    248, 257, 287, 333, 334
Diablo Canyon Nuclear Facility 195
Diaz, Nils 221
Dimona facility (Israel) 70
dirty bomb 3-5, 11, 29, 259-261, 271, 279, 296, 300
disused source 282-283, 290-291, 303-304
Dmitrovgrad, Bulgaria 157, 158
DPRK (see North Korea)
Dyson, Freeman 138

E

Egypt 21, 156
Eilabun facility (Israel) 70
ElBaradei, Mohammed 247, 274, 324
Electric Power Research Institute (EPRI) 214, 221-222, 244
Emergency Alert System 309
Emergency Broadcast System 309
emergency core cooling system 199, 201
Emergency Preparedness Review (EPREV) 247
Environmental Protection Agency (EPA) 228, 241, 292
EURATOM Treaty 12
European Police Office (EUROPOL) 287
Evan Mechan Eco-Terrorist International Conspiracy 195
export controls 153, 275, 300, 302, 323, 332

F

Federal Agency for Atomic Energy 110, 159
Federal Aviation Administration (FAA) 216, 239
Federal Bureau of Investigation (FBI) 80, 223, 239, 275
Federal Emergency Management Agency (FEMA) 81, 241, 239, 296
Fire Department of New York (FDNY) 91-92
Fissile Material Cut-Off Treaty (FMCT) 321
fizzle yield 135, 142
Food and Drug Administration (FDA) 297-299
Foreign Intelligence Surveillance Act (FISA) 81
Foreign Research Reactor Spent Nuclear Fuel Acceptance Program 160
former Soviet Union (FSU) 2, 11, 200, 223, 247, 278, 287, 304, 324,
    332
France 47, 62, 66, 68-69, 82, 110, 151-152, 162, 164-165, 197-199,
    207-208, 216, 230, 237, 243, 284, 322
FRM-II reactor 166
Fusion Task Force 82

G

G-8 151, 153-154, 166, 289-291, 301-302, 332
Garwin, Richard 132, 136, 233
gas-cooled reactor 198
General Accounting Office (GAO) 67, 72-75, 92, 143, 163, 206-207,
    220, 242, 291, 304-305
general license 265, 282, 300
Georgia, Republic of 130, 277, 286
Germany 82, 110, 142, 151-152, 156, 166, 208, 244, 282, 297
global cleanout 159
Global Partnership 153-154
Global Research Reactor Security 209
Global Threat Reduction Initiative (GTRI) 158-159, 160-161, 323, 326
Great Britain (see also United Kingdom) 62, 66, 68-69, 110, 162, 165-
    166, 200, 202, 208, 219, 243, 249, 322, 334
Greater-Than-Class-C (GTCC) waste 291, 303
Gun, Li 56
gun-type device 35, 134, 135, 137, 138, 141

H

Hanford Reservation 230
Harpoon cruise missiles 70
Hay, John 151
hazardous material (HazMat) 91

Health Physics Society 306
HEU Purchase Agreement 147, 149, 174
Heyl Pharmaceuticals 297
Hezbollah 19, 42
highly enriched uranium (HEU) 6, 8, 35, 67, 106, 107, 110, 115-124,
    127-133, 135-138, 141, 143, 145-147, 149, 150, 154-161, 163-
    164, 166-167, 171, 173-174, 176, 322--328
Hobson, David 206
Hollis-Eden Pharmaceuticals 298
Hungary 156, 201
Hussein, Saddam 35, 55, 124, 127

I

icebreakers (see Russian civilian)
Ignalina Nuclear Power Plant 224, 245
Immigration and Naturalization Service (INS) 299
implosion-type device 135, 138, 141
improvised nuclear device (IND) 3, 5, 6, 8, 10, 17-18, 20-23, 27, 31, 35-
    36, 51, 63, 79, 84, 87, 106, 108, 115, 117, 131, 141, 178, 194,
    259, 268, 270, 273, 279, 300, 321
Incident Command System (ICS) 92
India 47, 50, 52, 62, 66, 78-79, 80, 110, 162, 164, 166, 197, 208,
    301
Indian Point Nuclear Power Plant 220, 242
Indonesia 117, 141, 301
INFCIRC/225 (IAEA) 169
insider threat 73, 222-223, 247
Institute of Nuclear Physics in Ulugbek 130, 157
Institute of Nuclear Research and Nuclear Energetics (Bulgaria) 158
intercontinental ballistic missile (ICBM) 48, 319
International Atomic Energy Agency (IAEA) 9, 106, 144, 150, 152, 155-
    158, 166, 169, 173, 202-203, 212, 242, 246-247, 264, 274, 277-
    279, 283-289, 292, 294, 301-302, 304, 306, 324, 332
International Commission on Radiological Protection (ICRP) 305
International Nuclear Safety Group 247
International Physical Protection Advisory Service (IPPAS) 203, 246
INTERPOL 82, 287
Irish Republican Army (IRA) 19, 113
Iran 8-9, 21, 56-57, 116, 124-127, 145, 272, 300, 319
Iraq 8, 35, 55, 117, 124, 127, 137, 145, 242, 271, 274, 300
iridium-192 262, 264, 276, 303
Islamic Movement of Uzbekistan 118, 130, 157
Israel 42, 47, 50, 52, 62, 66, 70, 110, 162, 208, 301

J

Japan 16, 28, 54, 82, 110, 142-143, 151-152, 165-166, 197- 199, 208, 246, 322, 327
Japan Nuclear Cycle Development Institute 152
Joint Terrorism Task Forces 81

K

Kahuta, Pakistan 78
Kazakhstan 118, 153, 156-157, 172, 326, 328
Khan, Abdul Qadeer 9, 56, 57, 79, 82, 96, 116, 125, 127, 155
Khushab, Pakistan 78
Kidwai, Khalid 78
Kleine Brogel Air Base 68
Koeberg Nuclear Power Station 196, 223
Kurds 19, 113
Kyd, David 212

L

La Hague 208, 216, 230, 237, 243
Large, John 214
Lawrence Livermore National Laboratory (LLNL) 137
Lemoniz nuclear facility 24
leukemia 233
Levernier, Richard 162
Libya 8-9, 56-57, 116, 125-126, 145, 156, 158, 300
licensing fraud 270, 274-275, 300
light water reactor (LWR) 198, 201
Lithuania 201, 224, 236, 245
Lop Nur test site 69
Los Alamos National Laboratory (LANL) 67, 136, 141, 163, 290
loss-of-coolant accident 199, 210
low-enriched uranium (LEU) 110, 147, 164, 167, 174, 108, 147, 158-160, 172, 198, 273, 326, 327
Low Level Radioactive Waste Policy 303
Low Level Radioactive Waste Policy Amendments Act (LLRWPAA) 304
Lubenau, Joel O. 265
Lugar, Richard 1, 66
Lyman, Edwin 215

M

MAGNOX 198, 202, 249
Manhattan Project 134
Marcus, Gail 205

Maritime Transportation and Security Act (MTSA) 83
Mark, Carson 133, 136
material protection, control, and accounting (MPC&A) 143, 145, 147, 150, 152, 174-175, 291, 326, 327
Mayak Fissile Material Storage Facility 208, 237, 245, 327, 328
McGaffigan, Edward 211
Megaports Initiative 83
Meserve, Richard 191, 211, 212, 216, 223, 247
Ministry of Atomic Energy (MINATOM; Russia) 72, 110, 159, 244-245, 287-288
mixed oxide (MOX) fuel 108, 121-123, 151-152, 164-165, 208
Mohammed, Khaled Sheikh 194
Morocco 117
Musharraf, Pervez 1, 8, 56-57, 77-78, 96, 125

N

Narath, Albert 133
National Academy of Sciences 206, 229, 306, 308-309, 326
National Commission on Terrorist Attacks upon the United States (a.k.a. the "9/11 Commission") 82
National Council on Radiation Protection and Measurements (NCRP) 305, 306
National Joint Terrorism Task Force 81
National Nuclear Security Administration (NNSA) 67, 84, 161, 209, 230, 291, 303
National Oceanic and Atmospheric Administration 297
National Research Council 132, 205-206, 232, 262
National Strategy for Combating Terrorism 4
nationalist/separatist group 18-19, 24, 114, 270
Natural Resources Defense Council (NRDC) 141
Netherlands 82, 151, 166
Newly Independent States 144, 277, 287-288
Nigeria 2, 282
North Korea (DPRK) 8-9, 28, 47, 50, 56-57, 60-62, 66, 70-71, 81, 110, 116, 124-126, 131, 145, 156, 162, 208, 272, 300, 319
Norway 151, 153
Nth Country experiment 137
Nuclear Control Institute (NCI) 215
Nuclear Emergency Search Team (NEST) 42, 81, 84
Nuclear Energy Institute (NEI) 214, 220-221
Nuclear Regulatory Commission (NRC) 10, 167, 191, 202, 204, 206, 207, 209, 211-212, 216-221, 223, 225-229, 232, 237-242, 247-249, 257, 261, 265, 275, 291-294, 301, 304, 306, 311, 333-334
nuclear submarine 94, 153, 164
Nuclear Suppliers Group (NSG) 169, 203

Nuclear Threat Initiative (NTI) 157
Nuclear Weapons Storage Security Program 71
Nuclear Weapons Storage Site Security Protocol 73
Nuclear Weapons Transportation Security Program 72
Nuclear-Weapon-Free Zone treaties 12
Nunn, Sam 1, 46, 66

O

Oak Ridge National Laboratory (ORNL) 12, 67, 121, 163
Off-Site Source Recovery Program (OSR) 291, 303, 332
Office of Domestic Preparedness 81
Oklahoma City bombing 17, 217, 230
Ontario, Canada 2, 151, 240
orphan source 272, 277, 286-288, 292, 304
Orphan Source Initiative 292

P

Padilla, José (a.k.a. Abdullah Al-Mujahir) 23, 260
Pakistan 1, 7-9, 11, 16, 31, 46, 47, 50, 52, 55, 56, 60-62, 66, 77-
     80, 82, 84, 95-96, 110, 116, 124-125, 127, 130, 142, 154-155,
     157, 162, 167, 169, 172, 195, 208, 301, 319, 328-329
Palo Verde Nuclear Power Plant 195
Pan Am Flight #103 14
Pantex assembly/disassembly facility 67, 163
PATRIOT Act (see Uniting and Strengthening America)
Pentagon, U.S. 17, 20, 92, 117, 212, 214-215, 222, 297
permissive action links (PALs) 54, 61-66, 71, 76, 79, 329
Petten High Flux Reactor 166
Philippines 301
Pickering Nuclear Power Plant 242
Pierce, William 20
Pitesti Institute for Nuclear Research 157
Plutonium 108, 121, 143, 164, 328
plutonium 2, 6-8, 35, 67, 70, 107, 110-111, 117-118, 120-124, 127-
     128, 130, 134-137, 141, 143-145, 149, 151-152, 154, 163-167,
     174-176, 190, 197, 199, 207-209, 229-230, 264, 308, 322, 325,
     327, 333
plutonium disposition program 151-153, 175
plutonium-238 262, 264
Poland 82, 156
politico-religious terrorist group 18, 21-22, 192, 232, 270
Portable Downblending System (PDS) 176
potassium iodide 235, 241, 298
Powell, Colin 285

Presidential Nuclear Initiatives (PNI) 1, 77, 95, 321, 329
pressurized water reactor (PWR) 164, 198, 201, 204, 225, 236, 238
Project on Government Oversight (POGO) 141
Project Vinca 157
Proliferation Security Initiative (PSI) 81-82
Prussian blue 297, 298
Putin, Vladimir 78, 95

R

radiation emission device (RED) 3, 11, 36, 259, 271, 279
radioactive source 2, 10, 27, 32, 34, 36, 69, 150, 209, 280-281, 284-
    290, 292-294, 300-306, 319, 322-325, 332-333, 335
Radiogardase® 297
radioisotope 155, 209, 235, 251, 261-262, 263-265, 280, 283, 290,
    298, 303, 310
radioisotope thermoelectric generators (RTGs) 263, 276-278
radiological dispersion device (RDD) 3-5, 11, 20, 23, 29, 30-32, 36, 41-
    42, 135, 175, 209, 259, 261-268, 270-271, 274, 276-277, 279,
    283-284, 287, 289, 291, 294-299, 303, 308-309, 320
radium-226 262
Ramberg, Bennett 233
RBMK reactor 165, 199-202, 224, 236, 245, 249
reactor-grade plutonium 108, 135, 136
Ready.gov 309
Reduced Enrichment for Research and Test Reactors (RERTR) program
    160
reprocessing 108, 121-122, 124, 128, 153, 165, 175-176, 208-209,
    216, 229-230, 237-238, 242-243, 245, 322, 327
research reactor 10, 108, 110-111, 120-121, 123, 129-130, 146-147,
    151, 155, 156-161, 164, 166-167, 172, 175-176, 203, 209, 231-
    232, 237-238, 247, 249, 261, 272, 327, 334
Resolution 1540 (see UN Security Council)
Richardson, Bill 163
Ridge, Tom 195
Rogers, Harold 206
Rokkasho-mura 165, 208
Romania 156, 157
Rotterdam, Port of 83
Rumyantsev, Aleksandr 159, 244, 288
Russia 1, 2, 7-8, 29, 42, 46-47, 55, 58, 60, 62-63, 66, 71, 73, 75-
    77, 83-84, 94-95, 106, 110, 118, 128-130, 142-147, 149-160,
    162, 164-167, 171, 197-199, 201, 208, 236-237, 244, 287, 301,
    304, 319-323, 325-329, 334
Russian civilian icebreakers 108, 146

Russian Ministry of Atomic Energy (see Ministry of Atomic Energy)
Russian Navy 72-74, 94, 147, 164
Russian Research Reactor Fuel Return 160
Russian Strategic Rocket Forces 72, 73

S

safing, arming, fusing, and firing (SAFF) 61-62
Sandia National Laboratories 202, 277, 301
Sargodha, Pakistan 78
Saudi Arabia 21, 117, 224, 301
Savannah River Site 163, 230
Schumer Amendment 160
Second Line of Defense program 302
Sellafield site 202, 208, 214, 230, 237, 243
Senate Foreign Relations Committee 46
Sewell, Duane 278
Shays, Christopher 163
Sizewell B nuclear power plant 219
Slammer computer worm 224
Slovakia 201
specific license 265, 282
spent fuel pool 194, 204-205, 208- 209, 212-213, 225-229, 233, 236,
    238, 244, 248, 261
spent nuclear fuel 1, 120-124, 146, 151, 153, 158, 160-161, 164-165,
    175-176, 190, 203-208, 210, 214, 218, 225, 227-230, 237, 244,
    247, 261-262, 272, 323, 326, 334
Sri Lanka 19, 113
State Department, U.S. 272, 285, 300
strategic nuclear weapons 51, 53, 62
Strategic Plans Division 78
strontium-90 235, 262, 264, 277
submarine launched ballistic missile (SLBM) 48, 62
Sukhumi Nuclear Research Center 130
Syria 300

T

12th Main Directorate 71, 72, 73, 74
tactical nuclear weapons 1, 48, 53, 62, 66, 67, 70, 75-77, 95, 320-
    321, 329-330
Tajoura Nuclear Research Center 158
Taliban 8, 56, 116, 125
Tamil Tigers 19, 33, 113
Tashkent, Uzbekistan 130, 157, 158
Taylor, Theodore 122

Technical Area 18 (T.A. 18) 163
thallium 297
The Turner Diaries 20
Three Mile Island 200, 235
thyroid cancer 233, 235, 241, 298
Tokai-mura 208, 246
TOPOFF 295, 296, 307
Trabelsi, Nizar 68
Transportation Security Administration (TSA) 83, 216, 239, 240
Treaty on the Non-Proliferation of Nuclear Weapons (NPT) 172
Tripartite Initiative 287-288
Tripoli, Libya 158
Turkey 19, 113
Tuwaitha nuclear site (Iraq) 273, 274

U

U.S.S. Cole 17, 117
Ukraine 153, 156, 201, 234, 326
UN Committee on Sources and Effects of Atomic Radiation (UNSCEAR)
     234
UN Security Council Resolution 1540 170, 322
Union of Concerned Scientists 132
United Kingdom (see also Great Britain) 47, 68, 82, 151, 153, 207,
     214, 237, 244, 322
United States 1-10, 14, 23, 27-28, 31, 33, 42, 46, 47, 56, 62-64, 66-
     67, 71, 73, 77-78, 80, 82-84, 92, 94-96, 110-111, 125-126, 138,
     140-141, 144- 145, 150-151, 154, 157-160, 162, 166-167, 169,
     171, 173, 191, 193-195, 197-198, 202-204, 208-209, 216, 218,
     222, 226-227, 229-231, 235, 238, 242, 245-246, 248-249, 260,
     265, 272, 274-275, 278, 281-284, 287-288, 291, 293, 295, 298-
     299, 301-305, 307, 318-319, 321-330, 332-335
United States Enrichment Corporation (USEC) 147, 174
Uniting and Strengthening America by Providing Appropriate Tools Re-
     quired to Intercept and Obstruct Terrorism (USA PATRIOT) Act 81
uranium enrichment 9
uranium-235 107, 262

V

Vanguard ballistic missile submarines 68
Vietnam 156
Visitor and Immigration Status Indicator Technology (VISIT) 81
von Hippel, Frank 132
VVER-1000 165, 175, 176
VVER-440 165, 175, 201

W

weapons-grade plutonium 135-136, 150-153, 171, 174-175, 208
weapons-grade uranium 133
Westinghouse Savannah River Company 176
White House, U.S. 4, 132, 297
Wilkinson, Rodney 196
World Customs Organization (WCO) 287
World Trade Center 17, 92, 112, 117, 212-213, 215, 217, 222

X

Xinjiang province 69
Xinjiang separatist groups 69

Y

Y-12 plant 12, 67, 163
Yousef, Ramzi 217
Yucca Mountain 206, 207
Yugoslavia 156, 326
Yusko, James G. 265

About the Authors

Dr. Charles D. Ferguson is Scientist-in-Residence based in the Washington, D.C., Office of the Center for Nonproliferation Studies at the Monterey Institute of International Studies (MIIS). He joined CNS from the U.S. Department of State, where he was a Foreign Affairs Officer in the Office of the Senior Coordinator for Nuclear Safety in the Bureau of Nonproliferation. At the State Department, he helped coordinate U.S. government interagency nuclear safety policy on decommissioned Russian marine nuclear reactors, the Korean Peninsula Energy Development Organization (KEDO) light water reactor project, Indian and Pakistani commercial nuclear power plants, and Russian plutonium production reactors. He has also served as a nuclear arms control and non-proliferation analyst at the Federation of American Scientists, where he directed the Nuclear Policy Project. A United States Naval Academy alumnus, achieving a B.S. degree with distinction in physics and a commission as an officer in the U.S. Navy, he graduated from the Naval Nuclear Power School and the Submarine Officers School. While supervising an engineering crew of a nuclear power and propulsion plant on a fleet ballistic missile submarine, he also served as that ship's sonar and reactor controls officer. Dr. Ferguson has conducted scientific research at the Los Alamos National Laboratory, the Space Telescope Science Institute, the Harvard-Smithsonian Center for Astrophysics, and the Institute for Physical Science and Technology at the University of Maryland. He has a Ph.D. in physics from Boston University.

Dr. William C. Potter is Institute Professor and Director of the Center for Nonproliferation Studies at the Monterey Institute of International Studies. He also directs the MIIS Center for Russian and Eurasian Studies. Dr. Potter is the author or editor of thirteen books dealing with nonproliferation and national security issues. His present research focuses on nuclear nonproliferation issues involving the post-Soviet states. He is a member of the Council on Foreign Relations and the

International Institute for Strategic Studies, and serves on the International Advisory Board of the Center for Policy Studies in Russia (Moscow). From 1998 to 2003 he was a member of the UN Secretary-General's Advisory Board on Disarmament Matters and the Board of Trustees of the UN Institute for Disarmament Research. He has been a member of several committees of the National Academy of Sciences and currently serves on the National Academy of Sciences/Russian Academy of Sciences Joint Working Group on Nuclear Nonproliferation and the National Academy of Sciences Committee on Indigenization of Programs to Prevent Leakage of Plutonium and Highly Enriched Uranium from Russia. He was an advisor to the delegation of Kyrgyzstan to the 1995 NPT Review and Extension Conference and to the 1997, 1998, 1999, 2002, 2003, and 2004 sessions of the NPT Preparatory Committee, as well as to the 2000 NPT Review Conference. Dr. Potter holds a Ph.D. from the University of Michigan.

Dr. Amy Sands is Dean of the Graduate School of International Policy Studies at MIIS. Prior to this position, she served as Deputy Director of CNS. From August 1994 to June 1996, she was Assistant Director of the Intelligence, Verification, and Information Management Bureau at the U.S. Arms Control and Disarmament Agency (ACDA). Reporting directly to the ACDA Director, she was responsible for managing the development of verification and compliance policy for relevant arms control and nonproliferation activities, for ACDA's computer support and analysis activities, and for liaison with the intelligence community. Upon leaving the government, Dr. Sands received ACDA's Distinguished Honor Award and the On-Site Inspection Agency's Exceptional Civilian Service Medal. Before joining ACDA, she led the Proliferation Assessments Section of Z Division (Intelligence) at the Lawrence Livermore National Laboratory. In this position, she managed the research activities, publications, and numerous sponsors of Z Division's work relating to the spread of weapons of mass destruction. Dr. Sands holds a Ph.D. from the Fletcher School of Law and Diplomacy.

Mr. Leonard S. Spector is Deputy Director of CNS and heads the Center's Washington, D.C., Office. In addition, he serves as editor-in-chief of the CNS's publications. Mr. Spector joined CNS from the U.S.

Department of Energy (DOE), where he served as an Assistant Deputy Administrator for Arms Control and Nonproliferation at the National Nuclear Security Administration. His principal responsibilities at DOE included development and implementation of DOE arms control and nonproliferation policy with respect to international treaties; US domestic and multilateral export controls; inspection and technical cooperation activities of the International Atomic Energy Agency; civilian nuclear activities in the U.S. and abroad; initiatives in regions of proliferation concern, including the canning of plutonium-spent nuclear fuel in North Korea and Kazakhstan; and transparency provisions of bilateral agreements with Russia covering the purchase of weapons-grade uranium and the cessation of plutonium production. Additionally, Mr. Spector managed the Initiatives for Proliferation Prevention and the Nuclear Cities Initiative programs. Prior to his tenure at DOE, Mr. Spector served as Senior Associate at the Carnegie Endowment for International Peace and Director of its Nuclear Non-Proliferation Project. Mr. Spector also established the Program on Post-Soviet Nuclear Affairs at Carnegie's Moscow Center. Before joining the Carnegie Endowment, Mr. Spector served as Chief Counsel to the U.S. Senate Energy and Proliferation Subcommittee, where he assisted in drafting the Nuclear Non-Proliferation Act and the Nuclear Waste Policy Act. Mr. Spector has participated on the Senior Advisory Panels at the Sandia National Laboratories, the Los Alamos National Laboratory, and the National Research Council of the National Academy of Sciences. He has also served as Secretary and Member of the Board of Trustees of the Henry L. Stimson Center, and he is a member of the Council on Foreign Relations and the Washington, D.C., Bar. Mr. Spector holds a J.D. degree from Yale Law School.

Dr. Fred L. Wehling is Senior Research Associate and Education Coordinator for the CNS. In addition to teaching courses on nonproliferation issues and organizing the Center's educational outreach programs, he conducts research on fissile material security, exports of nuclear materials and technology from the former Soviet states, and transfers of weapons and related technology to the Middle East and South Asia. Before coming to CNS in 1998, Wehling was a consultant at RAND,

Coordinator of Policy Research for the University of California's Institute on Global Conflict and Cooperation (IGCC), and a researcher at the Cooperative Monitoring Center (CMC) at Sandia National Laboratories. His recent writings include *World Politics in a New Era,* 2nd ed., with Steven L. Spiegel (1998), *Irresolute Princes: Kremlin Decision Making in Middle East Crises* (1997), and various articles and reports for *The Nonproliferation Review.* Dr. Wehling has a Ph.D. in political science from UCLA.